Set in Stone

Set in Stone

Creating and Commemorating a Hudson Valley Culture

Kenneth Shefsiek

SUNY PRESS

Cover image: Memorial House, New Paltz, New York, postcard, c. 1920. Collection of the author.

Published by State University of New York Press, Albany

Printed in the United States of America

Excelsior Editions is an imprint of State University of New York Press

For information, contact State University of New York Press, Albany, NY
www.sunypress.edu

Production, Jenn Bennett
Marketing, Fran Keneston

Library of Congress Cataloging-in-Publication Data

Names: Shefsiek, Kenneth, author.
Title: Set in stone : creating and commemorating a Hudson Valley culture / Kenneth Shefsiek.
Description: Albany : State University of New York Press, 2017. | Series: Excelsior Editions | Includes bibliographical references and index.
Identifiers: LCCN 2016031459 (print) | LCCN 2016053185 (ebook) | ISBN 9781438464350 (hardcover : alk. paper) | 9781438464367 (pbk : alk paper) | ISBN 9781438464374 (e-book)
Subjects: LCSH: New Paltz (N.Y.)--History.
Classification: LCC F129.N53 S47 2017 (print) | LCC F129.N53 (ebook) | DDC 974.7/34--dc23
LC record available at https://lccn.loc.gov/2016031459

10 9 8 7 6 5 4 3 2 1

CONTENTS

List of Maps, Tables, and Illustrations		vi
Acknowledgments		ix
Introduction	New Paltz: Into the Mix	1
Chapter 1	The Walloons' English Town	17
Chapter 2	I Give Devise and Bequeath: Gender, Property, and Ethnocultural Creolization	37
Chapter 3	Halls, Windows, Hearths, and Barns: Architecture and Ethnic Culture	65
Chapter 4	"French, Dutch, and Tolerable English": Language Use in Early New Paltz	117
Chapter 5	Schism: Ecclesiastical Conflict in a Creolized Community	141
Chapter 6	"The precious germ of civil and religion freedom"	169
Chapter 7	Set in Stone	199
Notes		223
Bibliography		273
Index		295

MAPS, TABLES, and ILLUSTRATIONS

Maps

1.1	The Spanish Netherlands, Herman Moll, c. 1707	18

Tables

1.1	Genealogical connections of the New Paltz patentees	23
1.2	Marriage patterns, 1750–1800	30
4.1	Language of wills, 1676–1800	119
4.2	Language of financial receipts (I)	130
4.3	Language of financial receipts (II)	132
5.1	Members of the Second (Conferentie) Church of New Paltz	158

Figures

3.1	Progressive development of the *rookhuis*	67
3.2	Three variations of a *rookhuis* with an *insteek*	67
3.3	*Los hoes* (Johannes Winckelman barn/house, 1642, Achter Col Settlement, now the site of Bogota, Bergen County, New Jersey)	68
3.4	Structural framing of a rural Dutch-American house	69
3.5	Structural framing of a Dutch-American barn (Van Campen-Dewitt Barn, Wallpack Center Vicinity, Sussex County, New Jersey, early nineteenth century)	69
3.6	The Parson Capen House, Topsfield, Massachusetts, 1683, exterior	71
3.7	The Parson Capen House, Topsfield, Massachusetts, floor plan	72
3.8	Maria DuBois House, exterior, 1705	73
3.9	Maria DuBois House, interior	74

3.10	Five-plate stove, 1758 (at Schifferstadt, Frederick, Maryland)	75
3.11	Abraham LeFevre House, Gardiner, New York, addition c. 1758	76
3.12	Stairs (*wenteltrap*) to the attic in the Samuel Bevier House, c. 1731–1732	77
3.13	Daniel Hasbrouck House, 1721, c. 1728, c. 1734	77
3.14	Longitudinal section of Daniel Hasbrouck House	78
3.15	Samuel Bevier House (south façade), c. 1731–1732, c. 1735, with mid-eighteenth century addition	78
3.16	Samuel Bevier House (north façade)	79
3.17	Longitudinal section of Samuel Bevier House	79
3.18	Stairs to *opkamer* in Daniel Hasbrouck House	80
3.19	Deyo House at Bontecoe (in c. 1903)	81
3.20	Jacob Hasbrouck House, 1721	82
3.21	Jacob Hasbrouck House floor plan	83
3.22	Matthew Ten Eyck House, Hurley, New York, 1750	84
3.23	Matthew Ten Eyck House, Hurley, New York, floor plan	84
3.24	MacPhaedris-Warner House, Portsmouth, New Hampshire, 1718–1723	85
3.25	"Westover," Charles City, Virginia, c. 1730–1734	86
3.26	Cornelius Wynkoop House, Marbletown, New York, 1772	86
3.27	Abraham LeFevre House, Gardiner, New York, 1740–1742, c. 1758, c. 1794	87
3.28	Daniel Deyo House, c. 1763 (in c. 1903)	88
3.29	Freer-Louw House, 1762, 1763	89
3.30	Jacob Hasbrouck House reconstructed *kruiskozijn* window	90
3.31	Jacob Hasbrouck House reconstructed *bolkozijn* window	91
3.32	Daniel Hasbrouck House sash windows	92
3.33	Jambless fireplace, Jacob Hasbrouck House	92
3.34	Room in Jacob Hasbrouck House	94
3.35	Evert Terwilliger House, Gardiner, New York, 1738, with c. 1762 alterations	95
3.36	Evert Terwilliger House, Gardiner, New York	95
3.37	Evert Terwilliger House, floor plan of original condition	96
3.38	Evert Terwilliger House, floor plan after c. 1762 reconstruction	97
3.39	Evert Terwilliger House, stairs	98

3.40	Evert Terwilliger House, parlor fireplace	98
3.41	Evert Terwilliger House, mantel, second-floor bedchamber	99
3.42	Frederick Deyo House, "Thornwood," late eighteenth century	100
3.43	Jacob Hasbrouck Jr. House, 1786 (with later gables)	100
3.44	Abraham LeFevre House, Gardiner, New York, with c. 1825–1830 alterations	102
3.45	Cristoffel Deyo House, rear façade (original front façade), mid-eighteenth century	103
3.46	Cristoffel Deyo House, front façade (original rear façade)	103
3.47	Maria DuBois House, 1705, with c. 1830s additions	104
3.48	Stephen Goetschius House, 1791	105
3.49	Lucas Van Wagenen House, 1800	105
3.50	John A. Hardenbergh House (sometimes known as the "Col. Abraham J. Hardenbergh House"), late eighteenth century	106
3.51	Ezekiel Eltinge House, 1799	107
3.52	"The Locusts," 1826	108
3.53	Josiah Hasbrouck House, "Locust Lawn," 1814	109
3.54	Gideon Granger Homestead, Canandaigua, New York, 1816	110
3.55	Structural framing of Dutch-American barn (Van Campen-Dewitt Barn, Wallpack Center Vicinity, Sussex County, New Jersey)	112
6.1	Eighteenth-century chair, originally owned by Jacob Hasbrouck Sr. (one of six)	170
6.2	Josiah Hasbrouck House, "Locust Lawn," main hall	171
6.3	*Bust of Diana*, Joseph Mozier, c. 1850	171
6.4	Server, John Banks, c.1810	172
6.5	*Blanche and Fitz James*, needlework created by Hylah Bevier at the Litchfield Female Academy, c. 1811	173
6.6	Deyo House, before 1894	174
6.7	Deyo House, after 1894	174
7.1	Visitors to the Jean Hasbrouck House, c. 1897–1899	217
7.2	Unveiling of Huguenot Monument, September 29, 1908	220

ACKNOWLEDGMENTS

For a work of scholarship the origins of which are more than fifteen years in the past, many people and institutions have assisted me along the way. I first and foremost want to thank Jack Braunlein, Eric Roth, and Leslie LeFevre-Stratton (my favorite "Huguenot"), whose work for the Huguenot Historical Society both before and after I was employed there ultimately made my research possible. Jack's guidance and support, as well as his deep commitment to scholarship in the support of Huguenot Street, brought much-needed professionalism to the institution. He gave me the assistance I needed as I began my research into the history of New Paltz. Without Eric's superb archival organization, I am not even sure that this study would have been possible; and Leslie's scholarly curiosity about her family's heritage, her humor, and her friendship added great joy to my life in New Paltz (even though I know that my loud voice often got on her nerves). I cannot see a pink paperclip nor an "omnibus" sky without thinking of her.

I would also like to extend my deep gratitude to my many professors at the University of Georgia. I entered my graduate program there with little academic training in history but with practical skills in interpreting the past for the public; and the training and support they provided me changed my life. In particular, I would like to thank Allan Kulikoff, Peter Charles Hoffer, John Inscoe, Michael Kwass, Kathleen Clark, and Paul Sutter. They sometimes intimidated me, they consistently challenged me, and they gave me every opportunity to argue with them whenever I felt compelled (which, given my temperament, was often). I will forever be deeply grateful for their guidance and support. I would also like to thank the History Department at the University of North Carolina, Wilmington, most especially Paul Townend, for his efforts to provide me with the resources I needed to complete this work, and Tammy Gordon, who welcomed me to the university with open arms, making my transition to teaching far less stressful than it could have been. I extend my thanks also to Ted Bartlett, Neil Larsen, and Douglas Bucher, whose research on the Huguenot Street houses, Locust Lawn, and the Evert Terwilliger House I have drawn upon extensively, even if I drew my own conclusions based on their work. I would also like to thank Dennis Maika, David Voorhees, and Firth Fabend for the support they expressed for my work at the New Netherland Society's Emerging Scholars Roundtable in 2014. I also extend my gratitude to the State University of New York Press, particularly to Amanda Lanne-Camilli and Jenn Bennett. Amanda made a daunting process far less daunting than it might have been. I also want to thank Jan Davidson for her assistance in improving my manuscript, and Charlotte Hegyi just because. My gratitude also goes to Carrie Allmendinger, Bonnie Soper, Kenneth Snodgrass, William Charnock, Daniel Flebut, and Melanie Gettier who provided some of the many images used in this book.

Finally, I thank Paul, Karen, David, Mark, and the one who has been subjected the most to my prattling on about New Paltz, my partner, Terry. It is impossible for me to imagine my life without any of you. Without the love and support you have given me and continue to give me, I do not think I would have had the emotional strength to complete this book. Most especially, I thank Mowlee. If I have any ability to empathize with people past or present, if I can see the world at all through the experiences of others, it is because of her. She helped me to be a better person, and whether she knew it or not, a better historian. This book is dedicated to her.

Portions of chapters 1 and 6 were originally published in Kenneth Shefsiek, "Governing New Paltz: Scholarship and the commemoration of colonial New York ethnic heterogeneity," *New York History* 91, no. 3 (Fall 2010): 295–314.

INTRODUCTION

New Paltz: Into the Mix

> *I like middles. It is in middles that extremes clash, where ambiguity restlessly rules.*
>
> —John Updike[1]

It was in the early winter of 2000 that I first visited New Paltz, a small New York town on the west side of the Hudson River about midway between New York City and Albany. The historic village was founded in 1678 by twelve French-speaking Protestant men who, in 1677, had received a nearly forty-thousand-acre land grant from the royal governor, Edmund Andros. I knew virtually nothing about the town nor the area, but I had been invited for an interview for the position of curator of education at the Huguenot Historical Society, the institution founded in the late nineteenth century by the descendants of the town's founders to honor, preserve, and interpret their ancestral heritage. That heritage was primarily focused on a group of stone houses operated as museums that stand on Huguenot Street in the village's historic core—a National Historic Landmark District known throughout the Hudson River Valley—most of which reportedly had been constructed by the New Paltz founders. It was these houses that had most attracted me to the position, as I had recently completed a graduate degree in historic preservation, and I intended to make a career working in historic house museums.

Before the interview, I explored the historic village center, and what immediately struck me was the essential foreignness of the houses. I literally had never seen anything like them before, as the style in which they were built had not been addressed in any architectural history courses I had taken. Neither had I ever encountered anything akin to them in my travels around New England where I had been raised and where I had become familiar with colonial Anglo-American vernacular architecture. I was successful in securing the job with the Huguenot Historical Society, and during the few years that I worked for the institution, I came to understand that the style was a local manifestation of a Continental European architectural tradition most appropriately referred to as vernacular Dutch-American. However, upon seeing the houses for the first time, I simply did not know what to make of them.

As I walked around the neighborhood, I also saw evidence of how the town had commemorated and presented its past to the public, an activity in which descendants of the village's founders had been engaged since the turn of the twentieth century. One of those commemorative endeavors was the 1908 monument to the village's founders—the patentees—which descendants had erected in front of the most dramatic of the stone houses, the so-called Jean Hasbrouck House. That house was also known as the "Memorial House," a name it was given when the Huguenot Historical Society acquired it in 1894 for use as a museum. Before being invited for an interview, I had only a vague understanding of what a Huguenot even was—a Calvinist French Protestant—a condition I shared with most contemporary Americans. Those descendants who erected the memorial knew that many of their early twentieth-century peers did not have any knowledge of the Huguenots either, and they intended their monument to enlighten the uninformed, at least in part. That rough-hewn shaft of local granite, to which was affixed a large brass plaque, was dedicated "To the Memory and in honor of . . . the New Paltz Patentees, who, driven by religious persecution from their native France, exiles for conscience's sake, came to America." Many Huguenots had indeed come to the American shores after 1685, when Louis XIV revoked the 1598 Edict of Nantes, which made Protestantism illegal in France. The New Paltz patentees, however, had left their homeland decades before. Their commitment to religious liberty was supposedly so strong and the families so prescient, that they had sought refuge elsewhere beginning in the 1650s, decades before the Sun King began his persecution of the Huguenots and even before he began to rule his domain directly. Since the 1840s, the descendants of the patentees had been publicly claiming their supposed Huguenot heritage and commemorating what they perceived to have been their ancestors' great gift to the New World: their desire for religious freedom. Many of their twenty-first century descendants still hoped to preserve that legacy unimpaired for future generations.

The monument is not the only source of historical information on the street. In front of each of the houses stands a historic marker, most of which were erected by the State of New York in the 1930s. The markers provide construction dates for the houses ranging from 1692 to 1712, suggesting that they were built during the lifetimes of the patentees. I would later learn that with only one exception, all of these dates are wrong. Yet these early dates formed the basis of the Society's long-held (and erroneous) tagline: "The Oldest Street in America with its Original Houses." Promotional materials from the 1980s also claimed that these houses served as a "monument to the integrity, industry, and independence of the founders." The implication is that having established themselves during the nation's formative years, these founders made a significant contribution to the development of these core American values.[2]

A marker also stands near the site of the first stone church, which was dismantled nearly two centuries ago, although a conjectural reconstruction was erected nearby in 1972. The sign refers not to the site of a Huguenot but a Walloon church. I had never even heard of a Walloon before coming to New Paltz. I soon learned from the staff of the Society that nearly all of the founders of the village had not been from France, nor were they French. Rather, they were Walloons from the southern Spanish Netherlands near the northern border of France. Even so, as the Walloons spoke French, both amateur and professional American historians have tended to see the Walloons who founded New Paltz as essentially French. The result of this elision is that the European experience of the founders of New Paltz is falsely assumed to have been that of the French Protestants who faced persecution under Louis XIII and Louis XIV. The church marker itself obscures these ethnic distinctions, as the text also refers to the fact that the church was once "Called 'Our French Church.'" Who called it that, and in what context, is mysteriously left unsaid. In other words, the markers and the monument found on the street mention three groups—Walloon, Huguenot, and French—and in doing so, suggest that they were all one and the same, which they were not. If amateur and professional historians had faced the fact that the French-speaking Protestant Walloons from the Spanish Netherlands who founded New Paltz were not French Huguenots from France, they would have had difficulty sustaining their narrative of persecution under the French crown, and it was to just that narrative that descendants so tenaciously clung.[3]

Another historic marker that refers to the original government of the town stands near Huguenot Street, and it too suggests that there was indeed something special about this little village. That marker reads: "Die Pfalz a French Huguenot village governed by 'The Duzine,' a body of 12 men chosen annually. For 100 years the only form of government." Only later would I discover that this statement, while not completely fanciful, nevertheless refers to an aspect of the community's history that has been misinterpreted for generations. Why descendants found the Duzine to be important is that it suggested that the founders had governed themselves through a "pure Democracy," which again implies that the patentees had been bearers of political ideals upon which the future United States would be based. The so-called Duzine did exist, having been organized in the early eighteenth century, but it did not represent the village's government in any way. Nineteenth-century descendants of the founders of New Paltz misconstrued what the Duzine actually was—merely a group of elected representatives of the patentees' heirs charged with managing the land patent—in the interest of elevating the town and its founding families to an exalted, but unwarranted, position in American history.[4]

While the Huguenot Historical Society has been successfully bringing attention to the history of New Paltz since the late nineteenth century through its collection of house museums, little scholarly attention was paid to it in the twentieth century. Most of what has been said about the community's history was based on a local history written by a descendant and local newspaper editor, Ralph LeFevre. LeFevre's work was first published in 1903 and is based on a number of earlier publications, but it was his book that had the most staying power. His book also grounded the interpretation of the site through most of the twentieth century. Within the pages of that text can be found the essential elements of the traditional New Paltz narrative upon which the monument and the markers are based, concerning the flight of the descendants' supposedly Huguenot ancestors from religious persecution and their establishment of a French community uniquely governed by the Duzine.[5]

Elizabeth LeFever and Cornelia DuBois—contemporaries of Ralph

LeFevre—offered similar tales. They, too, stressed the desire of the founders to form a separate community in order to preserve both their devout religiosity and their French (rather than Walloon) culture, which descendants viewed as inextricably intertwined. Commenting on the experience of her ancestors in Dutch-dominated Wiltwijck (later Kingston, New York), where they had lived prior to establishing New Paltz, Elizabeth LeFever could not help but empathize with those "God-fearing Huguenots" who had little in common with the stereotypically commercial Dutch. The founders "doubtless found little to their liking [in] the riotous trading post . . . where the streets resounded from morning to night with the clattering tongues of Dutch housewives, and from night to morning with the brawls of drunken sailors." Cornelia DuBois likewise stressed the moral superiority of her supposedly Huguenot ancestors, noting that "whereas most of the Dutch Reformed churches sprang from the Dutch who came to America for gain, the New Paltz church claims as her forefathers those heroic souls . . . who fled from France because of religious intolerance." She further emphasized the sincere, but ultimately unsuccessful, effort on the part of the founders to preserve their French language as a means of anchoring their piety. She (erroneously) remarked that that "little village kep[t] up her mother tongue for nearly a century in the midst of a people speaking a different language." Unfortunately for them, they ultimately "had no weapons left with which to fight the calamity" of the loss of their Frenchness. According to DuBois, they must have experienced that loss as a great "tragedy," since she believed that the Frenchness of their ancestors, which was thoroughly aligned with their faith, represented the very core of their being. Those stalwart Huguenots, who had risked so much to form their own independent, French-speaking community in the wilderness, were apparently unable to defend themselves against the cultural onslaught of the irrepressible Dutch farmers who inhabited the region.[6]

Descendants likewise suggested that after the French tongue was lost to the Dutch that Dutch then persisted well into the nineteenth century. Ralph LeFevre incorrectly indicated that it is likely that most of the descendants of the founders began to learn English only when they went to school, but not before 1815, when the community supposedly hired their first English-speaking teacher, who was Irish. Cornelia DuBois echoed LeFevre, writing in 1915 that only when those of her grandparents' generation went to school did they learn English. Descendants did not offer much more about the transition from Dutch to English culture, as their primary concern was not the Dutchness but the supposed Frenchness of their ancestors. Nevertheless, descendants suggested that the members of the patentee families were ethnoculturally conservative regardless of which ethnic culture they aimed to preserve.[7]

The story the descendants formulated in the nineteenth and early twentieth centuries was further popularized beginning in the 1950s when another descendant, Kenneth E. Hasbrouck Sr., began his efforts to enlarge the architectural holdings of the Huguenot Historical Society from a single stone house to include the seven that remained standing in the historic core of the village. In his 1952 *The Street of the Huguenots*, Hasbrouck glorified "the story of this unique Street, which might be called 'one of the oldest streets in America with its original houses.'" He claimed it "had its beginning in 17th Century France where religious and political persecution made it necessary for many people to escape and find new homes in foreign lands," including his ancestors. He further (but incorrectly) elaborated that "the people owned the land in common, and by that arrangement the fruits of their labor went into a common store. For fifty years the heads of the twelve families met in legislative and executive session to administer the affairs of the Paltz. . . . The council was called the Duzine, meaning the twelve." These were the same points that LeFevre had stressed a half century before. Hasbrouck also alluded to the erroneous construction dates molded into the historic markers that stand before each of the stone houses, remarking that "when the early years of pioneering were over, the Patentees built homes resembling those they had left in France."[8]

Professional scholars rarely referred to the history of New Paltz before the 1990s, but when they did, the LeFevre/Hasbrouck interpretation was without question the source. According to Michael Kammen, who published his *Colonial New York: A History* in 1975, the "Dutch and French had been coming" in the late seventeenth century, "especially French Protestants after revocation [*sic*] of the Edict of Nantes in 1685. Many of them remained in New York City; but the most memorable made their mark upriver at New Paltz, where they built sturdy stone houses." Kammen seems to have been unaware of the fact that those famous "Huguenots" who settled New Paltz had left their homeland decades before the 1685 Revocation, an error which led him to the conclusion that persecution motivated their migrations. Kammen also accepted the construction dates of the houses as provided by Hasbrouck, as he did LeFevre's and Hasbrouck's explanation of the early town government. Kammen further commented that "their ethnic identity endures to this day," clearly referencing the activities of the Huguenot Historical Society. Alice P. Kenney in her 1975 *Stubborn for Liberty* similarly remarked upon the non-Dutch settlers of the Hudson River Valley in the seventeenth century. She noted that "the first of these groups were the Huguenots driven from France by the persecution surrounding the revocation of the Edict of Nantes in 1685. . . . Only some of them came to New York . . . but those who did . . . soon found places among the craftsmen of New York City or on the land at their settlements of New Rochelle and New Paltz. At New Paltz their stone houses, which reflect the medieval stone architecture of France, can still be seen in the only museum village in the country maintained by an organization of descendants of an ethnic group of original settlers." Clearly, Kammen's and Kenney's versions of New Paltz's past had been informed by the descendants' interpretation of their ancestors' migrations.[9]

This descendant-influenced interpretation of New Paltz still dominated when I began working for the Huguenot Historical Society in 2001, although the Society's professional staff was becoming increasingly engaged in both supporting and conducting new research. As a result of these endeavors, scholars were beginning to debunk or at least severely problematize many supposed "facts" concerning the history of the town. In so doing, they created the potential to undermine the traditional narrative. However, in their analyses of both the archival record and the material culture of the historic village, they consciously or unconsciously preserved the descendants' perspectives. Through these investigations, they concluded that the patentees and their eighteenth-century descendants were conservatives who consciously aimed to preserve their ethnocultural practices and traditions in a multicultural environment.

The most comprehensive of these recent interpretations is Paula Wheeler Carlo's 2005 study of New Paltz, in which she perpetuates the false assertion that the founders were "Huguenot Refugees," framing their experience in terms of "The Huguenot Diaspora," which was motivated by persecution in France. She does so in spite of the fact that she correctly notes that the founders (or at least most of them) were Walloons from the Spanish Netherlands, a point upon which some descendants had also previously remarked but never interrogated. Carlo's primary goal is to problematize Jon Butler's assertion that Huguenots who immigrated to cities in British colonial America quickly assimilated and disappeared as a distinct ethnocultural group. Although she accepts Butler's argument as it relates to urban Huguenots in America, Carlo's goal is to prove that assimilation did not occur at the same rate in rural locales, including New Paltz and New Rochelle, where she claims Huguenots perpetuated a distinct culture for far longer. In setting the stage for the ethnocultural experience of the founding families and their descendants, she preserves the nineteenth- and twentieth-century descendants' assertion that the founders established the town of New Paltz itself in order to preserve their culture through the creation of distinct and unique religious and governmental institutions, independent of both the Dutch in the region and the English who governed the colony. Carlo does, of course, acknowledge ethnocultural change in the eighteenth century, which she describes as "gradual acculturation," but she is rather imprecise about both the process and its timing. Yet, in establishing the founders as ethnocultural preservationists, she suggests that their immediate descendants were as well, and therefore that their gradual acculturation was something they had hoped to avoid.[10]

In a series of articles, Eric Roth has provided a similar interpretation to that of Carlo. In discussing poor relief in New Paltz, Roth somewhat hesitantly suggests that the patentees and their descendants remained committed to a particular Huguenot mission through the first half of the eighteenth century, evidenced by their willingness to provide for the poor independently of the local government. However, in discussing business connections between members of the patentee families and French speakers throughout New York, he takes a far bolder position, arguing that "for the first seventy-years of the town's existence, the population of New Paltz was dominated by French-speakers who were deeply committed to the retention of their language and culture."[11]

Architectural historian Neil Larson agrees with Carlo and Roth that the patentee families were committed to ethnocultural preservation well into the eighteenth century and perhaps even longer, although he suggests that the culture they were trying to preserve was neither French nor Walloon. Rather, he argues that the children of the New Paltz founders embraced Dutchness, which they demonstrated by willingly adopting the architectural traditions of the local Dutch, a practice that some descendants continued to follow into the early years of the nineteenth century. Larson maintains that in the early eighteenth century, that style "was consciously regressing to a more emphatic statement of cultural identity and resistance to change" in response to the "challeng[e] of British settlement." Even though many members of the second generation possessed parents who were both Walloons, they were apparently willing to abandon their culture in favor of that of the conservative Dutch. Larson therefore implicitly suggests that as Walloons they were progressive, but as people assimilating into the local Dutch, they were conservative. This is theoretically conceivable, even if it contradicts the arguments of Carlo and Roth, as the generations that followed the founders might have thought that they could benefit by culturally joining with the local Dutch population. However, he supports such a strong assertion with limited evidence, as he grounds his conclusions strictly in the architectural record of the community. Even so, Larson undermines his own argument for ethnocultural conservatism when he discusses the introduction of English architectural elements into a Dutch-American paradigm, which began as early as the 1730s. Based on his assertion that the New Paltz founding families were Dutch ethnocultural preservationists, he is forced to conclude that they only incorporated English architectural elements in the interest of modernization rather than as a means of Anglicizing. While this is indeed an arguable point, Larson implicitly suggests that cultural preservation mattered when the New Paltz families followed Dutch architectural traditions, but that culture was irrelevant when they adopted aspects of contemporary English architecture. Even though Larson does not agree with Carlo and Roth as to which culture the early descendants of the patentees aimed to preserve, all three scholars' assertions remain consistent with the descendants' traditional interpretation of the general ethnocultural conservatism of the patentee families.[12]

While both amateur and professional historians do not explain precisely when and how the descendants of the Walloon patentees adopted or adapted Dutch culture, all were certainly cognizant that they did, and in turn, that they also had to come to terms with English culture. As such, their interpretations of the ethnocultural history of New Paltz are not isolated from the broader historiography on the Dutch experience in colonial New York. They also share with that broader research similar perspectives and conclusions, which tend to accentuate ethnocultural preservation and resistance against what John Murrin has called English "ethnic aggression." Donna Merwick's recent research exploring Nieuw Nederland after the conquest is the most intriguing of the newer scholarship. She does not so much suggest that the Dutch of New York were resistant to change but that change was virtually impossible because of dramatic distinctions between the Dutch and English cultures that made cross-cultural communication and understanding almost impossible.[13]

In *Possessing Albany*, Merwick argues that the two cultures were "essentially" different, with the early modern Dutch being an urban, commercial, republican people who "navigated" the land, and the English being a rural, landed, and monarchical people who "occupied" the land. Such an argument suggests that both the rural Dutch farmers and the urban English merchants were strangers within their own cultures. Merwick also explores how the transition from Dutch and English rule left those active in the legal sphere without a place or the possibility of earning a living, apparently even motivating a former Dutch notary to kill himself. While he certainly took an extreme approach to his predicament, Merwick subtly suggests that his choice symbolizes the real impact of the loss of one's country and culture. Overall, Merwick suggests that the Dutch experience of English conquest was one of confusion and tragedy, and in such light, it is difficult to imagine how the former Nieuw Nederlanders could have successfully adapted to English culture even if they had so desired, which, according to Merwick, most had not.[14]

Those who have studied the Dutch Reformed Church in North America after the English conquest have similarly suggested Dutch conservativism and resistance. Randall Balmer argues that many urban Dutch Americans experienced marginalization as a result of the English conquest, motivating some to move to rural locations in New Jersey. There they apparently created a "frontier" society that made them prime targets for the anti-establishment perspective of Dutch Reformed pietists. According to Balmer, conflict between pietists and the orthodox erupted in the context of the Great Awakening, leading to the Coetus-Conferentie dispute, which pitted those who aimed to create an American classis against those who supported subordination to the Classis of Amsterdam. (In the presbyterian system of the Dutch Reformed Church, a classis is a regional ecclesiastical body that examines and ordains ministerial candidates and provides organizational and theological oversight of congregations and ministers in its region.) Balmer notes that the dispute paradoxically promoted ethnocultural change because of the ecumenical spirit of the Great Awakening, which brought Dutch Reformed Americans more closely into contact with English-speaking Protestants of a Calvinist persuasion. Nevertheless, Balmer claims that the roots of the conflict can be found among those who had suffered from the English conquest and sought the countryside in order to preserve their culture.[15]

Dirk Mouw successfully refutes Balmer's interpretation, arguing that the Coetus-Conferentie dispute was not predicated on a conflict between pietism and orthodoxy, yet Mouw also argues for ethnocultural preservation and resistance. He emphatically claims that both sides in the affair were attempting "to avoid the demise of their religion, culture, and ethnic identity" "in an increasingly diverse and ostensibly hostile environment" dominated by their English rulers. Firth Haring Fabend agrees that the New York and New Jersey Dutch were indeed ethnocultural preservationists. She argues that a distinct Dutch cultural identity survived well into the nineteenth century, primarily through a continued commitment to the Dutch Reformed Church. Nevertheless, her evidence might actually suggest the possibility that those of Dutch heritage were constructing a Dutch identity anew in the second quarter of the nineteenth century rather than preserving a living culture. As such, early nineteenth-century Dutch culture might have been more of a revival than a survival.[16]

Not all scholars have argued that the Dutch of New York and New Jersey were essentially conservative. Joyce D. Goodfriend successfully supports a model of gradual acculturation in New York City, as does David Narrett in his analysis of property rights, gender, and the family. But Goodfriend and Narrett would certainly argue that cultural processes in the entire Dutch cultural region cannot be extrapolated from those in New York City, nor that the study of one form of ethnocultural expression represents culture in its totality. Their findings, while important, therefore cannot explain the Dutch-American experience more broadly. More comprehensive is the work of David Steven Cohen, which reveals similar processes in rural material culture (including architecture), folklife, and the family. Importantly, all three of these authors' studies were published more than two decades ago, but this strain in the literature has been somewhat submerged in more recent formulations.[17]

An additional limitation of the historiography of Dutch New York and New Jersey is that many scholars have taken a regional rather than a local approach, including Narrett, Cohen, and John R. Stevens, with Fabend's study of the Haring family and Goodfriend's exploration of New York City being notable exceptions. Yet, except for a very small minority of the colonial population, most colonists lived geographically circumscribed lives, such that rural people in the Dutch cultural region would have made ethnocultural choices in the primary context of their communities rather than the region as a whole. As a result, a broad regional approach tends to obscure how individuals or particular communities experienced ethnocultural stasis or change on the ground. New Paltz was certainly not isolated, but it was decidedly insular, as were many early American communities. The farthest that the great majority of those who lived in New Paltz traveled was to the nearby town of Kingston, the seat of Ulster County. This is certainly not to suggest that regional studies are not valuable, nor that rural culture was not affected by changes in government and law made at the provincial level. Yet, many ethnocultural decisions remained in the hands of individuals at the local level, even when impacted by law. Perhaps one reason that many have taken a broad regional approach is that many studies address only one or two forms of culture, such that a wide evidentiary net must be cast. Again, exploring one form of culture in depth has its benefits, but care must be taken when drawing broad conclusions concerning ethnocultural strategies as a whole from more particular findings. To put this another way, a great deal of the literature is both geographically broad and ethnoculturally selective. There is therefore a need to reverse the balance through the use of a microhistorical approach that treats a limited area in a comprehensive manner, as such an approach can provide a clearer lens through which ethnocultural stasis and/or change as lived experience might be revealed.[18]

A further limitation of the historiography of colonial Dutch North

America is that many of the most compelling recent works address the Nieuw Nederland period, or at their broadest, the seventeenth century. Merwick's studies fall into that category, as do the works of Evan Haefeli, Susanah Shaw Romney, Janny Vennema, and Jaap Jacobs. There are far fewer recent studies that consider the eighteenth century—Dirk Mouw's being an important exception—such that the historiographical context for studies of the eighteenth-century Dutch-American experience remains that provided by such as Goodfriend, Cohen, and Narrett. Perhaps the limited attention recently paid to the history of Dutch culture in New York is due to the fact that post-conquest Dutch Americans have generally been seen as ethnoculturally conservative. Based on such an interpretation, the suggestion is that it is possible to see Dutch-American culture in the eighteenth century through that of the seventeenth. Even if Dutch Americans were conservative, they did not live in a static time, such that more attention needs to be paid to how they continued to respond ethnoculturally to changing social, political, economic, and cultural environments.[19]

In considering the history as told by descendants, as well as the scholarly explorations of New Paltz and the Dutch American cultural region more broadly, one notes that a general sense of ethnocultural conservatism pervades much of it. All have noted or discussed ethnocultural change—not to have done so would have been absurd—but investigations of change have often suggested that a great deal of ethnocultural change and acculturation was the result of ethnocultural pressure rather than willing choice. The studies of Goodfriend, Cohen, and Narrett do suggest otherwise, and their insights deserve greater attention.

Of course, the existing literature has many obvious merits. Still, it collectively does not provide an adequate lens through which to see the history of New Paltz, as the New Paltz patentee community was anything but ethnoculturally static or conservative over the course of the long eighteenth century. As much as some would argue otherwise, the history of the patentees of New Paltz and their descendants reveals active, conscious, and voluntary ethnocultural flexibility and change over time. The cultural process that best describes how the patentee families responded to their multicultural environment is creolization. "Creolization" is a fluid term for a fluid process. While scholars contest its precise meaning, it generally refers to the mixing of cultures, sometimes by force, sometimes by necessity, sometimes by choice, and sometimes for more than one reason simultaneously. Creolization is therefore characterized by individual and/or collective use of forms of cultural expression of more than one ethnocultural group, and/or the adaptation of available ethnocultural source material to create entirely new forms through hybridization.[20]

The parameters and purpose of creolization are heavily influenced by intergroup power relations, such that scholars have often approached the process through the experience of forcefully relocated, oppressed, and/or colonized peoples. Such people often could not avoid creolization, but they also might, in turn, become active agents in the process, sometimes using it subversively as a tool of resistance. However, creolization is not dependent upon such extreme power asymmetries, and neither is creolization a process experienced or created solely by the less powerful. The availability of more than one ethnocultural vocabulary can influence all involved, regardless of social position; in other words, creolization can be multidirectional. Power also can take many forms—a monopoly on the use of force, the ability to persuade, and the strength of numbers—with differing results. The power that influences creolization may also come not only from outside but also from within, such that intragroup relations might influence the process of creolization as well. The precise characteristics of creolization are therefore highly variable and situation specific.

To some extent, creolization was unavoidable for the patentees and their descendants, as they established their community after the English conquest. They therefore were forced to incorporate aspects of Anglo-American culture, particularly in law and government. In spite of this outside force, they collectively did not meet English power with cultural resistance, as they had never experienced English culture as aggressive. Some even began, by choice, to integrate elements of English culture into their ethnocultural expression in the earliest years of the community's history. Of course, English was not the only foreign culture the founders encountered, as they lived in a Dutch cultural region. The local Dutch therefore had power as well—the power of numbers. The founders and their descendants did not meet Dutch power with resistance either, so much so that the descendants of the Walloon founders became part of the local "Dutch" population. (By "Dutch," I am referring both to those whose heritage lay in the Netherlands as well as those people of non-Dutch heritage who had settled in Nieuw Nederland before the conquest and who essentially assimilated into a broader Dutch-American culture. "Dutch" also refers to those of their descendants who preserved such a "Batavianized" cultural orientation. But in becoming "Dutch," the Dutchness of the descendants was never stable nor complete. While it therefore may be possible to determine the ethnicities of the ancestors of a particular patentee descendant, such that a particular individual may have been, for example, genealogically one-quarter Walloon, one-half Dutch, and one-quarter German/"Dutch," from an ethnocultural perspective, it is often not possible to speak of an individual's having been distinctly Walloon, Dutch, or English in such a creolized environment.

In short, the patentees and their descendants accepted and became active agents of creolization in spite of the fact that there was outside pressure to do so. They were comfortable creolizing because precisely how they did so was substantially under their control throughout the long eighteenth century. Sometimes they creolized by taking advantage of the possibilities and choices that a creolized environment created, to individually select from and/or hybridize the cultures available as their beliefs and ideas dictated. At other times they responded pragmatically to the ethnocultural limitations they faced as a result of living on the ethnocultural periphery of an Anglo-American Atlantic world. In all, why the patentees and their eighteenth-century descendants made the ethnocultural choices they did within a creolized environment was therefore not monolithic. As a group, they generally approached their ethnocultural choices as matters of necessity and/or practicality, but as individuals, they were often able to make decisions according to personal desires; the variety of choices they made was therefore almost as extensive as the number of people within the community. Creativity was acceptable and prevalent, such that the availability of multiple cultures and the possibilities of hybridization represented opportunity rather than a threat, at least for most. To put this another way, ethnocultural conservatism apparently had less to offer the patentee community than did creative creolization, as the former limited while the latter enabled choice.

As much as ethnocultural creativity and change were ever present, the members of the patentee community effected change slowly and subtly. The result was that descendants maintained a creolized environment without ever producing a stable, bounded, creole culture. In other words, descendants never created one way of experiencing or directing the process of creolization. Because the patentees and their descendants had the power to substantially chart their ethnocultural courses and because they collectively did so slowly and sinuously, creolization rarely produced any noticeable conflict. The one conflict that did break forth in New Paltz was motivated by the goals of the few ethnocultural conservatives within the community, who, as exceptions, proved the rule.

In considering how members of the patentee families creolized, it is rarely possible to extrapolate from their behaviors to their self-constructed identities, as the evidence is relatively silent on this point. Members of the patentee families left no records in which they articulated what it meant to them to read from a French religious tract while living in a Dutch-American house, or to hear biblical passages spoken in Dutch in their church while following English gender ideals within the family. That they did freely choose from the multiple ethnocultural vocabularies available to them is clear, but the relationship between those choices and their ethnic self-perceptions is extremely opaque. Although it may be impossible to know why most made the ethnocultural decisions that they did, and what they thought about those decisions, it is still possible to appreciate the complex choices open to them as they selected marriage partners, built and lived in their houses, worshipped in their congregations, provided for the future of their families, and communicated with each other through their chosen languages. The choices they made, both consciously and unconsciously, but always actively, fluidly shifted their creolized environment for a century and a half.

Of course, the creolizing of three European cultures in the early years of the community rendered New Paltz atypical in the annals of early New York, but once descendants of the founders ultimately abandoned their Walloonness, they preserved a Dutch/Anglo-American creolized environment that survived even into the early nineteenth century. New Paltz is therefore linked to many communities that had been dominated by Dutch culture from the time of their founding. And like those whose ancestral origins were more closely linked to the Netherlands, the descendants of the founders ultimately abandoned Dutch cultural forms, integrating their ethnocultural expression into the dominant Anglo-American culture, a process that again they substantially controlled. Still, for at least a hundred years after this integration occurred, descendants never lost sight of the fact that their origins were not of the dominant population. They therefore felt the need to respond to the creation of a cultural environment in the nineteenth century that racialized and valorized the "Anglo-Saxon." Their response was to imagine themselves into being culturally distinct by creating persistent "Huguenot" and "Dutch" identities, even though their forbears had abandoned clear markers of those ethnic cultures sometimes generations or even centuries earlier.

The overall purpose of this study is not to suggest that the exact manner and timing of creolization in New Paltz is typical, as to claim that any New York town was typical would be erroneous, given the ethnic and socioeconomic heterogeneity of the colony and state. Rather, my primary goal is to explore the complex process of creolization as comprehensively as possible, as it is just such a lens that most effectively reveals the parameters of ethnocultural interaction in the ethnically diverse Hudson River Valley. Indeed, how the process played out in the various towns and cities would likely have been distinct, as the timing, place, socioeconomic structure, and ethnic composition of each was different; but it was just those socioeconomic and cultural forces that affected the ethnocultural environment of New Paltz as much as any other place. If a microhistorical investigation of one New York town, a type of study that has not been previously attempted, can reveal active, fluid, and voluntary creolization, perhaps the question of ethnocultural conservatism among non-English New Yorkers might be worthy of reevaluation, particularly in the case of rural environments.

It is worth clarifying that my intent is not to study New Paltz per se, but rather the patentees, their descendants, and those who became part of those families (most often through marriage) within the village. For almost a century, these families, which I have designated "the patentee community," were almost coextensive with the village, at least in terms of the free, white population. Even as newcomers eventually settled in New Paltz, the patentee community continued to comprise both the elite and the great majority of the middling population in the village throughout the long eighteenth century. I am indeed a bit hesitant to employ the term "community," based on recent usage. It is an excessively overused word, often suggesting a cohesive group with shared characteristics when no such cohesion actually exists (such as "the black community" or "the gay community"). Nevertheless, my use of "community" in this context is apt. The patentees and their eighteenth-century descendants were thoroughly linked through their congregation, their government (which the patentees and their descendants controlled), their management of the patent, their neighborhoods, and their continued patterns of intermarriage.

This attention to the patentee community leaves out the ethnocultural expression of those who lived among, but were not part of, that community, most particularly the many enslaved laborers in the village. Although fundamental to the village's economy and society, precise figures as to the enslaved population are only of limited availability. In 1703, enslaved laborers comprised approximately 7 percent of the population (nine out of 130) and 13 percent in 1790 (302 out of 2,309). In 1755, twenty-eight individuals—all members of the patentee community—possessed a total of seventy-eight enslaved laborers, further suggesting that a significant minority of the members of the patentee community owned human property. As for the origin of the New Paltz slaves, whether they were born in Africa, the Caribbean, or the North American mainland, very little is known, such that their ancestral culture cannot be discussed. As to their assumed creolization, only tidbits about their fluency in Euro-American culture have survived. Neither is there any evidence whether African culture influenced ethnocultural expression among the patentee community. In short, it would not be fruitful to explore the process and the influence of African-American creolization in New Paltz, as the evidence simply does not exist.

Neither do I train my focus on the ethnocultural experience of those free, white New Paltz residents who lived outside of the patentee community, many of whom were of Anglo backgrounds. In many ways, these families were even more peripheral than the enslaved people, as the latter at least shared the day-to-day lives of those who owned them, presumably for long periods of time. These Anglo people were also latecomers to the town, as their numbers only started to increase after 1763. Most were also relatively transient and lived on the socioeconomic, political, and geographic margins of the village, and as such, did not leave strong imprints on the historical record as to their ethnocultural expression. In total, it is virtually impossible to consider the ethnic culture of those who lived within New Paltz but were outside of the patentee community. Besides, if anything, the patentee community is a more defined and cohesive unit of analysis than the village of New Paltz was, as the patentee community was socially, culturally, economically, and even politically united throughout the long eighteenth century, far more than the village as a whole.[21]

I begin with an analysis of what motivated the families of the founders to leave their Walloon homeland for other European regions, ultimately settling in and around the city of Mannheim in the Palatinate (Die Pfalz). Contrary to the myths, their choice to leave had nothing to do with religious persecution. Rather, they fled because of difficult material circumstances brought about by war, as well as the attraction of economic opportunities abroad. Such factors also motivated some of those Walloon migrants to leave their home in the Palatinate for the New World, as did their decision to establish a Walloon community of their own in New York. That, too, was a decision motivated by economic opportunity—in this case, land acquisition—rather than a choice based on a desire for religious and/or political independence in the interest of preserving a distinct Walloon culture. From a religious or political perspective, doing so was simply impossible, at least when New Paltz was founded. What a separate community did allow for, however, was local economic dominance throughout the long eighteenth century, which considerably minimized outside pressure to conform to Dutch and English culture, except in limited and predictable ways. It was this local power and a lack of "ethnic aggression," which provided the context for the ethnocultural decisions that the patentees and their descendants made throughout the eighteenth century. It also affected how they would integrate themselves into the broad ethnic diversity of their region. To put this another way, the founders did not separate themselves into their own community in order to preserve their culture, but their economic power in their community allowed them to substantially determine for themselves to what extent they would preserve it, as well as how much they were willing to incorporate other ethnic cultures and people.

As the founders established a fluidly shifting, creolized, ethnocultural environment in the seventeenth century, their descendants willingly sustained such patterns throughout the long eighteenth century, although the cultural vocabularies that they creolized did change over time. Even the founders themselves let aspects of their Walloon culture slip into the past in favor of both Dutch and English culture, a trend that their children continued to effect into the early eighteenth centuries. The generations that followed then proactively let the Dutchness of the community continuously decline, causing little overt stress, at least for most. This shifting and willing creolization can best be seen through an exploration of architecture, gendered thinking as revealed in property rights, and language use, all three of which were forms of ethnocultural expression over which the patentees and their descendants had considerable, although not always complete, control.

Although most members of the community felt free to construct their own creolized culture, a few individuals did choose to openly resist ethnocultural change, while a few others actively encouraged it. Their polarized perspectives ultimately split the community apart. This division occurred in the context of the Coetus-Conferentie dispute in the Dutch Reformed Church in the 1760s, with those who promoted change seeking greater ecclesiastical authority for the American congregations and those who aimed to preserve Dutch culture hoping to preserve ecclesiastical connections with the church polity in the Netherlands. These divergent choices did not actually influence ethnocultural stasis or change in New Paltz to any noticeable extent, but whether the American congregations increased their authority or preserved limitations on their power did serve as a powerful symbol of ethnic identity for those who energetically promoted either position. Most members of the patentee families embraced the position of the most vocal proponent of American ecclesiastical authority, a community leader who actively embraced English culture. They accepted his position even though they continued to preserve a creolized ethnocultural environment in ways that he did not. They simply did not feel the need to preserve connections with the Netherlands in order to perpetuate a creolized culture that included Dutchness. Members of the founding families had always felt comfortable constructing their culture as they saw fit without the need for ethnocultural symbolism, and they would continue to freely draw from both Dutch and English culture for as much as a half century longer, in spite of their increased ecclesiastical distance from the fatherland.

Although the descendants of the founders had created and accepted an Anglo-American ethnocultural environment by the early nineteenth century, they never forgot that their heritage lay among the Walloons (whom they interpreted as having been Huguenots) and the Dutch. Beginning in the 1840s, they began to use that memory in response to the efforts of Americans of English heritage to create an Anglo-American identity grounded in a mythical Anglo-Saxon commitment to liberty and self-government that had supposedly burst forth anew in the wilds of the New World. This was a vision that nineteenth-century descendants of colonists whose heritage lay on the Continent could not countenance, encouraging some, such as the descendants of the New Paltz founders, to claim *their* centrality to the origins of American culture and political identity. These claims were highly charged, as they were grounded in a developing ideology of "race." Racial thinking was grounded in a belief that humans can be grouped according to physical characteristics linked to national, cultural, or geographic origins, which in turn can be linked to intellectual and moral capabilities and even ideological positions. As such, "Irish" and "German" and "French" and "Dutch" were considered "races" in the nineteenth century as much as "Negro" and "Indian" were. Upon such differences did many nineteenth-century Anglo-Americans, English, and Germans "scientifically" construct a hierarchy of human groups that became a central tenet of the culture of those who socioeconomically dominated in the United States. While this ideology affected American society and culture in multiple ways, its relevance to nineteenth-century interpretations of American history is that it suggested that political ideas, political culture, and even religious ideals were essentially grounded in biology.

Descendants of early American colonists of "Huguenot"/Walloon and Dutch origins, such as those in New Paltz, were less convinced as to the appropriateness of defining Americanness as being grounded in the Anglo-Saxon race's essential liberalism. In response, they began to forcefully argue that the true commitment to political liberty and self-government lay with the Dutch and religious liberty with the Huguenots. According to the descendants of the patentees, the founders of New Paltz were therefore much more suitable for ancestor worship than the Puritans of New England or the cavaliers of Virginia. This desire on the part of the descendants to celebrate their ancestors ultimately motivated them to form an organization—the Huguenot Historical Society—to protect and perpetuate that legacy through the creation of sites of public commemoration, including the Memorial House and the Patentees Monument. Later descendants added six more Huguenot Street stone houses and a reconstructed church to the society's holdings. However, in first constructing a history for themselves and then giving physical form to that history, the founders of the society fundamentally and thoroughly came to misunderstand the actual experience of their ancestors. They did so in a manner that continues to cloud an understanding of that history even today. Perhaps surprisingly, these descendants of non-English western Europeans struggled with their ethnocultural and ethnoracial identity, both personally and collectively, for more than 250 years after their ancestors came to the American shores. This fact suggests that New York's having once been Nieuw Nederland is not a story that ended in the seventeenth, eighteenth, or even nineteenth century. Through its many twists and turns, to be of northwest European birth or descent in an Anglo-American world continued to ramify for centuries after Dutch rule in North America had long since ended.

Chapter 1

THE WALLOONS' ENGLISH TOWN

In 1677, a small band of Walloon emigrants from Europe made the decision to establish a new community in the mid-Hudson River Valley in a Dutch cultural region within an English colony. To do so, twelve men purchased a large tract of land from the Esopus Indians, for which they were granted a patent the following year by the royal governor, Edmund Andros. The creation of this new village, which they named New Paltz, was the culmination of decades of migration in both Europe and America, motivated by ongoing wartime violence as well as a search for economic opportunity. Their search was ultimately successful, and they established a town, which they and their descendants socially and politically dominated for more than two hundred years. In creating their own town, however, they never intended to live in isolation from those of other ethnic groups. Because of their extensive local control, they never felt threatened by those who were not Walloons. They therefore allowed those of other ethnicities into their community, including those of British birth or heritage, as they could do so entirely on their own terms.

The Walloon Diaspora

The founders' heritage lay in the Walloon region of the southern Netherlands and northern France, which had been a politically unstable place since the mid-sixteenth century (see Map 1.1). The challenges the Walloons faced motivated many to seek better situations in other European regions, such as in England, the United Provinces (after the 1579 Union of Utrecht), and the Palatinate (Die Pfalz). The number of migrants sometimes made it possible to establish expatriate communities abroad, such as in Canterbury, England, the history of which is connected to the New Paltz story.

The earliest expatriates who relocated to Canterbury did so as early as the 1540s, having migrated for economic reasons. A few remained there even through the revival of Roman Catholicism during the reign of Mary I. After the 1558 accession of the Protestant queen, Elizabeth I, more Protestant Walloons from the southern Netherlands began to migrate to England to free themselves from the vicious persecution of the Catholic King Philip II of Spain, to whom they were subject in their homeland. In England, Walloons were permitted free exercise of their religion, as well as a number of privileges related to the manufacture and sale of goods, most importantly cloth. Some of this second wave of refugees settled in London, but in 1561, the queen

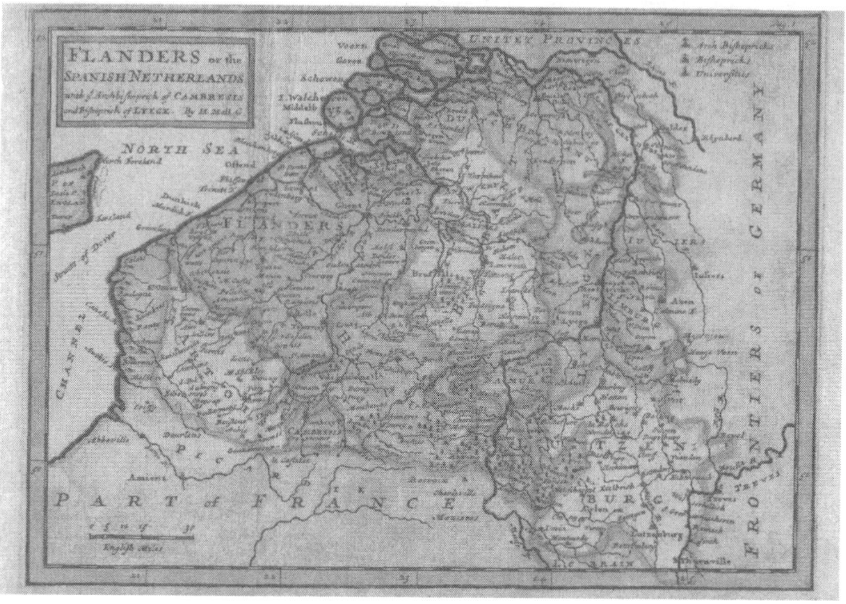

Map 1.1. The Spanish Netherlands, Herman Moll, c. 1707. *Twenty-four new and accurate maps of the several parts of Europe*. London: J. Nicholson, c. 1707. Collection of the author.

permitted twenty-five of these recently arrived households to relocate to Sandwich. The situation in the Netherlands became worse for Protestants in 1566, when Philip II sent the Duke of Alva to crush the Protestant movement there, motivating more Walloon religious refugees to migrate to England. By 1574, some of these new migrants had settled in Canterbury, joining the small number of Walloons who had been there since the 1540s. The size of the Walloon population in Canterbury grew even further when the queen directed a number of Walloons in Sandwich to relocate to Canterbury in 1575, as their numbers were growing beyond what the town of Sandwich could support. In 1579, the seven northern provinces of the Netherlands joined together through the Union of Utrecht in pursuit of independence from Spain, but the southern provinces remained under the unquestioned rule of Spain, and persecution under the duke continued. Expatriation for religious reasons went on unabated, such that by the end of the sixteenth century, the number of Protestant Walloons that remained in the Spanish Netherlands, as these southern provinces were then named, was "minuscule."[1]

As the Walloon population grew in Canterbury, it became clear that all had not migrated to the city due to religious persecution in their homeland. In 1582, Canterbury's Burghmote court noted that there were "so many as are alreadye here abydinge that are not come for theire consciences as protestants for defence of theire faith & of the worde of God. And whome the Elders of the said congregacion will not allowe of and answere for that they shall be sent awaye and not suffered here to tarrye." In spite of this protest, the number of Walloons in Canterbury continued to increase over the subsequent decades, such that by 1627, more than a thousand immigrants had settled there, mostly from a region extending from Armentières to Valenciennes. All did not remain, however, as some refugees returned home when the level of conflict in the continental Walloon region diminished in the opening decades of the seventeenth century.[2]

Unfortunately for the Walloons, this stability did not last, as in 1635, France declared war on Spain. This new conflict motivated Walloons once again to seek safety elsewhere in Europe, including England. This third wave of expatriation was motivated neither by economic nor religious reasons as in the past but by wartime violence or impending violence. On March 13, 1635, the mayor of Dover wrote to the Lord Warden, remarking that "near a hundred men, women and children, French and Dutch, all Protestants, some of them bringing with them their goods and household stuff whose dwellings were in and near Calais, but have lands and tenements in Flanders, and flee hither for security of the same in respect to the war likely to be betwixt France and Spain (as they say)." These new refugees were sent inland, including some to Canterbury. France invaded the province of Artois in the Spanish Netherlands in 1640 during the Thirty Years' War, such that the number of refugees from wartime violence increased even further. (France annexed Artois in 1659.) The records of the Burghmote in Canterbury, in an order dated September 21, 1641, note that since the reign of Elizabeth I, the Walloons "have lived peacablie and religiously and with their manufactures of spyneing and weaving by them introduced . . . . They therefore humbly desired this Court that in regard of the present Calamyties of warre in Picardie Arthois & fflandre many of the wallon people daily resort until this Citty and more daily are expected who being protestants and manufacturers in weaving desire to ioyne themselves unto the wallon Congregacon here."[3]

The Walloon community in Canterbury soon came to include Matthieu Blanchan and his family, who later would be linked to the history of New Paltz. Blanchan was born in the village of Noeville o corne in the province of Artois in the first decade of the seventeenth century. By 1633, he had relocated to the town of Armentières (near the city of Lille in Flanders), where he married Magdelaine Joire, a native of the village. The Blanchans remained there until at least August 1642, but by May 16, 1647, they had migrated to Canterbury. Why the Blanchans left their home in Armentières some time in the mid-1640s is unclear, as military conflict did not heavily affect Flanders until twenty years later when the French took Lille during the 1667–1668 War of Devolution, officially gaining the territory through the 1668 Treaty of Aix-la-Chapelle. Perhaps Blanchan was simply making a preemptive move, seeking a place of physical safety for himself and his family even before it was necessary, or perhaps his goals were primarily economic. In any event, his motivations were much more material than spiritual.[4]

Exactly how long the Blanchans stayed in Canterbury is not precisely known. They were still there in April 1649, but by 1652, Matthieu Blanchan and family had relocated yet again, possibly because England was suffering from a depression that began in 1646 and lasted until 1650. This time

Blanchan chose the German state of Die Pfalz, also known as the Palatinate, another region to which Walloons had been drawn since the mid-sixteenth century.[5]

In 1562, the Elector Frederick III, the ruler of Die Pfalz, had allowed sixty Walloon families to settle in a former monastery at Gross-Frankenthal, providing them with a charter that established the autonomy of their new community. The elector subsequently provided additional opportunities for Walloons to settle in his realm, and soon these refugees established a sufficient number of congregations to support the formation in 1571 of a classis of the Walloon Protestant Church. In 1607, another group of French-speaking Calvinists received a charter from Frederick III's successor, Frederick IV, to establish a community in Mannheim, but that community did not substantially grow before the advent of the Thirty Year's War. During that war, the Palatinate suffered extreme violence and depopulation due to emigration, military conflict, and famine, dramatically reducing the strength of its Walloon congregations.[6]

After the war's conclusion in 1648, the new elector, Charles Louis, aimed to rebuild his domain by attracting immigrants to his realm, particularly those with skills and resources, by offering a number of economic and religious freedoms. It was these freedoms and economic opportunities that apparently drew Blanchan, as they did a number of other Walloon migrants from the Spanish Netherlands, who strengthened the expatriate community in and around Mannheim. That community included many others who would later found the village of New Paltz, including members of the DuBois and Crispell families, both of which were originally from near Lille like Blanchan himself. It is not known exactly when members of the DuBois and Crispell families had relocated to Mannheim after the end of the Thirty Years' War, but they were soon united through marriage with the Blanchan family. Louis DuBois married Catherine, the daughter of Matthieu and Magdelaine Blanchan in October 1655, and in January 1660, Antoine Crispell was joined in matrimony with Catherine's sister, Marie.[7]

As the Palatinate had attracted the Blanchan family, so too did it attract the Bevier family, members of which had been migrating throughout Europe for reasons similar to those that had motivated the Blanchans. One of the Beviers, Louis, would eventually continue these migrations to the New World. Louis' father, also named Louis, was originally from Seloignes, one of the villages of Chimay in Hainault, a province of the Spanish Netherlands. As an adolescent, Louis the elder, along with his family of iron workers, had moved to Sweden in the 1630s to work in their trade; but Louis Sr. later relocated to the region around Mannheim and Frankenthal by 1645, where his son Louis was born. Louis the elder moved his family yet again around 1650, this time to Russia, in the employ of a Dutch businessman who was working to develop the iron and steel industry there. By 1655, however, he had returned to Die Pfalz, where Louis, his son, grew to adulthood and where he married Marie LeBlanc in 1673 in the town of Speyer.[8]

The other Walloons who later became involved in the New Paltz project also settled in the Palatinate after the Thirty Years' War, most likely because of wartime violence in or near their homeland. Christian Deyo and his family, from St.-Pol-sur-Ternoise near Arras in Artois, had emigrated to Mutterstadt in the Palatine before 1655 during the Franco-Spanish War, where most of his children were born. The brothers Jean and Abraham Hasbrouck and their father, natives of Calais, were also living in the Palatine towns of Mutterstadt and Mannheim by 1655. It is possible that these Hasbrouck brothers were cousins of Louis Bevier. Hugo Freer, a native of Herly on the western border of Artois, was also living in Mannheim by 1660, where he married his first wife. After her death, he married Jeanne Wibau, who was from near Tournai in the county of Hainault in the Spanish Netherlands; she was quite possibly the niece of Christian Deyo's wife Jannetje Wibau. The brothers Simon and Andries LeFevre also migrated to the Palatinate, presumably after the Thirty Years' War, although at what date is unknown. They originally hailed from Lorraine, a Walloon region that the French crown sought to gain beginning in the 1640s.[9]

Although Mannheim was growing and beginning to thrive, many of the early settlers chose not to stay. Matthieu Blanchan and his wife Magdelaine left in 1660, and there is nothing to suggest that anything other than economic opportunity motivated them to seek a new home yet again. Traveling aboard *De Vergulde Otter*, a ship of the Dutch West India Company, they and their three young children set sail on April 27, 1660, arriving in Nieuw Amsterdam in the Dutch colony of Nieuw Nederland several months later. They were accompanied by their daughter Marie and her husband Antoine Crispell. Louis DuBois and his wife Catherine Blanchan, along with their young sons Abraham and Isaac, arrived soon after. These three related families migrated to the Esopus, a region about halfway between Nieuw Amsterdam (later Manhattan) and Beverwyck (later Albany), to the town of Wiltwijck (later Kingston). By 1663, the Blanchan, DuBois, and Crispell family members had moved to Nieuw Dorp (later Hurley) about three miles south. They were apparently welcomed in this primarily Dutch region, as they were able to acquire land grants similar in size to those given to local Dutch men. As land was the basis of local social and political power, their acquisition of it allowed them to establish themselves as influential members of their new village. Louis DuBois's social position was reinforced when he was appointed a local magistrate after the English conquest.[10]

Those Walloons who remained in the Palatinate faced renewed violence when war broke out between the Holy Roman Empire and France in 1672. When the French military laid waste to a portion of the Palatinate in 1674, some chose to seek safety in the New World, including a number who later settled in the Esopus. That violence and the fear of violence motivated the migration of some Walloons to the Esopus is reinforced by the only surviving piece of direct evidence referencing the reasons why the future New Paltz founders relocated to America, a fragment of a 1676 letter sent from the town of Speyer in the Palatinate to America in 1676, which descended in the Hasbrouck family. In that letter, the unidentified author refers to the privations that his family faced as a result of the siege of the nearby city of Philipsburg. That city was under the control of French forces, as Louis XIV was attempting to increase his domain by seizing lands of the German states contiguous to France. The French occupation was contested by the forces of the Holy Roman Emperor, which, as an entrenched force, were causing material hardships and perhaps even presenting physical threats to the Walloons in Die Pfalz. The author writes, "As for us we have always great wars since your departure and we are still staying in this town [Speyer] waiting for better things. We have constantly lost our cattle and our harvest these two years past and this last summer were always with weapons in hand . . . if peace is not made we have nothing to expect in this quarter but all sorts of misery and poverty." The author further implores the recipient to "write us as quickly as possibly how it goes in your country and what there is of it, for if it is good I am always of the same intention as when you left here, to come and find you; but if it does not suit you well, I hope that you would return here near us," suggesting that safety and sustenance is what both the author and the recipient sought.[11]

Motivated by wartime violence, Christian Deyo and his son, Pierre, and daughters, Margaret, Elizabeth, and Maria, left the Palatinate for the New World in 1675. Like the Blanchan-DuBois-Crispell group before them, they first settled in Kingston, New York. There they anchored another node of interrelated Walloon families similar to that which centered around the Blanchan family. On the ship with the Deyos was Abraham Hasbrouck, who married Margaret Deyo in 1681, six years after their immigration to New York. When he and the Deyo family arrived in Kingston, they reunited with Jean Hasbrouck (Abraham's brother) and his wife Anna Deyo (the fourth daughter of Christian Deyo) who had come to North America in 1673. Hugo Freer and his second wife, Jeanne Wibau (possibly a niece by marriage of Christian Deyo), also came in 1677. The brothers Simon and Andries LeFevre had already immigrated to North America in the early 1660s, later settling in the Esopus. Andries never married, but he nevertheless became linked to many of the Walloons in the Kingston area through his brother Simon, who married Elizabeth Deyo, daughter of Christian Deyo, in 1676. Louis Bevier (who was possibly related to the Hasbroucks) and his wife Marie LeBlanc also immigrated to America in 1675; they were in Ulster County by 1678. Other French-speaking Protestant émigrés likewise established homes in the Kingston area, although they did not join themselves to the families who would soon found New Paltz.

Establishing New Paltz

The Blanchan, DuBois, and Crispell group were soon joined in Hurley by the Deyo, LeFevre, and Hasbrouck families, who also received land in the village. These families were apparently not satisfied with the quantity of land available to them in Hurley or Kingston, so this developing kin network looked to acquire additional land nearby, an endeavor which also attracted the Bevier and Freer families. Like Louis DuBois, Abraham Hasbrouck had been appointed a local magistrate by the provincial government; it is possible that they used their provincial connections in pursuit of their goal, which ultimately resulted in the creation of the village of New Paltz. That village began its life on May 26, 1677, when nine interrelated Walloon heads-of-families and the two sons of their leader, Louis DuBois, joined together to purchase from Native Americans of the Esopus tribe nearly forty thousand acres of land on the west side of the Hudson River, land that would ultimately become part of Ulster County in 1683 (see table 1.1).

This considerable plot of land was located approximately fifteen miles from what became the county seat (Kingston), on the edges of European-settled territory. In the following September, Governor Edmund Andros granted a land patent to these "partners," as designated in the patent, which included not only the purchasers as stated in the "Indian Deed," but the recently arrived Louis Bevier as well. These twelve men became the New Paltz patentees.[12]

Without a doubt, land, and thus economic opportunity, is what motivated the New Paltz founders to acquire a patent on the edge of European settlement. This is particularly clear for the Blanchan-DuBois-Crispell group, who were concerned not for their own but their children's future needs. One of the patentees Antoine Crispell never even moved to New Paltz, remaining in Hurley until his death in 1707, with his lands in New Paltz descending to a number of his heirs who had moved there. Patentee Louis DuBois did relocate to New Paltz, but only temporarily, returning to Hurley after he placed the new village and his sons on a sure footing. That land was on their minds is further reinforced by the fact that Matthieu Blanchan, the patriarch of the clan, did not even join in the New Paltz project, as he apparently felt

Table 1.1. Genealogical connections of the New Paltz patentees

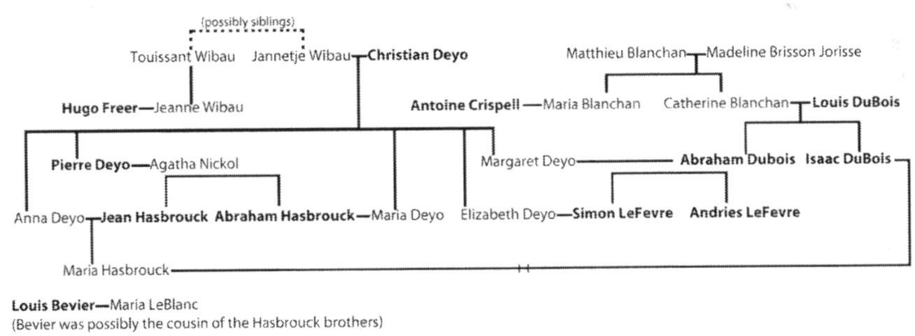

*Patentees in Bold
#Dotted lines represent possible genealogical connections

Patentee marriage dates and place of residence
Christian Deyo and Jannetje Wibau, Spanish Netherlands
Louis DuBois and Catherine Blanchan, 1655, Germany
Antoine Crispell and Maria Blanchan, 1660, Germany
Hugo Freer and Jeanne Wibau (second wife), Germany
Jean Hasbrouck and Anna Deyo, 1663, Germany
Louis Bevier and Maria LeBlanc, Germany
Pierre Deyo and Agathe Nickol, 1675, Germany
Abraham Hasbrouck and Maria Deyo, 1675, New York
Simon LeFevre and Elizabeth Deyo, 1676, New York
Abraham DuBois and Margaret Deyo, 1681, New York
Isaac DuBois and Maria Hasbrouck, 1683, New York

that he had sufficient land already. When the patent was acquired, all four of his daughters were married; he therefore needed to provide for only one son, and the patriarchal lands in Hurley were certainly sufficient for that. The acquisitiveness of the patentees is also reflected in the fact that some, including Abraham Hasbrouck, Hugo Freer, and Abraham DuBois, were not even satisfied with a one-twelfth share of nearly forty thousand acres. They continued to acquire substantially more land beyond New Paltz, upon which they settled some of their children. The patentee Abraham DuBois even acquired land in New Jersey, which he later bequeathed to his eldest son.[13]

It is not surprising that the New Paltz project involved families joined by ethnic culture and religion, even though the endeavor was primarily economic, as the creation of such linkages was typical among continental ethnocultural groups. As J. F. Bosher argues, Huguenots often engaged in economic activities with other Huguenots, as doing so supported an "atmosphere of personal trust based on a common religion." He clearly sees this among seventeenth-century Huguenot merchants, who formed a "Protestant international" in which "family life, and religion were interdependent." Susanah Shaw Romney likewise discusses how trade in the Dutch Atlantic world was supported by "intimate" family networks that facilitated economic relationships. While New Paltz was structured around land rather than trade, the same level of trust could reasonably be seen as desirable among a group of families engaged in a landholding partnership.[14]

While the establishment of new homes and farms on the edge of European settlement brought the patentees economic gains, moving beyond existing communities presented new cultural challenges. This was particularly so in the spiritual realm, as life on the frontier made it difficult for them to formally practice their religion. Since migrating to the Esopus region, the founding families of New Paltz had attended services and received the religious rites in the Dutch Reformed Church of Wiltwijck/Kingston, as they lacked a Walloon or French minister necessary for the establishment of an independent French-speaking congregation. Establishing New Paltz did not change that situation, but it did increase their distance from Kingston, making it even more challenging for the founding families to participate in church rituals and receive the edification they believed only a trained Calvinist minister could provide. They were still willing to travel in order to receive essential religious rites that required an ordained minister, especially baptism, but they nevertheless reduced their regular attendance in the Dutch church in Kingston. Instead, trusted men within the community read printed sermons in the French language to a gathered assembly. As a Calvinistic worship service was primarily structured around preaching, surely the reading of printed sermons did not provide particularly rewarding experiences. Apparently the patentees' desire for land outweighed their need for a deeper religious experience that a formally gathered congregation could offer.[15]

The primary reason that the patentee families could not establish their own congregation in New Paltz is that there were no Walloon or Huguenot ministers in the mainland British colonies at the time of the village's founding. Neither could they have anticipated that such a minister would ever become available. They therefore could not have presumed at the time of the founding that their independent control of the village could ever be translated into ecclesiastical independence. However, serendipity rather than design did enable them to establish their own independent congregation after a few French-speaking ministers immigrated to the American colonies in the early 1680s in response to growing persecution in France, which culminated in the Revocation of the Edict of Nantes in 1685. This unexpected immigration enabled New Paltz in 1683 to secure the services of a Huguenot minister, Pierre Daillé, which allowed for the formation of a congregation and its local governing body—the consistory—composed of the minister as well as elder(s) and deacon(s) selected from the congregation. Daillé served the congregation only until 1692, after which four years passed before they could acquire the services of another French-speaking pastor, David de Bonrepos, in 1696. He, too, served the New Paltz church only for a short time, leaving for other duties in 1700. The congregation never again secured the ministrations of another Walloon or Huguenot minister.

Even when the congregation was being served by Daillé and de Bonrepos, their ministers visited New Paltz only two to three times a year, when they preached the Word and baptized children of the New Paltz families. At all other times, local services still involved the reading of printed religious texts. The congregation also continued to rely on the Kingston church for most baptisms and for the Lord's Supper. While the patentee families apparently believed that a local congregation was desirable, creating one when the opportunity presented itself, they had initially believed that placing themselves far from the regular ministrations of a pastor and a consistory was a price worth paying in order to acquire a vast quantity of land.[16]

Governing New Paltz

The church was not the only institution that the founders created that bound themselves and their families together, as the patent stipulated that they establish a local government. Necessity also required them to create an institutional mechanism for managing joint ownership of that patent. Both were structured according to English colonial law, such that the patentees' shared Walloonness had no impact on how they might govern themselves. Still, while power was organized according to the English colonial government and its laws, local power was primarily held by the proprietors of the patent and their descendants throughout the long eighteenth century. Even when men from outside of the patentee families served in any institutional capacity, it was because members of the patentee community allowed them into their circle. In other words, English law defined the local government, but the patentee families controlled it on the ground. Institutional power was divided between provincial rule and local control, but that division was stable, predictable, and unthreatening, keeping at bay any actual, perceived, or threatened ethnocultural threat or pressure. The New Paltz founder families were simply not victims of "ethnic aggression."

In granting the patent, the English colonial government gave more than land to the patentees, as it created a new governmental jurisdiction that had to be organized according to English political and judicial structures. Governor Edmund Andros stipulated in the patent "that the plantacons which shall bee settled upon the said piece of land bee a Township." As a township, New Paltz had rights established in the Duke's Laws, including the right to elect four overseers and a constable. These officers possessed legislative authority for "the well Ordering [of] their Affairs, as the disposing, Planting, Building and the like, of their owne Lands and woods, granting of Lotts, Election of Officers, Assessing of Rates with many other matters of a prudentiall Nature, tending to the Peace and geod Government." They had the "power to Ordaine such or so many peculier Constitutions as are Necessary to the welfare and Improvement of their Towne; Provided they bee not of a Criminal Nature, And that the Penaltyes Exceed not Twenty Shillings for one Offence." The "Towne Court," in which the constable and overseers exercised their legally constituted power, also held limited legal jurisdiction as the lowest level of justice, meeting once every two, three, or four weeks, as they saw fit. Although there are no records that reveal whether the New Paltz patentees elected constables and overseers in the first years of the town's history, if they did, all town officers would have been New Paltz patentees, as in its early years, the patentee families comprised the entire town.[17]

Local government began to change soon after the village's founding when the provincial assembly created counties in 1683. New Paltz was located in what became Ulster County. In the same 1683 legislative session, the assembly also passed a law to "settle Courts of Justice" for each of the counties. Each county court was to be administered by a minimum of three appointed justices of the peace, although town courts were retained at the lowest level of justice. The assembly also enacted a law "for the Defraying of the publique & necessary Charge of each respective Citty, towne and County throughout this Province & for maintaining the poore, & preventing vagabonds." This law discontinued the use of overseers and required the electing of a new spate of town officers to assess and collect rates—an assessor and a treasurer—as well as the appointment of a supervisor to manage "publique affairs." The 1683 legislation was revised in 1691, but that second law was confusing and ambiguous. The assembly therefore passed a further revised statute in 1703, which remained unchanged throughout the remainder of the colonial period. That 1703 law required the "ffreeholders and Inhabitants" of towns such as New Paltz to elect a supervisor, two assessors and a collector on the first Tuesday of every April.[18]

The positions of supervisor, assessor, and collector did not exhaust the elected offices in colonial New York, as constables continued to be elected. In 1691, each town was also given the right to elect three surveyors empowered to regulate highways and fences, "with such orders to be recorded in the 'Towns book.'" Such a law was passed as towns "are soe Circumstanced as to have different and distinct wayes in their Improvements of Tillage and Pasturage." The assembly later separated the oversight of highways and fences, creating two separate offices, that of fenceviewers and overseers (or surveyors) of the highways. The final elected position that New Paltz voters were allowed to choose in the eighteenth century was the overseer of the poor, although when precisely such officials were first chosen is not precisely known.[19]

Due to the sparseness of early records, it is not clear exactly when New Paltz began to elect officers in accordance with English colonial law, but it is certain that New Paltz had a functioning town government designed according to provincial legislation at least as early as 1702. Such a government was the only government the colonial community ever possessed. In 1728, they did create another standing institution—the "Twelve Men" or the "Duzine" (based on either the French or Dutch word for "dozen")—that has sometimes been seen as the village's government. If it was, it was a unique form of government, as no institution identical to the Duzine was created in any other New York town. This fact encouraged nineteenth-century descendants and others to conclude that it was designed so as to allow for the autonomy of the Walloon community, an idea that still resonates among descendants today. In reality, the institution of the Twelve Men in no way had judicial or legislative authority within the town, as has been claimed, but merely provided a mechanism for managing and protecting what began as a jointly owned land grant in a manner inspired by English colonial law. Simply put, the basic form of the Duzine was not the brainchild of the Walloon New Paltz patentees nor their immediate heirs.[20]

Such an institution as the Duzine was required in New Paltz because of the vagaries of the laws related to joint ownership of land patents, which made their management quite problematic. One legal issue concerned how jointly owned land could be divided after the original patentees had died. In 1708, the province enacted legislation to allow for such division, but it remained in effect only through 1721 (with limited lapses in 1715 and 1718). A new law concerning the division of land was enacted in 1726, but it was repealed by the king on February 15, 1728, leaving the heirs of the New Paltz patentees without a legal means of dividing the undivided land in the patent. With the repeal of the 1726 law, neither did New Yorkers anywhere have a means of legally protecting the boundaries of patents, which, according to that law, were sometimes "incroached upon by others."[21]

During the lifetimes of the patentees, the patentees presumably managed the patent themselves, but questions must have arisen among the heirs as to how to divide the land and protect its boundaries as their numbers continued to grow while the number of surviving patentees shrank. They might have looked to provincial legislation, but after the king disallowed the 1726 law, they were left without efficient legal options. Nevertheless, when the number of living patentees had been reduced to one, he and the many heirs of the patentees chose to look to the previous provincial laws for guidance. In 1728, nearly fifty years after the founding of the town, patentee Abraham DuBois and the heirs formally decided that the patent would henceforth be managed by an elected body of twelve administrators, with each member representing the real property interests of the heirs of one of the patentees. The representatives chosen to serve as members of the Twelve Men were to be elected on the first Tuesday in April, which was the same day that the election of town officials was legally mandated. While the election of town officials was open to all "ffreeholders and Inhabitants," the election of the Duzine was open exclusively to those "owners and occupiers [who] hath a Right In each of the aforesaid Pattent[ee]s Shares." The number of New Paltz men unrelated to the patentee descendants by birth or marriage was small when the Duzine was created, but there were some in the community who had the right to elect town officials but not members of the Duzine. As the town grew throughout the eighteenth century through the in-migration of individuals unrelated to the patentee families, this gap continued to widen, reflecting the fact that the institutions were essentially separate.[22]

The threefold and limited purpose of the institution of the Twelve Men was to protect the legal title to the full patent, to confirm the divisions of the patent that had been previously made without legal deeds, and to divide the undivided land when they deemed fit and necessary. While all three issues were of considerable import, the last is most significant in terms of affairs within the community. According to the contract, when the Duzine determined that it was desirable or necessary to divide previously undivided portions of the patent, such land was to be laid out and distributed "in Twelve Equal Shares and Devisions soe that the one is not of more Vallue than the other and Then the aforesaid Twelve Shares or Devisions shall be numbered and then the aforesaid Twelve men shall Draw Lotts for the same and such Share or Division as falls to the Lotts of the aforesaid Twelve men Respectively." How each of the Twelve Men subsequently distributed the one-twelfth portion among those who had inherited any legal right to segments of that allotment is not known.[23]

While the founders did create a somewhat-isolated, ethnically homogeneous village, differentiated from both the Dutch in the immediate area and the English who controlled the colonial government, they simply could not, from a legal standpoint, have isolated themselves as a distinct people, just as they could not have initially separated themselves from the religious life of the region. It was simply impossible to be strictly local or strictly Walloon in a Dutch cultural region in an English colony, even if they had wanted to pursue such a goal. Having their own village did give the patentees political power, as well as ownership and control of a considerable expanse of land, but that power could not facilitate the expression of Walloon culture from either a legal or political perspective.

The Coming of Outsiders

Nevertheless, the patentees' ownership of all of the village's land, which then descended to the children, did profoundly affect ethnic relations within the community. As they controlled all access to the village's natural resources, and hence its wealth, so too did they control access to the town's government, its church, and its families, and they did so throughout the long eighteenth century. Whether the village remained ethnically homogeneous or incorporated those whose ethnocultural heritage was different from that of the founders was entirely within their hands. They were able to choose between endogamy and exogamy, and they had the option to restrict land ownership and use to members of their ethnic group, if they so chose. Ultimately, they did not. Neither did they turn in upon themselves in order to preserve a restrictive Walloon congregation, even though their church potentially could have been the strongest anchor of ethnic distinctiveness, if such distinctiveness was desired. They had no need to isolate themselves as Walloons because they controlled how other ethnic groups were allowed to join into the life of the community, a fact which continued to color ethnocultural relations and strategies throughout the long eighteenth century.

A primary way in which the lack of isolationism can be seen is through marriage patterns. Marriage patterns, however, do not incontrovertibly reveal acceptance of those of non-Walloon ancestry into the patentee *community*, as it was not a communal decision to pursue exogamous unions but rather a personal or, at the highest level, a family decision. Nevertheless, it is clear that a stigma was never attached to exogamy between a Walloon and a person of "Dutch" ancestry, and later between such a person and someone of British birth or descent.

The local "Dutch" and the Walloons in New Paltz joined together very early on in the history of the community. Of course, exogamy between Walloons and "Dutch" might have been influenced to some extent by the limited number of eligible French-speaking spouses in the region. However, there were additional possibilities for endogamous marriages that were not pursued, as the patentee families certainly did not comprise the full extent of Walloon or French families in the county. This web of ethnic intertwining began to develop as early as the second generation, resulting in a full incorporation, and practically an amalgamation, of the non-British ethnicities in the families of the New Paltz patentees. For example, three of patentee Pierre Deyo's four children married "Dutch" individuals. The cultural affiliation of the spouse of the remaining son is unclear, as her surname was recorded in both French (LeConte) and Dutch (deGraff). Of the six children of patentee Louis DuBois and his wife Catherine who were not patentees themselves, five married those of "Dutch" descent, while only one married a member of a patentee family. The children of other patentees did not contract marriages to those of "Dutch" descent to such a high degree. For example, two of Louis Bevier's children married those of pure Walloon background, one of full Dutch ancestry, and two of mixed French/Walloon and Dutch heritage. Similarly, of patentee Abraham Hasbrouck and his wife Maria Deyos's children, one married a person of Walloon background, two married within the "Dutch" families, and two married individuals of mixed French/Walloon and Dutch heritage. The fact that those of Walloon heritage did not shun "Dutch" marriage partners is not particularly surprising, as the Nieuw Nederland/New York Dutch generally accepted and incorporated into their society those of many continental ethnicities. This would have been particularly easy for Walloons and the Dutch, as they shared the Reformed religion.[24]

Marriage patterns become somewhat more opaque over time, as the intermarrying of people of multiple ethnicities makes it difficult to assign a particular ethnicity or ethnocultural orientation to most individuals. Nevertheless, the heirs of the patentees first incorporated the "Dutch" into the community through marriage, and less so but increasingly the British as well, as an analysis based on surnames reveals, even though there was no demographic pressure to do so. Between 1750 and 1800, 216 unions in which both of the spouses' birth surnames are known were recorded in the church records either through a marriage or the baptism of a child, of which 209 are useful for analysis. Over the course of the entire period, about one-quarter of those marriages were between a man and woman both with patentee surnames, and three-fifths between a person with a patentee surname and a person with a non-British surname, which in general means someone who had likely assimilated into the New York "Dutch" population. About only one in eight of the marriages involved one member with a British surname, basically divided between men and women. Over the course of the period, however, the number of marriages between a person with a patentee surname and a person with a British surname noticeably increased, particularly in the last quarter of the century (see table 1.2). Everyone in the community might not have been equally supportive of marrying outside of the traditional ethnic pool—the evidence is silent on this point—but when it came to seeking out a marriage partner, many individuals felt comfortable expanding their ethnic horizons to include Anglo-Americans.[25]

Marriage was not the only way that eighteenth-century descendants of the patentees allowed those of British birth or descent into their daily lives, as they also allowed them to share in the rites of their church, including baptism. Again, while it is impossible to determine the ethnic heritage of all who were married or had children baptized in the congregation, a host of surnames

Table 1.2. Marriage patterns, 1750–1800

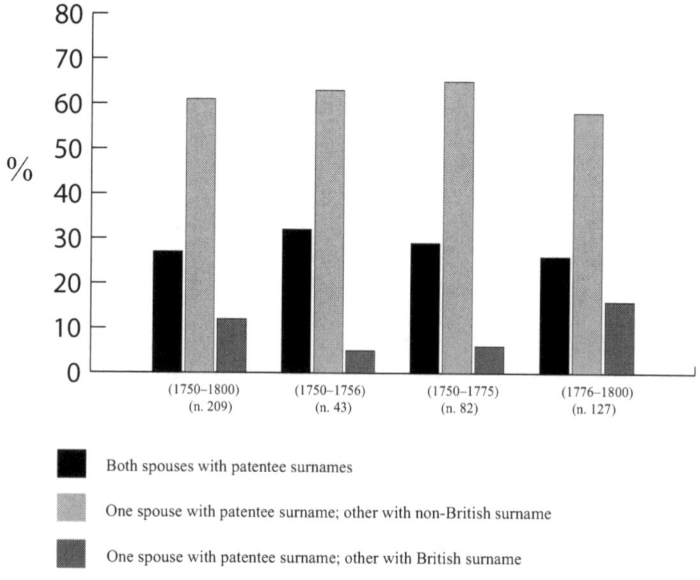

that suggest British ancestry appeared in the records. Many men were married to women of non-British ancestry, such that the continental ethnic heritage of their spouses might have led to the participation in the religious community. However, there were also marriages between individuals both of whom had British surnames, suggesting that the doors and the rites of the church were not closed even to those that may have lacked strong "Dutch" connections. This may not be much of surprise, given that at least some of the British people may have shared a Calvinistic faith with the non-British residents of New Paltz. Even if they did not, the services of no other ministers were available in the community, such that ministers of other denominations might have had to suffice. Nevertheless, it is clear that patentee descendants did not follow ethnically exclusionary practices within their congregation, the primary institutional anchor of their ethnocultural heritage.[26]

A primary reason that they did not restrict what the church could offer those without strong patentee family connections is that they controlled access to deeper engagement with the church through membership and service in the consistory. While 432 individuals baptized a child and/or were married in the church between 1750 and 1800, only 249 became members. Of the 101 of the 124 female members for which maiden names can be determined with certainty, only seven had British birth names, but six of these seven all had strong non-British connections. Only Elizabeth Wood, a young unmarried woman who became a member during the Great Awakening, lacked a solid non-British connection. Of the 125 male members, only eight clearly had British names, most of whom had patentee/"Dutch" connections. Again, only one man, Daniel Graham, did not have any clear "Dutch" connections that can be determined. In short, only two British individuals lacking clear non-British connections became institutionally connected to the community through church membership.[27]

Not surprisingly, holding an office in the church was an even more exclusive honor than membership. Of the 239 times New Paltz men were chosen to serve as elders and deacons between 1731 and 1800, just over three-quarters had patentee names, and many chosen served more than once. Other than Daniel Graham (deacon, 1778), Johannes York (deacon, 1797 and 1799), whose mother was a patentee descendant, and perhaps Hendric Smitt, (deacon, 1792 and 1794) whose ethnicity cannot be determined, the remainder of the church officers all had non-British surnames.[28]

A more common way that the descendants of the founders allowed those of British birth or ancestry into their midst was by permitting them access to land. Again, they apparently did not shrink from doing so because they were able to keep British newcomers on the margins, both geographically and economically, as the surviving tax lists demonstrate. This trend did not begin immediately, although nothing suggests that the slow start was the result of intentional design. The earliest list, from 1712, includes the assessments of twenty-two property owners, three-quarters of whom represented six of the seven New Paltz patentee families. The seventh, Antoine Crispell, was represented by his daughter, Lysbeth, the spouse of Elias Ean, who was likely of Dutch ancestry. A few other men of Dutch ancestry had also entered the community by that time through their marriages to women from patentee families. In total, approximately 90 percent of the New Paltz residents in 1712 belonged to the founding families by birth or marriage, with twenty heads of household holding virtually all of the wealth. There were two additional men in the community without any obvious connections to the founding families, but as they were of Dutch background, they would not have been isolated from the patentee community because of their ethnic heritage. Not much had changed by 1728, the year of the next surviving tax list, when 90 percent of the taxables were members of the community established by the founding families, by birth, marriage, or ethnocultural heritage. Again, this group held virtually all of the community's wealth.[29]

The next surviving tax list, that of 1765, however, reveals a pronounced change in the ethnic demographics of the village. Still, economic power remained in the hands of patentee descendants. Of the 112 individuals taxed, about one-half had patentee surnames. Another thirteen men with Dutch surnames were also members of the patentee families, as they or their fathers had married women descended from the founders. Four more "Dutch" men with long New Paltz connections from the Vandermark and Schoonmaker families can also be included in the patentee orbit, as well as three other "Dutch" newcomers who had no direct connections with the founding families. The patentee circle also embraced a few newcomers not of Walloon or Dutch ancestry, including Rev. Johannes Mauritius Goetschius (of Swiss birth), Joseph Coddington (of Anglo-American heritage), and the brothers Christian and David Auchmoody (of Scottish heritage). Goetschius and Coddington served the patentee community by providing religious and educational services, and the Auchmoody brothers were the sons of James Auchmoody and patentee descendant Maria Deyo. Together, the patentee circle consisted of about two-thirds of the taxables, rather than in the 90 percent range as before. Nevertheless, the patentee circle continued to hold most of the assessed wealth (95 percent). The decline in the patentee circle as a proportion of the entire population between 1728 and 1765 may have been over 20 percent, but the economic power of the group remained essentially unchanged.[30]

The remaining thirty-six individuals enumerated in the 1765 tax list represented thirty-four different family names with no discernible connections to the patentee family group by birth or marriage. Most of these newcomers were both poor and transient, such that they were relatively disconnected from members of the intertwined patentee circle. The one-third of the total New Paltz householders included in the "new" group were assessed for only about 5 percent of the wealth, and if the one individual in this "new" group of significant wealth is removed (Abraham Donaldson), that percentage is reduced to 4 percent. In fact, six individuals in the patentee group were each worth more than the total "new" group combined (less Abraham Donaldson). The ethnic origin of all of the names is not entirely clear, but many were clearly of British extraction. Others suggest a Germanic background or French or Walloon ancestry.[31]

These newcomers lived in a clearly defined neighborhood, one which had only been recently settled and which consisted primarily of relatively poor land. As a result, not only did they live on the socioeconomic margins of the community but the geographic margins as well. For most of the first hundred years, the patentee families and their descendants had congregated on the fertile flats along the western portion of the patent near the Wallkill River. They continued to hold almost the whole eastern side of the patent from the Wallkill to the Hudson in common, not needing it for agriculture. In 1745, they divided the land directly along the Hudson River, but it does not appear that this land was settled until somewhat later. In 1763 they surveyed and divided the swampy and hilly section of the patent between the older settlement and the lots abutting the Hudson River, in what they termed the "new division." This area was soon settled, as the patentee families leased or sold many of their portions to others. Apparently, the motivation to divide commonly held land was not land pressure that forced the descendants of the founders to farm the less desirable portion of their land, but the desire to profit financially from what had formerly served as the commons. It is on these lands that the newcomers settled, some apparently for only a short time. Thus, given the newcomers' overall transience, the geographic separation of their farms from the bulk of those traditionally tied to the community, and their low socioeconomic position, the fact that a not-insignificant number of such newcomers were of British backgrounds likely had little immediate impact on those village residents traditionally of a non-British orientation. Perhaps some of these newcomers portended the spread of English culture to the old village residents as the way of the future, but the village middling and elite certainly would not have felt any meaningful cultural pressure from those who lived on the geographic and socioeconomic edges of the village community.[32]

The ethnic and socioeconomic makeup of the community faced even more dramatic changes over the course of the next thirty years, although members of the patentee community clearly continued to dominate socioeconomically. In 1798, when the Federal Direct Tax schedules were prepared, the proportion of the patentee community in relation to the "newcomers" completely reversed that proportion as it had been in 1765. At most, the patentee group accounted for only just over one-third of the taxables, whereas in 1765 they had comprised approximately two-thirds. Of the many "newcomers," only about one in seven of which had last names that could be found in the village just over thirty years earlier, only a few could be considered "Dutch." However, an impressive number had names of English origin. Even if just the names beginning with B (Baker, Barber, Barns, Barret, Bedford, Benton, Bosworth, Brannen, Brown, Budd, Burnet, Bush) or S (Sammons, Seaman, Shearwood, Simmon, Sloan, Smith, Stanton, Star, Stephens, Stokes) are considered, the English influx is evident. The sheer number of names in 1798 that had not been represented in New Paltz in 1765 was staggering—166—as compared to only twenty-six surnames in the patentee group. Of the new names, about three-quarters were represented only once in 1798, which suggests that many of the newcomers were unmarried, had relatively young families, or did not have sons who could choose or had chosen to settle in New Paltz. The social structure in 1798 was also different than it had been in 1765. While two-thirds of the patentee group owned or leased houses valued at least at one hundred dollars, so too did just under a third of the newcomers. One-tenth of the newcomers even owned or leased houses worth $300; still, their numbers were fewer than the nearly half of the patentee group who did so as well. Nevertheless, the newcomers were not by definition all poor, as had been the case in 1765, but they were still clearly of a lower social position.[33]

Importantly, the patentee families were entirely responsible for the diversification of their community. The willingness of the landowners of the patentee group to lease and, even more significantly, to sell some of their lands to "strangers" had made this ethnic diversification possible. That they chose to do so suggests that the patentee group did not attempt to isolate itself from the English. One element that made this influx of newcomers acceptable, of course, was that the patentee group maintained its economic dominance, especially so as of 1765 although somewhat decreasingly by 1798. Nevertheless, even by 1798, the elite was still primarily composed of members of the patentee family group. As such, this ethnic diversification would not have appeared as a threat as it might have in places such as seventeenth-century New York City, where many Dutch indeed may have felt culturally threatened.

Even if the collective wealth of the patentee community declined proportionally relative to that of the newcomers, the patentee community retained all the reins of local political power, as the interrelated men of such families collectively formed an unchallengeable block. Thus, selling or renting land to newcomers of British birth or descent did not have the potential to undermine the authority of the patentee families. This is not to say that no one outside of the patentee circle served in political office. However, those that did so served in low-level positions, positions which existed only because the patentee men had created them.

Election records are scant for the first half of the eighteenth century, but they are extant from 1751–1766, except for one year. These records are particularly valuable because they span the period both before and after the 1763 "new division" of land to the east of the core of the New Paltz settlement, as that pivotal division was what resulted in the creation of a substantially British neighborhood between the original settlement and the Hudson River. From 1751 through 1759, virtually all elected officials, and even nominees, possessed patentee surnames or had intermarried with patentee families. Only four were not of the patentee circle. Beginning in 1760, however, some of the "new" group were nominated and elected to serve, but only for lower ranking positions, such as fenceviewer, pound master, constable, and surveyor of the highways. Individuals of the patentee group served in lower-status positions as well, but the higher offices—supervisor, collector, assessor, and overseer of the poor—were filled by men from only the patentee group. Importantly, higher offices were restricted to a particular number each year (one supervisor, one collector, and two assessors), while the town had the discretion to create as many of the lower positions as it saw fit. The village's leaders did expand the number of positions in the lower offices because the town had developed into two neighborhoods, the "paltz" side and the "river" side (as indicated in the election records); and they wanted the newcomers who lived on the "river" side of the town to be able to monitor themselves. The patentee families did not, however, allow newcomers to lead the government of the town as a whole. This again suggests that the newcomers impacted the ensconced families in only a minor fashion. If these British newcomers had been seen as a threat, the patentee families certainly might have resisted the British influx into the community, which had necessitated the incorporation of newcomers into the government. They did not.[34]

A snapshot view of a later period—the 1790s—reveals that the pool from which town officers were drawn had expanded to include more individuals from outside the patentee group, and in slightly higher capacities. Nevertheless, members of the patentee group still dominated, as they served as officers in numbers far outweighing their representation in the community. In the first half of the decade, one in four of those elected to serve in high office was not from the patentee group, a type of service that had not been possible for them in the 1760s. Nevertheless, the highest offices—supervisor and clerk—were still filled only by members of the patentee group. Of the seven newcomers who served, however, the highest office that five achieved was overseer of the poor, with only one of those five serving more than once. As for the other two, Peleg Ransom served four times as assessor and Jonathan Preslar as overseer of the poor (once), collector (twice), and assessor (twice). Ransom and Preslar were distinctive in serving so many times: from 1790–1795, no one else, including members of the patentee group, served in as many offices as Preslar and no one repeatedly served in the same office as did Ransom. In other words, members of the patentee group seem almost to have been seen as interchangeable, while only a couple of newcomers reached the inner circles of government, which again suggests that the power of the newcomers remained thin enough not to have presented any threat to the patentee circle.[35]

The peripatetic families of the founders of New Paltz were both fleeing material hardships and searching for economic opportunities. They, as Protestant, French-speaking Walloons, did form expatriate communities when possible, but their ability to protect and preserve their culture was not what fundamentally motivated them as they migrated through Europe and America. At least it was not their first priority. Had it been, the founders would likely have never left the Palatinate, as there they had successfully established a Walloon enclave. Of course, the Palatinate had become a physically dangerous place to live, but the New World was not particularly safe either. Whether they could establish a Walloon community in the New World would have been far from certain, as they migrated in small groups into either a Dutch colony or, after the conquest, a Dutch cultural region in an English colony. The first group to arrive—the Blanchan-DuBois-Crispell family group—could hardly have thought that they could protect and preserve a living Walloon culture by themselves, and theirs was not the beginning of an organized chain migration. For all they knew, they would remain relatively alone in the midst of the "Dutch" of Nieuw Nederland. Once in America, they and some of those Walloons who arrived soon after did begin to form a community in Hurley, and when they sought more land, united in their efforts to acquire it. Doing so, however, was primarily linked to a sense of trust grounded in family relationships and their shared language and religion. They did not join together to create an independent Walloon community. That was simply impossible, as they were required to structure their village as an Anglo-American town according to Anglo-American laws. It was also impossible to establish an independent Walloon congregation when the town was founded. They did create one when they could, but they were not prescient. They did not know they would ever be able to do so, such that the possibility of creating a Walloon congregation could not have inspired their actions either.

It is true that Dutch and English culture were forced upon the founders and their descendants in one way or another. But as much as it was forced upon them, they never responded by isolating themselves from either Dutch or English people, even to the extent that they could. This should not be overly surprising, especially when considering the founders themselves, as only people who were culturally flexible could have managed the challenges they faced as they moved through Europe and America. Of course, their children, grandchildren, and great-grandchildren may not by definition have embraced the flexibility of the founders. Yet they did as well, at least for the most part. Many of the founders' children reached out to "Dutch" partners, even though a greater number of endogamous unions was theoretically possible. Some of the generations that followed even married those of British heritage. They also allowed British people to share in the rites of the church, to buy or rent land in the town, and even to serve in government. Still, while intermarriage led to the integration of the Walloons into the "Dutch," they most often accepted British people into their midst by keeping them on the margins. British people held provincial power, but the local power of the founding families remained unchallenged because of their control of the town's lands. In other words, while the founding families began as an ethnic minority, they never became an embattled minority, as they had complete control over how those of other ethnic backgrounds would be allowed into their community. Their position was therefore nothing like that of the Albany Dutch, who struggled against the English-dominated provincial government. Neither were they in the position of the French or Dutch of New York City who might have faced marginalization if they had not culturally adapted to being in an English colony, at least to some extent. Interethnic interaction was therefore far from monolithic in ethnically heterogenous New York.

Allowing, and sometimes even accepting, those of different ethnocultural heritage into their community did not necessarily mean that the founders and the descendants were willing to integrate or accept their culture. Yet, they actively and willingly did that as well, and it was fundamentally because they possessed so much local power that they could feel comfortable adopting and/or adapting the multiple ethnocultural vocabularies available them. As we see in the following three chapters, they did so by creating a constantly shifting creolized culture in which their power was clear but in which ethnocultural "ambiguity restlessly rule[d]."[36]

Chapter 2

I GIVE DEVISE and BEQUEATH

Gender, Property, and Ethnocultural Creolization

English law substantially defined how New Paltz was governed as a town and how it was managed as a patent, but it also affected more intimate, domestic relations between men and women both as husbands and wives and as sons and daughters. It did so by regulating property rights and inheritance in highly gendered ways. These laws both reflected and affected how the English conceived of maleness and femaleness, the proper relations between spouses, and the structures of power within the family. Nevertheless, English laws of marriage and inheritance often provided for considerable, although not total, male discretion when it came to control over property. Female discretion was sometimes possible as well, and legal remedies also might exist to thwart even restrictive laws. As a result, English men never treated women in a strictly uniform manner.

The traditions and laws of the Walloons and the Dutch were also gendered, but in ways quite distinct from those of the English. Male members of the New Paltz founding families could, and often did, use the discretion English law provided to preserve non-English traditions. They nevertheless had to do so through the context of English law. If they wanted to perpetuate either Walloon- or Dutch-gendered thinking as reflected in property rights, they were therefore forced to creolize by hybridizing the various cultures. This was the case in spite of the fact that the 1664 Articles of Capitulation gave former Nieuw Nederlanders the option to preserve their traditional customs of inheritance. Some men, however, creolized not only because English law made doing so unavoidable; some creatively creolized even more than was legally necessary. Other men chose to adopt English cultural traditions or seek inspiration from the English laws of intestate succession. Issues of gender were complex within each culture itself but the complexity became even more intense when the three divergent cultural systems intersected. The result was a complex interplay of law, custom, and individual choice in the multicultural environment of New Paltz.

Gendered Cultures

Of the three cultural systems that potentially affected the ownership and control of property in New Paltz, it is most difficult to generalize about the cultural heritage of the Walloon founders. This is the case because their ancestry lay in a region that, according to Martha Howell, demonstrated an "unusual instability of law," as legal and customary practices in that area were changing as the late Middle Ages gave way to the early modern period. Additionally, as Howell notes, any generalizations that might be attempted are "only that: abstractions constructed from thousands of specific instances." Still, legal scholars have suggested that a general approach to the gendering of property rights existed in the Picard-Walloon region from whence the families of the founders of New Paltz came. That approach was quite different from those in the surrounding cultural regions inhabited by the French, the Flemish, and the Dutch, as well as the English.[1]

In the Walloon regions of Europe, marriage created a communal estate, encompassing both real and personal property, unless a couple contracted for a more complex system of ownership. In spite of this joint ownership, marriage was patriarchal, as a husband controlled all of the conjugal property, enabling him to do whatever he wished with any or all of it. However, upon the death of either spouse, this extensive power was transferred to the surviving spouse, either male or female, according to the principle of the *ravestissement*, provided that the couple had produced a child. Such power gave a widowed parent complete independence, grounded in his or her power over their children's potential future inheritance. Even if the couple did not bear children, the spouses could, and often did, legally grant the *ravestissement* to each other. Such control was permanent; it was not impacted by the widow's or widower's future marriage choices.

Walloon parents also prioritized their needs, desires, and rights over those of their children, such that parents used, alienated, and distributed the family estate as they saw fit. They generally followed a policy of preferential legacies, often favoring one or more children over the others. This pattern strongly suggests that children were not assumed to possess any claim on their parents' estate. Such a perspective is further demonstrated by the fact that among the Walloons, children of a deceased child of the testator did not inherit in the place of a parent. Of course, the purpose of preferential distribution of property might sometimes have been to prevent over-fragmentation of the family estate—an issue that many early modern Europeans faced—but to whom parents bequeathed the conjugal estate most often had a gendered dimension as well.[2]

In most ways, Walloon customs were at variance with both Dutch legal and customary practices in Nieuw Nederland, which in turn were based on Roman-Dutch law that obtained in the United Provinces. They did bear one important similarity, however, in that both Dutch and Walloon law dictated that all marital property was held communally, unless a premarital contract was executed. Dutch gendered ideals were also patriarchal, as a husband had control over the joint estate during marriage, as he legally held guardianship over his wife. In spite of wives' legal subordination to their husbands, scholars have suggested that in practice, Dutch women in both Europe and Nieuw Nederland often assisted quite substantially in their husbands' business and legal affairs. This relationship represents a form of matrimonial partnership particular to the Dutch, which gave women more extensive spheres of action within marriage than was evident among the Walloons or the English. From a financial perspective, such a partnership helped to prepare women for the real possibility that their husbands might predecease them. As a result, Dutch widows did not struggle with the management of family estates as much as widows in those cultural groups that did not adequately prepare women for potential widowhood.[3]

In contrast to the law among the Walloons, the Roman-Dutch law of intestacy dictated that upon the death of either spouse, the surviving spouse inherited only one-half of the family estate, but she or he owned it absolutely. The remaining half of both real and personal property descended equally to the deceased parent's heirs in a gender-neutral fashion, as heirs, regardless of biological sex, were customarily assumed to have an equal and permanent claim to part of each parent's half of the estate. This was a perspective that Walloons did not share. The Dutch, unlike the Walloons, also allowed the children of deceased heirs to inherit in the place of their parents. Each parent had the legal right to compose a will for his or her half of the estate, although most spouses composed a single joint will. When Dutch couples did so, they often chose to transfer control over the entire estate to the survivor, male or female, rather than provide the survivor with only half of the estate in accordance with intestacy law. The Dutch and Walloons therefore shared the belief that a woman could become an independent head of household upon her husband's death. Sometimes parents provided for such control only while minor children were at home, but spouses often provided the survivor with permanent control of the estate, provided he or she did not remarry. Upon remarriage, the Dutch then distributed the deceased parent's half of the estate to her or his heirs, such that the distribution of property due to remarriage reflected the laws of intestacy.[4]

Dutch law and custom, and the gendered thinking that both produced and was affected by it, bore few similarities with English law and tradition. Both were patriarchal, although the English form of patriarchy, which held that women possessed an inherently dependent nature, was so universalizing that it made any hint of gender neutrality inconceivable. English men constructed married property rights accordingly. According to English and Anglo-American common law, a married woman was a *feme covert*, a "covered woman," whose legal subordination to her husband was nearly absolute. All personal property brought to a marriage by both members of the conjugal unit, as well as any inherited after they were legally joined, became the property of the husband. In contrast, real property was owned by either the husband or the wife, whether they had acquired ownership of it before or after they married, unless purchased or inherited jointly during marriage, which was uncommon. Although a married woman continued to independently own any real estate that she had been given, she could not administer that property or derive its profits for herself, unless she and her husband had entered into a prenuptial contract that permitted her to do so, which was not common. Her husband, however, could administer and profit from her real property even after her death if they had produced a child together, according to the principle of the "curtesy," even if the child had not survived and even if the husband remarried. A wife was even denied the right to bequeath her real property as she wished, as according to English common law, that property would go to her heirs according to the laws of descent, regardless of whether she possessed any independent wishes of her own.[5]

Under English common law, a woman lost considerable control of any property she brought to a marriage, but her loss of rights was balanced to some extent by the rights she gained for support during her widowhood. According to English common law, a wife possessed a perpetual right of dower in her husband's estate, such that even her remarriage would not deprive her of that support. Dower gave a widow the right to use one third of her husband's real estate, permitting her the rents or income thereof. Such use rights allowed her some degree of authority, since she had the option to rent her dower land and the choice of to whom she would rent it; or she could continue to farm it herself (if the land was agricultural). In practical terms, however, she often had to rely on the assistance of her sons, placing her in a dependent position. What she did not have the right to do was sell any of her dower lands, such that they were "hers" in only a provisional sense. Neither did a widow have a legal right to stay in her home, although mothers were not typically dislodged from their homes by their sons or sons-in-law. During her husband's life, a woman could protect her right to dower, such that she generally had to agree to the *inter vivo* sale of her husband's property, as such sales could affect the amount of land a man held at his death and correspondingly the amount of income it could produce for his widow's support. A male testator could provide his widow with more than her dower rights but not less. If he did so, she could repudiate the will and claim her dower in court. In New York, a woman was also entitled to claim a third of her husband's personal property as her own, but only if he died intestate, such that if she repudiated his will, she lost any claim to personal property.[6]

Many men in New York and elsewhere took the opportunity to avoid the law of intestacy by composing wills. Many did so by providing their wives with an "honorable maintenance" instead of their thirds. Such an arrangement might have ensured that a widow received support, but such "maintenance" clearly made her as dependent as she had been when her husband was alive. Her dependent status was further enhanced by the fact that men who chose such an option often made the decision as to who was to provide that support and where their widows may reside. Even after a man died, he substantially defined his widow's future.

As Anglo-American law provided for a great deal of male discretion, a New York man could create a will to provide for his widow in either a Dutch or Walloon way, as either approach would result in her receiving more rather than less than her dower rights. If he instead chose to follow English gender ideals as inscribed in law or tradition, he did so entirely of his own volition. However, the Dutch system of joint estates simply did not apply. His land would always remain his land and her land would be hers, while all personal property was his. There simply was no "theirs" according to law, regardless of whether a husband preserved a Dutch perspective on gendered power. Neither could a female New Yorker make any claims outside of English law, as those laws substantially denied her agency when it came to issues of property. Dutchness was circumscribed by English law; it could survive only within a creolized Dutch-Anglo context.

Male New Yorkers had considerable freedom of choice in providing for their wives, but they had absolute power over the way they distributed their property to their children. It is, however, more difficult to delineate a "typical" English approach to the transfer of a patriarch's property to his children than it is to define a traditionally Dutch approach. Some English men accepted primogeniture—even to the point of placing an entail on land—while others allowed for partible inheritance. It is particularly difficult to define a typical English approach in New York because the law of intestacy, which directed male primogeniture (for real property), was generally thwarted by the many men who wrote wills. Still, English men typically associated land ownership with being male, and they generally bequeathed property to sons differently from the manner in which they provided for daughters, both in terms of amount and type. The English simply did not follow the principles of Dutch gender neutrality when it came to provisions for either widows or children.[7]

Of course, testamentary choices are not always strictly based on cultural traditions as represented in law or practice. Family relationships, the life cycle, demographics, the relative availability of land, the size of the estate and the types of property it included were all factors in will-making decisions. In other words, men legally possessed the right to manage the material needs of their families, and practicality more than cultural traditions might sometimes have influenced a husband and father as he planned for his family's future. Simple whim could impact choices as well. Nevertheless, the fact that different cultural groups within Western Europe constructed different forms of gendered power suggests that decisions regarding property rights and ownership were rarely based strictly on material or personal concerns. Even if a non-English man in New York chose to follow particular ethnocultural practices for material or personal rather than ethnocultural reasons, his choices produced ethnocultural change on the ground.[8]

The Founding Generation's Views on Gender and Property

Except for his eldest son Abraham, Louis DuBois was the only patentee who composed a will while his wife was still living, such that only he was required to provide for the future of his entire family through the distribution of his estate. He ultimately wrote three wills over the course of nearly thirty years, but the manner in which he distributed property changed over the many decades. He was aware of many legal possibilities and limitations, but the one possibility he did not choose was to preserve Walloon traditions. Instead, he selectively chose aspects of both Dutch practices and Anglo-American law, creating his own personalized Dutch-Anglo cultural hybrid. His changing approach to gendered property rights and the gendered order of the family suggests that the patentees and their descendants had to make complex decisions as they negotiated their creolized and creolizing environment.

In 1676, twelve years after the conquest and two years before New Paltz was settled, the soon-to-be patentee Louis DuBois and his wife Catherine Blanchan, both Walloons, composed a Dutch-style joint will. Their joint will—the only one composed by any member of the patentee families—was a type of legal instrument that was fast becoming antiquated in Anglicizing colonial New York. It represents the closest to a pure Dutch approach that any of the patentees ever followed, as it was based on the Roman-Dutch legal principle that held that a husband and wife owned the family estate jointly. Louis and Catherine also followed Dutch practices by providing for each other in an entirely gender-neutral fashion. Accordingly, upon the death of either of them, Louis and Catherine provided that the surviving parent would assume full ownership and administration of the family estate, provided he or she did not remarry. If that occurred, the survivor would retain ownership of only one-half of the estate, with the other half descending to their heirs, as in Dutch fashion. In spite of the overall Dutchness of their choices, perhaps a hint Walloonness still echoed, as they provided that the survivor had full control of the estate, as he or she was not compelled "to pay out anything to the children, no more than he or she pleases, either as a marriage-present or something else." Nevertheless, Louis and Catherine also stipulated that after their deaths their entire estate would ultimately descend in equal portions to their progeny, both male and female. These provisions for heirs were supremely egalitarian and gender neutral, again in accordance with Dutch traditions.[9]

Although Catherine and Louis initially embraced the traditions of their Dutch neighbors rather than preserve Walloon customs, Louis' commitment to Dutch gender neutrality in the control and transmission of marital property waned over time. In 1686, he wrote a second will, this time in his name alone. In doing so, he silenced his wife's legal voice. He also transformed what had once been their joint estate into his alone, as he chose to adopt English cultural practices, at least in part, which assumed that a husband and wife did not share equally in a married estate. He could do so because the Articles of Capitulation allowed but did not require the former Nieuw Nederlanders to preserve Dutch inheritance practices, and Catherine had no legal means of forcing him to do so. Louis did not nullify his earlier will out of necessity; his and Catherine's joint will could still have been probated legally. He chose to write a new will because his thinking had changed, and he redistributed what he had come to see as his property accordingly.[10]

Louis did not adopt all of the English cultural practices, however. If his widow remained a widow, Louis still provided that she would independently administer the entire estate upon his death, according to Dutch custom. If she did marry again, she was required to immediately turn over half of what was now his estate to his heirs, again reflecting Dutch intestacy law. However, exactly what rights she would retain over the remaining half are ambiguous. This ambiguity might have resulted from Louis' desire to reflect Dutch and English culture simultaneously, or perhaps from his misunderstanding of the English language. He first states, in English, that after his debts are paid, "what there shall be found Afterwards belonging to my Estate, shall be equally dealt among my children." Yet, he later indicates that if his widow remarried, "she shall have the one right half of the whole estate." By "have," did he mean absolute ownership, or was he simply suggesting use rights? If the former, the suggestion is that despite his growing Englishness, he was still willing to provide his widow that which she would have had if that property had been jointly owned, in accordance with Dutch practices. If he was suggesting that Catherine would only have use rights to half of the estate upon her remarriage—which is certainly possible given that he first stipulates that the entire estate would go to his children—then he was drifting much closer to the gendered traditions of the English.

Whatever Louis' intentions were in 1686, he clarified them in a third and final will in 1694, one which reflected Dutch-Anglo hybrid creolization that nevertheless tipped closer to Englishness. According to his final will, Louis still permitted his wife full administration of his estate during her widowhood, and again he stipulated that she would have to turn over half of the estate to his heirs upon her remarriage. If she did remarry, however, his final will clearly directed that she would only be entitled to lifetime use of part of her deceased husband's property ("om gedürende haer leven to mogen gebrüycken"). In other words, while Louis *may* have been willing to give his wife half of his estate in 1686, by 1694, he was clearly not willing to give her anything beyond use rights. In both 1686 and 1694, he also implicitly preserved his total power over the estate during his life even if his wife predeceased him, while limiting her power in a manner quite at variance with the provisions of the 1676 will. From his perspective, that was the way it should have been, since he now perceived the estate as his and not hers as well. While he may have ultimately chosen such a course because he did not want any of his estate to come under the control of his wife's potential future husband, if he had continued to perceive the estate as jointly held, such a concern would have been moot. If half were hers, she could do with it what she wished. If it were entirely his, he and only he would be the one to make the decision as to the future of his property. And making that decision is what he did.[11]

While Louis chose to modify his approach in providing for his widow in light of English law and custom, he remained committed to the Dutch principles of gender neutrality and equality in his provisions for his children, at least in terms of how much and what type of property his children received. According to all of his wills, all children, male and female, essentially inherited the same, in both real and personal property, except for a token gift to his eldest son that he added to his 1694 will. In accordance with Dutch customs, he also included an additional provision in his 1694 will to account for the death of his son Isaac, directing that Isaac's children would inherit in their father's place, once again repudiating Walloonness and following a Dutch practice. Louis did, however, make a distinction between how he distributed his property to his sons and to his daughter Sara. Instead of giving her property directly, he provided her only with the lifetime use and profits from that property by placing her share in a type of trusteeship for his grandchildren. It is possible that his purpose in doing so was not to restrict his daughter's property rights but to protect the property from her husband, as according to English law, her husband would gain the legal right to administer any land her father gave her directly. Her husband would also gain ownership of any personal property she received as well. Louis may not have viewed his daughter as being any less capable of owning and managing property than her brothers were, but because of English law, he was prevented from giving property directly to her if he also wanted to keep it from her husband's control. By placing Sara's share in a quasi-trust, he also allowed for his grandchildren to inherit immediately after their mother's death; had he not, and had their mother died before their father, Sara's share would have remained in her husband's control until he died, in accordance with English law. In other words, Louis may have attempted to preserve Dutch traditions in distributing his property to his children but was hampered by English law.[12]

No other patentee composed a will when his wife was still living other than Louis' son Abraham, but his relative age and the date of his will (1731) make it more appropriate to consider him as part of the second rather than the founding generation. Still, it is relatively clear that the patentees chose neither Walloon nor English practices when it came to the distribution of their property to their children. They chose instead to adopt the gendered egalitarianism of the Dutch. According to his 1698 will, Hugo Freer left his entire estate to his children in equal portions in both real and personal property. The estate was not to be divided, however, until his unmarried children received marriage portions of personal property, presumably because he had already provided portions to his older children. Similarly, when Christian Deyo wrote his first will in 1676, he stipulated that both his real and personal estate would be equally divided both by his daughters and son, and that each unmarried child would receive as much as the married children had in their marriage portions. When he wrote his second (and final) will in 1687, Deyo maintained his commitment to an equal division of his estate among his children, with the exception of the cancellation of a monetary debt that his only son owed to him, as well as a gift of forty pieces of eight and a small gun to his grandson Christian Deyo, possibly because Christian bore his grandfather's name. Neither Hugo Freer nor Christian Deyo indicated how their estates were to be precisely divided, suggesting that they did not consider any type of property in gendered terms, as the English did. Neither did patentee Antoine Crispell, although he did choose to be more precise in the division of his real estate in his 1707 will. Nevertheless, he gave both sons and daughters significant grants of real property, with one-third of his share in the New Paltz patent each going to the heirs of his eldest son collectively, his daughter Maria Magdelena, and his daughter Elizabeth. He also purchased a farm for his daughter Jannetje. He divided his lands in Hurley, where he had always lived, among the heirs of his eldest son, his son Jan, and his daughter Sara, although he required payment into the estate at least from Jan and Sara in commodity money (wheat). Although each of these four patentees chose a slightly different approach, they all bequeathed land to both sons and daughters in an egalitarian fashion, an approach which they adopted from their Dutch neighbors.[13]

Patentee Louis Bevier made a different choice, as he provided for his children in a hybrid Dutch-Anglo manner. According to his 1715 will, Bevier bestowed his estate equally to all of his children according to value.

Nevertheless, he distributed his real property only to his sons, stipulating that they make payments to their only sister, Esther, presumably to make the cash value of each heir's legacy equal. In doing so, he demonstrated Dutch egalitarianism but English gendering of real property. Louis Bevier made slight adjustments to his 1715 will in 1720, as in the meantime his son Andries had become mentally disabled, yet even that son was still to receive an equal portion of real and personal property. Upon his death, Andries's share would be divided into fifths, with each of his siblings, both male and female, receiving one portion. This meant that according to his 1720 will, Louis' daughter, Esther, was to receive a share of the real estate, which is something she would not have received according to her father's earlier will; however, that real property comprised only one twenty-fifth of her father's total real estate, much less than what her brothers received. Just like Louis DuBois, Louis Bevier blended ideas of Dutch gender equity with English traditions, forming a hybrid approach designed according to his own personal wishes and desires.[14]

Of the six patentees of the founding generation who composed wills, only Jean Hasbrouck might have aimed to create a hybrid Walloon-English approach. The English aspects of his will are seen in his gendering of real property, as well as his choice to distribute it in an unequal fashion. He privileged his son Jacob with all of his land—comprising almost a full one-twelfth of the New Paltz patent—as well as two male slaves, all but three books, and half of the personalty. Hasbrouck also directed that if his eldest son, Abraham, who had previously left New Paltz for parts unknown, returned, Jacob would be required to provide his elder brother with a horse as his birthright, as well as half of their father's landed estate. In contrast, Jean Hasbrouck did not give real property to either of his daughters, Elizabeth and Mary, the latter a widow. He did, however, deed land in 1705 to Mary's two sons when they were twenty and fourteen, which formed "part of said marys portion from her said father." If he had given that land directly to Mary, it would have eventually gone to his grandsons anyway, but his English gendering of real estate deprived his daughter of the control of land that many other early New Paltz fathers were more willing to provide to their female heirs.[15]

Hasbrouck did not deny all property to his daughters, but he was far less generous than he was to his son (or sons). It is also possible that he favored one daughter over the other. Elizabeth received £60 in current New York money, a female slave, three books, and the remaining half of her father's personal estate. To his other daughter, Mary, he gave only £57, a bequest that took the form of two separate debts owed to her father rather than cash in-hand. In addition, Mary was pointedly given the unnamed property that she had previously received from him ("all watt Zy voor dessen van myn heft genooten"). It is possible that Hasbrouck did not, through his will, give Mary any additional property because he had already given her what he considered her share. It is also possible that he gave Mary less because she was the widow of the patentee Isaac DuBois, such that she was already well provided for. It is also possible that he aimed to treat her sister preferentially in accordance with Walloon practices. Still, he allowed his grandchildren to inherit in place of their deceased parents, a practice common among the Dutch and English but not the Walloons. In all, the unique provisions in Jean Hasbrouck's will suggest a complex interplay of at least Walloon and English practices, but possibly Dutch as well. While it is difficult to know exactly which ethnocultural perspective(s) Hasbrouck aimed to express, it is clear that he chose not to follow the egalitarian approach of his fellow patentees who had adopted Dutch ideals.[16]

Because only one of the patentees of the founding generation wrote a will when his wife was alive, it is impossible to generalize as to which ethnocultural choices they might have made when providing for their widows. When it came to their children, however, it is clear that they abandoned Walloon traditions and adopted, or were at least strongly influenced by, the practices of their Dutch neighbors, the only possible exception having been Jean Hasbrouck. They nevertheless were also aware of English law. In that legal context, they either adjusted their practices in order to follow Dutch practices as best they could, or they creatively constructed a Dutch-Anglo hybrid that met their own particular desires.

To Women as Wives

Much more can be said about the patentees' children and grandchildren, whose actions reveal a great deal more about the gendered thinking of the next generations of men as it related to property. Some followed Dutch practices, at least to the extent they could, and others adhered to English common law traditions and/or were inspired by New York's Anglo-oriented intestacy laws. Many chose a hybrid, creolized path. Men were aware of the ethnocultural alternatives available to them, and they often creatively chose from among them, rendering the community as a whole decidedly hybrid and ethnoculturally fluid throughout the eighteenth century.

While English law did not countenance community property between husbands and wives, a husband could perpetuate a Dutch gendered perspective by granting his widow temporary control of the estate while minor children remained at home. He also had the right to make that control permanent, an approach chosen by many Dutch-oriented men in both the Old World and the New, provided their widows did not remarry. Such an approach created for a widow matriarchal status irrespective of the age of her children. The thirty-four-year-old Hendricus Deyo did just that in 1724, directing that his thirty-one-year-old wife, Margriste, "will remain in full possession of all my worldly goods in order to enjoy them peacefully during her widowhood without having to give account for them to my children." When he wrote his will, Hendricus and Margriste had minor children at home, but he did not circumscribe her control temporally, directing that she would be the head of household in perpetuity, unless she remarried. In 1738, Andries LeFevre also stipulated that his wife, Cornelia, would have full control over his entire estate, but only if she never wed again. He even directed that she would also have "all the Income of all my Money During her Widow Ship," an unnecessary order, given that he already provided for her total authority over the estate. Perhaps this point was meant to emphasize his wishes in no uncertain terms. Like Hendricus Deyo, Andries LeFevre might have been motivated to give his widow such control because they still had minor children at home, the youngest only ten. Yet, the eldest was twenty-nine and had been married for thirteen years. He certainly could have assumed the position of head of household either upon his father's death or when the youngest reached majority, in accord with English patterns. His father, however, followed a Dutch model, preferring that his widow maintain control regardless of what ages the children attained.[17]

Some men continued to follow this pattern into the closing years of the century. In 1747, Daniel DuBois directed that his wife, Maria, would have full possession of the entire estate during her widowhood, unless she remarried. He did so even though his children had reached the age of majority; the youngest child (a son) was already nineteen and married, while still living at home, and the eldest son was twenty-eight. Hendricus DuBois acted similarly in 1774, when his wife was sixty-one and his youngest child (a male) was twenty-three. In 1790, Abraham LeFevre likewise dictated that his wife Maria, then seventy-two, would have "the Use and Income of all my Real and personal Estate during her natural Life," even though their children ranged in age from twenty-seven to forty-six. Of those eighteenth-century men from the patentee families whose wills survive, approximately half followed such practices.[18]

The desire of some men to give control of their estates to their widows sometimes produced situations in which the administration of property descended from woman to woman, even when adult men lived within the household. When Andries LeFevre died in 1738, he gave his wife full administration of his estate during her widowhood, and directed that after her death, his real estate would descend to his two sons. One son, Simon, had married Petronella Hasbrouck the year before his father's death, after which the couple continued to live in the household of Simon's parents. Simon's mother was still alive and managing his inheritance five years later when he died in 1743 at the age of thirty-three. Shortly before his death, Simon directed that his widow, Petronella, was to manage his estate, just as his father had done, at least until their youngest child reached the age of twenty-one. That transition, however, could not occur until his mother's death, as his father's will still applied until that time. The date of his mother's death is unknown, but when she did die, the administration of the estate immediately passed to her daughter-in-law. The evidence even suggests that Petronella controlled the property until her 1774 death, long after she had been required to transfer control to her children. In short, although Simon inherited property, he never had the opportunity to manage it. By following Dutch practices, the LeFevre men produced a forty-year, multi-generational matriarchy, something not often found among the English.[19]

Noah Eltinge (grandson of patentee Abraham DuBois) also preferred that the women in his family control his estate. He did so by ensuring that his son-in-law, Dirck Wynkoop, the husband of his only child, Sara, would become economically dependent first on Noah's wife, Jacomyntje, and subsequently on Noah's *granddaughters* (and Dirck's daughters), Cornelia and Geertje. When Noah composed his will in 1775, his daughter, Sara, was already deceased, so he gave his property to his granddaughters. Following a typical Dutch practice, he nevertheless provided that his wife would remain in full control of his entire estate as long as she was a widow. He also directed that if his son-in-law "shall continue to dwell and live with my said wife on the farm whereon I now live and shall work manage and take the prudent and necessary care thereof in such manner as he . . . heretofore hath done since his marriage with my deceased daughter that my said wife shall allow and give unto him . . . the full and equal one half of the income issues and profits thereof." Importantly, Jacomyntje had to give her son-in-law income from the estate, rather than his providing his mother-in-law a sufficient maintenance, as an English man might have done. When Jacomyntje died, Dirck's daughters gained control of their inheritance. Cornelia inherited her grandfather's homestead farm when she attained the age of twenty, thus rendering Dirck dependent on his own daughter for his support. Such a situation was clearly an affront to English conceptions of patriarchy. If Noah had wanted to create a patriarchal family order rather than a Dutch matriarchy, he certainly could have placed his estate in the hands of his son-in-law in trust for his granddaughters. He chose not to.[20]

Other men provided their wives with the administration of the full estate during their widowhood, typical of Dutch traditions, but limited their power upon their remarriage in ways that strayed from Dutch ideals. The result was various Dutch-Anglo hybrids. In 1707, Hugo Freer Sr. (son of the patentee of the same name) directed that his wife Marie would have possession of his entire estate, but he reduced her rights to the use of one-third of his estate if she remarried, referencing the English principle of the widow's "thirds." Daniel DuBois was also influenced by English law and custom, but again only partially. In his first will (1729), he directed that his wife would have authority over his estate during widowhood. Yet upon her marrying again, she would receive a third of the income from his real estate, and use rights to one female slave, three or four cows, three horses, and all the household furniture, reflecting but not precisely following English principles. Henry DuBois (1784) gave his wife use rights if she remarried, but in a highly idiosyncratic manner; if she chose to remarry, she would receive one-seventh of the real estate, as did each of their six children, although hers was only a life interest. The 1743 will of Simon LeFevre also suggests a Dutch-Anglo hybridity. He stipulated that his widow would have control over the estate but only until the youngest child reached the age of twenty-one, suggesting Dutch practices. He nevertheless still produced a hybrid Dutch-Anglo result by directing that after his children matured, his wife was to receive one-third of the income from her husband's real estate, although without use rights, thus reflecting but not precisely following English dower law.[21]

Some husbands chose to hybridize Dutch and English cultures by giving their wives perpetual authority over the patriarchal estate as widows, in Dutch fashion, but also permanently providing them with some personal property and/or cash, an annuity, or income from real property, resources that would remain theirs even upon remarriage. Such latter provisions reflected Anglo-New York laws of dower and intestate succession. In his first will from 1720, Jacob Hasbrouck left his wife, Esther, all of his personal estate except two slaves—a generous bequest—but when he rewrote his will in 1732, he provided his wife with only the annual interest on 500 "pistoles." (A pistole was the French name for a Spanish gold coin, but Hasbrouck might have used the word to signify pounds). Andries LeFevre (1738) intended to transfer ownership of a slave and horse to his wife, and Jonathan DuBois (1746) gave his wife a slave named Judie and "as many cows and household goods she had in her portion when I married her." Jacobus Bevier (1774) gave his wife £40 "in lieu of dower," and in 1784, Daniel LeFevre wrote a will that would transfer to his wife the ownership of a slave.[22]

While a significant number of New Paltz men from the patentee families gave women usufruct rights over their estates during their widowhood, and at least something if they remarried, some nevertheless denied them everything if they wed again. These few men created a truly Dutch-American creole settlement, as both Dutch traditions and English law provided that a woman was entitled to something substantial and permanent even if she remarried. Joseph Hasbrouck (1724) directed that his thirty-nine-year-old wife, Elsie, was to have full use of the estate as a widow; but if she married again, then she would have such control only until the youngest child reached the age of sixteen, reflecting Dutch principles. However, if she remarried, he barred her from any inheritance, even though she had contributed to the value of her husband's estate through her labor, as well as through the marriage portion she most likely brought to their union. Abraham Deyo I also gave his wife, Elsie, total possession of his estate according to his 1724 will, but he required her to turn over the entire estate to his son if she remarried. Simon DuBois likewise indicated in 1756 that his "well beloved Wife," Catharyntie, who was only thirty-five at the time, was to have full control of her husband's entire estate. He nevertheless emphatically stipulated that "in case she shall happen to marry again, Then and in Such case to be utterly Excluded and Debarred of and from my Estate." Daniel Hasbrouck similarly provided for his fifty-one-year-old wife, Wyntje, in 1759, although he did so with a softer tone, merely indicating that upon her remarriage "that she shall then deliver up the possession unto my Children."[23]

Why these men chose to take such a novel approach is somewhat difficult to ascertain, but a possible explanation relates to the complexity of preserving Dutch traditions in an English legal context. According to English law, each spouse retained ownership of any real estate he or she brought to a marriage: if these men's wives did not contribute to a communal landed estate, which was impossible in colonial New York, their husbands decided that their widows should have no permanent rights to any of the patriarchal lands. This clearly represents a double standard, as the reverse was not the case: if these wives predeceased their husbands, their husbands did retain use rights over their wives' real property according to the curtesy, regardless of whether they remarried. This double standard, however, may have had less to do with keeping the patriarchal estate from a widow who chose to remarry than it did with keeping that estate away from the control or influence of a second husband. If this was the case, then the gendered thinking of such men may not have changed. Rather, they may have been navigating the difficulty of preserving Dutch traditions in a colony that was governed according to English law. To put this another way, if the law provided for communal property (as among the Dutch), then a widow would take only *her* half to a new marriage. Without community property (as among the English), had a man given his widow some type of permanent rights over his estate that remained if she remarried, she would then be taking such rights over *his* estate into the new marriage. This latter situation was unavoidable in English New York, unless a man denied his wife all property rights upon her remarriage, which is what some New Paltz men chose to do.

A woman who was displeased with her deceased husband's choice to eliminate her control over all property if she remarried could repudiate his will in order to claim her dower rights. However, if she had been given matriarchal status, she would have been required to give up that control as well, if she chose her dower rights instead. She also would have had to do so soon after her husband's death, rather than if and when she remarried. She therefore would have had to sacrifice her power as a Dutch matriarch in favor of English rights to permanent support. She could not have it both ways. Whether this was a difficult decision to make for women who were born to or married into patentee families remains a mystery, but this difficulty was clearly a result of the intersection of Dutch tradition and English law in a creolized environment.

Some men chose to combine ethnocultural traditions by encouraging their sons to provide for their widowed mothers, fulfilling English cultural ideals, while also providing for the possibility of greater independence for their widows, more akin to Dutch customs. In 1768, Jan Hasbrouck bequeathed to his "beloved Wife Rachel van Wagenen" some furniture, household goods, and her apparel, and further directed that his children were to supply their mother a place to live and "sufficient Support." Yet, he further stipulated that if she was dissatisfied with the support she was receiving, she could choose an annuity of £10 instead. He also provided a further option that would have allowed his wife to choose for herself where she would live. If she chose that path, she would then receive a £15 annuity, free firewood, use of half of the garden, the use of a female slave, and a cow, with pasturage and fodder, provided she did not remarry. Similarly, in 1776, Jacob Hasbrouck Jr. indicated that his wife Jannetje was to continue to live with his sons in their father's dwelling house, and the sons also were to provide their mother a "sufficient Maintenance, Suitable to her State and condition." However, if she was dissatisfied with such an arrangement, she still was entitled to one room in her deceased husband's house, as well as an annuity of £25, as well as a slave, kitchen equipment, and furniture. These two men preferred to provide for their wives in an English manner, but perhaps they believed that English ways might not have sufficiently protected the interests of women, so they provided a more Dutch-like back-up plan.[24]

Other men rendered their wives essentially dependent upon their children for support, but they did so in a manner that made them somewhat less dependent than English women commonly were. They did so by directing their heirs to provide their widowed mothers with a precisely valued annuity, which they could manage independently. Josiah Eltinge (1767), for example, directed that his widow Magdalena would receive a £20 annuity; and Peter Deyo (1791) ensured that his wife Elizabeth would be given a £15 annual allowance. Johannes Freer (1796) stipulated that his children would supply their mother Agetta £10 each year. The position of such women was a far cry from those whose husbands directed that their widows would maintain control of the entire estate if they did not remarry, reflecting Dutch ideals; yet such men did seek to provide their wives with a somewhat greater level of independence than English gender traditions generally assumed.[25]

Clearly, some men provided for their wives in what was essentially a Dutch manner, while others creatively combined Dutch and English ways in a variety of permutations across a spectrum that produced relative independence to relative dependence. Some, however, chose to provide for their wives in a decidedly English manner. Intriguingly, it was not later generations who introduced such practices in the village, as the first to do so was Abraham DuBois, the second youngest and longest-living patentee, who did so in 1731. He was a Walloon born in Mannheim in 1657, who came to Nieuw Nederland in 1661, who might have remembered the English conquest that occurred when he was seven years of age. Yet, at the age of seventy-four, he was on the cutting edge of ethnocultural change. He placed his widow, Margaret, in an uncompromising position of dependence according to the English law of dower, by directing that his wife would receive one-third of the income from his estate. Margaret did have an income over and above what her husband provided, as she, along with each of her siblings, inherited an equal share of her patentee father's estate; so she was not solely dependent upon support from her husband's estate. However, the issue at stake is not so much the extent of a widow's income but her control over her husband's estate, and thus her position within the family. And Abraham DuBois's position on that issue was clearly conceived of in English terms.[26]

Once Abraham DuBois had adopted and introduced such English traditions, other younger townsmen chose to follow suit, although those who followed a strict Englishness were few. Roelof Eltinge, the husband of Abraham's daughter Sara, for example, provided in his 1745 will that his son Noah was to furnish Sarah an "honorable maintainance." Sara, however, was in no need of a maintenance, as according to law, she would become independent upon her husband's death, as she had inherited land from her father. However, she did so in a somewhat unusual manner, as her father atypically gave land to her and her husband jointly. Because of this, Sarah would gain ownership of all of that land upon her husband's death, according to the principle of "tenancy by entirety." Still, like Abraham DuBois, Roelof *intended* to deny his wife authority within the family, in contrast to Dutch ways. In a similar fashion, Benjamin Hasbrouck in 1796 stipulated that his wife, Lydia, was to live with one of their sons of her choice, and the sons collectively were to ensure that "she be clothed, maintained and supported in a decent and comfortable manner," although he also gave her an annuity which provided her with a little more control of her affairs.[27]

These women were already elderly when their husbands provided for their future dependence, as Margaret DuBois was sixty-nine, Lydia Hasbrouck sixty-seven, and Sara Eltinge sixty-three. But it was perhaps not their age alone that motivated their husbands to render them dependent, as other men from the patentee families chose Dutch-style independence for their widows even if they were elderly. Jannetje DuBois was sixty-one in 1774 when her husband Hendricus DuBois wrote a will that allowed for her matriarchy as a widow, and Abraham LeFevre's seventy-two-year-old wife, Maria, was a decidedly senior citizen when her husband gave her power over the estate. Besides, if an elderly man could direct his estate, then his widow could as well, at least theoretically, and clearly some did. Elsie Hasbrouck managed the family farm when she was between the ages of thirty-nine and sixty-nine, and Petronella LeFevre was controlling the estate into her sixties, exerting more control than her husband had even intended. Margrietje Bevier began managing her children's patrimony only at the age of fifty-three; and she kept very close reins on that estate, holding her eldest son strictly accountable for providing her with the necessities of life in exchange for allowing him to stay in his deceased father's home. Clearly, a widowed Dutch matriarch could have been as economically powerful within the household as her husband had been, and it is partially so that she could assume such a role that Dutch girls were educated in business and financial management. In other words, a wife's advanced age alone did not necessarily motivate her husband to make her dependent, suggesting that ethocultural factors were also at stake.[28]

It is important to note that a man's ethnocultural gendered thinking was not necessarily fixed and unchanging. This issue, however, can be seen only in a few instances, as men very rarely composed more than one will. Other than Louis DuBois, Jacob Hasbrouck Sr. was the only other man from a patentee family that composed three, spanning nearly three decades (1720, 1732, and 1747). Through these wills, he revealed his changing assumptions concerning gender. The overall tone of his first will was far more Dutch than English. He directed that his wife, Esther, was to have full possession of his estate, "without giving Any Account to [his] Heirs"; if she remarried, she remained in control only until the children reached maturity. Nevertheless, he did transfer ownership of all his moveable property to her (except for two enslaved laborers who went to their son Benjamin) regardless of her future marriage choices. While such a provision did not reflect the idea of communal ownership of the conjugal estate in both real and personal property, the personal property his wife was to receive was certainly of significant value.[29]

By 1732, however, he had chosen to hybridize Dutch and English cultures. He still provided that his wife would be in full *possession* of the entire estate in her widowhood in Dutch fashion, but he only gave her permanent rights to the interest on 500 pistoles, suggesting the idea of English dower rights. However, in his last will, composed in 1747 when he was fifty-nine and his wife sixty-one, Jacob denied his widow the power to control the estate even during her widowhood, providing her an English-style maintenance instead. He nevertheless made her a co-executor in his 1747 will, suggesting that he believed she was capable of making financial decisions, but not of managing his estate, a somewhat contradictory position. Over the course of his life, Jacob reconceptualized the role and social position of his wife from an influential woman with significant authority, reflective of Dutch ideals, to a dependent person, but he never fully embraced the level of dependence to which English women were often subjected.[30]

Another clear manner in which a husband demonstrated his ethnocultural viewpoint as to his wife's position in the family and the community was whether or not he made her an executor of his estate, either alone or with others. Only Louis DuBois ever made his wife sole executor, but more than half of the women of the patentee families wielded significant influence as co-executors between 1724 and 1784. The others were denied such authority, reflecting the patriarchal values of the English. It is, of course, conceivable that a man might have denied his wife the role of executrix because of her age and physical health. However, neither Simon LeFevre, whose wife was only thirty-four when he wrote his will, and Daniel DuBois, who composed his first will when his spouse was just forty, provided for their wives' executorship, suggesting that some men were indeed motivated by ethnocultural concerns. Husbands who gave their widows full administration of the property (at least if they did not remarry) were two-to-one more likely to make them executrixes as well, which is hardly surprising. Importantly, when it came to the issue of executorship, men drew upon the ideals of both Dutch and English cultures in relatively unchanging proportions through most of the century. It would not be until 1784 that wives were universally denied the power of executrix, revealing an ethnocultural shift.

Overall, in comparing the choices that New Paltz men made in providing for their widows, the patentees and their descendants thoroughly abandoned their Walloon-gendered ethnocultural heritage. Instead, they created a broad spectrum of approaches. Some drew heavily on Dutch ways; others essentially followed English cultural formations. Many, however, charted an intermediate position between Dutch-style matriarchal independence and English-influenced female subordination and dependence, resulting in various Dutch-Anglo hybrid forms. Others created an ethnocultural approach that was none of the above, by granting their widows control of the family estates in Dutch fashion while denying them all resources upon their remarriage, a hybrid approach that likely represents a Dutch response to English property laws. When looking at how men navigated the issues surrounding women's inheritance rights, it is clear that the New Paltz community created paths of creolized ethnocultural complexity throughout the eighteenth century. It was an environment in which men felt comfortable choosing from the gendered thinking of multiple cultures in order to meet their own particular beliefs and needs.

The Women's Perspective

Because the law gave men the primary agency when it came to property, it is difficult to find evidence of women's reactions to their increasingly circumscribed role within their households and community. Women did not often compose wills, as they could legally do so only as widows or if given permission by their husbands. Even if they did write a will, they had the right only to distribute any personal property under their control. Nevertheless, the few women who did write wills clearly intended to exert their authority within the means they possessed, or at least within the means they believed they possessed. Catherine Blanchan DuBois, the widow of patentee Louis DuBois, attempted to write a will in 1712, some years after she married her second husband, Jean Cottin. That remarriage allowed her continued use of only half of her husband's estate according to her first husband's 1694 will, property that would after her death automatically descend to her children in equal shares. Yet she also mistakenly believed that she had a legal and transferable right to one-third of the profits that had accrued to her second husband's estate, although he was still alive. She would have gained transferable access to such profits only if her husband had predeceased her and had died intestate, such that through her will, she demonstrated her limited understanding of the law of dower. Nevertheless, Catherine attempted through a will to give money to her two female slaves (whom she intended to be freed after her death), as well as to her church in Kingston. She also attempted to bequeath her remaining personal property to her children, with one daughter receiving more than the others. She actually possessed neither money nor other personal property of her own to bequeath, in accordance with the terms of her first husband's will and the laws of the colony. Her children were aware that their mother's will was thus illegal and unenforceable, so they contracted among themselves to divide her estate equally, which is how their father had actually intended it to be.[31]

Other women made very different choices. Maria Deyo Hasbrouck gave all of her property in 1729 to a single child Daniel, as "he has taken care of me in my old age and has been my consolation." Catharina Freer, in 1781, chose to give her personal property only to her daughter and not to her sons. In 1787, Wyntje Hasbrouck gave to her only daughter, Elsie, her clothing and absolved a son and a son-in-law of debts they owed to her, while dividing her remaining property among all of her children equally. Given this diversity of approaches, meaningful conclusions as to women's views on gendered relations as defined by property rights are difficult to draw.[3]

If female property owners were more acted upon than actors, one may wonder how they felt about the choices their husbands had made to follow Dutch, English, or hybrid Dutch-Anglo gendered thinking. Perhaps surprisingly, some women did not necessarily resist the decline in Dutchness and female power. Some actively assumed the dependence that characterized the English male-female relationship as codified in New York law. However, they exerted their agency by making the choice to do so, rather than having greater dependence forced upon them. Elsie Hasbrouck, for example, was given full administration of her husband's estate for life, although she formally gave up that control when she was sixty-nine, allowing her son Abraham to take his inheritance. The sixty-seven-year-old Jannetje DuBois immediately chose not to maintain control when her husband, Hendricus, died in 1774, releasing it to two sons. In exchange, she retained the right to three rooms in the house in which she was living and all the basic necessities of life. She was not content, however, with merely giving away her rights in exchange for her maintenance; her son Methusalem bound himself to her in the amount of £1,000, which he would be required to pay if he did not live up to the agreement. Rebecca Van Wagenen DuBois did not choose to release control of the estate of her husband when he died in 1787 when she was likely in her forties, but she did release her powers as executrix.[33]

Unlike Rebecca DuBois, both Elsie Hasbrouck and Jannetje DuBois were admittedly rather old when they released control, but nevertheless they, as conscious actors, formally controlled the termination of their matriarchy in a *de jure* rather than a *de facto* manner. From an ethnocultural perspective, the meaning of this is unclear. Did their decision to release their control represent an acceptance of English female dependence? Or did their choice to give away their power merely represent the power they possessed as Dutch matriarchs, since the power to administer included the power to give up that administration? That Elsie Hasbrouck and Jannetje DuBois chose to relinquish power formally, when they easily could have done so informally, suggests at least an awareness of the real power they possessed. The evidence is unfortunately too limited to gather any more than a glimpse as to how women faced the creolized environment, but they certainly did choose to act within the field of action available to them. Whether that could be interpreted through an ethnocultural lens is difficult to say, although some clearly possessed the wherewithal not to become the stereotypically dependent English woman who struggled to manage her affairs after the death of her husband.

Stronger hints of women's perspectives through time can be garnered through an exploration of how women determined, or were allowed to determine, their role within the family in cases of intestacy, particularly when the courts did not play a role in the outcome. Isaac, son of Louis, was the youngest of the New Paltz patentees, having been born in 1660. He appears to have died intestate in 1693 at the age of thirty-three, leaving a young wife, the twenty-nine-year-old Maria Hasbrouck DuBois, and three young sons. Given that her sons were between the ages of four and nine, it is not surprising that Maria independently took control of the estate, but she also managed the estate almost as if it were her own. During her administration, she invested her deceased husband's legacy in the construction of a substantial two-room stone house in 1705, and she donated handsomely in 1717 for the construction of the village's first stone church. She retained control of her children's inheritance until 1719, when, at the age of fifty-five, she finally transferred the administration of her deceased husband's estate to their thirty-five-year-old, eldest son. Maria Deyo Hasbrouck, the widow of patentee Abraham Hasbrouck (d. 1717), also obtained control of her husband's estate when he unexpectedly died intestate from an "apoplectic fit" (possibly a stroke). Like Maria DuBois, Maria Deyo Hasbrouck used her control of the estate to donate funds in 1717 for the building of the church; her thirty-one-year-old second son, Solomon, who still lived with her, did not likewise donate, suggesting her position as head of the family. At the time, her youngest had already reached the age of twenty-one. Similarly, Lysbeth Crispell Ean, the daughter of patentee Antoine Crispell and widow of Elias Ean (d. before 1728), served as head of household, when she, but not her children, was taxed in 1728, even though her eldest son was twenty-eight and her youngest was twenty-three.[34]

Wives of men who died intestate at the end of the seventeenth century and into the first decades of the eighteenth apparently had sufficient influence to act as if their husbands had granted them authority over the estate along Dutch lines. Their sons also appear to have accepted their mothers' authority, as well as the gendered familial order of the Dutch, whether or not their fathers had specifically transformed their mothers into powerful matriarchs. In one instance, a man attempted to provide for his wife's ultimate dependence according to English traditions, but Dutch ways were nevertheless followed, again suggesting that at least one woman had the power to control the gendered order of her household after her husband's death. In 1743, shortly before he died, thirty-three-year-old Simon LeFevre composed a will, which stipulated that his wife, Petronella Hasbrouck LeFevre, was to remain in control of the estate only until the youngest child was twenty-one. After that milestone, her children were to ensure that she received income based on her dower rights. Yet in 1771, twenty-eight years after her husband's death, Petronella was still in control of his estate, even to the point of selling part of his land, something which she had no legal right to do. That year, the congregation of New Paltz acquired "a piece of ground bought of Petronella LaFevere located on the west side of the street," which either abutted or was part of the homestead lot of her husband. Surely Petronella's children knew the Anglo-style parameters of their father's will, as did the executors. Not only did her children not challenge the sale of their father's property, but the congregation apparently deemed it was hers to sell, suggesting a broad acceptance of gendered rights that strayed far from Englishness.[35]

To allow Petronella such authority in Dutch fashion as late as 1771, in spite of the legal limitations imposed upon her by her husband's will, perhaps reflects the fact that her position as head of household had been in place for almost thirty years. But by the 1790s, a man's widow and family could, as could the man himself, expect that English common law practices would be followed. Maria Low Eltinge's husband, Roelof Josiah Eltinge, died intestate in 1795; it is clear that she was not seen as the head of household after that point, as her family's house was listed as being owned by her sons Roelof and John in the 1798 Federal Direct Tax list taken three years later. It was also presumed that she would receive her thirds both in personalty and a life interest in real estate. Maria chose to increase her level of independence by releasing her dower in exchange for goods and the right to live in the family home and to use the barn, hay house, and wood lot. Maria might have been preserving a degree of Dutchness through the careful bargaining for her semi-independence, but the days of Dutch culture informing estate administration in cases of intestacy had passed; in its place, English patriarchalism had found a foothold.[36]

The changing contours of gender that are revealed in the rights widows gained or did not gain through the death of their husbands obviously impacted more than women as wives, but affected the whole family structure. Dutch-identified men could provide women with authority during widowhood only if they believed that the role of parent to a significant extent transcended gender, such that the family order was substantially unaffected by the father's death. As matriarch, a Dutch widow profoundly affected the lives of her children, particularly her sons, because a long-lived mother could keep her sons in a dependent position for a very long time. Of course, fathers could do so as well in either Dutch or English society. However, the English would have likely seen an elderly widow controlling a dependent adult son to be a reversal of the natural order, a situation that might have been uncomfortable or possibly even demeaning for a Dutch man in New York—if he was attempting to achieve acceptance among the English. Direct evidence for such a concern is admittedly slim. Nevertheless, given the extreme importance that patriarchy played in English culture, it is difficult to see how English-identified New York men might have raised an eyebrow at adult men who were dependent upon their Dutch-oriented mothers. Whether or not this might have affected the choices husbands made when providing for their wives is unknown, but it is certainly possible that any erosion of Dutch practices might to some extent have been influenced by fathers' concerns for the possible sociocultural position of their sons.

To Women as Daughters

Wives and sons were not the only ones affected by the ethnoculturally gendered decisions their husbands and fathers made, as daughters were impacted as well. But whereas men began to incorporate English culture in providing for their wives very early in the history of the community, they continued to provide for both male and female children in Dutch fashion for far longer. The dominant pattern was established by the Walloon founders of New Paltz, who, with the possible exception of Jean Hasbrouck, repudiated their native culture in favor of Dutch traditions by refusing to favor one child over another. For example, after providing small bequests to his son and his son's eldest son (the latter who was his grandfather's namesake), patentee Christian Deyo dictated in 1687 that "unto my five children all ye rest of my estate of lands, housings, chattels, and movable goods, to them." Hendricus Deyo continued in his grandfather Christian's footsteps in 1724, when he divided his real estate and personal property equally among his two sons and one daughter, with the exception of an additional horse going to his eldest son. According to his 1729 will, Daniel DuBois also distributed his entire estate in the same manner among both male and female children, although his eldest son was to receive his father's cavalry equipment over and above his equal share of the estate. He made only slight adjustments when he rewrote his will in 1747. Simon LeFevre (1743) also divided his real estate among his two daughters and one son. Rather than devising his personal property directly to his children, he stipulated that his moveable estate be sold after his wife received her portion, with the proceeds to be divided in an almost equal fashion; LeFevre directed that his two daughters pay their brother £20—the approximate value of one good horse and a milch (dairy) cow—suggesting that that payment represented his position as eldest (and only) son. Others, such as Simon DuBois (1756), Jan Hasbrouck (1768), and Hendricus DuBois Jr. (1784), provided similarly for both male and female children. The widower Hugo Freer Sr. (son of the patentee of the same name), writing in 1728, even stipulated that if the "fruit of the flesh" ("de Vleeschlycke Vreught") of Tryntie Van Cleck lived to the age of twenty, Freer's apparently illegitimate child would receive an equal portion of an extensively divided estate along with his or her thirteen half-siblings.[37]

Other Dutch-oriented fathers were careful to inform their children, male and female, that even if they were provided with specific bequests rather than equal fractional shares, their fathers did not intend to favor one child over the others. In his third will of 1747, Jacob Hasbrouck Sr. divided his land among his three sons, but "because [Benjamin's] proportion of land is esteemed better," he had to pay his brother Isaac £50 and his brother Jacob Jr. £40. Samuel Bevier, in 1750, equally distributed to his three daughters and to three of his six sons all of his land in New Paltz then in his possession, while he bequeathed another son Philip, land on the Hudson River. Samuel pointedly noted that he had already conveyed land to his two other children, Isaac and Jacobus, which made them "equal with the rest of my other children." Bevier also owned a share in the undivided lands in the New Paltz patent, but he bequeathed that share to only eight of his nine children, leaving out Jacobus. Given that Bevier pointedly noted that Jacobus's share was equal to that of his siblings, perhaps Jacobus's land was considered superior, such that he did not receive a share in the undivided lands. Noah Eltinge also was careful to provide for an equitable division to his two granddaughters as his only heirs, ordering one grandchild to pay the other £400 "to make them nearly equal" because "the proportion . . . given to my said grand daughter Cornelia Wynkoop is more valuable than that proportion given to my other grand daughter with respect to the buildings thereon and the goodness of the land."[38]

While some fathers clearly made little if any distinctions between the sexes of their children when dividing the patriarchal estate, some fathers were not as gender-blind when it came to their distribution of real property, suggesting the influence of English gendered culture. Yet, many nevertheless preserved a balanced division of real property by requiring male heirs who received land to make cash payments to their siblings, including their sisters. English men did not generally follow such an approach, suggesting another form of English and Dutch hybrid creolization. As noted earlier, patentee Louis Bevier in both his 1715 and 1720 wills divided his real estate among his sons, requiring that they each pay their only sister her equal share of the market value of all of their father's real property, while each child, male and female, also received an equal share of their father's moveable property. Clearly, his choice represented ethnocultural rather than material concerns, as his denial of land to his daughter could not have been based on a desire to prevent fragmentation of his land holdings, as he owned one-twelfth of the patent, or more than three thousand acres. Other fathers chose to be more precise as to the legacies their daughters were to receive, such as Andries LeFevre who directed in his 1738 will that all of his land would descend to his two sons, requiring them to pay their seven sisters £400. He, too, had extensive landholdings, as he had inherited a total of over 7 percent of the patent. In 1759, Daniel Hasbrouck's similarly devised all of his real property to his six sons, who were required to pay their only sister, Elsje, £200. If he could divide his land into sixths, he likely could have divided it into sevenths, if he had so wished. Instead, he gave his only daughter money. Some fathers followed a similar pattern even into the closing years of the century, including Solomon DuBois (1756), Abraham Bevier (1763), Hendricus DuBois (1774), and Benjamin Hasbrouck (1796).[39]

This is not to say that fathers ceased to give their daughters any land, but when they did so, they increasingly gave them small lots of undeveloped land in addition to cash payments from their brothers. Clearly, fathers increasingly gendered land in ways characteristic of English culture, while many nevertheless remained true to a belief in Dutch gender equity, demonstrating ethnocultural hybridization once again. This growing Englishness as reflected in the distribution of property to children was not forced upon members of the New Paltz patentee families in any way. A father had virtually unlimited power to distribute his property to his children as he saw fit, so if his choices reflected even touches of Englishness, he had made such choices willingly.

In distributing personal property, fathers tended to be less concerned about its precise division, although they attempted to allow for general equality throughout the first 125 years of the community's history. Like many of the patentees, a number of fathers, such as Samuel Bevier (1750), Hendricus DuBois (1774), and Benjamin Hasbrouck (1796), simply gave each child a share in his personal estate, without stipulating how precisely it would be divided. When fathers did devise personal property more precisely, distinctions as to type of property were often made between male and female children, as fathers often gave sons their farm equipment and daughters their household goods. Perhaps even when fathers did not stipulate what types of property were to be given to children of a particular sex, the expectations were that in practice, property would be apportioned by type, as the men and women had different daily relationships with different types of goods. To gender certain types of moveable property reflects neither Dutch nor English culture, as the gendered division of daily labor on a farm did not substantially vary between the two cultures. In short, while fathers increasingly divided personal property more precisely, this may not have indicated any change in the construction of gender per se, the reconceptualizing of which *had* undergirded the changes in presumed rights to land.[40]

When a father did privilege one son over his brothers and sisters, such a choice stands out as an exception that proves the rule. In 1724, Joseph Hasbrouck gave his entire farm at nearby Guilford, which he had received from his father, patentee Abraham Hasbrouck, to his eldest son, Abraham, who was required to pay £500 in current New York money to his nine brothers and sisters, each of whom would receive an equal share of that payment. This clearly had nothing to do with a potential fragmentation of landholdings, as the Guilford lands comprised two thousand acres; Joseph clearly could have created viable farms for at least some, if not all, of his six sons. Joseph Hasbrouck's creolized choice therefore suggests the flavor of English primogeniture combined with a Dutch commitment to equity. Cornelius DuBois (1780) also favored his one son, Cornelius Jr., but he did so only temporarily, by allowing his son to use all of real estate for life; after the death of Cornelius Jr., the land would be equally distributed to his six sisters or their heirs, both male and female. The most atypically advantaged heir was Levi Deyo, the third son and sixth child of Peter Deyo, who in 1791 became destined to receive all of his father's real estate in New Paltz comprising, in the father's estimation, twelve hundred acres. Additionally, Levi was to inherit all of his father's personal property and other land outside of New Paltz, except for that at Kinderhook. Peter gave the Kinderhook lands to his five sons (including Levi) and five daughters, but as his title to most of that land was questionable, that bequest potentially might have amounted to nothing at all. While Peter Deyo did not follow a practice of primogeniture, he nevertheless anomalously privileged one son in a manner fundamentally at variance with the choices made by his more Dutch-oriented neighbors and forebears.[41]

Fathers occasionally granted the eldest son an inheritance in cash or personal property above his siblings because of his birth position, but such gifts were often small. Their intention in doing so is not entirely clear. David Narrett argues that some men did so as a way of "affirm[ing] their right to avoid primogeniture." However, he also suggests that their doing so reflects an early modern Dutch practice of acknowledging "the eldest son's right to special treatment" while still providing for equitable divisions of their estates. If the intention was to thwart primogeniture, then such a token bequest was unnecessary, as the law of primogeniture applied in New York only when a father died intestate; even then, it does not seem that, in practice, the law was applied in New Paltz. Either interpretation, however, suggests the desire on the part of fathers to embrace or perpetuate Dutch culture. The first to bequeath a unique gift to an eldest son was patentee Christian Deyo, who gave his only son, Pierre, fifty rijksdaalders, each worth perhaps five or six shillings, that his son was indebted to him. That bequest, however, was perhaps more of a debt cancellation than a gift. Patentee Hugo Freer was the first to clearly note his eldest son's quasi-privileged position, as according to his 1698 will, he gave his firstborn male child ten pieces of eight. In 1720, Jacob Hasbrouck similarly gave a gift to his eldest, and he clearly pointed out that he should not claim anything more as his firstborn. Jan Hasbrouck (1768) gave a similar monetary gift of eight shillings to his eldest son, and Jacobus Bevier (1774) gave to his firstborn son forty shillings. Examples of similar bequests to eldest sons were those of Jonathan DuBois in 1746 (a "Large Dutch Bible"), Daniel DuBois in 1747 ("one horse . . . in consideration of being my Eldest son on which account he shall not have or pretend to have any thing more by any ways or pretences whatsoever"), and Abraham LeFevre (1790), who gave his eldest son a heifer. The only time a father gave a truly generous gift to his eldest son was Abraham DuBois in 1731, who gave to Abraham Jr. £200, but he noted that he did so not only because that son was the eldest but because he had been obedient to his father. In total, approximately two-thirds of the fathers provided a particular gift to their eldest sons (at least in one of their wills), but in doing so, they did not undermine the Dutch-style gender equity that prevailed in the community throughout the eighteenth century.[42]

Although Abraham DuBois bequeathed one son something more than the others because of his first-born status *and* as a reward for his behavior, fathers occasionally granted a child other than the eldest son something extra strictly for having provided them with a particular service. Such fathers nevertheless felt the need to explain to their other children why they had done so, and in doing so, they simply reinforced their general commitment to equity. For example, Antoine Crispell in 1707 bequeathed one daughter the monies that were due to him from a mortgage in payment for several years' board and for her "great services" ("groote dienste") to him. In his 1720 will, Louis Bevier allowed his third son, Samuel, to have first choice of for his portion of the estate, as Samuel had returned with his family to his father's house to assist him after Louis' daughter Esther married and moved out of the family home. Likewise, Hugo Freer Sr., in 1728, devised his weaver's loom to his second son Isaac "for his faithful service."[43]

The gendered thinking within the patentee families clearly demonstrated certain trends between the end of the seventeenth and the turn of nineteenth centuries. The first is the forceful repudiation of Walloon traditions. Second, the Dutch concept of community property during marriage was only loosely established and quickly jettisoned. Nevertheless, Dutch-gendered practices were strongly stamped in eighteenth-century New Paltz culture. Beginning with the first generation and continuing as late as 1796, some husbands gave their widows full control of their estates in typical Dutch fashion, which enabled them to retain a powerful matriarchal role even as their children reached maturity. That power was often reinforced by their widows' co-executorship. Matriarchal power, however, was often provisional, as it was often dependent upon the willingness of widows to remain widows. If they did choose to remarry, that matriarchy came to an end. Some women who remarried then received what constituted an English widow's thirds, an approach first seen in 1707, such that in total, their husbands had provided for them in hybrid Dutch-Anglo ways. Other wives who were destined to become Dutch matriarchs as widows were denied everything upon remarriage. This approach, first used in 1724, represents an innovative Dutch-American formation produced through the hybridization of Dutch and English ways. Some husbands might have chosen to follow such a path not because they aimed to deny their wives anything but because they simply could not accept the possibility that any part of their estate might come under the control of their wives' later husbands, which would be unavoidable due to English property laws.

As early as 1731, however, with the will of patentee Abraham DuBois, widows might also be treated strictly according to English law and traditions, rendering them dependent upon their children. Increasingly, widows were also denied the power of executorship; the first not to be granted that power was Margaret DuBois in 1731, and the last women to receive that power were Rebecca DuBois and Catharine LeFevre, both in 1784. By the closing years of the eighteenth century, most men only provided their widows with cash annuities, with or without some moveable property, rights to use of real property, or a maintenance from a child, all reminiscent of English practices.

Although the rights of widows of New Paltz patentee descendants contracted over the eighteenth century, most fathers nevertheless continued to devise to their children an equal, or at least equitable, division of property in accordance with Dutch customs. Yet, fathers increasingly ceased to perceive daughters and sons as interchangeable, by giving land to sons but not to daughters, a perspective that reflects English ideals. Still, many chose to effect an equitable division through cash payments from brothers to sisters, which was not a typical English practice. Again, the result was voluntary Dutch-Anglo hybrid creolization.

The ethnocultural orientation of the New Paltz patentees and their descendants as expressed in gendered inheritances practices and beliefs clearly demonstrates that New Paltz men created and maintained a creolized Dutch-Anglo culture throughout the first 125 years of the community's existence, even though Englishness was clearly advancing. Ethnocultural change did not proceed monolithically, however, as change affected women as wives more quickly than women as daughters. Yet, such generalizations are somewhat facile, as even with the limited number of wills available, the cultural permutations are almost endless, reflecting the fact that two cultural perspectives were available from which to choose, at least to some extent. Certain aspects of English law made the preservation of Dutch traditions impossible. As a result, it was impossible to preserve all of the conditions of Dutch law in an English context. Creolization was simply unavoidable. However, all men of the patentee families did not want to follow Dutch traditions, either wholly or in part, even if they could have. The result was that each man had many ethnocultural options from which to choose, and many constructed their own uniquely creolized approaches.

Why precisely they charted their own ethnocultural paths is impossible to decipher given the available evidence. We simply cannot know why a particular man did not allow his wife to administer the estate or even serve as one of his executors as Dutch women typically did. Maybe he did not give her such authority because he wanted to follow an English path. Or perhaps he did not think she had the appropriate skills to successfully manage an estate. Maybe she did not even want such power, preferring that their children take a more dominant role in the family. In most cases, we just cannot know. This is certainly not to say that women would have generally preferred a more dependent position. It is very possible, even probable, that many women balked as their husbands increasingly circumscribed female control of property. Those daughters who received their share of their father's estate in cash might also not have been pleased that their brothers received theirs in land, as these daughters knew that fathers in previous generations had not made such gendered distinctions. Dutch women had more power and agency than their English sisters, and "Dutch" women in New York would certainly have been aware that the spread of English gendered thinking was increasingly hemming them in.

What we do know is that men of the New Paltz patentee families did have considerable power to select between the gendered thinking of multiple ethnic cultures. They clearly made use of that freedom to choose in ways not generally possible in a monocultural environment in which options would have appeared more limited. Whatever their motivations, the positions of men and women in New Paltz marriages, families, and the community itself remained fluid in such a creolized environment, and the extent of change could not have been predicted. Still, English law gave most of the agency lay to men, even if they chose to follow Dutch ideals in whole or in part, such that the gendered aspects of Dutch culture could never be preserved intact in an English colony.

Chapter 3

HALLS, WINDOWS, HEARTHS, and BARNS

Architecture and Ethnic Culture

The structures that the New Paltz founders and their descendants built on the land they controlled reflected their creolized culture as much as had their approach to gender and property. Indeed, the houses that the New Paltz patentee families built and lived in mark the most overt, tangible, and lasting evidence that the New Paltz patentee community was built on Dutch roots. But upon those roots they grafted English architectural forms in a complex and fluidly changing manner. In the patentees' New World context, the availability of different regional architectural forms made architectural creolization possible, and the choices they actively made made that possibility a reality.

This is not to suggest that their agency was limitless. Just as gender performance was sometimes constrained by law, so too was architecture limited to some extent by the knowledge and the abilities of the regional artisans. This was particularly the case with stone houses, which required the work of skilled craftsmen, including masons, carpenters, and roofers; such stone structures represent virtually all surviving New Paltz structures of the eighteenth century. It is therefore likely that, to a significant extent, many buildings represent the ethnocultural traditions and orientation of the builders rather than those for whom they were erected. Still, those who contracted for the construction of a house certainly did have the opportunity to influence some design choices that reveal architectural creolization. This was particularly the case when it came to many secondary architectural characteristics, including windows, fireplaces, and passageways, all of which took different forms in Dutch and English architecture. The creolization of the community is also revealed through alterations made to existing structures. Such alterations merit particular attention because they would not have been made unless the owners specifically requested them, thus reflecting their agency.[1]

In describing architectural creolization, it is necessary to distinguish between creolization and hybrid creolization, both of which are demonstrated in the New Paltz architectural record. By creolization, I am referring to those situations when the members of the New Paltz patentee families simply inserted Anglo-American architectural elements into overall Dutch-American forms, producing a pastiche that included distinct elements of each. When they combined Dutch-American and Anglo-American architecture to produce fundamentally new forms, they were creolizing through hybridization. Ethnocultural change in New Paltz architecture began with creolization and then progressed into hybrid creolization, culminating in the eventual acceptance of truly Anglo-American forms. The creolization process in material culture is therefore different from the creolization of gender, which was always strictly hybrid, as Dutch gender ideals could be preserved only within the strictures of Anglo-American law.

Origins and Transference

Unfortunately, virtually nothing remains of the earliest domestic architecture of New Paltz, much of which likely was meant to serve only temporarily. In the early eighteenth century, however, the founders' children began to build, or had built, permanent houses, many of which still survive. These buildings clearly reflect the region's Dutch-American architectural idiom, a style which dominated both in New Paltz and in Ulster County more broadly. The houses that survive are virtually all of stone, which was the material of choice for the wealthiest third of New Paltz residents. All members of the patentee families therefore did not own a stone house, but most if not all of the stone houses were built for the patentees and their descendants.[2]

These houses, however, do not represent a simple transplantation of the architecture of the Netherlands. Most importantly, the Old World Dutch did not generally build in stone. The local practice of building in stone might have developed from the hybrid creolization of the Dutch and other continental Europeans who came to Nieuw Nederland and early New York. Such creolization was possibly facilitated by the fact that most of the continental Europeans who settled in the region would have drawn from architectural traditions "common throughout parts of present-day Belgium, Germany, and the Netherlands and possibly parts of northern France and areas farther abroad," according to architectural historian Jeroen van den Hurk. The choice to build in stone might also have resulted from adaptations made in a new environment. Perhaps both forces were at work. While this adaptation in a New World multiethnic environment possibly represents a form of hybrid creolization, the patentee families were not responsible for this basic change. Their acceptance of the standard local form therefore does not represent their own creolization. Rather, for them, the regional Dutch-American architectural paradigm served as a standard that they later adapted through

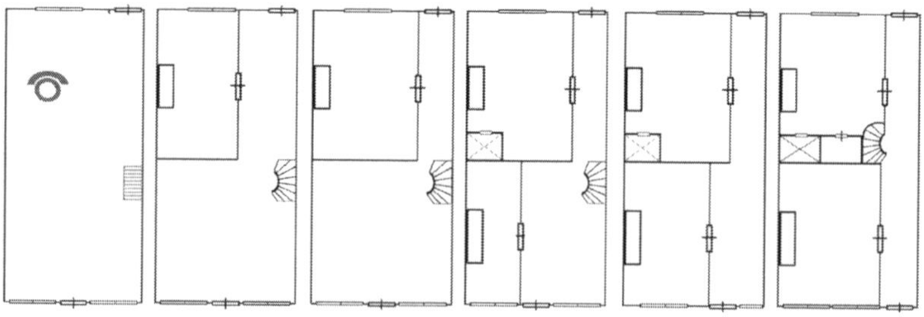

Figure 3.1. Progressive development of the rookhuis (the creation of the binnenhaard is depicted in the first three drawings, the development of the zijkammer on the right). After Zantkuyl, "The New Netherlands Town House," 143, 145.

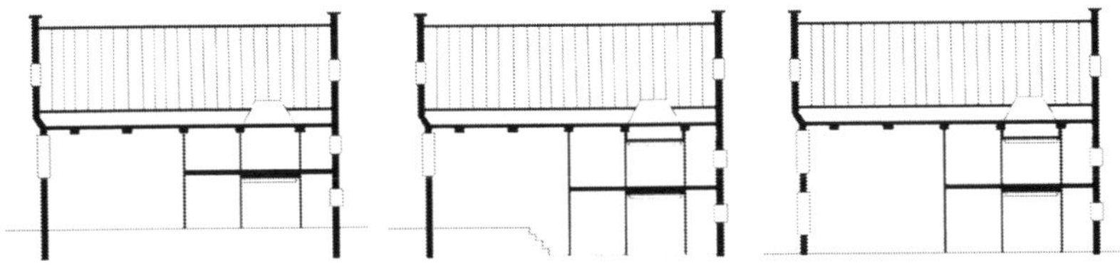

Figure 3.2. Three variations of a rookhuis with an insteek. After Zantkuyl, "The New Netherlands Town House," 145.

the inclusion of elements of English architecture.

While the materials do not represent the Dutchness of the buildings, their floor plans and the distribution of functions within the structures, as well as many secondary architectural features, can be closely associated with structures associated with Netherlandic forms. It is true that some attributes of the local architecture were also found among domestic structures of other continental Europeans. Still, the stone architecture of Ulster County was clearly associated with the local "Dutch," who followed patterns of form and function not found in contemporary English and Anglo-American domestic structures.[3]

Architectural historians have delineated two basic medieval architectural forms that served as source material for early modern Dutch and Dutch-American domestic architecture. These forms were the urban rookhuis ("smoke house") and the rural combination house-barn that housed both humans and their livestock. The rookhuis was originally a single open room with a firepit, the smoke from which escaped through a hole in the roof (see Figure 3.1). The firepit was later moved to a sidewall, and later yet, a chimney was erected above it. Initially, the single room served all household functions, but with the relocation of the fireplace, with its better means of exhaust, came the possibility of constructing a room around it. This new *binnenhaard* ("inner hearth") served as a cooking space and more private family space, while the remaining portion of the house—now referred to as the *voorhuis*—could function as a public space connected closely with the street. In addition to the partition for the binnenhaard, another room towards the front of the house could be sectioned off from the voorhuis. This small sideroom (*de zijkammer*) allowed the urban Dutch a comfortable place to observe activity on the street. Over time, the zijkammer was enlarged to create a more formal living and entertaining space, as well as to serve as the best sleeping chamber. The zijkammer might be left unheated so as to keep it free from "soot and stench," thus making it particularly suitable for displaying one's finest possessions. With the enlargement of the zijkammer, the voorhuis was essentially reduced to an entrance passageway, although the nomenclature remained the same.[4]

To use heat more effectively towards the rear of the house, the ceiling of the binnenhaard was sometimes lowered, thus allowing for the insertion of another room above, the *insteek* (see Figure 3.2). If there was insufficient clearance in each of the stacked rooms, the floor might be further excavated

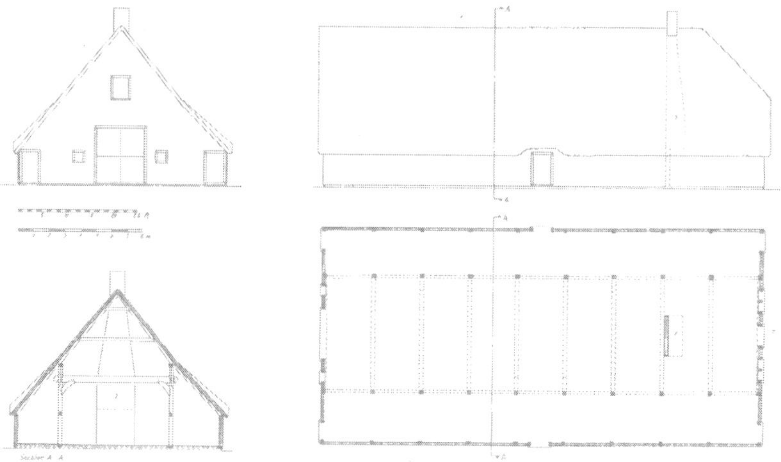

Figure 3.3. *Los hoes* (Johannes Winckelman barn/house, 1642, Achter Col Settlement, now the site of Bogota, Bergen County, New Jersey). Stevens, Dutch Vernacular Architecture, 179.

as well, so that the lower room was partially subterranean. Such an arrangement allowed light to enter into the lower room. With the inclusion of an additional room, the binnenhaard could then be reconceived primarily as a kitchen, while the insteek would be used as general family space and sleeping quarters, often with built-in, enclosed bed boxes.

In contrast, rural house forms developed from a three-aisled combination house-barn called a *los hoes* or, when the farm and living spaces were divided by a wall, a *hallenhuis* (see Figure 3.3). The large center aisle in such a house-barn—the nave—was functionally divided into two sections. The rear portion (*achterhuis)* was dedicated to farm activities such as threshing. Farm animals were housed in the side aisles, known as *uitlaiten* (singular: *uitlait)*. The front area (voorhuis) provided housing for humans, with sleeping boxes inserted through walls into the uitlaiten on each side of the nave. By about 1600, and increasingly so over the next century, the Dutch began to relegate domestic and farming activities to separate structures, although such house-barns in the Old World continued to be used by some families for centuries.[5]

The newly separate house (see Figure 3.4) and barn (see Figure 3.5) nevertheless retained similar structural configurations and profiles, and the house continued to be functionally divided. The rear room, which could sometimes be simply called the *kamer*, was equipped with a fireplace and used as daily living space, while the front area, the voorhuis, was used for higher status purposes. The front voorhuis might be divided into a primary area (sometimes with a second hearth), and a small entrance hall or vestibule (*portaal*). A cellar kitchen (*kelderkeuken*) was sometimes constructed below the *kamer*, although generally not fully depressed below ground level; when the basement kitchen was present, the kamer above would be known as the

Figure 3.4. Structural framing of a rural Dutch-American house. Zantkuyl, "The New Netherlands Town House," 152.

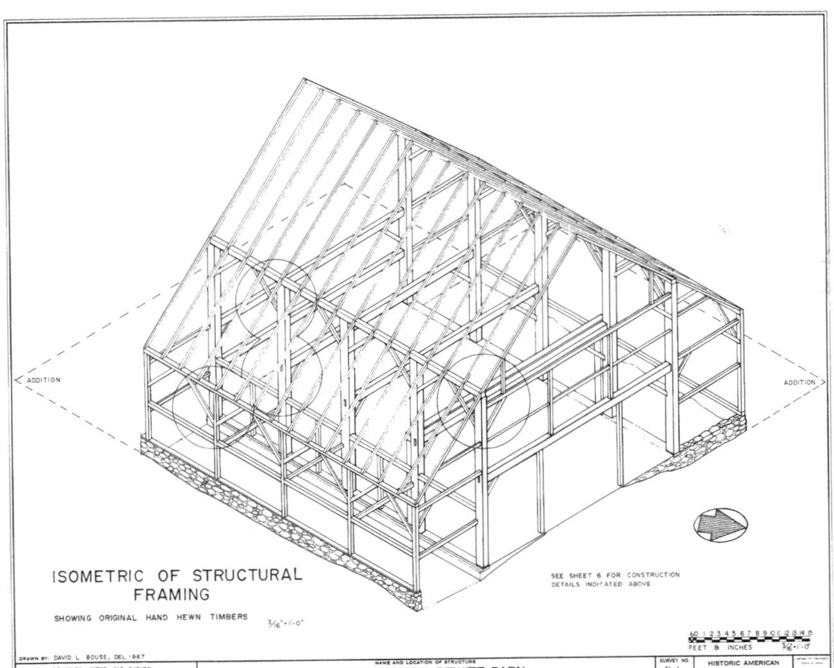

Figure 3.5. Structural framing of a Dutch-American barn (Van Campen-Dewitt Barn, Wallpack Center Vicinity, Sussex County, New Jersey, early nineteenth century). Library of Congress, Prints & Photographs Division, HABS, HABS NJ,19-WALPAC.V,3- (sheet 5 of 6) David L. Bouse, delineator, 1967.

opkamer or *boven kamer*. Such a configuration was similar to the insteek/binnenhaard combination. Rural houses sometimes had exterior doors in each of the rooms, and side aisles (uitlaiten), when present, provided another access point between the front and rear rooms. Uitlaiten could contain bed boxes inserted into them, as they had been in the side aisles of barns, but the Dutch increasingly dispensed with this architectural feature.[6]

As rural houses were separated from the barn and side aisles were abandoned, urban and rural houses increasingly came to look and function in similar fashions. The rear room in both was dedicated to daily family activities, including sleeping and cooking. When two rooms were set above each other, the one below was used for cooking and the one above for family space. (As for nomenclature, it is not entirely clear in the literature whether it varied between urban and rural houses. In spite of this ambiguity, I will henceforth use the terms "opkamer" and "kelderkeuken" when referring to two rooms stacked one above the other.) The front room was more publicly oriented than the rear, functioning as an entrance area and/or a public entertaining space. It could be entered directly from the street or through a sidehall or vestibule. Depending upon the size of the family, beds could be found in any room.[7]

Early modern Dutch architecture was at variance with contemporary English architectural principles in a number of ways. English architecture, however, was not uniform, so the most apt comparison of Hudson Valley Dutch architecture and early Anglo-American architecture is with that of neighboring New England. That architecture is considered basically late-medieval in form. A primary difference between Dutch and New English architecture is that the gable-end of the New England house was generally set perpendicular to the street, unlike the façade of the Dutch house, with its gable-end set parallel to the public thoroughfare (see Figure 3.6). Second, the entrance was not made into a room like the Dutch voorhuis, but merely a small space known as a "porch" or "entry," set in front of the massive center chimney stack (see Figure 3.7). From this small space both the hall, which generally served as family and cooking space, and the parlor, the more refined and special-use space, were accessed. The primary rooms did not flow into each other as did the rooms in a Dutch house. Elite seventeenth-century New English houses also might rise to two full and distinct above-ground stories, unlike multi-storied Dutch and Dutch-American houses which bore a one-story profile, since the lower level was at least partially subterranean.[8]

The structural framing of seventeenth-century English and Dutch houses was also different. In wood-framed Dutch houses, the load-bearing support is provided by a series of bents, consisting of beams set upon or into posts ("H-bents," see Figure 3.4), such that the weight of the house is carried and spaced across the length of the house. In a stone house, the work of the posts is performed by the stone walls themselves, upon which the heavy beams rest. (The Dutch are also known for their use of bricks, but in the seventeenth century, bricks were often not structural but merely used as a veneer over a wooden structure.) The primary load-bearing elements in English timber-framed architecture were the four corners, with further

Figure 3.6. The Parson Capen House, Topsfield, Massachusetts, 1683, exterior. Library of Congress, Prints & Photographs Division, HABS, HABS MASS, 5-TOP, 1–5, C. E. Peterson, photographer, 1935.

support provided by "summer beams," which stretched across the length of the house halfway between the front and rear walls. Those who built houses in eighteenth-century New Paltz remained committed to Dutch construction methods throughout the eighteenth century, so the issue of framing methods in domestic architecture need not be explored further.[9]

Little can be said about the shelters built by the New Paltz founders. Based on seventeenth-century comments by Cornelius Tienhoven (1650) and Jasper Dankers (1679–1680), architectural historians have suggested that the earliest Euro-American colonists in some areas of the Hudson Valley built pit houses, which are wood-lined holes in the ground covered by a roof. Over the course of the past decade, archaeologists have discovered evidence of such temporary structures in the historic core of New Paltz. They have also uncovered post-hole stains, which indicate the existence of early earth-fast houses (wooden structures built upon posts set in the ground). Earth-fast houses are more easily built than houses with foundations but are essentially temporary, as the wooden members of the structures decay relatively quickly through their direct contact with the earth. At least some of the founders also constructed wood-frame houses that served for several decades or more; building elements from such structures were reused in the 1734 portion of the Daniel Hasbrouck House (traditionally known as the Abraham Hasbrouck House) and the 1762–1763 Freer-Louw house.[10]

The only (non-archeological) physical remains of the first permanent house that survive are portions of the west and south stone walls and basement kitchen of patentee Jean Hasbrouck's house. Dendrochronological study of the structure suggests that it was built soon after the village was settled, making it the only seventeenth-century house that survives in any form.

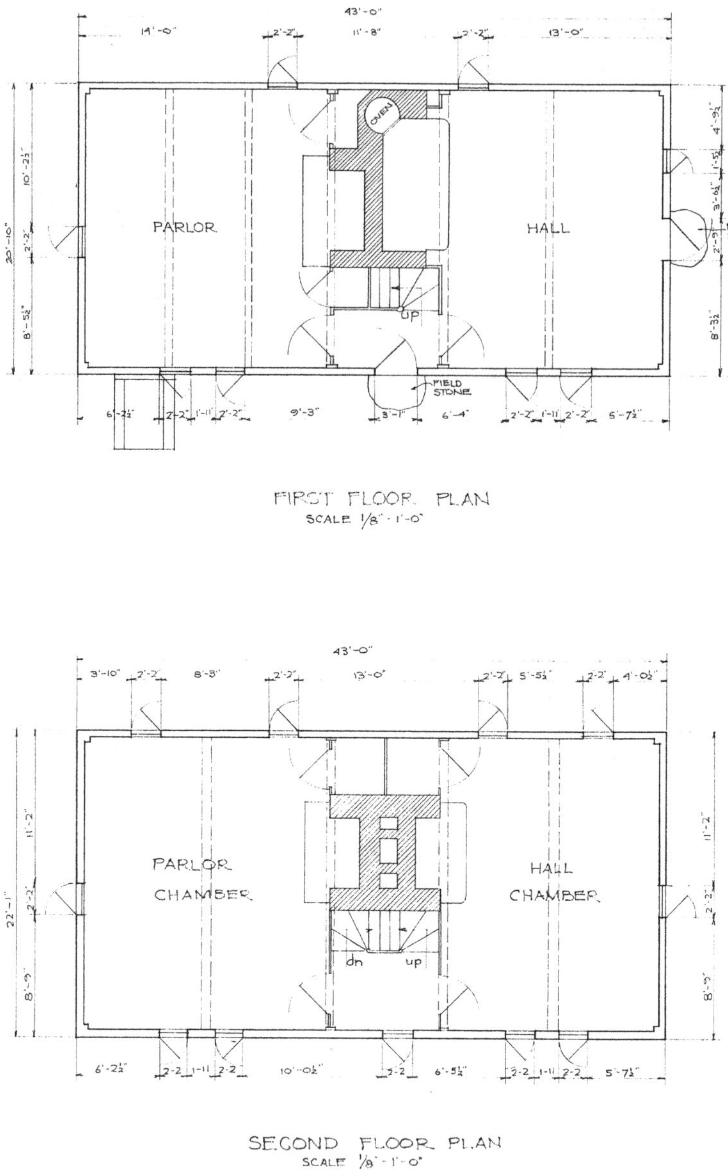

Figure 3.7. The Parson Capen House, Topsfield, Massachusetts, floor plan. Library of Congress, Prints & Photographs Division, HABS, HABS MASS, 5-TOP, 1-(sheet 3 of 3), redrawn by A. Craig Morrison, 1965.

The house included one above-ground, general-purpose living room, capped by a garret for storage of grains, and supported by a basement kitchen below, where the cooking was performed and where enslaved laborers were housed. The attic and basement were likely accessed by what were essentially ladders. Fragments of this house were later incorporated into the 1721 stone house built by Jean Hasbrouck's son Jacob.[11]

The only documentary evidence referencing a seventeenth-century New Paltz house is one listing in the 1798 Federal Direct Tax schedules, prepared by New Paltz resident Josiah R. Eltinge. That listing indicates that Ezekiel Eltinge (the brother of the surveyor) owned a house on the main street that was 113 years old. If the date provided was correct, then at least a portion of it had been built in 1685, making it almost twenty years older than any house that survives in New Paltz today. Such a date would indicate that it had been built by or for the surveyor's great-great grandfather, New Paltz patentee Abraham DuBois. The house was described as being "of Stone and Frame," with dimensions of 35x24 and 25x20. Excavations of the site suggest that the 35x24 portion of the house was a two-room stone structure that presented its short side, or gable-end, to the street. The wood-framed portion consisted of one room, set either to the rear or the side of the stone portion, although whether the stone or the wooden portion was constructed first is not known.[12]

Although the Abraham DuBois's gable-fronted stone house no longer survives, it is likely that it was similar to its near-neighbor, the Maria DuBois House (generally known today as the DuBois Fort [see Figures 3.8 and 3.9]). (That house survives today, but was extensively altered in the early nineteenth century.) This structure built for Abraham's sister-in-law, was

Figure 3.8. Maria DuBois House, exterior, 1705. John G. Waite Associates, "Dubois Fort: Historic Structure Report," (unpublished report for the Huguenot Historical Society, 2003), 76 (sketch by Douglas Bucher).

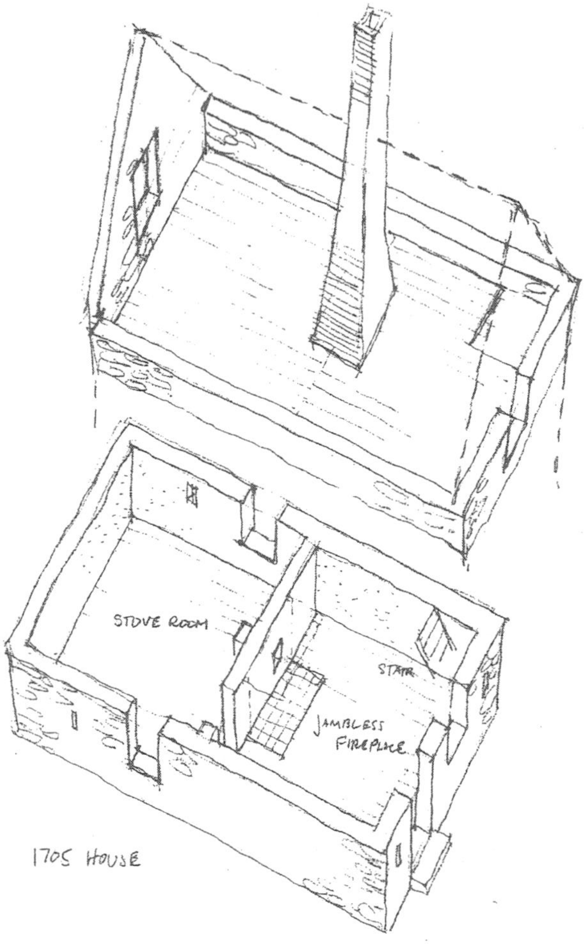

Figure 3.9. Maria DuBois House, interior. John G. Waite Associates, "Dubois Fort: Historic Structure Report," (unpublished report for the Huguenot Historical Society, 2003), 77 (sketch by Douglas Bucher).

constructed between 1703 and 1705. The two-room house presented its east gable end to the street, typical of Dutch houses, with the only door being on that elevation. Maria DuBois's house was of the two-room, unpartitioned Dutch form, either urban or rural (by "unpartitioned," I mean that neither of the two primary rooms was further divided). However, it represented a functional reversal of the typical Dutch plan, made possible by the use of a five-plate stove, a technological device of German origin, which was regularly used by the early Ulster County elite (see Figure 3.10). Such a device was essentially an open-backed iron box set next to a fireplace, which was fed through a hole in the fireplace's back wall and vented back

Figure 3.10. Five-plate stove, 1758 (at Schifferstadt, Frederick, Maryland). Schifferstadt, Frederick County Landmarks Foundation, Frederick, Maryland, photograph by Joe Sweeney.

through the fireplace's chimney. Stoves such as this made for cleaner and more pleasant spaces, characteristics usually associated with more formal functions commonly assigned to the front room. However, Maria DuBois reversed the typical room functions by choosing to heat the back room of her house rather than the front with a five-plate stove. As the front room included the only fireplace, it would have been used for multiple purposes including cooking. Maria DuBois's choice to reverse the functions of the two rooms suggests a willing flexibility in the placement of rooms within a domestic structure, a flexibility that became commonplace.[13]

Above the living space in the Maria DuBois House was a loft area, covered by a sharply pitched gable roof. The loft was unfinished, as it was primarily used for storing grain, which could be brought directly from the outside via a mow door on the front gable end. This feature was common in the region and was included in the nearby and contemporaneous Samuel Bevier and Daniel Hasbrouck Houses, as well as others in New Paltz, such as the Abraham LeFevre House (the upper-story window was originally a mow door [see Figure 3.11]). The Maria DuBois House was accessed by a steep ladder stair that intersected with a trap door, or by way of tightly wrapped enclosed

Figure 3.11. Abraham LeFevre House, Gardiner, New York, c. 1758 addition. Photograph by Bonnie Soper.

stairs (*wenteltrap*) above another stair to the cellar below, such as those that survive in situ in the Bevier House across the street (see Figure 3.12).[14]

The Maria DuBois House was distinctive in that it was constructed in a single building campaign. It was much more common for houses in the village, such as the Daniel Hasbrouck House (see Figures 3.13 and 3:14) and the Samuel Bevier House (see Figures 3.15, 3.16, and 3.17), to be built in phases, particularly in the early years. (The Daniel Hasbrouck House is generally known today as the Abraham Hasbrouck House, and the Samuel Bevier House is generally known today as the Bevier-Eltinge House.) Both were first built as single-room houses, the Daniel Hasbrouck House in 1721 and the Bevier House in c. 1731–1732. As single-room structures, each consisted of a general purpose room on the first floor, a garret for storage, and a basement below; enslaved workers likely slept in either the garret or the basement. The only major difference between the two houses is that the Bevier House presented its gable to the street, like the Maria DuBois House, while the gable of the Daniel Hasbrouck House was set perpendicular to the street. The latter orientation represents a variation of the Dutch house that became increasingly standard in the New World, although such an orientation possibly had European antecedents.[15]

Two more stacked rooms were added in the second phase of construction of both the Bevier and Daniel Hasbrouck Houses. This enabled the residents to

Figure 3.12. Stairs (wenteltrap) to the attic in the Samuel Bevier House, c. 1731–1732. Photograph by the author.

Figure 3.13. Daniel Hasbrouck House, 1721, c. 1728, c. 1734. Library of Congress, Prints & Photographs Division, HABS, HABS NY, 56–NEWP, 4–6.

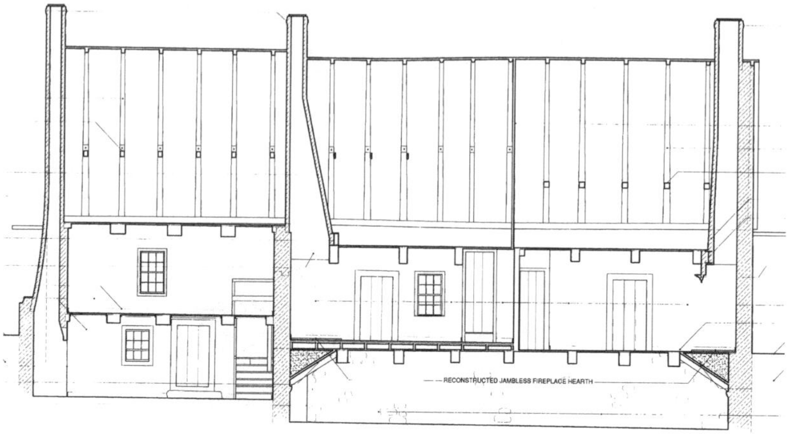

Figure 3.14. Longitudinal section of Daniel Hasbrouck House. Library of Congress, Prints & Photographs Division, HABS, HABS NY, 56–NEWP, 4- (sheet 7 of 19), prepared by Kenneth Hewes Barricklo Architect, P. C., January 20, 2003.

Figure 3.15. Samuel Bevier House (south façade), c. 1731–1732, c. 1735, with mid-eighteenth-century addition. Photograph by the author.

Figure 3.16. Samuel Bevier House (north façade). Photograph by the author.

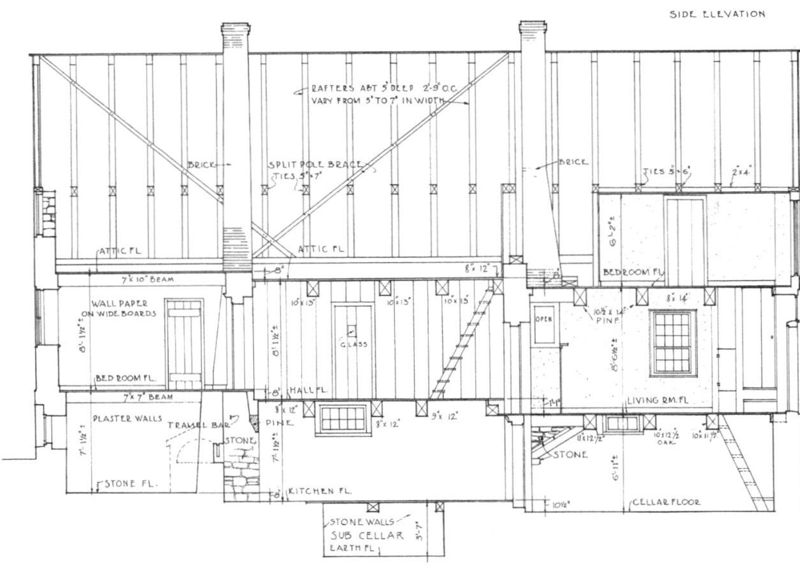

Figure 3.17. Longitudinal section of Samuel Bevier House. Library of Congress. Prints & Photographs Division, HABS, HABS NY. 56–NEWP. 2- (sheet 9 of 11). C. S. Keefe and A. Schrowang, Delineators, May 1934.

Figure 3.18. Stairs to *opkamer* in Daniel Hasbrouck House. Library of Congress, Prints & Photographs Division, HABS, HABS NY, 56–NEWP, 4–11.

redefine the original room in each house as a voorhuis. The Daniel Hasbrouck was first enlarged in approximately 1728 with a room to the north (left); the date of the second construction phase of the Bevier House is c. 1735. From the voorhuis in each house, a few steps *(bordistrap)* rose to an opkamer, heated by a five-plate stove (see Figure 3.18). The opkamer in each house was equipped with both interior and exterior entries, unlike the Maria DuBois House, which had only a single exterior entrance. Beneath the opkamer in each house was a cellar kitchen (*kelderkeuken*), partially depressed below ground level. The cellar in some New World Dutch-American houses such as the Bevier and Daniel Hasbrouck Houses functioned somewhat differently from Old World Dutch houses because of the presence of slaves, some or all of whom were likely sheltered in the kitchen. As a result, the distinction between upstairs and downstairs would have been much stronger among those New Paltz families who owned slaves than it would have been in Dutch houses in Europe. The lower rooms in both houses were also equipped with both interior and exterior access points, although the interior connection in the Daniel Hasbrouck House was not original. Old World cellar kitchens were also sometimes equipped with only an exterior entrance, which allowed for independent access. This restricted access to the kitchen might have served a particular purpose in households such as that of Daniel Hasbrouck, as it would have allowed slaves access to that room without going through their owners' family spaces.[16]

Since urban lots generally did not allow for side access points, the multiple exterior doors into the Bevier and Daniel Hasbrouck Houses suggest a rural inspiration. Both houses also included exterior side aisles (uitlaiten), constructed during their second phase of construction, which again suggests a rural heritage. Nothing substantial of the Daniel Hasbrouck House uitlait survives other than evidence of its early existence found in the rear exterior wall. The uitlait on the Bevier House is partially open like a porch; it might have been originally fully enclosed, such that it could also have served as an unheated room. Other early houses in the village were equipped with uitlaiten, including the 1738 Terwilliger House (discussed below). The mid-eighteenth-century section of the (possibly Benjamin) Deyo House in the Bontecoe section of New Paltz also had an uitlait (see Figure 3.19).[17]

Both the Bevier and Daniel Hasbrouck houses were enlarged in a third phase of construction to increase the size to a total of four rooms, with three being fully above ground. It is not clear exactly when this occurred in the Bevier House, but it certainly occurred fairly early on its history. The Daniel Hasbrouck House's fourth room was built in approximately 1734, when Daniel married his cousin Wyntje Deyo. Such linear houses were common in Ulster County, if not necessarily archetypical as some architectural historians have suggested. The third above-ground rooms of the Bevier and Daniel Hasbrouck Houses likely served different functions. In the Bevier House, the third room was unheated, suggesting that it was a sleeping chamber for children. The third room in the Daniel Hasbrouck House contained a fireplace, as well as the most modern windows in the house. It probably functioned as Daniel and Wyntje's sleeping chamber. A third above-ground

Figure 3.19. Deyo House at Bontecoe (in c. 1903). LeFevre, *History of New Paltz*, 272.

room was probably desired because Daniel's mother, Maria, the widow of his father, Abraham, still administered his father's estate. She probably utilized the *opkamer*, which was heated by a five-plate stove, as noted above.[18]

In total, the early architecture built by the children of the patentees was inspired by Dutch cultural sources, although with some minor New World adaptations. The functional design of each house was not fixed, as it could be adjusted to meet the particular demographics, needs, and desires of the families who built them. In other words, while the houses had similar functional spaces, the placement of those spaces could vary considerably. In contrast, the functional layout within Anglo-American houses was more rigid. The designs of the New Paltz houses were also sufficiently adaptable to allow for modifications based on New World forces, such as the presence of slaves and the availability of new technologies. A further possible modification of Old World traditions was the choice to orient the primary axis of the house parallel to the street, rather than perpendicular, although the reasons for doing so are not clear. Importantly, these modifications of the original Dutch sources were indeed something that could have been requested when owners contracted with craftsmen to build their houses, suggesting a lack of rigidity and a willingness to adapt traditions for current purposes.

The only early New Paltz house that strayed from typical Dutch-American patterns was the Jacob Hasbrouck House of 1721 (see Figures 3.20 and 3.21). (The Jacob Hasbrouck House is traditionally known as the "Jean Hasbrouck House" and the "Memorial House.") This house is unusual because it consists

Figure 3.20. Jacob Hasbrouck House, 1721. Library of Congress, Prints & Photographs Division, HABS, HABS NY, 56-NEWP, 3-3, Stanley P. Mixon, Photographer, July 25, 1940.

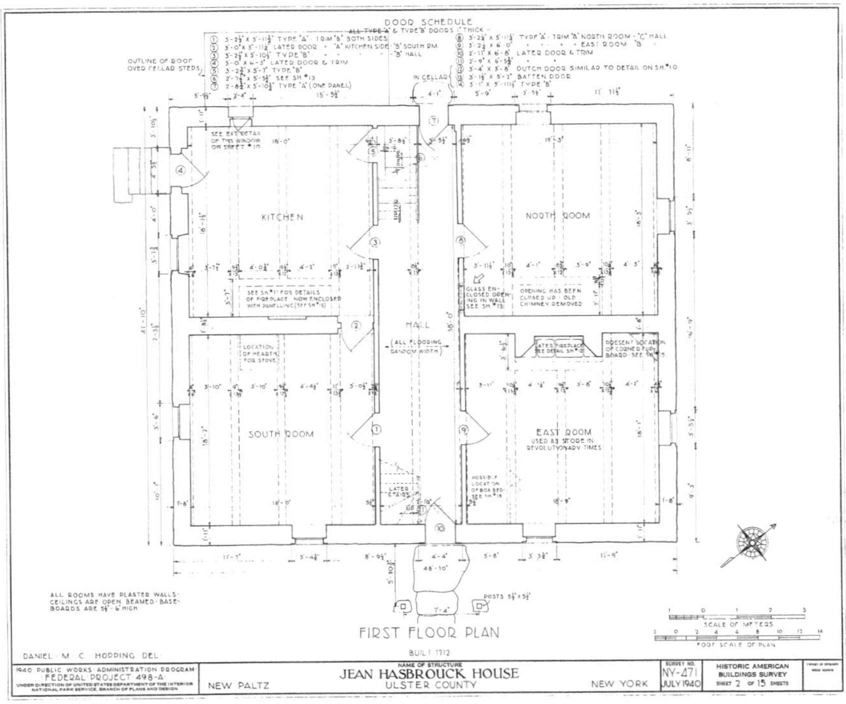

Figure 3.21. Jacob Hasbrouck House floor plan. Library of Congress, Prints & Photograph Division, HABS, HABS NY, 56–NEWP, 3- (sheet 2 of 15).

of four rooms built in a square. It was also built in a single building campaign (although with fragments of two walls and the basement of Jacob's father Jean's house), which was not typical for houses consisting of so many rooms. The decision to build such an unusually large house at one time presented both possibilities and challenges not found in other construction projects. The house includes a full basement and symmetrically paired above-ground rooms, capped by a massive two-level attic beneath an extremely steep roof, the sharp pitch of which was required for the roof's extension over the four-room structure. While the house is certainly much taller than was common in New Paltz, its overall appearance is nevertheless linked to its one-story neighbors, as the finished rooms are contained on only one floor. Such a house must have been an extreme rarity even in its time, as the only other surviving house in the region that employed a similar, but not identical, four-room plan is the 1750 Matthew Ten Eyck House in nearby Hurley (see Figures 3.22 and 3.23). (Figure 3.22 depicts the rear addition as well as the older central architectural block.) Evidence also suggests that the no-longer extant 1775 Hendricus DuBois House, materials of which were later reworked into another structure, also bore similarities to the Jacob Hasbrouck House.[19]

An important element of the Jacob Hasbrouck House, which sets it apart from even the similar Ten Eyck House, is that it incorporated a central

Figure 3.22. Matthew Ten Eyck House, Hurley, New York, 1750. Stevens, *Dutch Vernacular Architecture*, 226.

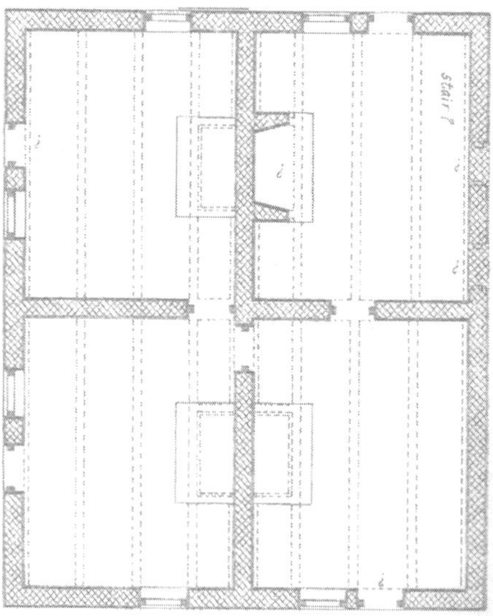

Figure 3.23. Matthew Ten Eyck House, Hurley, New York, floor plan. Stevens, *Dutch Vernacular Architecture*, 227.

hall. Such a hall, which resulted in a symmetrical façade, is something not found in other regional Dutch-American architecture. At least two explanations of this unusual feature seem possible. First, the central hall could have been inspired by new architectural fashions that were appearing both in the Netherlands and England in the late seventeenth century. Such an explanation, however, seems unlikely, particularly when considering the possible transference of Old World Dutch cultural innovations to the New; the stream of culture that connected the two was extremely weak almost sixty years after the English conquest of Nieuw Nederland. In contrast, the new "Georgian" architectural style of England, characterized by a central door and hall flanked by symmetrically paired windows in a rectangular block, did begin to influence American architectural design in the early eighteenth century. Important early examples of such a design approach are seen in the MacPhaedris-Warner House (1718–1723) in Portsmouth, New Hampshire (see Figure 3.24); and "Westover," the Virginia plantation of William Byrd II (c. 1730–1734 [see Figure 3.25]). Vernacular versions of the style also began to affect rural New England early in the eighteenth century. Still, it is unlikely that this new style influenced the Jacob Hasbrouck House either, as the Georgian style was only just reaching the British colonies in North America when Jacob Hasbrouck arranged for the construction of his new house, and

Figure 3.24. MacPhaedris-Warner House, Portsmouth, New Hampshire, 1718–1723. Library of Congress, Prints & Photographs Division, LC-D4-14997, Detroit Publishing Co., c. 1902.

Figure 3.25. "Westover," Charles City, Virginia, c. 1730–1734. Library of Congress, Prints & Photographs Division, HABS, HABS VA, 19-WEST, 1–3.

Figure 3.26. Cornelius Wynkoop House, Marbletown, New York, 1772. Library of Congress, Prints & Photographs Division, HABS, HABS NY, 56 STORI, 1–3.

there is nothing to suggest that he could have learned of the new fashions through such cosmopolitan places. Neither is it likely that the style could have spread from rural New England to the west side of the Hudson River Valley as early as the 1720s, as the connections between the regions were also quite weak. The earliest surviving house in the region that was clearly influenced by the Georgian style is the 1772 Cornelius Wynkoop House in nearby Marbletown, built more than half a century after the Jacob Hasbrouck House (see Figure 3.26). If the center hall of the Jacob Hasbrouck House had been inspired by English design, it was seemingly precocious to the point of being revolutionary.[20]

The center hall of the Jacob Hasbrouck House can be better interpreted through a Dutch architectural lens, suggesting that it was only coincidentally similar to progressive elite Anglo-American houses. Based on the Dutch model as described above, the center passageway can be seen as functioning as an *uitlait* serving two pairs of rooms. In other words, the atypical passageway was necessary to allow easy direct entry into any room—a traditional approach—which had been made complicated by the choice to configure four rooms in a square. Despite its uniqueness, the Jacob Hasbrouck House therefore still reflects the local Dutch-American architectural idiom, rather than contemporary English and Anglo-American stylistic trends.

Few in New Paltz other than Jacob Hasbrouck had the desire and the resources to construct such a dramatic statement in a Dutch-American mode, such that the linear paradigm of houses of two or three aboveground rooms without a central hall remained dominant for decades after its construction. For example, Abraham LeFevre and his wife, Maria Bevier, began to construct such a linear house between 1740 and 1742 in the Kettleborough region of the abutting town of Gardiner (see Figure 3.27).

Dendrochronological analysis indicates that like many of the New Paltz houses, the house originally consisted of one room. A large two-room addition was constructed in c. 1758 (also suggested by tree-ring dating). Both rooms in the addition were fully above ground, unlike in the Samuel Bevier and Daniel Hasbrouck Houses, but like them, the LeFevre House did not

Figure 3.27. Abraham LeFevre House, Gardiner, New York, 1740–1742, c. 1758, c. 1794. Photograph by Bonnie Soper.

include a passageway. After the addition was constructed, the original room became a general-purpose room in which the cooking was done. The abutting new room, with its more stylish fireplace, served as the best room of the house. The second room in the addition lacked a fireplace, although it is unclear why Abraham made the unusual choice not to provide a heating source in a primary room. The second room in the addition also contained a mow door and an entrance on the side gable wall, the appearance of which reflected the antiquated Dutch-American gable-fronted house.[21]

The house was enlarged once more in a linear mode with the construction around 1794 of a new kitchen abutting the original room opposite the earlier two-room addition. This second addition was built when Abraham's son Philip became master of the house. Both Abraham and Philip perpetuated the practice of placing exterior openings organically, rather than formally in the Georgian style, even as late as the end of the century. At that point, the front façade contained at least two and possibly three doors, plus an additional end-gable door, interspersed with windows in no particular pattern.[22]

There are other later examples in New Paltz of the linear Dutch-American paradigm without a passageway. Daniel Deyo's house, built c. 1763, was similar to the Daniel Hasbrouck House in its second phase, which had been completed about thirty-five years earlier (see Figure 3.28). The Freer-Louw House in the village center, built in two phases in 1762 and 1763 by Johannes and Rebecca (Freer) Low, similarly consisted of two above-ground rooms not separated by a central hall (see Figure 3.29). The

Figure 3.28. Daniel Deyo House, c. 1763 (in c. 1903). LeFevre, History of New Paltz, 267.

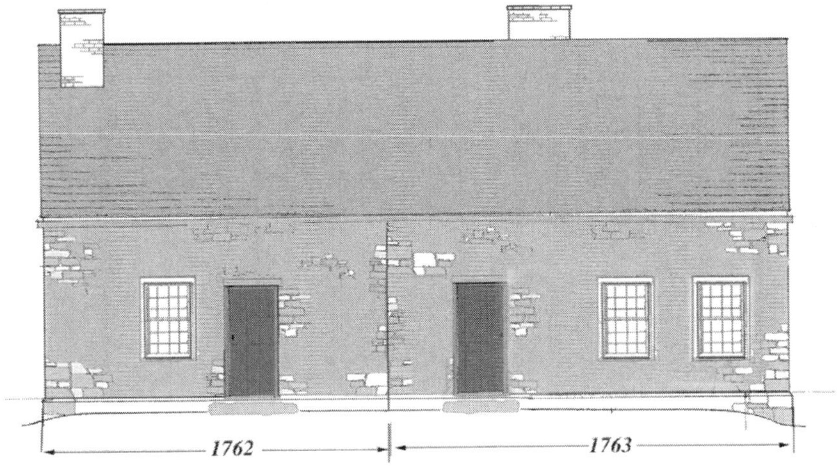

Figure 3.29. Freer-Louw House, 1762, 1763. Larson Fisher Associates and Ted Bartlett, for Crawford & Stearns, "Historic Structure Report for the Freer-Louw House," unpublished report for the Huguenot Historical Society, 2011.

conservative façade of the house was also asymmetrical, with a door and window in the north room, and two windows and a door in the south.[23]

In the closing years of the century, patentee descendants continued to build houses in a fashion very similar to those constructed many decades before. For example, two of Daniel Deyo's sons, Abraham D. (b. 1763) and Nathaniel (b. 1770) built their own frame houses on their father's land not long before 1798. Each of their houses was only thirty-five feet in length, with depths similar to the original block of Abraham DuBois's house, built about a century earlier. Given such dimensions, it is almost certain that these houses lacked central halls. The floor plan of these houses constructed just a few years before the beginning of a new century therefore continued to follow the designs of houses built nearly a century earlier, revealing the staying power of the Dutch-American architectural tradition.[24]

The Influence of Architectural Englishness

As powerful as that tradition remained, patentee descendants began to introduce English architectural innovations in secondary characteristics into a Dutch-American design paradigm as early as the 1730s, resulting in creolized architectural forms. One such innovation involved windows. Through most of the seventeenth century, when European-Americans fashioned moveable windows, they employed side-hinged casements, which swing in or out. The Dutch in Europe and America used three distinctive and different window forms consisting of combinations of shutters, fixed glazing, and moveable glazed casements. The most complex form was the four-part *kruiskozijn*, the

Figure 3.30. Jacob Hasbrouck House reconstructed kruiskozijn window. Photograph by the author.

center transom (horizontal cross piece) and mullion (vertical cross piece) of which formed a cross (see Figure 3.30). The two upper parts were formed with fixed windows of rectangular-shaped pieces of glass secured together with lead-came and reinforced on the outside with metal bars. The bottom two parts were composed of exterior shutters and interior-swinging casement windows or simply of shutters, the latter a less-expensive approach that remained popular in Dutch-American houses even though it was becoming antiquated in the Netherlands proper. The *kloosterkozijn* was essentially a two-part half version of the kruiskozijn, as it appeared and functioned as one side of the four-part cross window. The third window form was the *bolkozijn*, which was also a two-part form but divided vertically only by a mullion (see Figure 3.31). The bolkozijn was merely shuttered or included fixed or movable windows in combination with shutters.[25]

Evidence for the use of Dutch-style windows in New York is scattered and fragmentary, as by the middle of the eighteenth century, many houses were being retrofitted with more modern sash windows. Such windows were introduced into the American colonial architectural landscape by Anglo-Americans. The early history of the sash window is not entirely clear, although it seems to have been invented in England c. 1670 and then transplanted to high-style architecture of the Netherlands in 1686. Sash windows were first

Figure 3.31. Jacob Hasbrouck House reconstructed bolkozijn window. Photograph by the author.

used in America in the English colonies in the early eighteenth century, from where they soon spread into Dutch areas of New York. These new windows had certain mechanical advantages, as they could be easily raised and held at any height. Their adoption among the New York Dutch did not necessarily indicate a desire to Anglicize, as their functional superiority to casement windows could have been their primary attraction. Their gain in popularity, however, does suggest a lack of resistance to things English. This use of both Dutch and English elements produced creolized structures, even though the balance still favored regional Dutch models.[26]

Close study of the New Paltz structures reveals evidence of both the early use of Dutch-style windows, as well as the introduction of sash windows. In the Jacob Hasbrouck House (1721), the east (primary) façade and the north and south walls contained a total of four kruiskozijn windows, with bolkozijn windows used on the attic level. Each of the first two rooms of the Samuel Bevier House also originally contained a kruiskozijn window, one in the front gable façade and one on the south wall of the middle room. The Daniel Hasbrouck House also included Dutch-style casement windows in the first two rooms. In the earliest-built (center) room, a kruiskozijn was placed in the front (west) façade when constructed in 1721, as would be expected given that it was built in the same year as the Jacob Hasbrouck House. In the second phase, another Dutch-style window—a two-part bolkozijn—was

Figure 3.32. Daniel Hasbrouck House sash windows. Photograph by Bonnie Soper.

Figure 3.33. Jambless fireplace, Jacob Hasbrouck House. Photograph by the author.

installed in the north room built in 1728. However, when the final room was built in c. 1734—the room most likely built as a bedchamber for the newlyweds Daniel and Wyntje—the new-style vertically sliding sash windows were installed (see Figure 3.32). These sash windows represent the earliest known use of such an element in New Paltz, revealing an important architectural transition. The form soon became dominant.[27]

Even though Daniel and Wyntje Hasbrouck made the transition to sash windows in the third building campaign, they remained committed throughout to another Dutch architectural icon: the jambless fireplace. The jambless fireplace consists of an open hearth beneath an extremely large smoke hood and chimney (see Figure 3.33). Such a fireplace was distinct from the form of the English fireplace, which by the seventeenth century had been given side supports ("jambs") beneath the smoke hood, providing for a much-more enclosed and efficient heating space. Jambless fireplaces were likely constructed in all of the early New Paltz houses, at least through the 1730s. Thus, while Daniel Hasbrouck chose to install extremely up-to-date and efficient sash windows in the last room he built—the form of which had been introduced into the colonies by the English—he nevertheless retained a Dutch-style fireplace, which lacked the efficiency and cleanliness of the contemporary English form. He was not alone in making that choice.[28]

Abraham LeFevre also incorporated a Dutch-style jambless fireplace and English-inspired sash windows when he built the first room of his house in 1740. However, when he built a large, two-room addition in c. 1758, he installed a jambed fireplace with an elegant mantel instead, which was set back-to-back with the original jambless fireplace, an unusual configuration linking the old and the new. This gradual adoption of English secondary characteristics occurred even though houses continued to demonstrate a Dutch-American organic style rather than the formalism of the English Georgian style. The result was a Dutch-American house overlaid with an English veneer. This was a complexity that many owners consciously chose to include, which suggests neither resistance to, nor full acceptance of, English culture. Rather, they created a creolized architecture that was flexible enough to meet individual desires and needs.[29]

While Daniel Hasbrouck introduced English-inspired sash windows and Abraham LeFevre a jambed fireplace when they added on to their existing houses, others chose simply to replace some tell-tale Dutch features with modern English ones in their existing homes. In 1751, Louis Bevier III, grandson of patentee Jean Hasbrouck and patentee Louis Bevier, constructed an addition to an early eighteenth-century house that his parents had acquired from a previous owner, probably when they married in 1715. When he did so, he installed sash windows in the new addition, but he also replaced the Dutch-style windows in the original portion with sash windows as well. While Bevier did not live in New Paltz but in nearby Marbletown, this example is worth noting because the change can be dated precisely, which is rare. In the Samuel Bevier House, the kruiskozijn in the middle room was replaced with a double-hung sash window around the middle of the eighteenth century, quite possibly around 1760, when the house was acquired from the estate of Samuel Bevier by his neighbor Josiah Eltinge for his son Roelof Josiah Eltinge. It is plausible that the kruiskozijn in the front room was also replaced with a sash window at that time. The original jambless fireplace in the voorhuis, which Roelof Josiah used as a store, was also transformed into a jambed fireplace at some point during his occupancy between 1760 and his death in 1795, possibly around the same time he altered the windows.[30]

The 1721 Jacob Hasbrouck House down the street was also modernized, probably by the builder's grandson, Josiah Hasbrouck, soon after his father, Jacob Jr., built a new house for himself in 1786. This modernization involved the replacement of the Dutch-style windows with sash windows and the intrusive demolition of the back-to-back double jambless fireplaces in the north rooms. In the front room of the northern half of the house, in which Josiah began to operate a store, he installed a simple firebox. Josiah later transferred the use of the house and the operation of the store to his daughter and son-in-law, Josiah DuBois. When Josiah DuBois moved the store from the house in 1811, he made the former store room more elegant with a paneled chimney breast (see Figure 3.34).[31]

Similarly, Simeon Low, who inherited the 1762–1763 Freer-Low House from his father, replaced one of his two jambless fireplaces with a jambed fireplace around 1800, in what became a parlor. The Dutch-style windows of the Daniel Hasbrouck House were also modernized with replacement sash windows between 1801 and 1830 when the widow Maria Bevier Hasbrouck (Daniel's daughter-in-law) managed the

Figure 3.34. Room in Jacob Hasbrouck House. Library of Congress, Prints & Photographs Division, HABS, HABS NY, 56–NEWP, 3–9.

Figure 3.35. Evert Terwilliger House, Gardiner, New York, 1738, with c. 1762 alterations. Photograph by the author.

Figure 3.36. Evert Terwilliger House, Gardiner, New York. Photograph by the author.

property. While these changes clearly reflect attempts at modernization, it was a modernization that could not have been seen as anything but English-inspired.[32]

Around 1762, Jonathan Terwilliger did not just modernize his house. Rather, he rebuilt it in an attempt to reflect the English Georgian style. Jonathan had inherited the 1738 house built by his parents, Evert and Sarah (Freer) Terwilliger, a two-room stone structure along the Plattekill River on land abutting New Paltz (see Figures 3.35 and 3.36). With its gable end to the street—a form that had already become rather antiquated—the Terwilliger House represents a high degree of conservatism, as its design was very similar to that constructed by Maria DuBois thirty-three years earlier. The Terwilligers' house consisted of two rooms, with the front voorhuis heated by a comfortable and elegant five-plate stove and the rear *kamer* with a jambless fireplace, preserving the Dutch tradition of a more formal space in the front. The front façade had three openings: a door with a leaded-glass transom, a Dutch casement window on the first floor, and a mow door under the eaves, providing exterior access to the loft. Internally, the typically unfinished

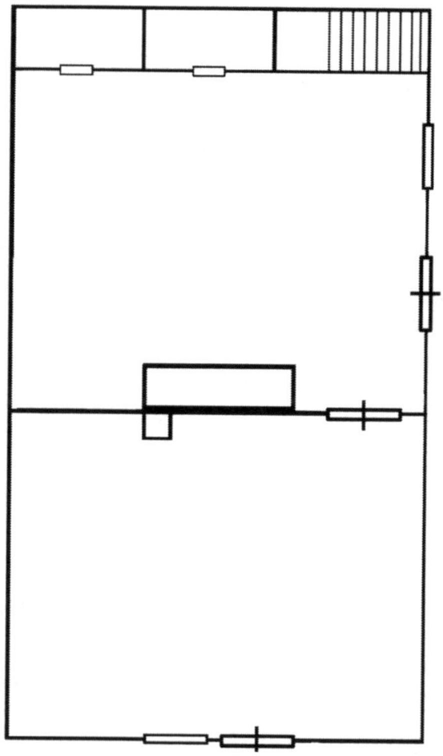

Figure 3.37. Evert Terwilliger House, floor plan of original condition. After Crawford & Stearns and Neil Larson, "Historic Structure Report for the Evert Terwilliger House," 1.4.

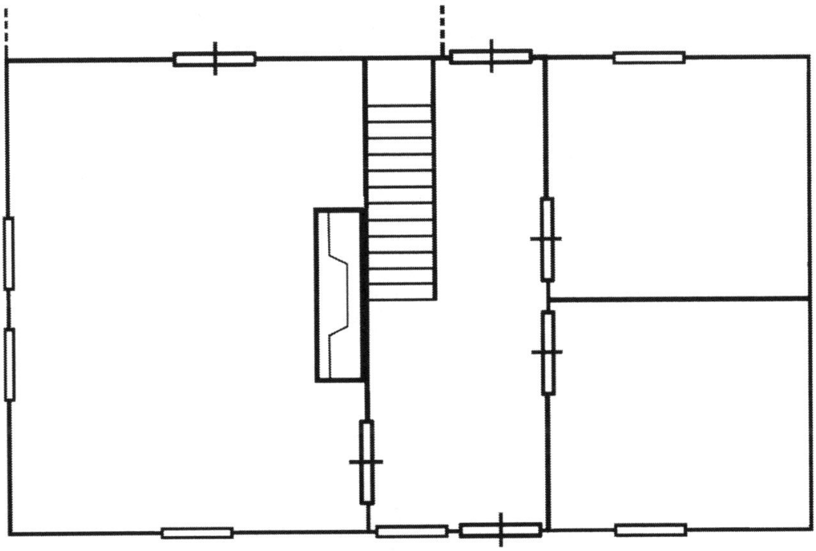

Figure 3.38. Evert Terwilliger House, floor plan after c. 1762 reconstruction. After Crawford & Stearns and Neil Larson, "Historic Structure Report for the Evert Terwilliger House," 1.13.

attic was likely accessed by way of a ladder stair. Access to the basement and rear room was via an *uitlait*. There was also an interior opening between the primary rooms (see Figure 3.37).[33]

The Terwilliger House, however, existed in this traditional Dutch form only for a short time—possibly not much more than twenty years. In 1762 Evert conveyed his stone house to his son Jonathan as his inheritance, one year after Jonathan's marriage. Shortly before or after, Jonathan embarked on its dramatic reconstruction (see Figure 3.38). The primary entrance of the house was relocated into what had been a side door in the uitlait. This reoriented the front façade of the house from its gable end to the long side. With the new entrance being in what had once been the uitlait, that space ceased to have its traditional Dutch function, becoming more of a piazza (or porch). In the former kamer (the rear room), a new partition wall was built to the right of what was now the primary front door, creating a new center hall. This hall included a new, (relatively) elegant stairway, providing access to the attic, which nevertheless remained an unfinished space (see Figure 3.39). These new stairs were a bit odd, as they seemed to be going nowhere just for show, but they suggested the elegance of a Georgian stair hall. To the right of the hall, what remained of the kamer was further divided into two unheated, small sleeping chambers. Additionally, the original jambless fireplace in the former kamer was demolished and the five-plate stove in the voorhuis removed; a new jambed fireplace was constructed in this former front room, which now served as a parlor (see Figure 3.40). The parlor's original front entrance and Dutch-style window were converted to sash windows; the mow door to the second floor was also fitted with a new window. A new frame kitchen (no longer extant) was also built adjacent to

Figure 3.39. Evert Terwilliger House, stairs. Photograph by the author.

Figure 3.40. Evert Terwilliger House, parlor fireplace. Photograph by the author.

the rear of the parlor. These interventions were both destructive and invasive, as the reconstruction required the insertion of new support beams and the rotation of some of the original ones.[34]

Jonathan and his wife, Mary, continued the transformation of their house in the 1780s, when they created a sleeping chamber in the second floor over the parlor. This newly finished bedroom conversion on the second floor included a relatively stylish mantel, suggesting that they created the new room for themselves (see Figure 3.41). As primary bedrooms in Anglo-American house were increasingly being placed on the second floor for the sake of privacy, the Terwilligers' choice to follow the practice again reflects a forward-looking mindset. Overall, Jonathan Terwilliger's interventions required a great deal of effort, as they involved skilled builders and financial resources, suggesting that Jonathan was highly motivated to culturally transform his house. His efforts to reconstruct his father's house in light of English forms nevertheless resulted in a less-than-successful product, stylistically speaking. From the exterior of the reoriented front façade, the house appeared relatively balanced according to Georgian design principles, but internally it was now unbalanced, as the hall and sleeping chambers had been made from a single room that originally matched the size of the other room. The product was rather awkward, at least as compared to mid-eighteenth-century English elite stylistic ideals, and thus it represented a Dutch house "trying

Figure 3.41. Evert Terwilliger House, mantel, second-floor bedchamber. Photograph by the author.

to be" English. The result was also quite different from the modifications in many other houses, which combined discreet Dutch and English elements in creolized fashion. In the Terwilliger reconstruction, the result was a messy ethnocultural hybrid; as a totality, it was neither Dutch nor English, but an amalgamation of two architectural paradigms into a unique Dutch-American form. Perhaps Jonathan's ethnocultural persona was similar. One is tempted to theorize that Evert and Sara Freer Terwilliger's extreme architectural conservatism might have produced an equally extreme progressivism in their son, motivating him to invest always-scarce resources into the transformation of his Dutch-style home to an English version—at least to the greatest extent possible.[35]

Little is known of Jonathan Terwilliger to reveal where he acquired these non-Dutch ideas, but his acceptance of elite English design principles occurred at least a decade before Cornelius Wynkoop constructed his two-story central entrance Dutch-Anglo house in 1772 in Marbletown, the earliest surviving example of such a form in the immediate environs of New Paltz, (see Figure 3.26). The Terwilliger House rebuilding, then, seems to have been relatively precocious, although more extensive investigation of other houses (with accurate dendrochronological dating) would be necessary to determine how precocious he was within the New Paltz community.[36]

Others attempted to bring in the modern English-inspired hallway without even a nod towards balancing the façade by building an addition, such as in the Frederick Deyo House, known today as "Thornwood" (see Figure 3.42). Likely built in the mid-eighteenth century, this house began as a one-

Figure 3.42. Frederick Deyo House, "Thornwood," late eighteenth century. Photograph by the author.

room stone house that was soon expanded with another room built of stone. By 1798, however, a wood-frame addition had been added, which consisted of a room with a jambed fireplace and a new passageway with a curving stairway into the attic. To create the passageway, the stone wall of the earlier part of the house that abutted the addition was demolished and the earlier room decreased in width by about one-fourth. This change was not as invasive as that which had been undertaken in the Terwilliger House, but it nevertheless involved careful reconfiguring of space. It, too, was awkward from a Georgian perspective, as it clearly presented an unbalanced aspect, with its joining together of frame and masonry rooms.[37]

Some descendants also began to introduce the hall or passageway in new construction without challenging the structure's basic appearance as a Dutch-American house. Such is the case with the house Jacob Hasbrouck Jr. built in 1786 (see Figure 3.43). Jacob Jr. had inherited his father's house (the 1721 Jacob Hasbrouck House), but he made the rather unusual decision to build himself a new home when he was in his fifties, leaving his father's home to his eldest son, Josiah. Jacob Jr.'s new house was in keeping with the linear plan of the typical Dutch-American houses in the community, much moreso than his father's imposing house had been, as the profile was only one-room deep. Jacob Jr. included a passageway in his house, based on English precedents, although it was not centered, as it would have been in a contemporary Anglo-American home of similar size; it was simply inserted between the south and center rooms, the latter which abutted the north room. That both the function and the design of this house were still strongly Dutch is further supported by the fact that in the 1806 estate inventory of Jacob Hasbrouck Jr., one room was described as the "fore

Figure 3.43. Jacob Hasbrouck Jr. House, 1786 (with later gables). Photograph by the author.

room," which may have been used as an English approximation of voorhuis. The use of an Anglo-American passageway within a Dutch-American form, as well as sash windows and jambed fireplaces, represents another strong example of creolization without hybridity.

For those who, for whatever reason, did not construct new houses, some continued to engage in major redesign projects into the 1820s and 1830s, although the result still fell shy of English symmetry. For example, between 1825 and 1830, Abraham LeFevre's son Philip replaced the doors in the façade in the east and west additions of his father Abraham's house with windows, leaving the only entrance in the original room, which placed it left of center (see Figure 3.44). The original room was divided into two, which created an entrance room or hall at an approximately center location, quite possibly for the purposes of dining, as was becoming common in the Federal period. A similar updating for a center entrance occurred in the mid-eighteenth century, three-room (possibly Cristoffel) Deyo House, when two doors in the original primary façade (each of which provided access to a single room) were replaced with windows (see Figure 3.45), with the surviving door in the opposite side of the middle room becoming a center entrance on a reoriented façade (see Figure 3.46). The location of the windows, however, was still more organic than balanced. One of Maria DuBois's descendants altered her 1705 house even more dramatically, reorienting the entrance to a long side of the house and creating a new center hall, while also raising the height to a full two stories to create finished second-floor rooms (see Figure 3.47). While the alterations of the Abraham LeFevre and Cristoffel Deyo Houses

Figure 3.44. Abraham LeFevre House, Gardiner, New York, with c. 1825–1830 alterations. Photograph by Bonnie Soper.

Figure 3.45. Cristoffel Deyo House, rear façade (original front façade), mid-eighteenth century. Photograph courtesy of Daniel Flebut and William Charnock.

Figure 3.46. Cristoffel Deyo House, front façade (original rear façade). Photograph courtesy of Daniel Flebut and William Charnock.

Figure 3.47. Maria DuBois House, 1705, with c. 1830s additions. Photograph by Bonnie Soper.

represent creolization, the dramatic changes to the Maria DuBois House suggest a form of hybrid creolization even more fundamental than that of the Terwilliger House.[38]

The construction of houses with original center halls did become relatively common around the turn of the nineteenth century, even though the Dutch-American architectural profile was often maintained, with the result being hybrid creolized forms. Rev. Stephen Goetschius and his wife, Elizabeth DuBois (great-granddaughter of patentee Louis DuBois), built a stone house in 1791 with such a hall, flanked by a room on each side (see Figure 3.48). Benjamin and Maria Hasbrouck likewise constructed a one-and-a-half story house around 1798–1800, and in doing so preserved aspects of the Dutch-American house, but they also included a center hall, which balanced the overall form along English lines. However, they also preserved the Dutch-style basement kitchen, although instead of raising an *opkamer* above it by a few steps, as had previously been common, they fully excavated the area around the basement kitchen. Perhaps the oldest center-hall frame house in New Paltz is in the old village center, which was built by Lucas Van Wagenen in 1800 (see Figure 3.49). This careful balancing of the traditional Dutch one-story plan and modern English architectural styles produced hybridized forms that were much more cohesive than in those Dutch-American structures into which English architectural elements had simply been inserted, as in other structures discussed above.[39]

One of the more unusual houses of the late eighteenth century is that of John (or Johannes) A. Hardenbergh (grandson of Johannes Hardenbergh, a

Figure 3.48. Stephen Goetschius House, 1791. Photograph by the author.

Figure 3.49. Lucas Van Wagenen House, 1800. Photograph by the author.

patentee of the Hardenbergh Patent) and Rachel DuBois (the great-granddaughter of patentee Louis DuBois [see Figure 3.50]). Hardenbergh was a member of the town's highest elite. As a member of the elite, he was likely to have been aware of current provincial fashions, which were essentially English by the closing years of the eighteenth century. His house did reveal fashionable English tendencies, even as it still had much in common with older Dutch-American houses. The brick house had a balanced façade, with a center entrance flanked by paired sash windows, presumably lighting primary rooms on the right and left of the center hall. It also had a gambrel roof, another stylish feature that came to New York via its New England neighbors, which allowed for the spanning of deeper structures. The depth of the Hardenbergh House was thirty-three feet—an unusual depth for a regional Dutch-American house, which suggests that the house had a row of rooms of lesser depth behind the principal front rooms. The gambrel roof also expanded the depth of the loft, which might have allowed for finished spaces in the attic. Again, this was not a common Dutch feature, as attics were generally used for storage. Yet, since the principal rooms were on one floor, which also contained the only openings in the façade, the house still reflected the profile of Dutch-American stone houses in New Paltz. That one of the largest houses in the town, built by one of the wealthiest residents, retained a strong sense of Dutch character is illustrative of how powerful architectural Dutchness remained even at the end of the eighteenth century. Still, the house as a totality clearly reflected ethnocultural hybrid creolization.[40]

In 1799, Ezekiel Eltinge (b. 1763) built the first truly Anglo-American

Figure 3.50. John A. Hardenbergh House (sometimes known as the "Col. Abraham J. Hardenbergh House"), late eighteenth century. LeFevre, *History of New York*, 459.

Georgian house to appear in New Paltz (see Figure 3.51). (The Ezekiel Eltinge House is sometimes known as the "LeFevre House.") His house, with its symmetrical five-bay façade rising to a full two stories, was unlike anything before seen in the town. Its atypicality was further accentuated by its uncommon brick façade (it being only one of four brick structures in the village at the time) and its stylish Anglo-American gambrel roof, later lost in a storm. Its roof spanned a structure that was two-rooms deep, as in the Hardenburgh House, again something very rarely seen in the village.[41]

The Anglo-American character of the exterior of Ezekiel's house was reflected internally in its architectural plan, but its internal functioning was not. Instead, Ezekiel organized his house in a manner similar to the Dutch-American house of his youth. The result was a hybridized Dutch-Anglo house, although one that tipped closer to Englishness than any other New Paltz house that had come before. Entering the front door, a visitor or resident came into a center hall flanked by a pair of rooms to the left and the right, a characteristic floor plan of most larger Anglo-American houses of the time. Such rooms in a typical Anglo-American home would have served as a parlor and dining room or as a pair of parlors. In Ezekiel's house, however, a parlor stood to the right; but to the left was a public room where he operated a store and from which he conducted his business affairs. To the rear of the parlor was a dining room, but to the rear of the store was a storeroom, making the northerly half a public space and the southerly half family space. Ezekiel's second story was similarly divided, with storerooms above the store and bedrooms above the family rooms below, an even more unusual configuration. Ezekiel had been raised to adulthood in a Dutch-American-style

Figure 3.51. Ezekiel Eltinge House, 1799. Photograph by the author.

house that had been similarly divided—the Samuel Bevier House—which the Eltinge family had acquired in 1760. That house was oriented with its gable end to the street and consisted of three aboveground rooms. Ezekiel's father Roelof Josiah operated a store and tavern in the front room, with the two rear rooms for family use; the attic was used for storage. Ezekiel chose to perpetuate this internal division, masking it within an envelope of Anglo-American Georgian symmetry.[42]

Ezekiel Eltinge possibly learned of contemporary Anglo-American architecture when he traveled to New York in the early 1790s on several buying trips for his father. Ezekiel eventually took over his father's business and later expanded his own profit-making ventures by joining with two of his kinsmen in 1798 to purchase the Dashville Falls, a few miles north of the village. There they constructed grist, fulling, and woolen mills. He built his new house the following year, which served as a statement of his wealth and cosmopolitanism. His house likewise demonstrated to his community that he was an Anglicizing man of Dutch descent. Still, he was only willing to go so far in becoming an Anglo-American, retaining aspects of his creolized heritage even into the early years of the nineteenth century.[43]

Others followed Ezekiel Eltinge's lead, such as his third cousin Peter Eltinge, who built in 1826 a late Georgian or Federal house, now known as "The Locusts" (see Figure 3.52). These Anglo-American houses were fashionable and grand, but they were put to shame by the dramatic and refined Federal mansion constructed in 1814 for Congressman Josiah Hasbrouck, the great-grandson of patentee Jean Hasbrouck (see Figure 3.53). Josiah Hasbrouck's genteel and imposing house, "Locust Lawn," was based on a design from a noted pattern book of Connecticut architect Asher Benjamin. Josiah's architectural showpiece brought a truly revolutionary architectural profile to the community, and nothing about this structure in either form or function was Dutch-American in any way. The same design was chosen

Figure 3.52. "The Locusts," 1826. Photograph by the author.

Figure 3.53. Josiah Hasbrouck House, "Locust Lawn," 1814. Library of Congress, Prints & Photographs Division, HABS, HABS NY, 56–NEWP.V, 1–1.

by United States Postmaster General Gideon Granger, who built a similar house in Canandaigua, New York, in 1816 (see Figure 3.54). Hasbrouck likely knew Granger, as both served in Washington in the years of the Early Republic, Hasbrouck as congressman from 1803–1805 (and also again from 1817–1819) and Granger as postmaster from 1800–1813. If Ezekiel Eltinge had become familiar with Georgian architecture on a few trips to New York, Hasbrouck had even greater opportunities to familiarize himself with contemporary fashions when he served in the highest halls of government. There he brushed elbows with some of the wealthiest men in the nation, most of whom were Anglo-Americans by both birth and heritage. Although of a different ethnocultural heritage than most of his political colleagues, Locust Lawn demonstrates that Josiah Hasbrouck aimed to be one of their number.[44]

This analysis of domestic architectural adaptation and change in New Paltz highlights how ethnocultural creolization in the patentee community occurred in the realm of material culture. When the founders and their children began constructing permanent houses, they built according to a regional model, most aptly described as "Dutch-American." That model was based primarily on Dutch Old World domestic architecture, although possibly influenced by other regional continental architectural sources, particularly in the use of stone as a building material. The regional approach also involved New World adaptations, including the use of Germanic five-

Figure 3.54. Gideon Granger Homestead, Canandaigua, New York, 1816. Library of Congress, Prints & Photographs Division, HABS, HABS NY, 35–CANDA, 2–1, photograph by W. H. Cassebbeer, 1937.

plate stoves and the transformation of basements from family space to spaces for enslaved laborers, at least for those families that owned slaves. While a few gable-fronted houses, which better reflect Netherlandic models, were built in the early years, it soon became the norm to orient the long axis of the house perpendicular to the street, although the overall Dutchness of the house remained fundamental.

The early generations also preserved Dutch-style jambless fireplaces and casement windows, clear markers of the regional Dutch-American style. By the 1730s, however, patentee families began to insert English architectural elements into new construction, first with the use of sash windows and somewhat later with jambed fireplaces. By the 1750s, owners of some houses also began to retrofit existing houses with these English features. Such selecting from two ethnocultural architectural idioms reflects creolization but without hybridization, as together they did not produce new architectural forms. As the general form and function of the houses changed little through the remainder of the century, creolization continued to favor Dutchness rather than Englishness, at least for most people.

Stylish, new English-inspired Georgian central halls flanked by symmetrically paired rooms were nevertheless introduced in the 1760s. The earliest dated example involved the rebuilding of a traditional Dutch-American home rather than new construction. It appears that it was not until after the Revolutionary War that newly constructed houses might be built on balanced principles. One such house is the Hardenbergh House, which represents an essentially new Dutch-Anglo hybridized form. But even after the Revolution, a man at the pinnacle of local society, Jacob Hasbrouck Jr., Anglicized only to the point of incorporating the English-introduced internal passageway within a one-story Dutch profile, resulting in what remained an essentially creolized English and Dutch structure. It was not until the very end of the century that a two-story symmetrical house with a central hall was constructed on principles that had been brought to America through English agency, yet even that house substantially functioned in a traditional Dutch way. Even after such a house was constructed, Dutchness still prevailed over the New Paltz ethno-architectural landscape. However, this Dutchness was not "pure," as the English "Georgian" symmetry was incorporated into a Dutch profile, producing hybrid creolized forms. This continuity made the first truly English house inside and out—the 1814 Josiah Hasbrouck mansion—seem almost "avant garde," in the apt words of architectural historian Neil Larson.[45]

It is certainly possible that the new architectural elements and form were adopted simply for their modernity rather than in the interest of becoming more English. They provided greater privacy, differentiation of space, cleanliness, and convenience. However, it was a modernity introduced by the English, and as such, it is clear that the patentee descendants did not, by definition, resist such architectural Englishness, creating an ethnically creolized architecture in the process. This architectural change over time was relatively slow and smooth, such that the process of architectural Anglicization would have been far from unsettling. It was also a process in which the New Paltz builders were active agents, as they accepted and incorporated change on their own terms and by their own volition. When it came to domestic architecture, the English was blended into the Dutch, but only slowly.

Barns

The house was not the only architectural form on the New Paltz landscape, as each farm was also equipped with at least one barn. The Dutch and the English designed and constructed such structures in noticeably different ways. Like the Dutch-American house, the source of the Dutch-American barn was not strictly the Netherlands but western continental Europe more broadly. The Dutch-American barn (see Figure 3.55) generally was square or when slightly rectangular, wider than it was deep. Its primary entrance was on a gable end, it had relatively low side walls, and it generally consisted of three aisles, with the largest in the middle. The form developed from the *hallenhuis* tradition, and the structure of the building was based on the H-bent or anchorbeam system. This structure consisted of a series of structural supports that extended parallel to the gable end; each of these H-bent supports consisted of two vertical columns connected by a horizontal anchor beam. These columns extended above the anchor beams and were joined by purlins to which was connected a relatively light roof structure. The space above the anchor beams was used for storage of crops, the side aisles used for stabling of livestock, and the wide central nave used for threshing.[46]

The English timber frame barn stood in sharp contrast to that of the Dutch. It was longer than wide, and its four corners stood as the primary structural supports. The primary wagon entrance was located on the long

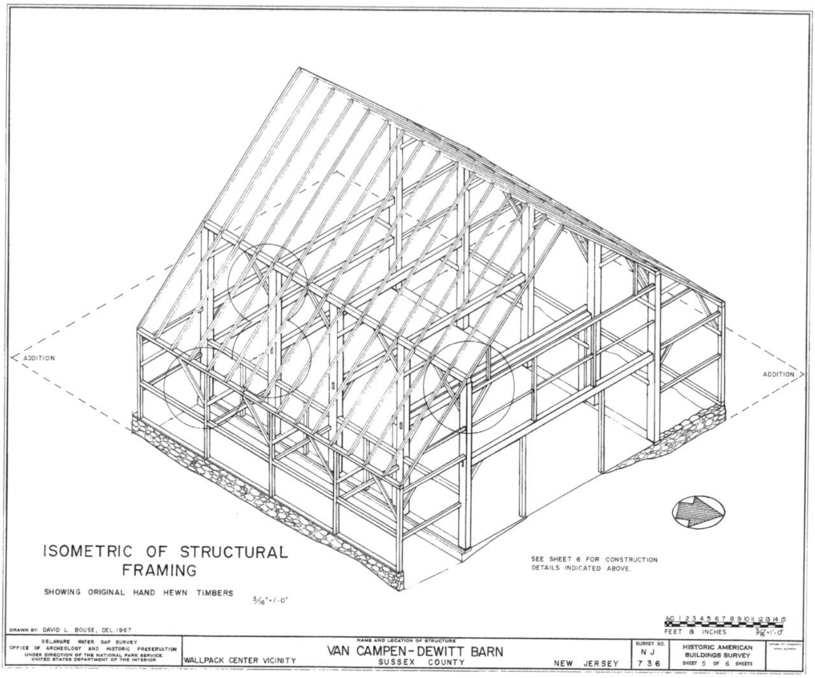

Figure 3.55. Structural framing of Dutch-American barn (Van Campen-Dewitt Barn, Wallpack Center Vicinity, Sussex County, New Jersey). Library of Congress, Prints & Photographs Division, HABS, HABS NJ,19–WALPAC.V,3- (sheet 5 of 6) David L. Bouse, delineator, 1967.

side, which allowed internal access for the unloading of livestock fodder, the storage of which was the primary purpose of the barn. That fodder was stored in the extensive areas to the right and left of the center floor.

No early barns survive in New Paltz, but the 1798 Federal Direct Tax schedules for New Paltz provide a record of all 204 barns in existence at that date. Tax assessor Josiah R. Eltinge clearly indicated which barns he perceived of as being *Dutch barns* (n. 88) as opposed to barns of another form, including *log barns* (n. 22) and *frame barns* and *barns* (n. 94 together). (The surveyor's nomenclature is indicated in italics.) Although Eltinge's use of such nomenclature is not without ambiguity, as discussed below, he clearly was aware that Dutch material culture was at variance with that of the English. This unique record therefore makes it possible to analyze ethnic culture as expressed in the architecture of barns within a single town in an uncommonly comprehensive way.[47]

In New Paltz, Dutch barns literally dominated the physical landscape. They also dominated "socially." They were large, ranging in size from 60 x 50 feet (a 3000-square-foot footprint) to 30 x 29 (870 square feet), with an average footprint of 1935 square feet. This was more than twice the size of an average barn (962 square feet), and about four times the average log bar*n* (415 square feet). Dutch barns were also more often associated with the wealthier residents of New Paltz. The barns themselves were not assessed a particular value, but the average assessment of the houses associated with Dutch barns was $377, while the average for those with barns was $183, or less than half; the average value of houses associated with log barns was only $45. Nearly three-quarters of the Dutch barns also appeared on farms with stone houses, which on average were assessed at one-third more than farms with frame houses. Most of the owners of the Dutch barns were members of the patentee community (sixty-four out of eighty-eight, or 73 percent). In contrast, members of the patentee community owned only 18 percent each of log barns (four of twenty-two) and barns (seventeen of ninety-four). Of those seventeen barns, ten bore dimensions similar to Dutch barns yet not noted as such. To put this another way, the larger and more valuable the barn, the more likely it was a Dutch barn, and the greater likelihood that it was owned by a member of the elite New Paltz patentee community.[48]

Importantly, a significant number of the barns might also have borne Dutch characteristics, with the result being creolized forms. The "classic" Dutch barn has a square to just slightly rectangular footprint. (Terms placed in quotation marks refer to the nomenclature of architectural historians.) The average width-to-length ratio in the New Paltz Dutch barns was 1.13 to 1, as opposed to a 1 to 1.32 width-to-length ratio for barns. However, the dimensions of twenty-two of the ninety-four barns (23 percent) had footprints similar to those of Dutch barns, in that they were square or only somewhat rectangular. Eight of these were extremely substantial in size, covering as much ground as the most substantial Dutch barns. Seven of this subgroup were within a foot of being square, which was simply not a characteristic of English barns, and the eighth was 45 x 50, such that its dimensions were very similar to eight of the Dutch barns. Seven of these eight large, almost-square barns were owned by old New Paltz families, as were the Dutch barns.[49]

Why the surveyor, Josiah R. Eltinge, did not choose to describe those barns that bore dimensions of Dutch barns as Dutch barns, is not entirely clear. However, one architectural historian suggests that these were possibly barns of a type that has been referred to as "true hybrid Dutch-Anglo" barns. The design of such barns was based on a combination of Dutch and English barn forms as a result of hybrid creolization. These barns were distinct from those "classic" Dutch barns that were modified into hybrid barns in the nineteenth century, a not uncommon process. The framing of such "true hybrid Dutch-Anglo" barns was based on the Dutch H-bent or anchorbeam system, although sometimes with modifications. However, many other aspects of the barn reflected English design, including the placement of the primary entrance on a side elevation. These "true hybrid Dutch-Anglo" barns also had more area for crop storage in the left and right bays than did "classic" Dutch barns. The "true hybrid Dutch-Anglo" barns were probably not the only hybrid creolized barns in the community; it is highly likely that at least some of the "classic" Dutch barns had also been modified with the insertion of a side entrance into a building that had originally contained only a gable entrance.[50]

The construction of "true hybrid Dutch-Anglo" barns or the modification of "classic" Dutch barns into hybrid forms was likely motivated by the need to expand a barn's storage capacity rather than reflecting a desire to advance Englishness. Many farmers in the region were shifting from grain production to dairy in the late eighteenth century and needed to store increased amounts of hay for livestock fodder. As such, those who chose to adapt the "classic" Dutch barn along English lines may not have intentionally chosen to embrace English material culture. They nevertheless produced a creolized material culture in the process.

Although the purpose of these hybrids (both "true hybrid" and modified "classic") was to increase fodder storage, there appears to have been a Dutch alternative, designated by the 1798 surveyor as hay houses. It is therefore likely that the owners who had not remodeled a "classic" Dutch barn or built a new "true hybrid Dutch-Anglo" barn built hay houses. Of the eighty-eight Dutch barns, thirty of them (or 34 percent) were accompanied by hay houses of significant length (one each was sixty feet, forty-seven feet, and forty-five feet long, eight forty feet, and sixteen were between thirty and thirty-nine feet long), with widths commonly of eighteen to twenty feet. In contrast, only four of the twenty-two possible "true hybrid Dutch-Anglo" barns (18 percent), had separate structures for hay storage, an almost two-to-one difference, as the increased storage area of hybrid barns sometimes made an additional storage structure unnecessary.

Since the hay houses were most often coupled with Dutch barns, it is quite possible that these hay houses were, in fact, built utilizing Dutch framing methods, resulting in what would be single-aisle Dutch barns. Such barns, which essentially consisted of the central nave of a Dutch barn without side aisles, generally served as "accessory buildings and are often adjacent to the main classic or true hybrid barns at particular homesteads." Single-aisle barns were "fairly often built" in the Dutch cultural region, yet oddly none were recorded in the 1798 tax list in New Paltz. The likelihood, then, is that the surveyor noted only the fully developed three-aisle barn as a Dutch barn, since he based his nomenclature not on framing but form.

If the hay houses were, in fact, Dutch-style single-aisle barns, they would bring the total number of barns to 238, about one half of which were originally constructed in accordance with New World Dutch principles and the other half according to English models. However, a significant number of the fifty-eight Dutch barns that lacked hay houses might have, in fact, been modified into Dutch-Anglo forms, as otherwise their owners might have found it difficult to meet the storage needs that were increasingly necessary. In total, New Paltz barns owned by members of the patentee community included Dutch barns; Dutch barns paired with Dutch hay houses; Dutch-Anglo barns, both "true hybrid Dutch-Anglo" barns and "classic" Dutch barns modified into hybrid forms; and English barns; which together produced a strongly creolized built environment.[51]

This creolization of agricultural structures was likely pragmatically determined, in contrast to the creolization of domestic structures, which seems to have resulted from personal choice. Still, taken together, the sources strongly reveal the continued Dutchness of the architectural landscape created by the descendants of the patentee families. High-style English domestic design and traditional English agricultural design clearly affected patentee families' architectural choices as early as the second quarter of the eighteenth century, but architectural Englishness had not overshadowed Dutchness even at the end of the eighteenth century.

It is not surprising that architecture might have been slower to change than other forms of cultural expression, given that buildings had a very strong staying power. In an age when teardowns and new construction were not the norm, and when architectural modifications were often resource intensive, the architectural landscape as a whole would have been more static than some other forms of cultural expression. The architectural landscape might also have been slower to change because it was dependent upon the availability of builders who worked in particular ethnic idioms. Furthermore, vernacular housing tends to change at a relatively slow pace, as it requires not only stylistic changes but alterations in domestic functioning and the social organization of domestic space. In other words, greater stasis might not signify overall ethnocultural conservatism, particularly if architecture is compare to other forms of cultural expression. Even if architecture changed more slowly, the patentee families did effect material ethnocultural change over the eighteenth century. The result was a creolized Dutch-Anglo built environment, even if the emphasis remained strongly on the Dutch side. And just as with issues of gender and property, that change did not proceed monolithically, but complexly.[52]

Chapter 4

"FRENCH, DUTCH, and TOLERABLE ENGLISH"

Language Use in Early New Paltz

In about 1735, Abraham Hasbrouck, a grandson of the patentee of the same name, wrote of his father Joseph (1684–1724) that he "spake French, Dutch and tolerable English." This trilingualism represents considerable skill indeed, but it was also a matter of necessity for a leading male member of the New Paltz patentee families, who was also a member of the regional elite. French, of course, had been the language of Joseph's parents, the patentee Abraham Hasbrouck and his wife, Maria Deyo, both of whom were Walloon émigrés from Europe. French was therefore the language of Joseph's youth. It was also the language first used in the New Paltz congregation, remaining so throughout Joseph's lifetime. Still, monolingualism would not have been possible for Joseph, as Dutch was the native language of his wife, Elsie Schoonmaker, who, like himself, had been born in Ulster County. It is possible that she might have learned at least a little French herself, as she, too, was a member of the New Paltz Walloon congregation. Even if Elsie was bilingual, it is quite likely that Dutch was an important, if not the primary, language of Joseph and Elsie's household, as Dutch was the lingua franca of the region and therefore the language of Joseph's children's future. Of course, French and Dutch were not the only languages used in the colony or even the region, as English was the language of the provincial government. Given his untimely death, Joseph was never directly involved in provincial affairs, but his father, Abraham the patentee, served as a representative from Ulster County to the provincial Assembly. Such service would certainly have required Abraham to develop at least "tolerable" English like his son Joseph. It is quite possible that Abraham would have ensured that his eldest son Joseph developed sufficient skills in English, possibly so that he might one day follow in his father's footsteps.[1]

This one example alone clearly reveals that members of the patentee families, both individually and collectively, had to make complex choices when it came to which language they would use, choices that were even more complex than in the contexts of gender and material culture. Whereas French or Walloon culture had had little or no impact on architecture or gender ideals, the French, Dutch, and English languages were all used in significant ways at some point in the history of New Paltz; and never during the long eighteenth century was one language employed to the exclusion of all others. New Paltz began as a multilingual community and remained so even into the nineteenth century. According to Ralph LeFevre (b. 1844), bilingualism survived in some form even as late as the 1850s, as during his childhood, "it was the custom for the old people to talk in Dutch when they did not want the children to understand what they were saying." The patentees and descendants did not create a hybrid creolized language, but they nevertheless creolized their community by using multiple languages concurrently for nearly two hundred years.[2]

Joseph Hasbrouck's experience also suggests that the choice of language varied depending upon context, whether governnmental, legal, business, religious, or personal. The rate of change also varied according to the milieu, such that a primary characteristic of multilingualism in New Paltz is that the pace, timing, and process of change were extremely uneven. Sometimes the use of a particular language was required. Sometimes the language of choice was a matter of practicality. At other times, individuals were entirely free to express themselves in the language of their choice. It was the very fact that language use varied between different aspects of individual and community life that produced the complex linguistic environment in New Paltz that obtained throughout the long eighteenth century.

Collective Language Use

Government and the Law

As New Paltz was founded more than a decade after the English conquest, the language used in governmental and legal contexts was almost universally English. With only one exception, documents related to the establishment and management of the patent—the legal basis for which stemmed from the English colonial government—were in English, including the papers of the Twelve Men/Duzine, the earliest of which date to 1728, the year the institution was formed. The records of the town government were also recorded in English, as were official land deeds and court records produced for the county, which was created by colonial legislation in 1683. Given that the Dutch language was actively used in Ulster County even into the early nineteenth century, it is certainly conceivable that Dutch was used in spoken communication within a legal setting after 1683, but this is impossible to confirm. There is no evidence that French was ever used in such official environments.

The only use of Dutch in a corporate document was the town's very first—the so-called "Indian Deed"—which confirmed that the Esopus Indians had transferred land to Louis DuBois "and his associates" ("en syn participanten") in exchange for a wide variety of Euro-American material goods. This document was used for provincial purposes, as Governor Andros would grant a patent for land only if Native Americans had already transferred it to Euro-American settlers, such that at least a verbal translation into English might have been necessary at some point. The transfer was nevertheless recorded in Dutch. Dutch might have been chosen because it was the European language with which the Esopus Indians were likely most familiar, as there were so few French- or English-speakers in the region when the deed was drafted. It also might have been recorded in Dutch because the local witnesses who signed the document were Dutch. Perhaps they would have been willing to sign it only if they also could read it.[3]

The patentees and their heirs occasionally, but rarely, composed documents of a legal nature in French, but only when they were drafted for their own use. Such documents include a 1707 contract with their schoolmaster, fencing agreements from 1708 and 1712, and a road construction agreement from 1739. A handful of early, undated documents written in French also survive, including a land division agreement (c. 1710), one election list for the Twelve Men, and a contract to buy button and ladle molds. Given that descendants who collected these documents in the late nineteenth and twentieth centuries were particularly enamored of anything related to the Frenchness of their ancestors, they collected whatever French documents they uncovered. Even so, the results of their search were meager.[4]

The one type of legal document that apparently allowed for greater linguistic flexibility was the last will and testament. Of course wills, which were created by individuals or their agents, had a legal function, but they were not necessarily entered into the official county records. When not submitted to the county government, it seems that they were informally probated within the family of the testator. As such, many functioned as personal rather than official documents, which perhaps explains why such linguistic flexibility was permissible. Of the forty-seven wills composed before 1800, five were in French, twelve in Dutch, and thirty in English (see table 4.1). Not surprisingly, all of the French wills were composed in the early years of the community (before 1732), but so were ten of the twelve Dutch wills, including the earliest of all, written in 1676. Even English was sometimes used in the early life of the village, as Louis DuBois composed his second will in English in 1686, suggesting that the founders themselves did not assume that any particular language was the language of testation. Testators were also not necessarily consistent; of the five individuals who composed more than one will before 1750, only one testator used the same language in all of his wills. However, with only one

Table 4.1. Language of wills, 1676–1800

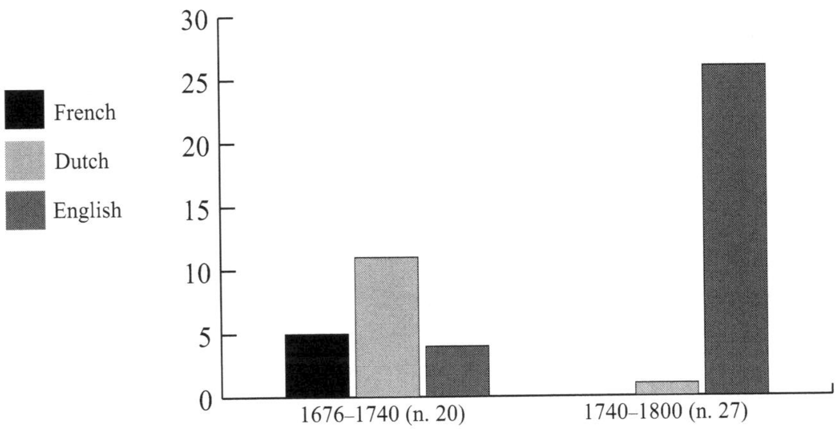

exception, English became the exclusive language for wills by 1743. This transition was entirely a matter of choice, as it was not in any way required by law, nor is there anything to suggest that a Dutch will could not still have been successfully probated throughout the century. In total, it is clear that French was never much used in legal documents, with Dutch only modestly more, while English was adopted in a legal context even when linguistic flexibility remained possible.[5]

The Language of Religion

Although the founders could not preserve their native tongue in legal and governmental contexts, they initially did preserve French in their church, at least until about 1730. The community founded a congregation in 1683, five years after the town was settled. Only then were the New Paltz founders able to secure the services of a French pastor. Initially, they considered their church an independent Walloon Reformed congregation, but they eventually became Dutch Reformed in the 1750s. Their first pastor was Pierre Daillé, who served until 1692, during which time his presence in New Paltz was only intermittent. He was succeeded as minister by another Frenchman, David de Bonrepos, but his period of service was also minimal and sporadic, lasting only from 1696 to 1700. From that date until 1731, the congregation was without ministerial leadership.

This is not to say that the New Paltz founding families were unchurched during the first three decades of the eighteenth century, as they traveled to the Kingston Dutch Reformed Church to receive the rites of marriage, baptism, and, for church members, Holy Communion. They also maintained institutional religious life within their village itself even without ministerial leadership, and the local language of religion remained French. As members of the patentee families later informed the Dutch Reformed Classis of Amsterdam, "besides maintaining Family Worship, they [had] in their midst public service of pure Religion. . . . Whenever there was no minister a sermon was read in French." They even pooled scarce resources to build an imposing stone church, the 1720 completion of which they noted in French in their congregational records. In addition to the use of French in church services, several of the patentees and their children owned printed religious materials in French, which they passed down to their descendants, who used them at least for a time. Jean Hasbrouck owned at least three French religious books, which he bequeathed to his daughter Elizabeth in 1714, including a book of sermons, the Psalms, and a book entitled *La Pratique de Piété*. It is quite possible that the book of sermons once owned by Jean Hasbrouck could have been that (or one of those) used in the New Paltz church into the 1720s. Jean Hasbrouck also owned a French New Testament that included a metrical version of the Psalms set to music, which likely passed to Elizabeth as well. These books were not merely tokens of the past, as Elizabeth and her husband, Louis Bevier II (son of the patentee), recorded family records in *La Pratique de Piété* soon after her father's death. When he composed his will in 1724, Abraham Deyo I, son of patentee Pierre Deyo, likewise bequeathed

French religious texts to his daughters, Marie and Wyntje, which they received the following year after his death. Marie inherited a French New Testament; a book of sermons and a book of Psalms she received might have been in French as well. Wyntje also received a French Testament, as well as "le pratique de piete" and, as her father described it, "le vieux bible francoij" ("the old French Bible"). In 1738, Andries LeFevre, son of patentee Simon LeFevre, also gave to his eldest son his "beg French bible," which he likely inherited from one of his parents. He gave an additional French Bible to his younger son Mattys.[6]

French did not remain the language of religion, but the transition to Dutch occurred incrementally. By the end of the 1720s, the congregation began to offer afternoon services in Dutch in addition to their morning French services. Both of these services were led at that point by lay persons. It is certainly possible that members of the congregation participated in both the French and Dutch services, given that it was common for Calvinists of the time to attend church both in the morning and the afternoon. Doing so would not have been too difficult, as it is likely that members of the second generation did have at least some familiarity with Dutch. Even before the congregation began to offer Dutch services, the schoolmaster Jean Tebenin anticipated that French was likely soon to be abandoned in the congregation. He directed in his 1719 will that if the congregation ceased to employ the French language in worship, then his French Bible should be sold and the proceeds used for the poor. He repeated this directive in his 1730 will, suggesting that a complete transition from the use of French still had not yet occurred. Nevertheless, his Bible was indeed sold after his death in about 1733 according to his wishes; it descended in the family of Jacob Hasbrouck Sr., the son of patentee Jean Hasbrouck.[7]

New Paltz did finally secure the ministerial leadership of a member of the ordained clergy, Johannes van Driessen, in 1731. Several historians have claimed that van Driessen originally hailed from the region that is today Belgium, concluding that French was his native language and thus the language of church services during his tenure in New Paltz. Such a contention is based on a misinterpretation of his certificate of ordination. Even if he was from what would eventually become Belgium, his first language could have been French, Flemish, or German, depending upon where in that region he was raised. His place of birth is actually unknown, but it is highly likely that he was from the Netherlands, such that his native language would have been Dutch. He claimed to have been educated at Monnickendam and Hardenwyck (both near Amsterdam), Utrecht and Leyden, and he was certainly a student for a time at the University of Groningen, all of which were Dutch towns. In the New World, van Driessen preached in Dutch in the Dutch Reformed congregations of Kinderhook and Claverack, New York, where he served between 1728 and 1735, both before and during the time he served in New Paltz. He subsequently served a Dutch congregation in Aquackanonck (modern Passaic), New Jersey. He also composed a letter in Dutch to Jacob Hasbrouck in 1748, even though Jacob's first language was French, a fact which van Driessen would have known. If van Driessen had been fluent in French, and if he had used that language when he served in New Paltz, he presumably would have used it in his missive to Jacob, but he did not. Johannes van Driessen's older brother, Petrus, was also a Dutch-speaker, who reported to the University of Groningen upon his matriculation that he was from Coevorden in the Province of Drenthe. Petrus was sent by the Classis of Amsterdam to serve as the pastor of the Albany Dutch church in 1711, where he remained until his death in 1738. The only suggestion that Johannes van Driessen might have used French in New Paltz is a couple of simple entries in the church records in French, and van Driessen's 1734 reference to the New Paltz church as "our French Church." However, that reference might have had nothing to do with the use of the French language in the church but simply a reference to its being, at that time, independent of the Dutch Reformed Church.[8]

Another indication that Dutch replaced French in church in the 1730s is that Dutch Bibles and other religious works first appeared in New Paltz in the second quarter of the eighteenth century. The last French Bible that can be confirmed to have been used in New Paltz was printed in 1712. The earliest print date for a Dutch Bible that can be verified as having been used in New Paltz was 1720, being that of Petrus LeFevre (1720–1806), although the dated records inscribed in that Bible do not begin until about 1760. The earliest confirmed ownership and use of a Dutch Bible and other religious texts are those of Abraham Deyo I, neither of whose parents were native Dutch speakers. Although Abraham owned French religious texts, which he bequeathed to his daughters upon his death in 1725, he also gave to his daughters Wyntje a Dutch prayer book ("un Livr de priere flament") and Marie a Dutch Bible ("le bible flament"), suggesting that a language transition began to occur in this family perhaps even before the 1720s. Abraham also tellingly characterized the French Bible he bequeathed to Wyntje as "old" ("vieux'), while he applied no adjective to the Dutch Bible he gave to Marie. Jan Ean (son of Elias Ean and Elizabeth Crispell, daughter of patentee Antoine Crispell) also acquired a 1724 Dutch Bible in 1730. His wife, Caty Van Wagenen Ean, also possessed a 1737 Dutch prayer book that tradition states was used in the New Paltz church. Other early Dutch religious works used in the community included the Bible of Evert Terwilliger and Sara Freer (printed in 1730, in use by about 1737), a Dutch Bible first used in 1733 by Hendricus DuBois, and a book of Psalms owned by Josiah Eltinge (a grandson of patentee Abraham DuBois) and his wife, Magdalena DuBois Eltinge (printed and first used in 1734). Mattys LeFevre also received a Dutch Bible (as well as a French Bible) in 1738, according to his father Andries's will. Clearly the schoolmaster Jean Tebenin was correct in anticipating that French was soon to be replaced with Dutch in the church.[9]

Dutch continued to be heard in the church for another eighty years through a number of pastorates. Van Driessen possibly served as late as May 1736, followed by more than a decade in which the congregation occasionally received the services of supply ministers. In 1741, the New Paltz congregation, in conjunction with three other nearby churches, called Domine Johannes Casparus Fryenmoet, but to no avail; the congregation at Minisink on the Delaware River, where Fryenmoet was the settled pastor, was able to thwart the New Paltz call. In 1749, a new minister, the Rev. Johannes Henricus Goetschius, came to New Paltz, visiting the town sporadically until 1753. Goetschius (originally Goetschi) was born in 1718 in Zurich, Switzerland, and educated in his hometown. The native tongue of the Goetschi family was German, although Johannes's father, Maurice, was skilled in a number of languages. The family migrated to America in 1735 when Johannes was only seventeen, after which he soon began to preach in German churches in Philadelphia and the surrounding area, even though he was not ordained. He was ordained six years later in order to serve several Dutch-speaking Reformed congregations on Long Island (1741–1748). He later moved to New Jersey, where he served as pastor in the Hackensack and Schraalenberg Dutch Reformed congregations from 1748–1774. It is not clear when Goetschius attained fluency in Dutch, although he surely must have, as he became not just a preacher for but a member of the Dutch communities in which he served. Goetschius undoubtedly conducted services in Dutch in New Paltz, as the records of the congregation were kept in that language during his time there, and there is no suggestion anywhere in the record that Goetschius had any skills in French. In 1753, the New Paltz congregation installed Barent Vrooman, who without any doubt was a Dutch speaker, having been born in Schenectady (1725), educated in Utrecht (1750–1752) and ordained by the Classis of Amsterdam (1752). During Vrooman's short stay in New Paltz, the congregation abandoned its denominational independence and officially became Dutch Reformed.[10]

Dutch remained the exclusive language of the New Paltz church through the tenure of the brother of J. H. Goetschius, Johannes Mauritius Goetschius, who served from 1760–1771, and into the early years of the pastorate of Rev. Stephen Goetschius, son of J. H. Goetschius, who served from 1775 to 1796. According to Charles Stitt, a nineteenth-century New Paltz pastor writing in 1860, "Toward the latter part of his ministry at the Paltz, in order to meet the wants of the younger portion of his audience, he [Stephen Goetschius] preached alternately in Dutch and English. As his congregation was nearly doubled when he preached in English, he used to vary his services, so as always to secure a respectable house." Although the congregation began to embrace English during the tenure of Stephen Goetschius, they continued to use Dutch for church records throughout his period of service. It was not until 1800 that the church records were kept in English during the ministry of his successor, Rev. John H. Meyer, who was nevertheless required to preach one half of his services each in Dutch and English. That the transition from Dutch to English was progressing during the last quarter of the eighteenth century is also clear from the fact that Stephen Goetschius's 1775 call was written in Dutch, as was a revised agreement from 1784. However, Rev. Meyer's 1799 call was recorded in English. Meyer served until only 1802, but his successor continued to alternate the use of Dutch and English in church services from 1808 through 1814, when he removed to New Jersey. Beginning in 1817, at the commencement of the ministry of William R. Bogardus, English became the sole language of the church.[11]

To summarize, French was the language of religion from the founding of the community through the early 1730s. Nevertheless, Dutch was introduced into family worship and formal afternoon services in the 1720s, but it is likely that many engaged in religious activities in both languages. With the arrival of the Rev. Johannes van Driessen in 1731, the congregation made the transition to the sole use of Dutch in religious services. As the use of French overlapped with the use of Dutch, so did Dutch and English, the latter of which was introduced probably by the 1780s. Again, ministers continued to alternate between both languages for several more decades. By 1817, Dutch was no longer heard from the pulpit.

The Language of Education

Shortly after the community formed a congregation, they also established a school. As with religion, the language of education was also initially in French, and remained so through at least the 1730s. That the language of both school and church was simultaneously French for a number of decades is hardly coincidental. A primary purpose of the school was surely to teach the children to read, a skill they would need if they were to fully participate in spiritual activities in both the home and in the church. If French was the language of religion, so too would it need to be the language of education.

The patentee community initially chose to hire native French-speaking schoolmasters. The first was Jean Cottin, a native of Bohain in the northern French province of Picardy, who was hired at least as early as 1689. He probably served through 1695. Cottin remained committed to French throughout his life, as he kept his account books in that language until his death in 1721. Following Cottin, the community hired Jean Tebenin, whose origins are not known. Nevertheless, French was clearly his first language as well, as demonstrated by his 1730 will. It is unclear how long Tebenin served as schoolmaster, but there is no record of any other schoolmaster in New Paltz until after his death in the early 1730s.[12]

The patentee community remained committed to teaching French at least through the 1730s. References to two other teachers with French surnames from the 1730s—Pierre Simon and Jean Meschines—have survived, although virtually nothing is known about either of them. If they were young and had had strong local connections before the 1730s, it is possible that their first language may not have been French, but nothing can be said with certainty. Whether the first language of the teachers who served in the 1730s was French or not, an early ciphering book created by another Abraham Hasbrouck (b. 1722) proves that French was the language of instruction at least into the early 1730s. The dates of the school exercises are not recorded, but Abraham's father, Solomon, also used the book between 1731 and 1733 for keeping poor-relief records in his capacity as deacon. The book also includes a 1739 reference to Meschines, to whom the next deacon, Jacob Hasbrouck, paid tuition for educating one of his sons.[13]

The documentary record concerning the community's school unfortunately becomes murky for several decades after 1739. Between that year and the mid-1760s, the school made the transition to Dutch, as attested to by Benjamin Hasbrouck's (b. 1748) ciphering book dating from 1764 to 1766. Philip Deyo (b. 1752) also began to keep a ciphering book in Dutch in 1768, but he used Dutch only on the first page, after which he transitioned to English. Peter LeFevre Jr. (b. 1759) used English exclusively in his 1773–1775 ciphering book. Although evidence of Dutch language instruction therefore exists only for a short period time in the middle-to-late 1760s, it is highly likely that it was introduced much earlier. There would have been no practical purpose for teaching French by the 1740s at the latest, as French was no longer the language of religion nor the medium of communication in any other of life's activities, as is demonstrated below.[14]

The village schoolmaster in the 1760s who taught in Dutch was Joseph Coddington, the first of that surname to live in the vicinity of New Paltz. Coddington, whose native language was not Dutch but English, hailed from an Anglo community in New Jersey. He relocated to Rochester, a town near New Paltz in Ulster County, sometime before February 1753, when he married Catherine van der Marken, whose family was associated with New Paltz as early as 1728. The Coddingtons were linked to the New Paltz community through the congregation, as he and his wife baptized a child in the New Paltz church in November 1756. They had moved to New Paltz by 1765, when Coddington was listed as a "freeholder or inhabitant." During this period of more than a decade, Coddington must have developed a certain level of Dutch proficiency, which is not surprising given that he had moved to a generally Dutch region where he married a woman of Dutch descent. It is intriguing that the community hired a non-native speaker of Dutch to teach in that language, as there certainly must have been other local men capable of instructing the community's youth. Perhaps Coddington's fluency in English created the possibility of bilingual education, or perhaps he was employed in order to facilitate the transition to English that soon occurred.[15]

The transitions from French to Dutch and from Dutch to English in both the school and the church therefore correspond temporally, which is likely not a mere coincidence. For the first three decades of the eighteenth century, the community lacked clerical leadership, such that parents directed spiritual concerns at home and trusted men in the community led within the church. Either by choice or necessity, these men would likely have perpetuated religious instruction in French, as that had been the language of religion and of the religious texts bequeathed to them by their parents. To perpetuate this way of managing their religious needs, fluency in written French was needed, which probably motivated them to continue to have their children instructed in that language. When the congregation was finally able to hire a minister after a gap of over three decades, that individual was a Dutch speaker. His entrance into the community also coincided with the appearance of Dutch religious texts. After decades of no leadership at all, the hiring of a Dutch-speaking minister must have led to the realization that French pastoral leadership had come to an end. Without a practical reason to continue with French-language instruction, the language of the founders was fully phased out in the schools, and replaced with Dutch, the new language of religion.

Similarly, the transition to English in education in the mid-1760s corresponds with a transition in the New Paltz congregation as well as in the Dutch Reformed Church in America as a whole. This transition involved what is known as the Coetus-Conferentie dispute, which led to the separation of the American Dutch Reformed congregations and their ministers from the authority of the Classis of Amsterdam. The controversy was several years in the making, but it came to a head in 1764, when the majority of the American Dutch ministers and congregations finally declared their independence from Amsterdam, in part because they hoped to educate and ordain ministers in the colonies. As future ministers presumably would be born in America, it was highly likely that they increasingly would be native English speakers, as the use of Dutch language in the colonies was clearly on the decline, and the American congregations would need to prepare for that eventuality.[16]

The New Paltz congregation followed the Americanizing wing of the colonial congregations, although a small splinter congregation was formed in New Paltz in 1767 that retained ties with the Classis of Amsterdam. Soon after the American congregations parted ways and the New Paltz congregation split, the patentee families allowed for the transition from Dutch to English in education, motivated at least in part by the need to prepare the succeeding generations for American-born, English-speaking ministers. In doing so, the patentee families created a self-fulfilling prophecy. Those children who first received their education in English in the late 1760s very likely became those members of the "younger portion" of the congregation to which Rev. Stephen Goetschius referred, who, in the 1780s, asked their minister to begin to introduce English-language services. They must have done so simply because they preferred English, as there was no way that these congregants would not have at least spoken Dutch. Overall, the choices the community made concerning language use in the church and correspondingly in the school suggest a significant degree of pragmatism, rather than a strong commitment to any particular ethnic culture.

If anyone was ethnoculturally rigid in religious and educational affairs, they were clearly in the minority. Otherwise, these linguistic transitions could not have been effected. It is also likely that the desire for change was cross-generational, as the younger generations probably could not have thwarted the older generations if the latter meant to resist ethnocultural change, given the generally deferential character of colonial families. This suggests that even the elder members of the church were looking more to their children's future rather than to their own past, and they saw no need for ethnocultural rigidity in the present. These transitions also suggest a creolized sensibility, in that the community accepted Dutch in a religious context even as they still considered themselves an independent Walloon church. Similarly, when they transitioned to English, the congregation remained Dutch Reformed, although it was now independent of Amsterdam and part of the new United States of America. As much as language and denominational affiliation in the Reformed tradition were historically integrated in Europe, those links might be abandoned in America in creolized communities such as New Paltz, which felt comfortable making use of various ethnic cultures.

Individual Language Use

The choices the New Paltz patentee community made in terms of language use in church and school reflect only how they collectively and formally decided linguistic aspects of their ethnocultural behavior. Language use, of course, was nevertheless subject to the choices of individuals every day in myriad ways. Unfortunately, we will never discover more than mere hints as to when French, and later Dutch, was last spoken aloud in New Paltz. Neither will it ever be possible to unravel fully the linguistic complexity of street and home life in the years when languages intermingled. Nevertheless, the archival record offers glimpses of the choices individuals made in circumstances less formal than the church or the school. Truly informal written communications such as personal letters and diaries are unfortunately few. However, family records inscribed in Bibles and records of casual business transactions are far more plentiful, and these sources hint at the language choices of everyday life. What these sources reveal is that many individuals began to transition from the use of one language to another before the community as a whole chose to do so, adding another layer to the complexity of the creolized environment that the patentee community created and sustained for well more than a century.

The Language of Life's Milestones

The Bible obviously stood at the heart of New Paltz's religious life, and copies of the Holy Scriptures would likely have been found in each patentee household, as well as those of their descendants. Psalm books and prayer books were also used by many in the community. In these texts, individuals and families often recorded births and deaths, baptisms and marriages. As these events were infused with great spiritual meaning, records of these events sometimes seem to have been entered in a formal and ritualistic manner. Yet, sometimes records seem to have been haphazardly and almost indiscriminately made, and as such, appear rather casual. This heterogeneity in style suggests that these genealogical records reflect language use less formal than that of the church, but not quite as informal as that of everyday speech.

Not surprisingly, the language of the earliest family records of the community recorded in religious texts was French. Patentees Louis Bevier and Jean Hasbrouck recorded their family records in French in French Bibles, as did Jean Hasbrouck's children. His son Jacob inscribed such records both in his father's Bible and in a book of martyrs (printed in French in 1582), while his daughter Maria recorded her family records in her 1712 French Bible. Maria's son Daniel later noted in his mother's Bible "moy Daniel du bois Je suis marrie le uien 18 lan 1713," but his is the only French family record from the third generation that has survived. Unfortunately, few Bibles or other religious works that were used by those in the first two generations have survived. Still, it can safely be assumed that the other patentees also utilized French in their family records, since that was their first language. It would not have been unlikely for the children of the patentees to have done so as well, at least to some extent, given that that was the language of the church and the school until about 1730. However, without surviving records, the extent of French use by the second generation can only be speculated.[17]

By the beginning of the 1730s, if not before, Dutch had become the language of genealogical records. Dutch was used exclusively until the mid-1750s, yet it remained common until the end of the century. The earliest Dutch records can be found in the Bible of Jan Ean, grandson of patentee Antoine Crispell, who acquired his 1724 Bible in 1730, an event noted in Dutch within. In 1733, Hendricus DuBois recorded in Dutch his marriage to Jannetje Houghtaling, and subsequently in the same language the births of his nine children (and the deaths of two of them). When he died in 1780, his widow, Jannetje, recorded so in Dutch, and she continued to choose Dutch when she entered the deaths of two more of their children. Although Magdalena DuBois and her husband, Josiah Eltinge (grandson of patentee Abraham DuBois), did not record family events in their 1734 book of Psalms, which they acquired the year of their marriage, they did use Dutch to indicate their ownership of the book. Of these five individuals, four descended from one or more patentee families, and the other married the grandson of a patentee. These individuals who began to write in Dutch in their Bibles had been born between 1699 and 1713, such that they learned Dutch even when the language of education and religion was still French. Their ultimate choice to have their children educated in Dutch was therefore a response to rather than a precursor of a linguistic transition that they had already made in their private lives. This transition from French to Dutch occurred as intermarriage between Walloons and members of the local "Dutch" population became commonplace. This is not surprising, as if one of the spouses needed to be bilingual, it would have been quite unlikely for a "Dutch" spouse to learn French rather than the reverse, considering the fact that French-speakers were clearly in the local minority.[18]

Although the transition from French to Dutch in family records seems to have been relatively abrupt, the transition from Dutch to English for Bible records was quite protracted, again revealing the creolized nature of the patentee community. The last time Dutch was used was around 1800, when Abraham Ean, the great-great-great-grandchild of patentee Antoine Crispell, made note of his own 1791 birth. During those seventy years between 1730 and 1800, the use of both languages was relatively balanced. The surviving Bibles and religious texts indicate that twenty-four or twenty-five patentee descendants and two or three spouses of patentee descendants used Dutch for family records. During the same time period, another eighteen individuals chose to begin recording important family events in English. Not surprisingly, many of the earliest English users were members of the first generation to receive an education in English, and were also members of the "younger portion" of the church congregation who preferred religious services in English. Still, the transition was not strictly generational but temporal as well. The first person to use English was a member of the third generation, Jacob Hasbrouck Jr. (1728–1806), who recorded in English the birth of his son Josiah in 1755. He was a member of a generation that had been educated in Dutch, but he chose to begin using English more than a decade before it was taught in the village school. This again suggests that transitions in language use in education followed rather than preceded shifts in the community at large. Unlike the transition from French to Dutch in family records, the switch from Dutch to English was not heavily influenced by the intermarriage between the patentee families and those of English birth or descent, suggesting that free choice rather than necessity drove the second transition.[19]

The creolized linguistic character of the patentee community is also demonstrated by the fact that virtually all patentee descendants who used English in the second half of the eighteenth century to record important family events in their religious texts did so within Dutch texts. It is not surprising that the patentee descendants continued to use Dutch texts even as they were making the personal choice to utilize English, as Dutch was the exclusive language of the church from the early 1730s into the 1780s, and it was still being used for some worship services until 1817. Additionally, Bibles and prayer books were often passed down from parent to child. For example, Josiah Hasbrouck (1755–1821) used the 1690 Dutch Bible once owned by his father-in-law, Cornelius Decker and Jacob LeFevre (1760–1817) used his father's 1720 Dutch Bible. For a person writing in English alongside pages of the scriptures printed in Dutch, this linguistic contrast could hardly have passed unnoticed. For some, at least, the use of English suggests a conscious choice and thus personal preference within a bilingual environment.[20]

Creolization is also evidenced by the fact that a few individuals used both English and Dutch in their genealogical records. For example, Caty Van Wagenen Ein (b. 1743) recorded the births of her first three children (1767, 1768, and 1770) in Dutch and of her youngest three children (1774, 1777, and 1781) in English. Others did not make such a precise transition, as they casually or perhaps even unconsciously flipped from language to language. As noted above, Jacob Hasbrouck Jr. used English to record in his Bible the birth of his son Josiah in 1755; he also used English when he noted the 1767 birth of another son, Jacob J. Hasbrouck, in a separate family register. Yet, Jacob also used Dutch in that register to record the date of his marriage, the birth and childhood death of his son Louis, and once again the birth of Josiah. In a similar fashion, Petrus LeFevre (1720–1806) also interspersed Dutch and English. Jacob Hasbrouck Jr.'s son Josiah, who became a United States congressman, also used multiple languages in his family record; but he did not make the transition to English until the 1790s, almost forty years after his father had first used English in his records. These individuals more than anyone reveal how complex this creolized linguistic environment actually was.[21]

The Language of Business

Another group of documents that can provide insight into language choice in day-to-day life are financial receipts. Like Bible records, financial receipts manifest to some extent the formal and institutional, as their language is generally quite formulaic. It is also conceivable that they might someday have been used within the ritualistic environment of the court. Still, the language used was so simple that the receipts could have been easily translated, even if they had not been written in the language of the law. A relatively low level of formality is also reflected in the fact that they were literally written on scraps of paper. In other words, financial receipts reflect everyday speech more than any other documents available, except for those few that were truly of a personal nature. Receipts also reveal a great deal more about language within a community than do Bible records, as the greatest extent of the audience for the Bible records was the family to which they referred. In contrast, the receipts held by an individual represent a whole network of financial relations of both creditors and debtors, both local and more distant.

The three earliest groups of receipts are those of patentee Pierre Deyo, patentee Louis Bevier, and Hugo Freer Sr. (son of the patentee of the same name), all three of which reveal the linguistic complexity of the founders' society (see table 4.2). The earliest receipts are those of Pierre Deyo, reflecting a relative balance between French and English. The French receipts each involved a different individual, all of whom were likely of French-speaking ancestry (except for one that is anonymous). The English receipts provide a record of financial transactions with several New York City merchants and apparently their agent in Kingston. Just a couple were recorded in Dutch, one with a local resident and the other with a trader in New York City. The ethnic heritage of all of these individuals with whom Pierre Deyo engaged in business is not precisely clear, but it appears that the receipts likely reflect the ethnic heritage of the other party. In other words, Pierre may not have chosen the language of the records, such that they do not demonstrate whether he was fluent in multiple languages. Nevertheless, it is clear that he did interact with others in languages other than his first. The receipts of Louis Bevier, like those of Pierre Deyo, are somewhat limited in number, with about half each in Dutch and French. Again, the language of the receipts generally reflects the ethnicity of the person with whom Louis transacted

Table 4.2. Language of financial receipts (I)

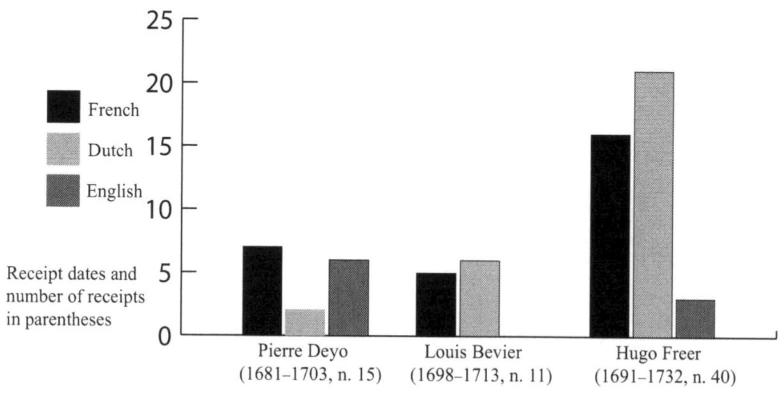

business. The lack of English receipts therefore suggests that either none survived or perhaps that Louis simply did not financially interact with those of an English ethnocultural orientation.[22]

The receipts of Hugo Freer are more numerous and cover a longer period. Although multiple languages are also reflected in these receipts, they do suggest the beginnings of a linguistic shift. A little under half of the documents are in French, recording business with numerous individuals. Not surprisingly, the other parties in these transactions, when they are known, were of Walloon or French background. In contrast, the many Dutch records document business affairs with people with surnames that demonstrate great ethnic diversity, including Dutch, Walloon, German, French, and English. This suggests that the language of business was changing and that the choice of language was increasingly less influenced by the ethocultural heritage of the parties involved. Almost half of the French receipts are also inscribed with short notes, generally identifying the documents as receipts. These notes were written in Dutch, presumably by Hugo Freer, suggesting that while he might have been able to conduct business in French, his preferred language was Dutch. The few English receipts also suggest a shift in language, as two of the three English receipts in which the name of the other party is noted indicate that such other parties were French speakers.[23]

The receipts of Hugo Freer extend into the second quarter of the eighteenth century, but the only other surviving receipts from that period—although few in number—are those of Daniel DuBois Sr. (b. 1684), son of patentee Isaac DuBois. They represent only twelve transactions with at least six individuals between 1718 and 1752. Again, the language use is diverse, including French, Dutch, and English, with the ethnic heritage of the other party often, although not exclusively, being determinative. It is nevertheless difficult to offer a definitive statement about language use in business between 1725 and 1750, although clearly many languages were still possible. However, the largest group of documents—those of Hugo Freer—do suggest the general adoption of Dutch even before patentee family members began to use it in genealogical records.[24]

The records become much richer beginning with the third quarter of the century, revealing a strong linguistic shift towards English as the primary language of business. It is difficult to say if this shift was abrupt or gradual, but it was nevertheless strongly apparent after 1750 (see table 4.3). This can be seen in the records of Simon DuBois (b. 1718), which recorded thirty-five exchanges with almost as many people. The parties involved never used French and rarely Dutch. Although a small number of the numerous English receipts involved transactions with men with Anglo surnames such as Green or Graham, the remaining participants who recorded their transactions in English had either Dutch or Walloon surnames, demonstrating a clear trend towards Englishness. Similar evidence can be found in the receipts of "Abraham Deyo" (probably both Abraham Deyo II b. 1710 and his son Abraham III b. 1734). Just a few of these were in Dutch, referencing business conducted with individuals possessing Dutch surnames, as might be expected. Most were in English and most were signed by those with non-Anglo names.

Table 4.3. Language of financial receipts (II)

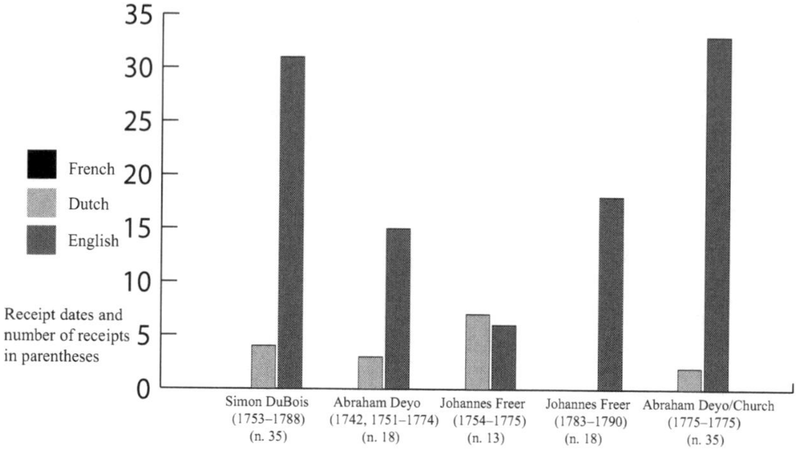

again revealing the spread of Englishness in business. A contemporaneous group of receipts are the documents produced by and for Johannes Freer, dating from 1754 to 1790. Those from the third quarter of the eighteenth century are almost evenly divided between English and Dutch. Those dating from the last quarter are all in English.[25]

Another more focused group of receipts was kept by Abraham Deyo II (b. 1710) in his capacity as manager of the construction of the New Paltz congregation's second stone church between 1771 and 1775. Only two are in Dutch, involving payments to Cornelius Beekman and Nicolas Vanderlyn. The others are all in English, recording transactions with a wide variety of individuals who possessed Anglo, Dutch, and Walloon surnames. By the end of the third quarter of the eighteenth century, the language of business had clearly become English. This conclusion is reinforced by the many receipts of William Deyo (b. 1761), great-grandson of patentee Pierre Deyo. His receipts begin in 1786 and were exclusively composed in English. Likewise, those of Daniel DuBois Jr. (b. 1750), which record transactions beginning in about 1790, were composed only in English.[26]

In general, the language of business from the founding of the town through the first quarter of the eighteenth century included French, Dutch, and English. Initially, the language of choice often depended upon the ethnicity of the other party or parties in the transaction. This increasingly became less relevant, as individuals even without Dutch surnames began to record business affairs in Dutch. English was rarely used through 1725, as were transactions with Englishmen. Unfortunately, the records for the second quarter of the eighteenth century are too few to draw strong conclusions, although those that do survive indicate the continued use of both Dutch and English. A substantial shift nevertheless did occur by or in the period from 1750–1775. Of the eighty-six receipts referencing transactions in which seventy-five individuals were involved, less than a fifth were recorded in Dutch. The records from the church construction reveal that by the end of the third quarter of the century, Dutch was indeed rarely used; it was never used in the last quarter.

Clearly, the language of business in the community was constantly in flux. Never was French the only language used, and while the use of Dutch in business transactions in the second quarter of the century was extensive, its use was never stable. Like the transitions from French to Dutch and Dutch to English in family records, transitions in business preceded those in education and the church. In fact, they occurred even earlier. Such diversity of language would not survive, as over the subsequent half-century, those children that were born and educated when English had become the primary language of business would seek to linguistically unify their lives, first within the family (as seen in the Bible records) and then eventually in the church itself.

Private Language

Personal records such as letters and diaries are exceedingly rare, and as such, cannot reveal general trends. They do, however, further demonstrate the creolized environment of New Paltz. One group of documents of a personal nature is that of Louis Bevier III (1717–1772), grandson of the patentee of the same name. He moved as a young adult to nearby Marbletown, although he maintained close connections with New Paltz. Bevier was trilingual, and even with only a handful of records surviving, the linguistic complexity of his environment is evident. The most significant records are two account books, one in French and one in English. His personal accounts he kept in English, yet the 1742–1750 accounts he kept on behalf of his disabled brother Andries were in French. As Andries lived in New Paltz with his sister Esther and her husband, Jacob Hasbrouck (son of patentee Jean), it is possible that the accounts were in French to meet either Esther's or Jacob's needs, which were at variance with Louis' own linguistic desires. Two French letters written by Louis Bevier also survive; both are to his father-in-law, Philip DuBois (born in 1689, son of patentee Isaac DuBois), who lived in nearby Rochester; one letter was undated, but the other dates to 1763. In contrast, he also composed a letter to his cousin Abraham Hasbrouck (1744) in English and one in 1761 to Moses Depuy, Esq. (also a Rochester resident) in Dutch. These records suggest that Bevier's personal choice was English, but he could also compose financial records and correspond with others in Dutch and French, with the language of choice presumably that of the intended reader. The suggestion is that linguistic flexibility in personal communication in the mid-eighteenth century was a continuation of a similar flexibility in language in business transactions that had existed earlier in the century.[27]

Louis Bevier's French documents of a personal nature are the only French ones in existence, but a few personal documents in Dutch produced by others have survived. Jacob Hasbrouck Sr. received a Dutch letter from his former minister Johannes van Driessen in 1748. In 1760, Tryntje Low Bevier (b. 1727) wrote a letter in Dutch to her uncle Cornelius DuBois (b. 1707) concerning a meeting of the heirs of her grandfather Solomon DuBois. Andries

LeFevre kept an account book in Dutch from 1755 to 1791, as did Jannetje DuBois from 1773 to 1791. Her son, Hendricus, did so as well from 1768 to 1795. There also exists a reference to a 1752 letter in Dutch from Rachel DuBois of Perkiomen, Pennsylvania, to her grandfather Solomon DuBois of New Paltz, but the whereabouts of the document are currently unknown.[28]

Two brothers in the Eltinge family, great-grandsons of patentee Abraham DuBois, represent an important transition point from the use of Dutch to English for personal communication and records. Solomon Eltinge, the younger brother, was born in 1742. During the Revolutionary War, he was exiled to New York City as a loyalist. Six letters home during his years of exile (1776–1783) survive, four in Dutch and two in English. The Dutch letters were collectively written for his entire family, as well as to his "Vrienden" (friends), while the two in English were addressed exclusively to his father, Josiah. A plausible interpretation of this evidence suggests that English was his father's preferred language, or at least that they generally communicated in English, while the community as a whole perhaps preferred Dutch. If these letters written essentially to the community were to be read aloud, quite likely to a mixed-aged audience, this is not surprising, since English fluency might not have been prevalent in an older generation. Solomon Eltinge's elder brother, Roelof Josiah (b. 1737), however, maintained all personal and financial records in English in his capacity as the first resident merchant in New Paltz. The earliest records for his store date from 1768 and the last from 1795, the year of his death. Roelof Josiah Eltinge also used English in a personal diary he began to keep in 1776 in connection with his treatment by the Ulster County Committee as a loyalist and his later banishment to British-controlled New York City. He also composed two letters in English to his family written during his exile, one likely directed to his eldest son, Ezekiel, and the other to his wife, whose age indicates that she, like her husband, learned English without having been educated in that language in school.[29]

Like Roelof Josiah Eltinge, his elder kinsman Colonel Abraham Hasbrouck preferred English. Born in 1707, Hasbrouck began to keep a personal diary in approximately 1735, the year he relocated from his farm in Guilford (a separate patent abutting New Paltz) to Kingston to begin a second career as a merchant. Soon after, he became the representative from Ulster County to the Assembly, as had his grandfather before him. As a man rising in social status, he embraced the language of political power in the colony, precociously choosing to compose his diary entirely in English. He recorded both mundane facts such as weather, as well as family history and memorials to departed loved ones, suggesting that he kept this diary for himself as well as for succeeding generations. Abraham likely chose English because he anticipated that it would be the primary language of the future, even though it had yet to be utilized in the school. Likewise, all of the other surviving documents that Abraham Hasbrouck produced, including a 1748 letter to a brother-in-law, are in English. A few other scattered letters in English survive written by and for patentee descendants, with the earliest possibly being 1753, but given the limited examples of this type of evidence, and the fact that the analysis of each document requires a host of qualifications (author, audience, purpose, date/dates of composition), any conclusions would be a bit suspect.[30]

In spite of the incremental transition from Dutch to English that spanned a century and required the active participation of generations of patentee community members, the linguistic environment was still complex even at the turn of the nineteenth century, but not for much longer. How complex it was can be attested to by the experience of an enslaved African-American woman who began her life with the name Isabella. Isabella was born in approximately 1797 to an enslaved couple, Betsey and James Baumfree, who were owned by Johannes Hardenbergh III (1729–1799) in Rosendale, New York, immediately north of New Paltz. The Hardenbergh family was one of the wealthiest and most illustrious families in the area. Johannes III was the grandson of Major Johannes Hardenbergh Sr., one of the patentees of the approximately two-million-acre Hardenbergh Patent granted by the Queen in 1708. He was also the son of Colonel Johannes Hardenbergh Jr., who was a representative to the colonial assembly from 1743 to 1750, a member of the first Provincial Congress, and a member of the state legislature in 1781–1782. The mother of Johannes III was Maria DuBois Hardenbergh (b. 1706), the granddaughter of a number of New Paltz founders, including Louis DuBois and Abraham Hasbrouck. The wife of Johannes III, Maria LeFevre (b. 1732), was also a patentee descendant like himself.

Many slaves in Ulster County such as the Baumfrees lived in the domestic structures of their owners, but Johannes III had given Isabella and her family a separate structure near the big house. They lost this level of privacy when Johannes died in 1799, whereupon the ownership of Isabella and her family was transferred to his son Charles (1765–1806), who moved the Baumfrees into his own house, where also lived Charles's wife, Annetje LeFevre Hardenbergh. Charles lived only a few years longer, and in order to settle his estate, Isabella was sent to the auction block. The auction block was surely a terrifying place for any enslaved person, but that was not the end of Isabella's suffering. The couple that purchased Isabella, the English-speaking Mr. and Mrs. Neely of Kingston, were unable to communicate with her, as they did not share the same language. Isabella's only language was Dutch, and while Mr. Neely could at least understand that language which was not his own, he could not speak it. Mrs. Neely did not even possess that level of fluency, and she became enraged with Isabella for her lack of comprehension of the English language. Isabella's not being able to understand her new master and mistress resulted in repeated violent and dehumanizing beatings, which left her physically and emotionally scarred throughout her life. Isabella eventually began to grasp some English during the few years that the Neelys owned her, but she never achieved even reasonable fluency in their household. As a result, when the Dutch-speaking Martinus Schryver offered to purchase her, she eagerly embraced the opportunity of escaping the Neelys' violent household. Schryver owned Isabella for only about two years, as in 1810, she was sold once again, this time to John Dumont of New Paltz. In his household she continued her slow progress towards English fluency. She eventually did manage to master spoken English, but she never lost her Afro-Dutch roots, as her English would continue to be inflected by a Dutch accent throughout her long life as the great orator, abolitionist, and women's rights activist, Sojourner Truth.[31]

That Sojourner Truth had not learned English in the household of her birth says a great deal about the choice of language in the homes of patentee descendants such as Charles and Annetje (LeFevre) Hardenbergh. Given the provincial importance of Charles's family, it would have been impossible for him not to have been fluent in English. Annetje would have been so as well, as she was presumably educated in New Paltz when the language of instruction was English. She was also of that generation that asked Rev. Stephen Goetschius to sometimes conduct church services in English, a request which he obliged. But if Isabella/Sojourner had not picked up any English by the time she was sold to the Neelys, it must have been that Dutch was the spoken language of her owners in a domestic setting, even though they were using English in more public arenas. William Strickland, who traveled through the region in 1794–1795, was therefore incorrect when he said that Dutch was spoken only by "some old people chiefly residing in retired and unfrequented places," as that certainly did not describe either the Hardenberghs or the Kingston–New Paltz region of Ulster County, where wealthy patentee descendants in the prime of their lives continued to use Dutch, but not exclusively. Mr. Strickland may not have been aware of this because he had not been privy to either domestic communications or church services. Mr. Strickland's comments were therefore premature, but what he said soon did come to pass, if we are to trust Ralph LeFevre. The "old people" of whom he spoke, who were using Dutch in the 1850s when they did not want the young folk like LeFevre himself to understand what they were saying, would have included the younger members of Annetje LeFevre Hardenbergh's generation and the older members of that of her children's. They would be the last to speak Dutch, and they may not have even been able to read it. The use of the Dutch language would therefore pass away with them.[32]

A Linguistically Creolized Community

If the full breadth of the evidence concerning language use is considered, the complexity of the linguistic environment comes into focus. First, not surprisingly, English was the language of government and the law from the very beginning of the village. Only in wills was there some degree of linguistic flexibility, but even then, many soon adopted English even without a legal compunction to do so. In communal institutions outside of those grounded in the provincial government—the church and the school—the patentees and their children preserved the French language for a bit over fifty years. That they preserved it so long was due primarily to necessity, as they were forced to be fully responsible for their religious lives throughout the first three decades of the eighteenth century, due to the fact that they lacked ministerial leadership. As the language of religion and the books that supported it had been French, they simply retained that which had been bequeathed to them. They facilitated the use of French in their spiritual lives through French language instruction in school. Even so, they began to offer Dutch services in the late 1720s, and when they hired a Dutch minister in the 1730s, their first in minister in many years, they began to purchase and use Dutch Bibles and prayer books. Outside of the church and school, French was used in only rare instances beyond the1730s, and only in personal communications and records produced by and for a few members of the second generation.

In the second quarter of the eighteenth century, Dutch not only became the language of the church and the school, but also the language of business and genealogy, and it remained alive in the community into the early nineteenth century. Yet, as the patentee descendants increased their use of Dutch, they never did so in a stable fashion. Some adaptable individuals began to incorporate English into their everyday lives even as early as the second quarter of the eighteenth century, particularly in business. This trend increased over the third quarter of the century, while at the same time, some also began to use English in the records of their families. In both cases, they did so entirely by choice. It was also in the third quarter of the century that the community began to have their children educated in English, hiring a bilingual schoolmaster to do so. This choice was probably pragmatically motivated, as these children would need to be prepared for native English speakers as their future pastors. After English overtook Dutch in both business affairs and formal education, the community began to increasingly diminish the use of Dutch in the church, eventually abandoning it in 1817.

If the oldest members of the congregation in 1817, who were born perhaps before 1750, were willing to accept this shift, they must have been fluent in more than one language, probably having become so as children, just as their parents had been. This suggests that the transitions from French to Dutch and Dutch to English in communal affairs were reactions to linguistic shifts that had already been occurring in everyday life rather than precursors of change. Furthermore, the choices to preserve and not to preserve a particular language seem to have been pragmatically driven rather than statements of ethnocultural identity, which again suggests that ethnocultural rigidity was generally unnecessary and undesirable.

It is not particularly surprising that the generations that followed the founders did not perpetuate French in a significant manner, given that the descendants of the Walloon founders lived in a sea of non-French speakers. However, French theoretically could have survived longer than it did, if the desire to perpetuate it existed. It did not. On their own volition, the descendants chose to let their use of the French language drift into the past. It is also quite logical that when the French language was abandoned, Dutch became the primary local language, given the regional ethnic environment. Still, some developed significant English skills quite early in the history of the community, particularly those individuals who had connections beyond the local, who provided necessary services to the New Paltz farmers who were engaged in a provincial economy. What is perhaps surprising, however, is that in or by the third quarter of the eighteenth century, the community clearly accepted the English language in casual business transactions, regardless of one's ethnic heritage. This transition was neither necessary nor required. It was a question of choice, and as such, it shows a general lack of resistance to things English. Still, while they accepted English in business, they simultaneously preserved Dutch in church for a half a century longer, at least in part, resulting in the continuation of a creolized linguistic environment. In the end, patentee descendants ultimately chose to fully adopt English even though nothing had prevented them from perpetuating the use of the Dutch language in their community, if not forever, at least for a longer time. In short, the choice of language was constantly shifting throughout the long eighteenth century, as the members of the New Paltz community intentionally created a linguistically creolized environment that lasted for almost 150 years, the decline of which was not a necessity, nor was it forced.

The choices members of the patentee families made in their language, architecture, and gender ideals created a fluidly shifting creolized environment throughout the long eighteenth century. During that time, no one experienced ethnic monoculturalism. They simply could not isolate themselves from other cultures, but neither did they try to. For the founders, Dutchness was all around them, but neither they nor their children ever perceived it as oppressive or aggressive. Neither did they experience English culture as aggressive, even if it was to some extent forced upon them. As a result, they met neither English nor Dutch culture with resistance. They did not feel the need to resist, as they remained substantially in control of their culture and society. The patentees initially owned the town, which gave them the power to govern it. That initial ownership also gave their heirs the power to choose whether to allow those of other ethnicities into their community, by giving them access to land and perhaps allowing them into the governing process. They indeed chose to rent and sell land to ethnic "others," but they did so on their own terms and in their own ways. They even let them into their church and into their government. Their collective wealth allowed for such control.

Neither did the heirs of the patentees isolate themselves from either "Dutch" or English people in the deepest of relationships, those of the family. The children and grandchildren of the patentees soon began to marry into the local "Dutch" population, producing children who were "Dutch" themselves. Some even began to marry those who were not "Dutch." Nevertheless, over time, the entire patentee community embraced Englishness and abandoned Dutchness, but they did so slowly and incrementally. Through these ethnocultural changes, the descendants of the Walloons eventually became Anglo-Americans, but that intensely complex and fluid process took nearly a century and a half to complete. But to focus upon the totality of that lengthy process is to look at the experience from the outside looking in, rather than from the perspective of those who lived it. The end of the process as it unfolded was not preordained, and it was the choices the descendants of the founders made that ultimately turned them into Anglo-Americans. Theirs was a creolized environment, where flexibility and ethnocultural complexity was a way of life—a way of life that theoretically could have continued indefinitely, or at least much longer than it did.

The great majority accepted and preserved this creolized way of life, even if they continued to allow it to fluidly change. A few others, however, were not so sanguine about the future, if that future might mean that their community might become less and less Dutch and therefore more and more Anglo-American. A few ethnocultural conservatives would try to place the brakes on ethnocultural change and, in doing so, tore their community apart. In the end, all that those few conservatives could do was marginalize themselves, proving that ethnocultural rigidity could never gain a permanent foothold in eighteenth-century New Paltz. It is to that story of division that we now turn.

Chapter 5

SCHISM

Ecclesiastical Conflict in a Creolized Community

In his final years, Hendricus DuBois (1710–1780) worshipped alone on Sundays in an empty Dutch Reformed church that stood near his home in New Paltz, New York. The church was not old, having been constructed only in 1766 to serve a small, newly formed congregation, the Second Church of New Paltz. That congregation had seceded from the First Church (also Dutch Reformed) whose members were part of a movement to separate the New World Dutch Church from its subordination to the Classis of Amsterdam, the ecclesiastical governing body that claimed oversight of the denomination's colonial congregations and ministers. After much internal strife, the Dutch Reformed Church in America did confirm its independence with the approval of the Amsterdam church polity in 1772, but it was several years before the New Paltz schismatics again found themselves in the bosom of their village's original congregation. Hendricus, a "pertinacious and bitter man," however, never returned. Even after his death in 1780, his spirit supposedly haunted the church at night, possibly raising his ethereal voice in communion with the mysterious calls of his neighbors, the owls, who were said to congregate around the nearly abandoned, forlorn structure. Locals even warned neighborhood children that Hendricus's ghost would throw unsuspecting passersby into the nearby Wallkill if they attempted to traverse his posthumous home. Of course the folk story was just that, a story, but it nevertheless tells of how Hendricus's refusal to accept change had made him a subject of community ridicule, making him a lonely man in life—and in death. For an ethnocultural conservative such as Hendricus, it is no wonder that his soul was not, as he might have said, "In Den Heeren Ontslapen."—"In the Lord Asleep."[1]

Hendricus's decision to depart from the village's congregation in 1765 had little direct connection to the ecclesiastical controversy that centered around the relationship between the colonial congregations and the Classis of Amsterdam and the authority of the latter over the former, which came to be known as the Coetus-Conferentie dispute. It is difficult even to imagine that Hendricus would have much cared about that relationship from an ecclesiastical perspective, since the New Paltz congregation had only become a Dutch Reformed Church twelve years earlier in 1753. Previous to that date, it had been an independent congregation of the Walloon Reformed Church. Nevertheless, the controversy in the religious sphere brought to the fore potential or latent ethnocultural conflict, something that had never before arisen in the community. This was the case because the connection between the American

Dutch Reformed congregations and an Old World classis represented the last bond with the origin and source of Dutchness, a bond that helped to anchor the Dutch element in a creolized culture that was continuing to tip towards Anglo-Americanness. That was a bond that an ethnoculturally rigid man such as Hendricus aimed to preserve. He nevertheless did so in vain. His goals came into conflict with those of the Anglicizers who worked to break that bond, as well as those who simply did not need to tie themselves to the fatherland as a means of preserving their creolized culture as it continued to sinuously change.

While the Coetus-Conferentie dispute was a defining event in the experience of eighteenth-century Dutch Americans, it remains only partially understood. What scholars have argued simply does not apply to the New Paltz experience. The long-standing interpretation is that the conflict substantially represented a contest between pietism and orthodoxy within the context of the Great Awakening, an event heavily influenced by socioeconomic stress and, for Dutch-Americans, ethnocultural marginalization within an English colony. The work of Randall Balmer represents this view of the religious dispute in its strongest form, as he argues that the middling and lower class Dutch were prone to accept the supposed anti-establishment and anti-authoritarian stance of pietistic ministers as a result of their long experience of social and cultural dislocation and alienation. This argument suggests that those who wished to advance pietism sought greater freedom from Amsterdam, a center of orthodoxy, in order to control doctrine, ministerial education, and ordination. Linked to the pietistic movement was a spirit of ecumenism that supposedly supported the Anglicization of the Dutch population, furthering a process that had been rapidly advancing by the middle of the eighteenth century. According to this interpretation, ethnocultural change was not at the heart of the religious dispute for pietists, but it nevertheless served to encourage such change. For their opponents, the traditionalists, both pietism *and* ethnocultural declension were to be resisted through continued subordination to Amsterdam. According to this formulation, those that supported pietism and Americanization of the church formed the Coetus party, while the orthodox and the ethnoculturally conservative comprised the Conferentie faction.[2]

This interpretation simply does not apply to the New Paltz experience. Although the Coetus-Conferentie dispute resulted in a local schism, there was no contest over theology and/or "style of faith," as pietism was embraced by all involved in the local dispute. Neither had the patentee community ever faced alienation, marginalization, or socioeconomic stress that might have led them to accept the pietism of the Great Awakening. This does not necessarily suggest that Balmer's interpretation is inaccurate, but it does suggest that such an interpretation cannot be universally applied.

Recently, however, Dirk Mouw has forcefully argued that Balmer's interpretation of the ecclesiastical controversy is simply untenable. Mouw argues that those on both sides of the dispute sought to reinforce the Dutch Reformed Church in an Anglo-American environment, although the two factions advocated for different means of doing so. Mouw further maintains that the controversy was grounded in an essentially Dutch cultural milieu, with both sides aiming to reinforce ethnocultural Dutchness and identity within a politically and culturally antagonistic Anglo-American world. In other words, he argues that those on both sides of the controversy—which essentially comprised all Dutch Americans in one way or another—aimed to resist ethnocultural change. This interpretation does not reflect the New Paltz experience either, as the patentee community had never experienced Anglo-American culture as antagonistic and had never met it with resistance. That is except for a small faction that formed in the 1760s, a faction that ultimately failed to forestall continued ethnocultural change.[3]

Although neither Mouw's nor Balmer's interpretation accurately reflects what occurred in New Paltz, their suggestion that ethnocultural expression and religious institutions intersected in the context of the Coetus-Conferentie dispute does provide a context through which the New Paltz experience can be explored. This is far from surprising, given that the church remained the only institution that could facilitate the preservation of Dutchness in eighteenth-century New York, as Joyce Goodfriend and Firth Fabend have suggested. As the church could be both a center of ethnocultural expression and a tool of identity formation, it could also be a cultural space for ethnocultural conflict. In New Paltz, the Coetus-Conferentie dispute was indeed not about religion at all. Rather, it represents the one time any of the patentee descendants attempted to stop the creolization process. They nevertheless failed in their bid to halt change, and their failure reveals how ethnocultural rigidity was a negligible force in a community whose culture had been changing ever since its founders had landed on the American shores.[4]

From Walloon Reformed to Dutch Reformed: The Transformation of the New Palz Church

The process by which the independent Walloon congregation of New Paltz became a congregation of the Dutch Reformed Church, and therefore involved in the Coetus-Conferentie dispute, was a rocky one, involving two highly controversial ministers, Johannes van Driessen and Johannes Henricus Goetschius. Although Paula Carlo has argued that the congregation accepted such outsiders as a statement of their congregational and ethnic independence, this was not the case. Rather, as an independent congregation without access to the support of an international ecclesiastical network, the congregation of New Paltz had to take whom they could get. This is not to suggest that the congregation did not value and respect those whom they did attract. They were particularly thankful for the services of Goetschius, a pietistic minister who led the congregation down the path of spiritual rebirth. That was a path that future members of both the Coetus and Conferentie in New Paltz willingly and gratefully followed.[5]

As discussed previously, the Walloon Reformed congregation of New Paltz was established in 1683 when the patentee families were able to secure the services of a French-speaking Protestant minister, the Rev. Pierre Daillé, who had recently fled France in response to revived persecution of the Huguenots. Between 1683 and 1700, however, the congregation received only occasional ministerial visits, first from Daillé and later from the Rev. David de Bonrepos, another of the small number of French Protestant ministers in the northern colonies. Even though the congregation could not secure French ministerial leadership after 1700, they did not dispense with local worship. In fact, they apparently desired it so greatly that they wanted to give it a permanent home, by funding and constructing a substantial stone church beginning in 1718. Without a minister, they continued to read printed sermons during Sunday worship, as they often had during the brief period of occasional French clerical leadership. For sacramental observances, New Paltz residents generally traveled to Kingston, where some also chose to be received as members.[6]

One wonders whether the patentee families constructed a stone church in hopes of attracting a minister, as the structure itself was a demonstration of the community's wealth. That in turn might have convinced a potential minister that they actually could support him, which was something many communities in the region were unable to do. They finally did secure ministerial services by March 1731, when the controversial domine Rev. Johannes van Driessen agreed to preach and offer the sacraments three or four times a year. They formally called him to serve in 1733. The presence of a minister made it possible for the New Paltz congregation to elect and install a new consistory, making their church once again fully functional, a situation that had not existed since the opening years of the century. While the New Paltz congregation was pleased with van Driessen, they ultimately discovered that he was a man of questionable credentials and morals, a situation that created local, regional, and even transatlantic tensions that lasted for decades.[7]

Johannes van Driessen first pursued ordination from the Classis of Amsterdam in 1719. Classis, however, denied him promotion to the ministry, due in part to his extremely poor performance at his examinations. Worse yet, Classis discovered in the course of his examinations that he had submitted forged certificates from two professors at the University of Groningen. As a result, Classis reprimanded him and recommended that he never again seek ordination. Van Driessen later migrated to North America, where he found his brother, Rev. Petrus van Driessen of Albany, supportive of his career in the church. The manor lord Robert Livingston also supported Johannes van Driessen, whose services he hoped to secure for his manor. Petrus encouraged his brother, Johannes, to seek ordination from the Presbytery in Philadelphia, but Livingston recommended that he turn to the Congregational ministers at Yale instead. He chose to follow Livingston's suggestions and was ordained by the Congregationalists in 1727, again making use of his fraudulent documents. Livingston then encouraged the Dutch Reformed congregations of Claverack and Kinderhook to extend a call to van Driessen, although Livingston stipulated that van Driessen must live directly on his manor. The congregations of Claverack and Kinderhook objected to such a requirement, so Livingston chose to step aside, allowing Claverack and Kinderhook alone to call the new minister. He was then installed in the two congregations by his brother. While members of the Kinderhook congregation were satisfied with his behavior and performance, Claverack soon dismissed him for his "unchristian life and behavior," according to an opponent, Rev. Petrus Vas of Kingston. New York ministers Gualtherus DuBois, Vincentius Antonides, and Henricus Boel likewise reported to Classis that van Driessen lived a "grossly offensive life." What precisely concerned them was not stated in the records, but his mere presence began to send shockwaves through the congregations in the region.[8]

Even if van Driessen's moral reputation had not been tarnished and his educational certificates had been legitimate, he would have remained controversial for both ecclesiastical and economic reasons. The principal reason for this was that the Classis of Amsterdam did not consider ordination by the Congregationalists sufficient for service within the Dutch Reformed Church. According to the ecclesiastical structure of the Dutch Reformed Church, the authority to examine and ordain ministerial candidates for the denomination lay with a classis, a regional body consisting of ministers and representatives from the congregational consistories within the region. By the late 1620s, the Classis of Amsterdam had claimed and exerted the primary control over colonial congregations throughout the world, maintaining that ministerial candidates in the colonies had to be ordained in Amsterdam. The Classis of Amsterdam nevertheless did reserve the right to delegate this authority to colonial Dutch Reformed ministers, but only in specific instances. Most senior ministers in the colonies likewise believed that ordination by a classis was required, but the power of the Classis of Amsterdam in the colonies was neither absolute in theory nor practice. This was the case because the colonial congregations had never been formally incorporated into the Classis of Amsterdam, nor into any other classis for that matter. As a result, it was not uncommon for both ordained and lay members of the Dutch Reformed congregations in North America to act outside of classical authority, as did Petrus van Driessen and the congregations of Claverack and Kinderhook. Neither was it uncommon for North American participants in Dutch Reformed congregations to ignore the guidance and opinion of the Classis of Amsterdam when offered. However, when colonial ministers and congregations acted against the wishes of Classis, conflict with other colonial ministers and church members was often the result.[9]

One minister who strenuously opposed Johannes van Driessen was Rev. Petrus Vas of Kingston. While Vas believed that van Driessen's ordination by the "Independents" of New Haven did not make him a lawful minister in the Dutch Reformed Church, van Driessen posed an even greater problem because he challenged Vas directly by injecting himself into the Kingston church. He did so without the approval of Vas as the settled minister, which was a clear offense against Dutch Reformed Church order. Even more problematic for Vas was that some Kingston church members apparently even welcomed van Driessen. Perhaps the most troubling issue for Vas was van Driessen's attempt to infiltrate the congregations in other Ulster County congregations, including New Paltz, the consistory of which eventually called him to be their settled minister. The Kingston minister's particular concern was that his ability to ensure his own income would be adversely affected if van Driessen was allowed to serve in the region. Vas claimed that Kingston "with all the surrounding villages in this our County of Ulster, as one body," including New Paltz, "have for some time past, had one pastor and teacher. For his support we have combined together and paid his salary, each locality according to its ability." If Vas acquiesced to van Driessen's serving in local congregations, Vas's livelihood would be at stake.[10]

Vas and his consistory were so troubled by the presence of van Driessen in their midst that they held a hearing in Kingston in an attempt to discredit both him and his brother. According to those who opposed van Driessen, that meeting became so contentious that van Driessen partisans from Kingston and nearby congregations "even threatened to drag certain members of the [Kingston] Consistory through the church by their hair." Vas went even further by banning New Paltz church members who supported van Driessen from participating in the Lord's Supper in Kingston, an act which New Paltz believed was inappropriate and illegal according to church order.[11]

The New Paltz congregation objected to Vas's interpretation and Kingston's pretended authority, maintaining that they were independent not only of Kingston but of the Dutch Reformed Church as a whole. In a later letter to the Classis of Amsterdam, the New Paltz congregation remarked that it was an independent "Reformed Walloon Church" not "under the jurisdiction of any other Dutch Church." They rightly claimed that they had the authority to accept the advice of any Protestant pastor, including that of Petrus van Driessen, who claimed that the ordination of his brother, Johannes, was legitimate. They later "assert[ed] that they were ignorant of the fact that John van Driessen was not a lawful minister." Neither were they aware of any unacceptable personal behavior on his part because his "conduct in these regions had not yet then become open to remarks." New Paltz stated simply that they accepted van Driessen because they "were desirous of having services at the Paltz." New Paltz's comments were perhaps a bit disingenuous. Even if New Paltz was unaware of the controversy surrounding van Driessen when he first came to the village in early 1731, there is no way they could have continued to have remained ignorant of his questionable credentials and reputation. Nevertheless, as the New Paltz congregation was independent of both Kingston and Classis, whether other Dutch Reformed ministers or Classis approved of van Driessen as a legal minister was irrelevant, since New Paltz had the authority to accept whomever they judged to be legitimate and morally acceptable. In short, New Paltz in no way sought van Driessen's services because he was an outsider, as Paula Carlo has argued, but because he was available.[12]

Van Driessen departed for New Jersey in 1736. Vas responded by removing the ban on all those in New Paltz who would repudiate van Driessen, allowing them back into the life of the Kingston church. The conflict over van Driessen, however, was far from over. It percolated up once again in the late 1740s when another controversial minister, the pietist Rev. Johannes Henricus Goetschius, offered his services to New Paltz.[13]

Rev. Johannes Henricus Goetschius (1718–1774), the son of the Rev. Moritz Goetschi (1686–1735), emigrated with his family from Switzerland to Pennsylvania in 1735 when he was seventeen. The elder Goetschi had organized a group of four hundred Swiss who intended to migrate to the Carolinas by way of Rotterdam, but resources were unavailable to support the journey. Goetschi was nevertheless able to secure payment from the States General to immigrate to Pennsylvania with his family alone, so that he could gather information on the German Reformed churches in the colony for the Synods of North and South Holland. The Synod of South Holland desired such information because it had agreed to provide support to the colonial German Reformed congregations in response to a 1728 request from the consistory of Heidelberg, which hoped but was unable to look after the American congregations. Unfortunately for both the Synod of South Holland and Goetschi, he was never able to provide that information, as he died the day after his ship docked in Philadelphia.[14]

According to the younger Goetschius, the German Reformed congregations in Pennsylvania had believed that his father had been sent to them as their minister, such that his death represented a substantial blow. In their need, they turned to Moritz's unordained son, Johannes, who soon began preaching and catechizing in a number of German Reformed congregations in and around Philadelphia. In order to further his ministry, he turned to the Presbyterian Synod in Philadelphia for ordination in 1737, as there was no German Reformed ecclesiastical body in the colony that possessed the right to ordain. The Synod referred him to the Presbytery of Philadelphia for examination. While the Presbytery did find him to be "well skilled in the learned languages," they found his general academic and divinity training lacking, so they declined to ordain him. They did not discourage him in his quest for ordination, however, suggesting that he place himself under the tutelage of another minister. The Presbytery also noted that he could continue to preach in the nearby German Reformed congregations, who desperately desired his services.[15]

Goetschius soon gave up his ministry and undertook additional studies in Neshaminy, Pennsylvania, with Rev. Petrus Hendricus Dorsius. Dorsius had been ordained in 1737 by the University of Groningen—the only non-classical authority in the Netherlands that possessed the right to ordain—so that he could serve Dutch Reformed congregations in Pennsylvania, which had been seeking ministerial services for some time. Goetschius was soon called by four united Dutch Reformed congregations in Queens County, Long Island, in October 1740, although his service was not slated to commence until he had completed his studies with Dorsius. Six months later, on April 7, 1741, Dorsius, along with the Revs. Theodorus Frelinghuysen Sr. and William Tennant, ordained Goetschius. He was then installed in the Queens County congregations by Rev. Bernardus Freerman (or Freeman), a Dutch Reformed minister ordained by the Classis of Lingen, who had been serving on Long Island since 1705.[16]

Dorsius's ordination of Goetschius was ecclesiastically questionable, since, with the exception of the University of Groningen, only a classis could ordain new ministers. A classis could, however, authorize other minsters to do so in its place. Dorsius claimed this right; and it is possible that he did so because he truly believed that he had been authorized to ordain by the Synod of South Holland, the Classis of Schieland at Rotterdam, or the University of Groningen. He also might have believed that he had the right to ordain because his charge lay outside of any classis. Several influential colonial ministers first accepted Dorsius's claim. Even the Classis of Amsterdam initially believed that it was possible that Dorsius had the authority to ordain. Classis, however, ultimately came to the conclusion that Dorsius had never been authorized to examine and ordain candidates for the ministry, such that his ordaining of Goetschius was illegitimate.[17]

News that the Classis of Amsterdam considered Goetschius's ordination invalid reached his congregations on Long Island in the fall of 1742. This information motivated his consistory to seek advice from the ministers and consistories in New York City and Kings County, Long Island, as to whether their minister's ordination was indeed invalid, and if so, what could be done to rectify the situation. After hearing testimony from Goetschius, the Revs. DuBois, Antonides, and Arondeus (along with members of their consistories) determined that he had not been legally ordained, and ordered that he desist from preaching and administering the sacraments. Goetschius chose to ignore their advice and continue his service.[18]

Goetschius did not follow the direction of the ad hoc committee of colonial ministers not because he resisted "high-church authority," as Randall Balmer argues, but simply because the committee had no formal authority. According to church order, such advice could only be controlling if provided by a classis, or by a committee authorized by classis, such that the opinion of any informally organized committee was nothing more than advisory. Nevertheless, ignoring the opinion of these more-senior ministers was extremely unwise, as they expected that Goetschius would defer to them even if they could not compel him to do so. Goetschius chose to ignore them in no uncertain terms. He aggressively remarked that he felt justified in doing so because the committee did not provide "proof obvious to us that your Reverences have any authority to interfere with me in my duties and services . . . and to set yourselves up as judges." The committee interpreted his unwillingness to follow their directive as representing his "inten[t not] to obey any ecclesiastical rules whatever," but this was far from the case. He simply believed that the legitimacy of his ordination was beyond question and that the committee was in error. In fact, he explicitly informed the ad hoc committee that he was ready and willing to follow the directives of the Classis of Amsterdam, provided that Classis "would be pleased to take [him] as a member under its protection." If so, then he was willing to subordinate himself not only to Classis but to the committee as well, provided that the latter "receive[d] the authority to act." Until that time, he "[did] not recognize you as a Committee, nor as judges, nor as mediators," which, in fact, was a decidedly legitimate position according to standard church order.[19]

Goetschius's refusal to defer to the more senior ministers initiated an extremely heated controversy that lasted six years, resulting in almost irreconcilable differences in his congregations, as well as great misery for himself. Ultimately, that dispute came to encompass issues of ecclesiastical order, Goetschius's pietism, interpersonal vitriol, alleged moral turpitude, vengeful behavior on the part of God-fearing Christians, and Goetschius's own commitment to his sacred duty; but it all began with the questionable status of his ordination. Goetschius ultimately did come to accept the position of his opponents and the Classis of Amsterdam that his ordination by Dorsius was unauthorized and therefore illegitimate. Goestchius also came to regard the Classis of Amsterdam alone as possessing formal authority over the American congregations (even though such a position was certainly not beyond debate). In such a light, Goetschius humbly informed Classis that "I feel myself most strongly bound to agree with everything which your High Revs. may be pleased to advise my humble self, concerning either my ordination or my ministry." With Goetschius's willing cooperation, Classis transformed what had been an ad hoc committee into a formal one, granting it the authority to investigate the dispute and inform Classis of its findings. After the committee gathered further evidence and submitted it to Classis, Classis formally determined that Goetschius would have to undergo examination and ordination once again. He did so without complaint. As the controversy moved towards resolution, Classis nevertheless came to the sad conclusion that the divisions on Long Island were such that Goetschius could no longer effectively serve them. Classis therefore recommended that he seek a new call. One soon came from Hackensack, New Jersey. Goestchius was subsequently examined, ordained, and then installed in his new charge in September 1748.[20]

Although Goetschius had finally been legitimized as a minister in the Dutch Reformed fold and placed himself under the authority of the Classis of Amsterdam, his painful experience apparently caused him to remain skeptical of ministers who claimed authority beyond what he believed was ecclesiastically legitimate. As a result, religious conflict once again burst forth in Ulster County when some members of the New Paltz congregation invited him to come and preach to them in 1749. However, the revived local controversy had nothing to do with New Paltz's desire to seek ministers on the fringe, as Paula Carlo has argued. If they did have such a desire, they would not even have accepted Goetschius, as he had already become part of the Dutch Reformed ecclesiastical establishment, even if his theology was more pietistic than that of some of his ministerial peers. New Paltz simply lacked the services of a minister, and if Goetschius was willing to help them, the New Paltz congregation was willing to accept his ministry. As an independent Walloon congregation, it was entirely within their purview to do so.

In preparation for his ministerial visit to New Paltz, Goetschius traveled to Kingston in June 1749 to inform the community's Dutch Reformed minister, Rev. G. W. Mancius, that he intended to preach at New Paltz. This angered Mancius exceedingly, as he maintained the position of his predecessor, Rev. Vas, that New Paltz was part of the Kingston congregation. Mancius therefore informed Goetschius that he could not preach in New Paltz without his approval. Goetschius also learned from Mancius that Vas had disciplined church members from New Paltz for accepting Johannes van Driessen as their minister and for allowing him to install a consistory. Mancius also made Goetschius aware that he maintained Vas's ban on those who refused to repudiate van Driessen. For Goetschius, this was not the first time that he had come into conflict with colonial Dutch Reformed ministers who attempted to expand their authority beyond that which church order allowed. With his nerves still raw from his struggles on Long Island, Goetschius angrily retorted that the Kingston consistory had no right to discipline church members of an independent New Paltz congregation. He further maintained that the consistory installed by van Driessen was "as lawful as that of any regular, orthodox, Dutch Church." In response to Goetschius's complaints, Mancius wrote to both Classis and a loose organization of colonial Dutch Reformed ministers called the "Coetus" (the organization of which is discussed below), complaining of the actions of the New Paltz congregation, once again arguing that New Paltz was not independent of Kingston and thus subject to the discipline imposed by the Kingston consistory.[21]

The ministers of the Coetus referred the question as to the relationship between New Paltz and Kingston to Rev. J. C. Fryenmoet, from the nearby congregation of Minisink. The Coetus authorized Fryenmoet to investigate the situation and install a new consistory if he determined that New Paltz was indeed independent of Kingston. If he did install a consistory, the congregation would be placed on a firm ecclesiastical footing. Fryenmoet traveled to New Paltz to take testimony from Elder Samuel Bevier and Daniel Hasbrouck as to the history of the relationship between the New Paltz and Kingston congregations. They argued to Fryenmoet that the New Paltz church "as a French Reformed Church, had always been accustomed to be provided with a minister and consistory of its own," and that Goetschius was correct in accepting the consistory established by van Driessen as "lawful." "Therefore," Bevier and Hasbrouck reported, "we are of opinion that the conclusion of Rev. Mancius is wrong. From the foregoing explanations it clearly appears that the Paltz was always a Church and congregation by itself and so independent of Kingston." Fryenmoet duly agreed with this interpretation and installed a new consistory, which therefore had the right to accept the services of Goetschius or any other legal minister. From the perspective of New Paltz, Fryenmoet's decision obviated the discipline that Kingston had illegitimately imposed upon those church members who had not repudiated van Driessen. Mancius nevertheless continued to maintain his position to Classis, at least temporarily. He also noted that Kingston was willing to consider New Paltz independent, as long as the separation was effected according to church order.[22]

While Classis acknowledged the reasonability of Mancius's interpretation of the historic relationship between his church and that of New Paltz, they thought it appropriate to give New Paltz the opportunity to respond directly to Mancius's assertions. After further communications between Kingston, New Paltz, and Classis, Classis constructed a solution aimed to establish peaceful relations between the two communities without seeming to take sides. Classis precisely acknowledged neither that New Paltz was nor was not historically part of the Kingston church, arguing simply that it would be more practical if the two congregations be separated due to distance. That division was possible because New Paltz, unlike many other communities, had the financial means to support its own minister. In other words, since a separate future made better sense, the past situation was essentially moot. Classis also acknowledged that even though adherence to van Driessen normally would be grounds for censure, New Paltz church members apparently followed him not out of some desire "to embrace or give encouragement to some heresy, but rather from the conviction that New Paltz ought to be recognized as an independent church."[23]

Based on this finding, Classis determined that the discipline that Kingston had placed on New Paltz was inappropriate, although to some extent, that was beside the point. As the churches were now held to be separate, any discipline could be amicably set aside, provided that the New Paltz church members publicly agreed to accept the Heidelberg Catechism, the Netherlands Confession of Faith, and the Church Order. If they chose to do so, they would transform their independent Walloon congregation into an orthodox congregation of the Dutch Reformed Church. Rev. Goetschius recommended that they do so, in spite of his previous struggles with Classis. The members of the New Paltz congregation were happy to follow what Goetschius advised, as he was "the man who took pity on us in our misery, and whom, next to God, we have to thank, for the deliverance thus far brought us." In a December 10, 1751, letter, the New Paltz congregation informed Classis that they intended to do as Classis advised, remarking that "the consistory of the Reformed Walloon church at New Paltz, having a short time ago placed ourselves under the direction of the Rev. Coetus at New York, and so under that of your Reverences." This relationship was further confirmed when they called Barent Vrooman to be their domine. Vrooman, a native of Schenectady, subsequently traveled to the Netherlands for examination and ordination by the Classis of Amsterdam, which represented the most orthodox of paths for colonial ministers. Classis ordained him in July 1752, and he was installed in the New Paltz congregation in August 1753. Several days later, the church members made public note of their acceptance of the tenets and order of the Dutch Reformed Church. Vrooman, however, served New Paltz only a short time, as by March 1754, he had relocated to Schenectady to serve the congregation there.[24]

Not only did Goetschius bring the New Paltz congregation into the fold of the Dutch Reformed Church, but his sporadic service in the years between 1749 and 1754 initiated a dramatic spiritual awakening. Somewhat atypically, the awakening in New Paltz united rather than divided the community, which set its experience apart from the many American congregations that experienced conflict during the era of the Great Awakening. Goetschius's fiercely pietistic preaching probably first graced the New Paltz pulpit on June 4, 1749, and he began to offer the Lord's Supper by April 1750. From that point on, Goetschius ushered in many new members who had experienced the new birth. The first group joined in April 1751, when he accepted eighteen new members into the New Paltz congregation, seventeen by confession of faith, which was required of them because they had not previously been members of any other Reformed congregation. Such a large number of new members might have reflected a backlog, as no one had joined the church since 1736. However, a spirit of revival seems to have persisted in the community, as eight more individuals joined on December 8, 1751, and eleven (seven by confession, four by certificate) on May 30–31, 1752. A great harvest of souls occurred on November 25, 1752, when the church received twenty-one new members (sixteen by confession and five by transfer). One of that number was Jacob Rutsen Hardenbergh, a great-grandson of patentees Louis DuBois and Abraham Hasbrouck, who was later ordained and subsequently became the first president of Queens College, now Rutgers University. On July 1, 1753, three additional individuals joined upon confession of faith and twelve by transfer. (Those who transferred had previously been members of the Kingston Dutch Reformed congregation.) Again on April 3, 1754, twenty-three more individuals joined the church upon confession, bringing the grand total of new members in the years 1751–1754 to an astounding ninety-six, seventy-four of whom had become church members for the first time. As there were only seventy-six households in the patentee group over ten years later, clearly the Great Awakening had touched a great majority of the patentee descendant community.[25]

The Coetus-Conferentie Dispute

The unifying spirit that graced New Paltz as a result of Goetschius's service would not remain, as the congregation, and thus the community, divided in the context of the Coetus-Conferentie dispute in the 1760s. That wrenching conflict had been in the making since the 1730s, almost two decades before the New Paltz congregation had joined itself with the Dutch Reformed Church. Even though New Paltz joined the struggle only as it reached its climax, its lateness did nothing to quell the zealousness of its participants.

Within the Reformed Church, much ecclesiastical authority rests with a classis, composed of ministers and consistorial representatives from within particular geographic regions. A classis has the authority to examine and ordain ministers, rule on questions of church order, and make doctrinal pronouncements. All authority, however, does not rest with a classis, as it is in turn subordinate to a regional synod, composed of a number of classes. The Classis of Amsterdam had assumed primary authority over colonial American congregations during the Nieuw Nederland period, and it attempted to retain that right after the English conquest. It consistently struggled to do so, however, as all colonial church members, congregations, and ministers did not fully acknowledge the power of the Classis of Amsterdam to control them. Even when they did accept the Classis of Amsterdam's authority, it was difficult for Amsterdam to provide oversight of the American congregations due to their distance from the Netherlands. This distance became a particular problem when Classis was called upon to resolve disputes within and between colonial American congregations, as it met the almost intractable problem of gaining accurate and timely information. This challenge was only compounded by the fact that Dutch Reformed Americans consistently did not speak with a singular voice. This problem had become quite clear in the 1720s, when Classis attempted to resolve controversy in New Jersey that surrounded the pietistic minister Rev. Theodorus Frelinghuysen Sr.[26]

In light of these challenges, the Classis of Amsterdam suggested in 1735 the formation of a coetus in the colonies. A coetus is an ecclesiastical assembly that allows ministers and elders from multiple congregations to interact and consult with each other, but it is an assembly that lacks formal authority. That remains in the hands of a classis or a synod. A coetus can act with authority when authorized to do so by a superior ecclesiastical body, but otherwise it remains only deliberative or advisory. Classis believed that such a collective body in the North American colonies might be able to represent the colonial churches to Classis more accurately and effectively than then possible.[27]

Classis's recommendation that a coetus be formed initially met with relatively lukewarm support from some ministers and most of the laity. Most American church members and ministers viewed the problems that had motivated Classis to suggest the formation of a coetus as localized conflicts that did not affect the colonial church more broadly. As a result, many Dutch Americans simply did not feel that such a joint effort was needed. Other American ministers refused to support the concept because they believed that many of those colonial ministers who did support a coetus did not intend for the assembly to remain inferior to Amsterdam.[28]

In spite of this less-than-vigorous support, a significant number of colonial ministers and elders met in 1737 and 1738 to discuss Classis's recommendation. They formulated an organizational plan for a coetus, which was approved by Classis in 1739. In encouraging and supporting such an initiative, Classis pointedly and repeatedly stressed the limitations imposed on the body: it would remain subordinate to rather than co-ordinate with Amsterdam; it could not comment on doctrine; and it did not possess the right to examine and ordain candidates for the ministry. In other words, Amsterdam stressed that the coetus must remain an informal body that would never seek to elevate itself to the position of an American classis.[29]

Although support among the clergy for such an assembly did grow after 1739, that support seems to have been more broad than deep. There was even less interest among the laity. As a result, the body languished, a situation which continued to trouble Classis. When further disputes in the British colonies in America developed in the 1740s, with the most vexing being the Goetschius controversy on Long Island, Classis pressed colonial ministers to reinvigorate the Coetus in order to streamline operations and communications that would enable Classis to resolve disputes. As an incentive for colonial ministers to organize themselves into a functional body, Classis even allowed the ministers of the Coetus to reexamine and reordain Goetschius and two others. Classis did so because they believed that such temporary authority might be seen as elevating the status of the Coetus, making it seem more worthwhile to less-enthusiastic colonial ministers. Classis nevertheless continued to insist that the Coetus would never be granted such authority as a matter of course. Classis also continued to pressure those ministers who refused to support the Coetus to reconsider their opposition. Such opponents included Kingston's Mancius, to whom Classis explained that the dispute between Kingston and New Paltz in the early 1750s could have been more easily resolved if he had been willing to work with the Coetus. Classis used this example to emphasize its belief that a colonial assembly was highly desirable or perhaps even necessary.[30]

The Coetus was finally revived in 1747 and continued to function as designed through 1754, during which time it facilitated the resolution of the conflict between Kingston and New Paltz. However, its limited authority presented a number of seemingly intractable challenges affecting the Dutch Reformed Church in New York and New Jersey more broadly. Among these included the Coetus's inability either to amicably resolve or pronounce judgment on various congregational disputes. The Coetus also could not respond to the ongoing dearth of ministers in the colonies, as American congregations had difficulty managing the cost of sending ministerial candidates to Amsterdam for examination and ordination, a process that also took a great deal of time. This challenge was further highlighted by the deaths of two Frelinghuysen sons during a 1753 trip back from Amsterdam, where they had just been ordained. The Coetus as then organized also could not formally speak on behalf of all the American Dutch Reformed ministers to the controversy over the chartering of Kings College (now Columbia University) and the possible appointment of a professor of Dutch Reformed divinity. These many challenges led some members of the Coetus to consider ways to enhance its functionality in order to provide greater support to the Dutch Reformed congregations in America.[31]

The solution that some sought beginning in 1754 was the transformation of the Coetus into an American classis under the authority of the Synod of North Holland. This was a development that some colonial ministers had always anticipated and feared and which Classis was most decidedly unwilling to countenance. The primary power that supporters of the establishment of an American classis sought to attain was the authority to examine and ordain ministers in and for the colonies. American ministers also hoped that they could establish a college suitable for the education of potential Dutch Reformed ministers in America. If either goal was achieved, the relationship between the Dutch Reformed in the New World and the Old would become even more attenuated, which Classis felt would result in the devolution of the Dutch Reformed Church in America.[32]

The ministers of the Coetus who advocated for the transformation of the Coetus into a classis captured control of the local ecclesiastical assembly in 1755. Those ministers who opposed such goals joined together to send a protest to Amsterdam, and in doing so, laid the groundwork for an opposition party. That group came to be known as the "Conferentie" (meaning "little conference"), which desired continued subordination and dependency on the Classis of Amsterdam itself. As Dirk Mouw so deftly argues, both groups of ministers sought the same thing—the strengthening of the Dutch Reformed Church in America in a time of great challenge and stress—but they differed as to the best method for doing so. Those of the Coetus promoted increased local control and those in the Conferentie hoped to foster even greater dependence on Amsterdam.[33]

Crisis

The denominational schism in the American Dutch Reformed Church that began to develop in 1755 did not immediately impact the New Paltz congregation. Nevertheless, the direction that the conflict might take in New Paltz was both foreshadowed and the seeds of conflict planted in 1760 when the congregation called as their settled minister Johannes Mauritius Goetschius (1724–1771), the younger brother of Johannes Henricus Goetschius. The "Doctor Domine," as he was called in New Paltz, was only eleven when he arrived with his family in Philadelphia in 1735. He probably began to study theology under his brother, but he returned to Europe with Dorsius in July 1743, most likely for the purpose of studying theology and medicine. His return to America likely occurred in 1744, after which he practiced medicine, later returning to the study of theology under the tutelage of Rev. Theodorus Frelinghuysen Jr. in Albany.[34]

In 1755, Mauritius requested that the Coetus seek permission from "Holland or the Classis of Amsterdam" for his ordination in America. He was soon called to serve the primarily German Reformed congregation in Stone Arabia, New York, which was then under the oversight of the Dutch Reformed Church, provided that he could be ordained. The Coetus agreed to seek such authority, arguing repeatedly to Classis that if it did not grant the request, the congregation at Stone Arabia might "become totally scattered," as it lacked the means to support Mauritius's return to Europe for ordination. Classis nevertheless denied the request, and in response, the Stone Arabia congregation abandoned their relationship with the Dutch Reformed Church. Mauritius was thereupon released from Stone Arabia in order to accept another call from the German and Dutch Reformed congregations in Schoharie. So that he could fulfill the call, the Coetus took it upon themselves to ordain Mauritius in October 1757, even though it had never been given authority by Classis to do so. Mauritius served in Schoharie only until 1760, when he accepted a call from New Paltz (and neighboring Shawangunk), where he remained until his death in 1771. Because he had been ordained by the Coetus without the approbation of Classis, Mauritius became an ardent supporter of the Coetus party, which would have implications for the future of the New Paltz congregation.[35]

The early years of Mauritius's ministerial life was a period of considerable conflict in the Dutch Reformed Church in the colonies, with both sides in the Coetus-Conferentie dispute seeking support of their position from colonial ministers, the laity, and the Classis of Amsterdam, as well as the Synod of North Holland. Classis continued its opposition to the establishment of an American classis. The Synod of North Holland was of the same opinion. Still, the Coetus yet aimed to receive classical and synodical approval for its plan for the establishment of an American classis. Colonial divisions nevertheless deepened in the early 1760s, in part due to the publications of tracts by ministers of both parties, which helped to bring the laity more fully into the controversy. In 1763, the Coetus authorized Rev. Jacob Rutsen Hardenbergh, the great-grandson of New Paltz patentees Louis DuBois and Abraham

Hasbrouck, to take its case directly to the Classis of Amsterdam and the Synod of North Holland. His journey met with much disappointment, as Classis and Synod once again categorically denied the request of the Coetus to establish an American classis. Both Classis and Synod further threatened to cut off contact with the American ministers and congregations unless they altered their seemingly intractable position. Even worse, the Synod informed Hardenbergh that the American congregations would never be able to form themselves into a classis. Synodical opinion held that a Dutch Reformed classis is directly connected to a civil government, such that a classis of the Dutch Reformed Church can never be formed within a foreign government. If the American congregations could not combine into a classis, they never could become a constituent member of a synod. In other words, with synodical membership not possible, there could be no classis. This placed the American ministers and congregations in an untenable situation, as it suggested that the American congregations would remain in a permanently dependent position, requiring them to submit to a classical authority without being able to participate in that authority. Such power was something not denied to their Old World brothers, as it is upon that participatory power that the governing order of the Dutch Reformed Church is essentially grounded.[36]

Not long after Hardenbergh's ill-fated audience with the Classis and Synod, the American ministers and congregations nevertheless still attempted a rapprochement. On June 3, 1764, the congregation of New Paltz authorized their minister, Johannes Mauritius Goetschius, and an elder Jonas Freer to attend a meeting of the Coetus and Conferentie parties to be held on June 19 and 20, 1764, in New York City. Reconciliation was once again attempted but to no avail. At the conclusion of the two-day meeting, the loose body of those who had opposed the establishment of an American classis formally organized themselves into "an assembly, subordinate to the Rev. Classis." With the division between the two parties now crystal clear, and with Johannes Mauritius Goetschius as their ministerial leader, the majority of the New Paltz congregation took the side of the American contingent that no longer held itself subject to the authority of the Classis of Amsterdam and the Synod of North Holland, setting the stage for a wrenching community crisis.[37]

Support for the Coetus was not universal in New Paltz. In July 1765, Hendricus DuBois, the fifty-five-year-old grandson of patentee Louis DuBois, was called before the consistory on the charge of a "complaint of discomfort by a few members against you." Refusing to respond, he was again asked on August 3, 1765, to appear "to answer to and about the vexation of strife and schism which you have caused in your community." The consistory was also displeased because DuBois had uttered "scornful remarks" against them and had "defamed" and "slandered" them. DuBois apparently felt no compulsion to answer these claims, ignoring a final request from his "soul loving friends" to come before the consistory on August 31. His refusal to address the consistory compelled them "to deal with [him], following God's Word and Rules of the Church." On that day, the membership of the church "[took] note of him and declare[d] him censured; [they] refuse[d] to admit him to the seal of the covenant at the Supper of the Lord and declare[d] him unworthy to receive it." This application of discipline within the New Paltz congregation appears to have been a unique occurrence in the community: at least no other record of discipline in either the seventeenth or eighteenth centuries has survived.[38]

After his censure, DuBois followed through with his schismatic tendencies. On August 29, 1766, he and a small group of discontents came together to pledge funds for the construction of a new church building, even though the services of a minister had not yet been secured. This Second Church congregation represented a distinct minority within the community: only thirteen people donated for the construction of the new church, while eighty-six individuals in the original congregation donated for the construction of a new First Church just six years later. The schismatics' stated reasons for creating a new congregation were that the "congregation of the New Paltz . . . ha[d] separated from the orderly subordination to the Reverend Classis of Amsterdam under which the Nether Dutch Reformed congregations in this province have belonged from olden times and still ought to belong." Furthermore, the schismatics remarked that as of June 3, 1765, such a congregation "cannot be recognized as lawful," according to the Classis of Amsterdam, and that "the afore mentioned subordination [was] lawful, beneficial and necessary for the maintenance of the pure doctrine and discipline of our Reformed Nether Dutch Church." This was a somewhat odd position for the new congregation to take, as New Paltz had been under the authority of Amsterdam for only just over a decade, suggesting that something more was at stake.[39]

The construction of the Second Church began in September 1766 and was substantially completed by December, although the congregation still lacked ministerial leadership. They did not gain that until August 29, 1767, when Domine Isaak Rysdyk, Conferentie pastor of Poughkeepsie and Fishkill, New York, met with the schismatics at the home of Hendricus DuBois to bless and approve the establishment of the Second Church of New Paltz. Mouw argues that Rysdyk was a partisan minister who fanned the flames of division within congregations in order to advance the Conferentie party's interests. Even if that is true, it was not the case in New Paltz, as Rysdyk merely assisted an already-divided laity in a *fait accompli*.[40]

Even if pietism influenced the Coetus-Conferentie debate more broadly, it had nothing to do with the schism in New Paltz, as those who separated themselves from the original congregation had been inspired by the pietistic Goetschius brothers as much as those who remained in the bosom of the First Church. The leader of the schismatics himself, Hendricus DuBois, had confessed his faith on July 1, 1753, as did his wife, Jannetje Houghtaling, when Johannes Henricus Goetschius was serving in the New Paltz pulpit. Hendricus's former brother-in-law Petrus Low and Low's second wife, Deborah Van Vliet, who joined Hendricus in his new congregation, also became church members during the period of J. H. Goetschius's service. Also among the schismastics were two of Low's sons Salomon and Isaak, the latter who had previously been accepted as a member by J. H. Goetschius on April 3, 1754. Neither had Hendricus DuBois and his former brother-in-law opposed the call of Johannes Mauritius Goetschius, whose ordination had not been authorized by Classis. The future schismatics had not been concerned when their congregation called a minister whose promotion so greatly troubled both Classis and the Conferentie ministers. Many of the fourteen other New Paltz residents who joined with DuBois in becoming original members of the Second Church had previously been members of the Kingston rather than the New Paltz congregation, but nothing suggests that any of them had been troubled by the pietistic Goetschius brothers, nor did they resist Mauritius Goetschius because of his unauthorized ordination by the Coetus.

The members of the Second Church of New Paltz remained a distinct minority in the community. In addition to the few members received in 1767, sixteen more joined on May 2, 1768, with only four more joining after that date. Although many family names were represented in the congregation, the core membership centered around closely related branches of the DuBois, Eltinge, and Low families, all of whom were members of the New Paltz patentee community (see table 5.1). The congregation was also short-lived, although it survived even after Classis and the Coetus ministers and congregations negotiated a resolution to the conflict that was formalized in June 1772. It nevertheless took time before all congregations were reunited. The Second Church of New Paltz stubbornly resisted reunification, even to the point of calling the Rev. Rynier Van Nest as their first and only resident minister in 1774, two years after the denomination breach began to be healed. Some of those involved in the Second Church nevertheless began to drift back to the original congregation. Finally, on May 25, 1783, "The Second Church of the

Table 5.1. Members of the Second (Conferentie) Church of New Paltz

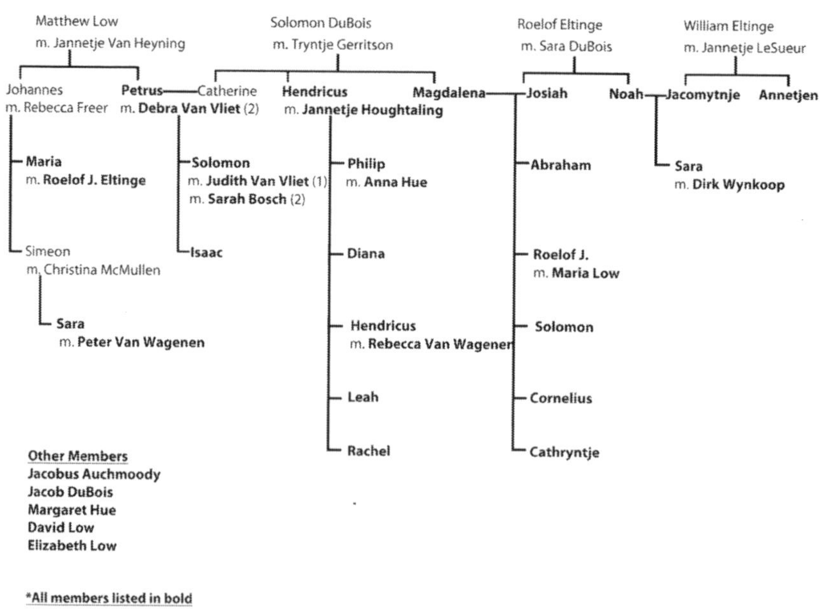

Paltz after preliminary deliberation and discharge by the Reverend particular assembly held at Mormelton [Marbletown, NY], the second Tuesday of May in the year 1783, was in the fear of god in love and mutual friendship united to the old congregation of the New Paltz." Hendricus DuBois had been presumably resisting that reunion for years: after his death in 1780, the conflict apparently mellowed, paving the way for his children and his many nieces and nephews to return to the congregation that their family elders had once so forcefully rejected.[41]

The Conferentie Leadership in New Paltz: The Preservation of Dutchness

Those patriarchs of the DuBois, Eltinge, and Low families who formed a new congregation must have been a highly motivated group if they were willing to undermine the cohesion of the patentee family community. Although they were joined by their wives and children, it is difficult to say whether their families shared their husbands' and fathers' perspective on the ecclesiastical controversy or simply deferred to their male elders. In any event, the creation of the Conferentie church was certainly a family affair. What motivated these men to lead a schism was that the ecclesiastical connection to patria represented the final surviving link to the source of Dutchness in a creolized local culture than continued to be less Dutch and more English with each passing year. That link, however, could serve only as a symbol of Dutchness, as it did not provide a strong mechanism for its preservation. Even as a symbol, these leaders of the local Conferentie congregation sought to maintain their connection to the Netherlands, as they were ethnocultural preservationists within a creolized culture. They represent the proud and the few who were struggling to maintain their Dutchness as their friends and extended families were increasingly allowing it to slip away.

One clear manner in which senior male members of the Conferentie party expressed their commitment to Dutchness was in their gender ideals. Hendricus DuBois directed in 1774 that "[his] wife Jannetie shall remain in the full possession of my whole Estate . . . during her lifetime," even though she was sixty-one years of age at the time he composed his will. Ironically, his wife, who also became a member of the Conferentie church, did not even want such jurisdiction, releasing control to her sons, Hendricus Jr. and Mathusalem, soon after her husband's death in 1780. That she did so suggests that Hendricus's decision to provide her with the rights of administration was aimed at meeting his ethnocultural needs rather than hers. Nevertheless, she carefully controlled how she released the administration of the estate to her sons by stipulating precisely what rights she would retain. She also maintained her agency by ensuring that the terms of the contract be met, by requiring that her son Mathusalem provide a £1,000 bond that he would have to pay if he did not comply with the agreement he made with his mother. Clearly, she was not comfortable relying on her sons simply to provide her an English-style "honorable maintenance," suggesting her commitment to female power within the family, more akin to a Dutch rather than an English household.[42]

Noah Eltinge, another wealthy member of the Conferentie church, also provided that his wife would remain in full control of his estate as long as she was a widow in Dutch matriarchal fashion. Noah did permit his son-in-law to work and manage the farm as a means of supporting both his family and his mother-in-law. Yet, his son-in-law would do so under the authority of her as a Dutch matriarch, as Noah required that his widow pay half of the income from the farm to her son-in-law, rather than the other way around. Noah also directed that his granddaughters would fully inherit and thus control their grandfather's estate after the death of both of their grandparents. As a result, Noah's son-in-law's dependence upon his mother-in-law would then be transferred to his own daughters. It would be up to them as to what authority, if any, they gave to their father over their inheritance. Noah could have placed his granddaughters' inheritance in trust, with the girls' father as trustee, if he had desired an English-style patriarchy. That is something he did not need or want, choosing instead to provide for his wife and grandchildren in a manner that represents an absolute reversal of the English gendered order.[43]

Josiah Eltinge was somewhat less committed to Dutch gendered ideals than his brother Noah, as Josiah chose to deny his wife, Magdalena, the administration of the estate. However, he bequeathed her a £20 yearly annuity (to be paid equally by their children) rather than simply directing his children to support their mother, as English men often did. As a result, he gave her the legal ability to compel her children to provide her with that income, over which she had complete discretionary control. Her level of independence was therefore greater than a typical English widow who often had to rely on an ambiguous "sufficient maintenance" provided by her children.[44]

Although Josiah circumscribed his widow's independence, suggesting that his commitment to the gendered ideals of the Dutch was not as strong as that of his fellow Conferentie supports, he inconsistently placed his only daughter, Catharyntje, in a position of authority. He did so by making her a co-executor of his estate along with her four brothers. This was a pattern that English fathers generally did not follow. She also had to pay an equal share of her mother's annuity. At the time her father wrote his will, she was legally able to fulfill both terms, as she had not yet married. However, Catharyntje married in 1772, with the result being that her new feme covert status made it impossible for her to independently fulfill the terms of her father's will. Nevertheless, her father, Josiah, never rewrote or composed a codicil to his will after her marriage, even though he ultimately lived twelve years after that event. He presumably believed that she would be able to fulfill the responsibilities he devolved upon her even as a married woman, suggesting that her husband would abide by the decision of his father-in-law. Such an assumption suggests that Josiah still acknowledged the influence of women within marriage in Dutch style, even if English law circumscribed their legal power and rights. In total, while Josiah did not adhere to Dutch gendered ideals as closely as did his brother, Noah, or his brother-in-law, Hendricus DuBois, his creolized approach still bore more many hallmarks of Dutchness.[45]

Hendricus DuBois and his household were also committed to preserving the Dutch language. Although he had been educated in French as a child in the 1720s, he claimed Dutch as his primary language, which became the language of his household as an adult. This is not surprising, given that Dutch was clearly becoming the dominant language in the community by the time of his youth. Yet, he remained committed to Dutch as English was advancing in the village. All four of the letters from the congregation to DuBois that precipitated the schism were composed in Dutch, presumably because that was his chosen language. His son, Hendricus Jr., and his wife, Jannetje, also remained committed to Dutch in their personal financial records, even after English had become the dominant language of business, suggesting that Dutch was the primary language of Hendricus's household. Hendricus Jr. (1743–1784) kept an account book in Dutch until 1783, and Jannetje (1713–1792) continued to use Dutch in her financial records until she died. Josiah Eltinge appears to have been somewhat more flexible than Hendricus, as he utilized both languages, as evidenced by the six letters his loyalist son Solomon sent him during the Revolutionary period, four in Dutch and two in English. It is likely that Solomon had intended that the letters would be shared with his family, suggesting that the Eltinge household still used Dutch in family situations.[46]

The leaders of the Conferentie faction were also committed to Dutch-American architecture. Hendricus DuBois made a strong statement in this vein in 1775 when, as an elderly man of sixty-five, he built a new house for himself. Although it no longer survives, investigations of a later house that included repurposed materials from the 1775 structure reveal that it was substantially similar to the Jacob Hasbrouck Sr. House built over a half-century before. Noah and Josiah Eltinge were also satisfied with the traditional architecture, perhaps even moreso than Hendricus, as they simply stayed in their ancestral homes, even though they had the means to build new like Hendricus, had they so desired. Noah lived in the house his father had built in the first decades of the eighteenth century. Josiah's was even older, as he lived from about 1735 until his death in the home built by a New Paltz patentee, his grandfather Abraham DuBois, which was possibly the oldest home in the village at the time of the church dispute. The 1798 Federal Direct Tax, the surveyor for which was Josiah's grandson, indicated the house was 113 years old, which meant that it had been built in 1683. At the time of the direct tax, the house was apparently so antiquated and/or in such poor condition that Josiah's grandson, Ezekiel, used it as a granary, although not for much longer. The entry in the tax list was crossed out and no valuation given, presumably indicating that the house was no longer in existence when the tax list was submitted. It is therefore highly unlikely that Josiah had ever upgraded the house in an English vein, as many others had been doing; he clearly must not have been concerned with the modern Anglo-American conveniences and style. The Conferentie leaders' satisfaction with and preservation of Dutch-American architecture therefore reflected their commitment to the Dutch language and Dutch gender ideals. This ethnocultural conservatism was in turn reflected in their attempts to preserve connections with the Dutch fatherland through their continued subordination to the Classis of Amsterdam.[47]

The Coetus Leadership in New Paltz: Increasing Englishness

The leading members of the community who continued to support the Coetus First Church, which advocated for domestic control of the Dutch Reformed congregations in America, pursued fundamentally different ethnocultural strategies. Leading men such as Major Jacob Hasbrouck Jr. and his second cousin Colonel Abraham Hasbrouck accepted and even promoted English culture. Their leadership within the congregation is evidenced by Jacob Jr.s' substantial donation to the effort to build a new church building that began in 1771; his gift was half again as much as any other donor. The next highest donation was that given by his cousin Abraham. Abraham was domiciled in Kingston, where he followed his chosen career as a merchant, facilitating commerce between Ulster County and New York City. He nevertheless remained closely connected with New Paltz through his ownership of the two-thousand-acre Guilford Patent in the New Paltz precinct, which he had inherited undivided from his father. The Hasbrouck cousins were also both political leaders. Jacob Jr. served as town supervisor from 1762–1765, and again from 1771–1776 as the movement toward revolution progressed. He later became one of the highest-ranking militia officers living in New Paltz during the Revolution. Colonel Abraham's political position was even higher than Major Jacob's. He was elected as a member of the colonial assembly in 1739, continuing to serve on and off through the late 1760s. His status as colonel is also a demonstration of his status in the province.[48]

Colonel Abraham Hasbrouck was also a vigorous proponent of the Coetus in the Kingston congregation, of which he was a member. He was willing to use whatever means he had at his disposal to advance its interests. The majority of the Kingston congregation supported the Conferentie, although the congregation never officially split. To avert such a disaster, the Kingston congregation required that their new domine, Rev. Hermanus Meyer, whom they had called in 1763, remain neutral in the controversy. Abraham Hasbrouck, however, was unwilling to support such neutrality, but as he was not a member of the consistory, he lacked congregational authority to force the issue. Without ecclesiastical power, he attempted to use his political power to sway the congregation. With the support of justices of the peace Louis Bevier (Abraham's cousin) and Colonel Levi Pawling, Hasbrouck convinced, cajoled, or forced Rev. Meyer in 1764 to take an oath of allegiance to King George, an oath which required Meyer to deny the authority of any foreign ecclesiastical body in the British colonies. Nothing suggested that Meyer's allegiance was in any way suspect, but by requiring Meyer to take the oath, Hasbrouck and his supporters forced Meyer to take a stand against the Conferentie. This act was aimed at pushing the congregation into the Coetus camp.[49]

As a local leader of the Coetus party, Abraham Hasbrouck was also a vigorous proponent of English culture. Like the leaders of the Conferentie faction, Abraham had been educated in French in the village's school, but he certainly would have spoken Dutch as well, as that was his mother's tongue as well as the lingua franca of the region. Yet, beginning in the 1730s, he chose to begin to compose a family history and personal diary entirely in English, rather than either of the languages of his youth. Such a linguistic choice was clearly no accident, as English would not become a primary language in New Paltz until the third quarter of the eighteenth century. What might have encouraged Hasbrouck to adopt English earlier than many of his patentee family peers is that he did so at the time he launched his career as a provincial merchant. Such a career connected him closely with New York City, where the English language was gaining ground faster than in the countryside. Of course, his role as an Ulster County representative in the Assembly certainly required English proficiency as well. Perhaps one reason he chose to write his diary in English was as a means of practicing his adopted language. He would have needed that practice, given his socioeconomic and political goals, which took him into the heart of life in the provincial capital.[50]

Abraham Hasbrouck also embraced the architecture of the provincial rulers. For a substantial portion of his adult life in Kingston, Abraham Hasbrouck resided in a one-story linear house built in the Dutch-American mode, which was destroyed in an October 23, 1776, fire (although later rebuilt and occupied by his son Jonathan). Even before that fire, however, Abraham had made plans to move to a more modern structure, which appears from written descriptions to have been much more English in form. Hasbrouck had purchased this second Kingston house from Robert G. Livingston in 1759, and "several years before" the 1776 fire, Abraham constructed a two-story addition to its north end. Following some health concerns that both preceded and succeeded the fire, Abraham moved himself and his family into that house on May 1, 1777. He described the house in his 1785 will, in which he indicated that his wife, Catherine, would have use of the new addition, which included a room on the first floor, the room above on the second floor, and the garret and cellar above and below. She also had use of the room over the entry and the use of the two runs of stairs that stood in that entry. These stairs provided access to the basement and the second floor, indicating that the entry was in fact an entry stair hall that separated the new addition from the original portion of the house, both of which were two stories. Such a structure was in no way modeled according to the regional Dutch-American idiom. Although it is not known if Hasbrouck's addition resulted in a perfectly balanced Georgian façade, it was nevertheless a structure that possessed many hallmarks of English architecture.[51]

Major Jacob Hasbrouck Jr. likewise did not end his days in an antiquated house, although his choices were not quite as progressive as those of his cousin Abraham. At the time of the New Paltz church dispute, Major Jacob Hasbrouck Jr. was living in the 1721 house of his father, Jacob Hasbrouck Sr. (the so-called Jean Hasbrouck House). Although idiosyncratic in some respects, that house had most of the telltale signs of Dutch architecture, including its basically one-story profile, its use of three Dutch-style jambless fireplaces, and its many elegant *kruiskozijn* casement windows on the first floor. Also present in the house was an enclosed box bed for the use of the heads of household, a Dutch-style feature that cannot be confirmed as having been included in any other New Paltz house. These Dutch features were becoming decidedly antiquated in New Paltz when Jacob Jr. inherited the house in 1761. In 1784, Jacob idiosyncratically chose to build a new home at the relatively advanced age of fifty-nine, at which time he left the old house to his eldest son, Josiah, who immediately attempted to modernize it. Jacob's new house down the road basically followed the Dutch one-story linear plan, but was nevertheless devoid of Dutch-style casement windows and jambless fireplaces, and he and his wife slept there in a proper bedstead rather than in an antiquated enclosed Dutch box bed. The new house also contained a passageway, reflecting a desire for levels of stylishness, cleanliness, comfort, and privacy suggestive of English taste. Granted, this home was not built until decades after the church dispute, but it nevertheless suggests the tendency of Jacob Hasbrouck Jr. to accept innovative architectural elements, even though English in influence. Why Jacob Jr. did not modernize his father's house as many individuals did is not entirely clear. Perhaps the construction of an entirely new house enabled him to distance himself more firmly from the more rigidly Dutch design elements that graced the home of his youth.[5]

The Hasbrouck cousins also provided for their wives in English fashion. In his 1785 will, Abraham stipulated his widow's rights to portions of the family house, barn, and garden, and also her right to the annual interest on £400. As she was not an executor, she would have had no authority over the investments, nor could she have been assured of what her annual income would be. Thus, she was dependent on the financial acumen of her male kin, which they hopefully employed in her best interests. Jacob Hasbrouck Jr. similarly did not provide for his widow's power and influence, as he too strayed from Dutch practices. In his 1776 will, he directed that his wife, Jannetje, would continue to live in the family home with their sons, Josiah and Jacob, who would provide her "a good and sufficient maintenance." He did provide an alternative if she was unhappy with the arrangement; in such case, she could have a room in the house and £25 per annum from the estate. While she had options, the options had been specifically determined by her husband, but his clear preference was that his sons dutifully and respectfully provide for their widowed mother according to English customs. In sum, Jacob Hasbrouck Jr. and Abraham Hasbrouck placed their widows in dependent positions or at least severely limited the control they had over their own future, as was common among Anglo-Americans. Their Anglo gender ideals therefore reflected their commitment to a greater Anglo element in their architecture, a commitment that is also evidenced by Abraham Hasbrouck's precocious embrace of the English language.[53]

It is clear that the congregational schism was not predicated on a dispute over doctrine, style of faith, or ecclesiastical structure. Leaders of both parties had previously accepted ministers who had participated in the rupture that brought the majority of American congregations and ministers into conflict with their more conservative brethren, as well as with their supposed superiors, the Classis of Amsterdam. What did divide them were their divergent approaches to managing the creolizing process in which they and their parents and grandparents had been involved since the founding of their community. The Conferentie supporters, led by Hendricus DuBois, attempted to halt the growing acceptance of English culture, while the leading Coetus members accepted and perhaps even promoted the opposite.

Local Men and Provincial Players

What also marked the leaders of both groups different from each other was that the Conferentie leaders lives' revolved around their local, rural community, while the leading Coetus members reached beyond New Paltz, even though all were wealthy members of their communities. For those that stayed local, their Dutchness marked them as typical, even if they tended toward a more conservative position than some of their friends and families. For those that reached outward, their Dutchness would have been a blemish that they might have tried to jettison or at least obscure.[54]

The leaders in the church dispute were all wealthy men, and as was typical, they were all elected to serve in government. However, the service of the Conferentie leaders was strictly local and also not at the highest level. Between 1751 and 1765, Hendricus DuBois, Noah Eltinge, and Josiah Eltinge stood in a majority of the elections, and each was elected five times (although the records for 1759 are not extant). The offices they occupied included overseer of the poor (DuBois and Josiah Eltinge), tax assessor (DuBois and Noah Eltinge), constable (DuBois), and fenceviewer (Noah Eltinge). None of the Conferentie leaders ever served in the highest town offices of supervisor, who represented their town at the county level, or even clerk. The only other office that required participation at the county level was the constable, and only one of the three men served in that role, and he did so only once.[55]

Economically, the leaders of the New Paltz Conferentie faction were also locally oriented. Hendricus was a substantial yeoman farmer, having inherited considerable property from his father. The precise size of his landed portion is unknown, but Hendricus likely received a bequest similar to his brother's three-thousand-acre inheritance. He probably farmed only a portion of that land, given his available labor force; but even so, Hendricus could have potentially produced considerable surpluses. Typically, such Ulster County men vented their surpluses into an American and perhaps even an international market; but most did so indirectly, by selling or consigning them to a local merchant, who then took them to market in the city. Due to the limits of the evidence, very little can be said about the trading activities of Hendricus Sr., but the records of his son, Hendricus Jr., reveal the local orientation of the DuBois household, the members of which operated within a traditional community economic network. Hendricus DuBois Jr. (1743–1784) lived within his father's household during the ecclesiastical controversy, and he remained subordinate to his father in that household until his father's death in 1780. In the 1770s, Hendricus Jr. worked as a local shoemaker, occasionally supplementing that income through occasional daywork for others. He also traded small amounts of agricultural produce locally. His economic activities off the farm, however, were extremely limited, presumably merely supplementing his labor on land he would one day inherit. Since the economic dealings of Hendricus Jr. were suggestive of a traditional, locally oriented economy based on community exchange networks rather than market oriented, it is likely that those of his father were similar.[56]

The financial activities of Josiah Eltinge, a Conferentie supporter, also revolved around the community. He styled himself a yeoman farmer, although his wealth might have placed him above that social category. Like many in the community, he produced agricultural surpluses for the market, but he also made significant profits as a local creditor. When he died in 1784, he had £3,580 in bonds lent out at interest dating back to 1760, indicating his acceptance of long-term credit relationships, typical of traditional lending practices.[57]

The political and economic lives of the Hasbrouck cousins, whose wealth also placed them at the top of local society, diverged substantially from those of the leaders of the Conferentie faction. This was particularly the case with Abraham Hasbrouck, whose life choices took him from New Paltz to Kingston, and most importantly, to the wharves, counting houses, and halls of government of New York City. Hasbrouck was truly a man of the province, with a farm in New Paltz, a house and much additional property in Kingston, and even a house near the wharves in New York City. He was also one of the few elite rural merchants who developed close business relationships with members of the New York City merchant elite, such as William Bayard, Henry Cruger, and Oliver DeLancey, who provided local merchants with foreign goods and credit. As a provincial assemblyman, he was also one of the highest-ranking politicians in the colony.[58]

Given his "Dutch" ethnocultural background, Abraham's chosen path may not have been an easy one, as he would have faced a persistent English anti-Dutch bias that very well might have challenged him in his pursuit of social, economic, and political advancement. The essence of that bias was that the Dutch were essentially greedy, ruthless traders who aimed to advance their own economic self-interest above any other consideration, including the needs of their community and nation—and even their very souls. Such a bias first developed in England in the early seventeenth century, but it grew dramatically in the context of the Anglo-Dutch conflicts over the place of each nation in global trade. It also grew within England itself, as the English increasingly struggled with incorporating both trade and traders in their traditionally landed culture and society. These English perceptions of the Dutch were transplanted to the colonies and persisted even into the nineteenth century, posing a view of "Dutch" New Yorkers that was anything but favorable.[59]

As the English stereotyped the Dutch as greedy, unpatriotic traders, a "Dutch" merchant such as Abraham Hasbrouck would have had to overcome a great deal if he was to find acceptance among the Anglo-American New York elite. He might have been particularly sensitive to this issue because he was one of those Dutch men who might have been emasculated by a woman. In his case, it was his mother, as his father had given her control of Abraham's landed estate in New Paltz for as long as she wished. Perhaps that is the reason he embarked on a career as a merchant in nearby Kingston.

And Abraham was clearly a status-conscious man who sought power and influence. During the heat of the Coetus-Conferentie dispute in the Kingston church, a supporter of the Conferentie noted how he aimed to force his ecclesiastical position, remarking that "The Col., it seems, will now endeavor to gain the Honorable seat of a Pope." Of course, this came from one of his opponents, but Hasbrouck later declared his desire for rank and power himself. When he was passed over for the commission of militia general in favor of (future governor) George Clinton in 1775–1776, Hasbrouck refused his commission as colonel; the legislature deemed his response "childish." To advance his position among the provincial Anglo-American elite, he might very well have felt compelled to distance himself from his Dutch heritage. In order to do so, he gained English fluency, provided for his wife according to the gendered ways of the English, and built for himself a house that reflected contemporary English design.[60]

Hasbrouck also might have advanced the Coetus position in order to demonstrate his selfless patriotism, even though he was not willing to leave the Dutch Reformed Church itself. Doing so would have been difficult for him, since he was a devout man, and at the time, there were no other churches in Kingston or New Paltz. However, by using the Coetus controversy in Kingston to compel the minister to take an oath of allegiance to the king, Hasbrouck implicitly demonstrated his own ability and willingness to be a loyal subject of the English crown. In doing so, he might have aimed to convince his Anglo-American peers that he had transcended the supposed greediness of his "Dutch" forebears, whom the English believed were unable to be good subjects or citizens of any type. Hasbrouck could then appear as an Englishman while remaining a member of an Americanized Dutch Reformed Church.

The concerns that the Hasbrouck cousins faced as they constructed lives beyond the village of New Paltz were not those of the great majority of the patentee family community. They nevertheless shared the Hasbrouck cousins' commitment to the Coetus. Most lived lives that revolved around the local, such that their lived experience was far more similar to that of the Conferentie schismatics than to that of the leading Coetus members. Yet, the majority did not follow the ethnocultural paths of either faction. The great majority of the patentees and their descendants had never been vigorous promoters of either ethnocultural assimilation or preservation. They had established and maintained a creolized culture that remained essentially fluid throughout the long eighteenth century. Neither were they as sensitive to the increasing decline of Dutchness as were the leaders of the Conferentie faction. The majority therefore did not need to maintain a connection to Amsterdam as a symbol of their Dutchness. The majority had accepted Dutchness and could continue to maintain it to the extent that they wished, with or without a connection to Amsterdam. Neither would the separation of the American Dutch Reformed Church from Amsterdam imply that the New Paltz patentee family community would have to embrace English culture more fully, even though the leading Coetus members in their community were doing just that. The patentee families had been in control of their own independent creolized culture since their ancestors founded the community and would remain so whether their church was linked to the Old World or grounded in the New. Remaining in a congregation that supported the Coetus was the path of least resistance, at least in New Paltz. Since that path also did not prevent them from preserving a creolized culture as they saw fit, it was also the most logical path to take. In contrast, it was the behavior of that most vocal of Conferentie supporters, Hendricus DuBois, whose behavior was illogical. He felt the only way he could take a stand in favor of Dutch ethnocultural preservation was by resisting Englishness and radically splitting the local congregation. Most members of the patentee family community knew that a more moderate approach was possible, as many had had been following such an approach for as long as any of them remembered.

Chapter 6

"The precious germ of civil and religion freedom"[1]

As the drama of the Coetus-Conferentie dispute faded from recent memory, so did the lived creolized Dutch-American culture. It seems to have done so not with a cry but a whimper. Descendants in the nineteenth century occasionally referenced the disappearance of the French and Dutch languages, but they suggested that the transition to English had been necessary and unavoidable, not something by which to be particularly troubled. The gendered ideals of the Dutch as enacted in New Paltz drifted away without comment, and the influential Dutch matriarch was simply forgotten. Many of the Huguenot Street houses remained but passed out of family ownership, including the Freer-Louw House and the Daniel Hasbrouck House, as the street became a less-than-desirable place to live. The Abraham DuBois House was simply demolished in 1798, as was the LeFevre House, also on Huguenot Street, the latter to make way for a new Greek Revival-style church in 1839. This decline of the houses was a slower process because they, unlike gender ideals and language, had both a physical presence and an economic value. Nevertheless, early houses throughout the town also began to fall into decay and eventual demolition by neglect. The Dutch-American architectural idiom also was fast becoming stylistically obsolete. The last of the new houses built by descendants in such an idiom was constructed in the first quarter of the nineteenth century. Even then, a number of descendants had chosen to build in the contemporary American Federal style. A lived creolized culture had become a thing of the past.[2]

It is not surprising in the least that when the Dutchness of the community finally faded away by the early nineteenth century, it did so with little overt struggle. As the church schism demonstrates, most people had accepted the separation of the church from the Netherlands either because they promoted English culture or because the creolized culture allowed for a steady and gradual process of ethnocultural change, even if it led to the passing of Dutchness. Only a distinct minority of the community's elders had resisted Americanization of the church and the severing of the final cultural connection with the fatherland, but they had all died by the end of the eighteenth century. Many of their children, who had also been members of the Conferentie church, had also died or were reaching the end of their lives by the early nineteenth century, such that their influence was quickly disappearing as well.

This loss of Dutchness did not mean that descendants uniformly lost all connections with their past. Some intentionally preserved physical reminders of the past as part of a lived present. When United States Congressman Josiah Hasbrouck built Locust Lawn in 1814, the grandest and most forward-looking house in the region, he nevertheless preserved the antiquated stone Terwilliger House on his property, a striking contrast to his new architectural showplace. He likewise retained ownership of his family's ancestral home, the Jean/Jacob Hasbrouck House. His choice to preserve the stone houses was a conscious one, as he and his wife, Catherine Decker, also remained committed to showcasing antiquated Dutch-American furnishings in the splendor of their new up-to-date mansion. Such furnishings included his grandfather Jacob's country Hudson Valley Queen Anne-style chairs (see Figure 6.1) and an eighteenth-century tall-case clock, which they placed in the stairhall of his mansion (see Figure 6.2), a room used for entertaining and dining. They also placed a number of eighteenth-century Dutch-style *kasten* (a piece of Dutch cabinet furniture used for the storage of linens) in the family bedrooms. His son and heir, Levi Hasbrouck, and his wife, Hylah Bevier Hasbrouck, continued to follow Josiah's practices. As a kinsman noted, "During his life time [Levi] would not allow any important changes to be made in the appearance of the old homestead [the Jean Hasbrouck House]." Levi and Hylah also continued to use the outdated Dutch-style furniture as physical reminders of the past, as they joined them with stylish new furnishings such as the *Bust of Diana* (see Figure 6.3) and furniture

Figure 6.1. Eighteenth-century chair, originally owned by Jacob Hasbrouck Sr. (one of six). Photograph by the author.

Figure 6.2. Josiah Hasbrouck House, "Locust Lawn," main hall. Photograph by the author.

Figure 6.3. *Bust of Diana*, Joseph Mozier, c. 1850. Photograph by the author.

Figure 6.4. Server, John Banks, c. 1810. Photograph by the author.

produced by elite New York City cabinetmakers (see Figure 6.4). Hylah also hung her Litchfield Academy needlework (see Figure 6.5) in close proximity to both the family antiques that anchored their history and the new consumer goods that bespoke wealth and status, another clear demonstration of her elite social position.[3]

Other descendants chose to keep their ancestral homes, not as primary homes and not necessarily intact, but rather as physical links to the past. This was a trend that developed over the course of the nineteenth century. As early as 1860, Abraham Bruyn Hasbrouck (1791–1879), the grandson of Colonel Abraham Hasbrouck (of Coetus-Conferentie dispute fame), a graduate of Yale College, a student of Tapping Reeve at Litchfield, a United States congressman, and president of Rutgers College from 1840–1850, made mention of patentee descendants' strong attachment to their ancestral homes. Although he was born and died in Kingston, New York, he nevertheless preserved a deep, personal relationship with New Paltz, remarking that "I cannot but feel for that ancient village, the special reverence which, by an impulse of our nature, ever clings to the early homes and sepulchres of our fathers." He was not alone. Mary DuBois Berry (1838–1902), who in 1853 inherited the 1705 DuBois House in which she had been raised, retained ownership of the house, although rarely living there as an adult. During the one extended time when she was in residence (1887–1896), she invested heavily in rehabilitating and furnishing her ancestral home. When her daughter Marie married in 1905, her nuptials were held "in the old historic mansion of the DuBois family, which is the pride of our village."[4]

Jesse Elting (1838–1922) also remained attached to the home of his forebears. He owned, but did not live in, the Bevier House, which had been in

Figure 6.5. *Blanche and Fitz James*. Needlework created by Hylah Bevier at the Litchfield Female Academy, c. 1811. Collection of Locust Lawn. Gift of Annette Innis Young.

his family since purchased by his great-great-grandfather Josiah Eltinge. He chose never to update it with modern conveniences. In the opening years of the twentieth century, he rented the house to a number of different men for the production of what Ralph LeFevre noted to be either survivals or revivals of handcrafts, including baskets and rugs, possibly for the tourist trade. Jesse Elting eventually gave the house in the same condition to his daughter Lanetta Elting DuBois, who kept it as a summer retreat. The Abraham Deyo House on Huguenot Street also remained in the family throughout the nineteenth century as a touchstone of the past. In 1894, Abraham Deyo Broadhead, a descendant of the builder, invested heavily in creating a Queen Anne-style house out of the old stone house (see Figure 6.6), which involved the encasing of the old within the new, linking the past and the present in an unusual but intentional way (see Figure 6.7). Although clearly overstating his case, Ralph LeFevre remarked in 1903 that "at New Paltz, as in no other place in our country, the homesteads have been handed down in the family ever since the first settlement. . . . the Huguenots kept their grip on their own old homesteads, and their conservatism we consider a more remarkable point."[5]

Descendants did not cling only to the houses but to stories of the past as well, stories that they trusted and upon which they built their identity. A. Bruyn Hasbrouck remarked that a study of New Paltz and the region's past offered "a wide field of research, rich in historical facts, and richer still in

Figure 6.6. Deyo House, before 1894. LeFevre, *History of New Paltz*, 262.

Figure 6.7. Deyo House, after 1894. Photograph by the author.

traditionary lore." He himself learned "in direct hereditary descent from my progenitor, who was one of the *twelve patentees*," about how New Paltz was acquired. He also often heard the story of how the patentees read a psalm to honor their arrival in their new home, which "may perhaps be considered less a fancy's sketch, than a probability nearly historical." In 1875, the Rev. Robert Patterson Du Bois likewise told of that event, remarking that "tradition tells us that that exiled band gathered close together on the first evening of their arrival here." In 1886, Irving Elting also commented on the importance of "tradition, both trustworthy and direct." Newspaper editor Ralph LeFevre likewise relied upon and gave credence to oral histories provided by a small group of elderly informants, stories which he collected and upon which he based his published historical sketches. LeFevre noted that "the best of all history is what we get from tradition, when we can confirm it by documentary evidence." Ralph LeFevre even suggested that New Paltz was exceptional in its powerful commitment to both its physical heritage and its traditions, holding forth that "we think it will be demonstrated in a few years that to scholars and literary people there is no place in our country quite so interesting as New Paltz, with its wealth of tradition, its fine old houses and its mass of valuable papers and documents." The Rev. Anson Du Bois summed it up well when he commented that the patentees' "descendants are in every part of the United States, and hundreds of these scattered families are cherishing as their most precious heirlooms traditions of those heroic days of their ancestors."[6]

These recorded comments are significant not only for their references to contemporary and past practices involving the perpetuation of tradition. Their very recordation demonstrates an important new stage in the importance and role of history in the community. By the mid-nineteenth century, descendants were no longer satisfied with telling stories just within their families, or even within their community; they eventually sought to usher their traditional lore into the public sphere. The beginnings of this trend were modest and regional, but ultimately culminated in the creation of a museum and a monument, which descendants intended to serve not only themselves but the broader public as well.

The history that descendants constructed, and the commemorative activities in which they engaged, were fundamentally organized around their particular ethnocultural heritage, which marked them as a distinct minority in the United States. Paradoxically, they began to think and talk about the historical non-Englishness of the community only once they had fully assimilated into Anglo-American culture. Only after that did their non-English heritage become an important marker of their identity. This was the case because just when the descendants had finally let their creolized culture fully pass into history, nineteenth-century Americans began to perceive culture as biologically predetermined. This new ideology suggested that even political and religious culture hereditarily inhered in bodies in a literal but mysterious way. The descendants' ancestral heritage therefore did not represent merely the past but a lived present as well—both a history and a biological birthright—which they believed was linked to a continually unfolding American story. The purpose of the descendants' historical and commemorative efforts was to remind both themselves and others of their ancestors' supposedly unique contribution to American greatness, and by extension, their own as well.

The Unfolding Anglo-Saxon Exceptionalist Myth

In arguing for the value of their ancestors, and thus themselves, the descendants of the New Paltz founders entered into a national dialogue about the origins of American politics, culture, and identity, which in the nineteenth century, revolved around an Anglo-Saxon exceptionalist myth. This myth posed a distinct challenge for those ancestor-worshipping Americans with other than English roots, as it hegemonically defined the intellectual environment in which they explored their heritage. Historicizing descendants of the patentees accepted the theoretical premises of Anglo-Saxon exceptionalism but claimed that their non-English ancestors bore the characteristics, abilities, and desires of the Anglo-Saxons even more than the Anglo-Saxons themselves. They supported their arguments through misinterpretations of the archival record and by citing traditional, yet often highly questionable, family lore. In doing so, they found in their ancestors the soul of America.

The Anglo-Saxon myth had a deep history, as it first began to develop in England in the early seventeenth century. It was grounded in a belief that the English people demonstrated a peculiar attachment to individual rights and the desire and aptitude for collective self-government. They claimed that the origins of these values and abilities could be found in the ancient Teutons, as described by Tacitus (56–117). Their distinct commitment to freedom and liberty was supposedly brought to the English shores by the Anglo-Saxons, one branch of the Teutonic people. These principles were said to have perpetually guided the Teutons' descendants in England, surviving even as their freedom and liberty was compromised by the Norman invasion, which led the English monarchs on the path towards absolutism and tyranny. They claimed that that commitment to liberty could survive even in the midst of the growing monarchical tendency towards absolutism because the English people supposedly represented the most vigorous branch of the Teutonic tribes. Such a perspective served to ground the struggles between parliament and the Stuart kings and was ultimately employed to explain and justify the Glorious Revolution. The more conservative Whigs claimed that the Glorious Revolution had finally purified the English constitution of its Norman infection, but more radical Anglo-Saxonists did not agree that it had effected sufficient reforms. Nevertheless, English Anglo-Saxonists collectively embraced the assertion that English liberty derived from the ancient German woods.[7]

The Anglo-Saxonist/Teutonic ideology was enhanced and strengthened in the early nineteenth century under the influence of romantic nationalism. Romantic nationalists believed that each cultural group possessed a *Volksgeist*, or spirit of a people, as defined by Johann Gottfried von Herder. This collective spirit was the result of long-term interaction between groups of people and their particular physical environments. Romantic nationalism developed independently in both Germany and England; but considering the perceived genealogical connections between the ancient Teutons and the Anglo-Saxon people, the ideas cross-pollenated. The belief in a Teutonic-Anglo-Saxon political legacy found particularly fertile ground in the United States in the early years of the republic, as the success of the revolutionary movement against tyranny, and the rearticulation of the search for liberty and individual rights, lent credence to the exceptionalist myth.[8]

The myth burgeoned further in the middle years of the nineteenth century through the work of such historians of the United States as George Bancroft and Francis Parkman. The American historian of the Netherlands, John Motley, also claimed a liberty-loving Teutonic heritage for the Dutch republicans who had fought so hard and for so long against Spanish tyranny. Such romantic historians clung to the progress of liberty as a grand and moral narrative and saw in the Teutonic blood the roots of that dramatic story. The tale was wrapped in sentimental and emotional tones, such that it appealed to both the heart and the head. As David Levin argues, such "literary" historians spun stories replete with "remarkable, vigorous characters act[ing] heroically on the largest possible stage." Such historicizing was characterized by "poetic" incidents and "scenery that had to include something of the picturesque, and as much of the sublime as possible."[9]

The exceptionalist myth was given further power when linked to Christian millennialism. This connection suggested not only that Anglo-Saxons had a particular desire and gift for self-government but that God had ordained it to be so. American historians contended that Anglo-Saxon Americans were His tool to advance liberty and self-government, leading the United States to its ultimate destiny as a republic of liberty and the salvation of humanity. Such a providential interpretation of American history obviated the need for proof of historical causality, since God, of course, acted in mysterious ways. All that American Anglo-Saxon nationalists needed to do to claim that God used the Anglo-Saxons to advance his divine plan was to assert that he did. The theory therefore only needed to be invoked or implied rather than explained. Dorothy Ross argues that this belief in American exceptionalism, as an extension of Teutonic Anglo-Saxonism interpreted through a Protestant millenialist lens, "quickly entered into popular literary, religious, and political discourse, and was so widely diffused that its premises often went unstated and its conclusions were often merely celebrated." When the advancement of freedom was pursued, God was there, and the Teutonic-Anglo-Saxon-Americans by definition led the way.[10]

Common Lands and the Roots and Rebirth of Self-government

As social scientific positivism undermined a belief in an interventionist god in the later nineteenth century, this providential mode of scholarly historical interpretation declined. This trend tended to sap the American version of the Anglo-Saxon myth of its overt religious underpinnings in intellectual discourse. However, following the arguments of English historians Henry Maine and Edward Freeman, a number of American historians offered a new interpretation of the development of Anglo-American self-government, which nevertheless continued to rest on the Teutonic heritage of the Anglo-Saxons. Influential scholars in this vein included James K. Hosmer at Washington University in St. Louis, Herbert Baxter Adams at Johns Hopkins, and Henry Adams at Harvard. These scholars formulated a new model of "scientific" historical inquiry based on the study of the history of political institutions. This model gained strength from, but was not dependent upon, Darwinian and Spencerian evolutionary theories, grounded in a belief that "the entire universe—including all human life—was governed by deterministic laws discoverable only through scientific inquiry," in the words of T. J. Jackson Lears. Their primary interest was the intersection of land tenure, political participation, and political institutions, as created and transferred from the Continent to England, and ultimately to the United States through an irrepressible yet vaguely conceptualized "germ." This new model was soon discredited by other academic historians. It nevertheless cast a long shadow, continuing to influence popular constructions of history for many years, in part because it was embraced by a number of leading politicians including Theodore Roosevelt, John Hay, Henry Cabot Lodge, and Albert Beveridge.[11]

Teutonist scholars argued that the primary unit of social organization of ancient Germany was a communally owned area of land called the "Mark." Out of this communal ownership arose stronger proprietary rights to portions of the Mark, although such rights were far less than ownership in fee simple. The freemen of the Mark allotted and farmed plots of arable land in "shifting severalties," as plots could be re-allotted as necessary to meet the needs of freemen families in the community, some of whom may not have been original members of that community. The land was initially distributed in equal portions, but Herbert Baxter Adams points out that even in the time of Tacitus, land was apportioned according to "dignity or title." Reassignment of arable plots occurred at increasingly broader intervals as time went on, a process that ultimately resulted in private ownership of land. Meadowlands were also subject to shifting severalties, but after harvest, the enclosures were removed and the land made available for common grazing. Lands not used for tillage or hay production, such as for timber and firewood, were commonly available to all within the community.[12]

More important perhaps than the communal rights to land were the means by which the ancient Teutons managed the arable land. It was those methods that supposedly led to the development of democratic political rights and the institutions of self-government. Even though individual families farmed strips of land, the community managed the arable land cooperatively, making individuals subject to the will of the majority in determining which crops would be planted, what land would lie fallow, and when the land would be planted and crops harvested. Collective land management by and among the freemen became a primary aspect of self-determinative government. The body of freeman, however, did not restrict their collective efforts to land management, as they also joined together to enact laws and mete out appropriate justice. It was through this communal ownership and management that "liberty was nurtured." These Teutonic principles cast a long and earth-shaking shadow, as "Magna Carta and the Bill of Rights are only the development of those germs of liberty first planted in the communal customs of our Saxon forefathers" who carried the Teutonic "germ" to England and later to America.[13]

The simple proof that the Teutonic ideals traveled to England and from thence to America was that common lands and communal regulation were once widespread in England, as they were in early New England. Herbert Baxter Adams describes the New England town as being

> like that of their Old English and Germanic prototypes . . . [being] a village community of allied families, settled in close proximity for good neighborhood and defense, with homes and home lots fenced in and owned in severalty, but with a common Town Street and a Village Green or Home Pasture, and with common fields, allotted outside the Town for individual mowing and tillage but fenced in common, together with a vast surrounding tract of absolutely common and undivided land, used for pasture and woodland under communal regulations.

He further asserted that "town institutions were propagated in New England by old English and Germanic ideas, brought over by Pilgrims and Puritans, and as ready to take root in the free soil of America as would Egyptian grain which had been drying in a mummy-case for thousands of years." The Pilgrims originally even went so far as to dictate communal labor in addition to communal ownership of land. As Freeman erroneously contended, "The most notable thing of all, yet surely the most natural thing of all, is that the New England settlers of the seventeenth century largely reproduced English institutions in an older shape than they bore in the England of the seventeenth century. They gave a new life to many things which in their older home had well nigh died out." Scholars did not articulate what the germ precisely was, but they believed it represented objective reality rather than metaphor. Teutonists did not endeavor to determine precise historical causality any more than the providential historians had, as they believed that the germ always survived in an active or latent form. They therefore interpreted similarities as causation. Brahmin historians such as Hosmer and the Adamses further contended that the Teutonic germ was most strongly stamped upon the Anglo-Saxon settlers of New England. New England, therefore, represented the ultimate source of American culture and identity.[14]

Those influential academic American Teutonists who argued that the American commitment to freedom and self-government originated in early New England were clearly reacting to the contemporary ethnic/racial context of their current or ancestral home—Boston. In the closing decades of the nineteenth century, elite Bostonians of English heritage were losing their hold on their society, local culture, and the municipal government in the face of waves of immigration, most notably of the Irish. It was not that they were troubled only by the loss of their local political power. They also feared that the future of their political culture and even the self-governing and liberty-loving nature of the nation might be in peril. The logic of this fear was inescapable. If the principle of self-government was uniquely inscribed in them as Teutonic Anglo-Saxons, the non-Anglo-Saxons that were advancing in power could serve only to threaten the political soul of the American people. One way to protect the dominance of Anglo-Americans was through the public commemoration of their heritage through the erection of monuments and the preservation of early structures, which could help educate and acculturate immigrants who did not bear the same roots.[15]

All Americans who described themselves as Anglo-Saxons, however, did not agree with the Brahmin historians and their amateur followers that New England represented the essence of America. Some white, elite Southerners refuted the Brahmins by arguing that it had been *their* particular Anglo-Saxon ancestors, not the Puritan founders of New England, who had actually paved the way for the founding of the American republic. Some Southern writers and historians even claimed that the founding of Jamestown itself had been motivated by the desire to flee monarchical tyranny. They also cited the many Virginians who had taken leadership roles in the Revolution and the Early Republic in the protection of the liberty and rights of Englishmen. Their parents and grandparents had also remained true to their Anglo-Saxon heritage by resisting northern tyranny during the Civil War and Reconstruction, after which they achieved success through Redemption. The efforts of the former Confederates suggested that Southerners might have been the most vigorous of all of the descendants of the ancient Teutons.[16]

It was not only in the context of regional pride that white Southerners asserted their Anglo-Saxon heritage, but also in the context of racial conflict and challenges to white supremacy. They aimed to protect and preserve political Anglo-Saxonism, not simply whiteness, by establishing Jim Crow. Some Northerners even argued that white Southerners were perhaps more purely Anglo-Saxon than those above the Mason-Dixon line because they had been so successful in creating and preserving the color line. Neither had the South been invaded by the immigrant hordes as in the North, which protected Southern Anglo-Saxon purity, a purity not only seen among the Southern elite, but among the rural folk of southern Appalachia. While Northerners and Southerners may have argued as to which of them were the most Anglo-Saxon of all Americans, they nevertheless shared the belief that American culture, politics, and identity were undoubtedly a testament to their Teutonic-Anglo-Saxon roots. Even those of British extraction on the West Coast shared in the promotion of Anglo-Saxonism, as Westerners were struggling with their own immigrants from Asia.[17]

The nineteenth-century conflict over the origins of Americanness was not simply a result of boosterish regional pride. It was invested with great significance because it was a conversation based on the developing concept of race. According to George Frederickson, the significance of "race" and racial classifications in the United States grew dramatically, beginning in the early nineteenth-century, as a direct result of the establishment of an enlightened nation supposedly predicated upon a belief in equality. As Frederickson argues, if one posits human equality within a culture in which some are "so despised or disparaged that the upholders of the norms feel compelled to make them exceptions to the promise or realization of equality," then one has to form a new worldview based on the proposition that those "others" are "less than fully human." "White" Americans—an ambiguous grouping itself—therefore began to construct fixed racial classifications in order to justify the institution of slavery, as well as support a racial caste system within free states. This new order was supported by scientists, both professional and amateur, who aimed to classify physical differences among groups of humans whose origins were in various geographic regions. In particular, they noted variations in skin tone and the shape of the body, particularly the head, which they then correlated with the divergent cultures of different groups. They further extrapolated from these variations in physical appearance and culture to moral condition and degrees of intelligence. To those involved in this intellectual project, these descriptions and correlations suggested that all of these characteristics are linked and permanently fixed in the body. If such separate groups, or "races," of humans demonstrated various degrees of morality, intelligence, and even beauty, they could therefore be arranged hierarchically based on fixed and immutable biological natures.[18]

Race in the nineteenth century was also much more than a classification system that separated humans into a handful of broad groups, as it would later become in the twentieth century. As David Roediger has argued, the distinctions that twentieth- and twenty-first-century Americans have made between ethnicity, generally perceived to be grounded in cultural differences, and race, generally thought to somehow relate to biological variations, simply did not exist before the early twentieth century. Race-thinking in the United States was therefore used to discuss the distinctions even among European ethnocultural groups, including the Irish and the "new" immigrants from southern and eastern Europe. In other words, "Anglo-Saxon" was not simply a synonym for "white"; it was used to define a very specific ethnocultural group. The members of that group perceived themselves as essentially superior to everybody, and as they represented the dominant "racial" group in the United States, all Americans were affected by such a belief in some way or another. The impact on dark-skinned Americans was violence and oppression, but for those who descended from early light-skinned American colonists who were not of Anglo-Saxon heritage, it was marginalization. That was something descendants of the New Paltz founders were unwilling to accept. They simply would not believe that their ancestors had been less important than Anglo-Saxons in creating the United States as a nation of liberty, freedom, and self-government.[19]

The descendants of the New Paltz founders therefore faced their own "race problem," but one that had little to do with that problem as experienced by those with colonial British forebears in the Northeast, South, and West. The descendants who became most active in preserving, interpreting, and celebrating their past, most of whom continued to live in or near New Paltz, virtually never even mentioned any concerns brought upon by contact with "others." The personal challenge patentee descendants faced was that they were not of English heritage, which was a problem because the Anglo-Saxon myth dominated any contemporary discussion concerning the development of American government, culture, and identity. If the New Paltz descendants were to find a place for their continental European ancestors, and thus themselves, in the annals of American history, they would be forced to counter Anglo-Saxonist claims. They did so by constructing their own equally questionable myths.[20]

They also faced a challenge that the Anglo-Saxonists had not, which is that they did not have a single "racial" heritage to honor. They had two. This complexity produced vigorous and contentious arguments among the descendant community itself as to which of their non-English forebears was central to the American story. These arguments suggest that the effort to define American identity upon a racialized view of the past and present was a high-stakes struggle for rhetorical dominance even among those that would later be considered simply "white." By engaging and constructing myths concerning the ethnocultural origins of America, descendants continued to address the challenges of not being ethnically English in a supposedly Anglo-American nation, a challenge that their ancestors had faced ever since the founding of their village.

The Dutch and the "Huguenots" in an Anglo-Saxon Culture

The various modes of historicism—romantic, providential, and racial—all inspired patentee descendants as they interpreted their heritage over the course of the nineteenth century. However, as new approaches to the past were introduced, older models were not always fully abandoned, as they were not mutually exclusive. Individual descendants sometimes did privilege one approach to historical interpretation more than another, but the three approaches continued to remain vital in descendants' understanding of both the past and present throughout the nineteenth century and into the twentieth.

The earliest written history of New Paltz consists of a four-part series on the history of the "Huguenots" of Ulster County that appeared in *The Christian Intelligencer*, a weekly publication of an "Association of Members of the Protestant Reformed Dutch Church," in April and May 1846. Although the authorship of the series was not noted, the editor of the magazine at the time was Rev. Johannes Hornbeck Bevier (b. 1805), a descendant of patentees Louis Bevier and Louis DuBois, among others. The source material for this history included general histories of the Huguenots in France and traditional family narratives that presumably were transmitted orally from the founders to the present day. Later family historians similarly claimed that their history had been passed down through the generations. It cannot be ascertained whether the patentee families had, in fact, created and sustained a rich oral tradition since the community's founding, suggesting at least the possibility that their traditions, or at least aspects of those traditions, were more recently invented. There are also subtle indications that certain elements of what would become their "traditional" narratives developed only as descendants formed and transformed those very narratives.[21]

The series on "The Huguenots of Ulster County" includes the earliest use of the ethno-religious term "Huguenots" in reference to the founders of New Paltz, establishing or perhaps reinforcing an erroneous belief that descendants never subsequently questioned. If the founders were Huguenots, descendants assumed that they must have faced religious persecution in France under the Catholic French monarchs, which the author claimed was encouraged by the pope. The author of the series therefore grounded his narrative in something that the Walloons who founded New Paltz had not faced. It is not clear when most nineteenth-century descendants of the New Paltz founders forgot that their ancestors had been Walloons. Even those few who seemed to have been aware that the founders were not French considered the Walloons from the Spanish Netherlands and Huguenots from France as essentially one and the same, both culturally and historically—which they were not. Descendants apparently found no need to be more precise.

The author interpreted the story of his Protestant ancestors' escape from persecution as a manifestation of God's divine plan to make the United States a haven for and beacon of civil and religious liberty, reflecting the providential millennialism of a number of contemporary American historians. He remarked that if the history of the New Paltz founders had been more carefully preserved, it would have "furnished many an example of patient and cheerful endurance, and numerous evidences of the care and faithfulness of God, and his gracious providence toward the posterity of his devoted servants." The author of the series also used the story of the New Paltz families to ground a vigorous anti-Catholic polemic in an era when verbal and even physical attacks on Catholics and Catholicism were widespread. The author cast the worst blame for the persecution of the founders' families on the pope, reflecting the popular critique of "papism" of the early nineteenth century. The author noted that "in 1656, Louis XIV, in compliance with the urgent solicitation of the Papal clergy, revoked the declaration of St. Germain, and soon afterwards enacted a law of great severity on Protestants." That was just the beginning. According to the *Intelligencer*, "The ever restless priests forced their way into the chambers of sickness," and "annoyed the dying with their arguments and entreaties, to renounce the Protestant faith. The utmost efforts were made to strengthen the Papacy." The editor of the *Intelligencer* series would most certainly have agreed with his first cousin and childhood neighbor, Abraham Garrett Bevier, who wrote in the same year as the *Intelligencer* articles that it was the "Pope of Rome and his emissaries [who] compel[led] them to bow down and worship the Beast with seven heads and ten horns, whose name is '*Blasphemy*.'"[22]

The author of the series nevertheless considered the crown's denial of religious and civil freedoms for the Huguenots of France to have been a relatively mild aspect of their persecution. Far more egregious was the physical violence that the Huguenots supposedly suffered after the Revocation of the Edict of Nantes, the horrors of which the author strained to sufficiently describe. The author distressingly tells the story of how

> men and women were hung up by their hair, and smoked with wisps of wet hay. They were thrown into fires, and when partly burnt, taken out. Wine was forced down the throats of some until

> they became intoxicated, and their consent was obtained to join the Papists. Infants were taken from their mothers, and placed in near apartments, where their cries could be heard, and there kept until famine put an end to their sufferings. . . . The sick and dying were tormented by the beating of a dozen drums around their beds . . . so that the poor wretches, if not released by death, became insane. If all of these . . .did not compel submission, they were thrown into prisons, such as we would fain hope are not to be found in modern days. Those who attempted to flee, were pursued and hunted like wild beasts.

Many of the Huguenots nevertheless fought on, driven by their undying commitment to their faith, subjecting themselves to what the author transparently likens to the sufferings of the martyrs of old. The editor of the *Intelligencer* series was not alone in his sentiments, as his cousin A. G. Bevier offered similar words: "Their ancestors had sacrificed their estates in a foreign land, and endured unparalleled privations and sufferings; all of which they might have avoided, by consenting to have '*the mark of the Beast* in their foreheads or their rights hands,' but they chose rather to die than to deny their Saviour."[23]

As the author of the *Intelligencer* series well knew, however, the founders of New Paltz had left a number of years before such horrors commenced. (He nevertheless failed to understand that the founders were not even from France.) Luckily, they appear to have been prescient, as their "shrewd minds discerned the tokens of a tempest gathering." But such shrewdness did not rest within themselves alone; it was God himself who inspired them to flee their homeland in anticipation of mounting oppression. As their coreligionists suffered and died, the New Paltz refugees were "quietly located on the banks of the Wallkill, breathing the balmy atmosphere of civil and religious freedom . . . and worshipping God according to the dictates of their conscience, without the . . . contravention of either kings or bishops. . . . It was God alone who caused the difference. . . . His everlasting arms were underneath and around them; and in due time he brought them to their desired haven—far out of the reach of their Popish oppressors." In claiming that God had saved his ancestors from the cruelties of the pope and Louis XIV, the author elevated himself and his kinspeople as God's chosen people. He believed that God had indeed chosen the patentees and their families to bear religious and civic liberty to the New World, thus placing them at the core of American exceptionalist ideology.[24]

In order to establish such a commendable position for his ancestors, the author of the *Intelligencer* series had to carefully and selectively engage the evidence, as a critical assessment of it would have seriously undermined his interpretation. He simply *knew* that his ancestors had fled religious persecution, so he interpreted all evidence through such a lens, setting a pattern to which later descendants closely adhered. This was particularly so when he addressed the dates of his ancestors' migrations. He asserted that "according to the best authorities extant, it is beyond all doubt, that the greater part arrived, *not only after the surrender* of the Province by the Dutch to the

English . . . [in] A.D. 1664; but even after its re-capture by the Dutch, in 1673; but the majority of them arrived in July 1675." The author is partially correct, as some of the founders did not arrive until the 1670s. However, he categorically dismissed an alternative history that he knew was then circulating, which "stated that the party to which Louis Dubois was attached, reached this country as early as 1660." "[T]he correctness of this [story]," he claimed, "is, to say the least, *questionable*," as it "was not fortified by collateral facts." He was, in fact, in error, but he simply had to dismiss any evidence that might have suggested that the first patentees had arrived in 1660. Had he not, he would have been unable to account for another aspect of the Huguenot story that he did correctly note, which was that between "the death of Louis XIII, A.D. 1644, under the administration of Cardinal Mazarin [1644–1661], their [i.e., the Huguenots'] condition was comparatively happy." If he had accepted the assertion that DuBois left during Mazarin's administration, he could not have argued that he had fled religious persecution. Of course, DuBois was not even from France, so he never faced either Mazarin's administration or the rule of Louis XIV, but given that the author believed that DuBois had faced French rule, he had to misinterpret the evidence in order to save the overarching theme of his narrative.[25]

In noting that his divinely guided ancestors had had the foresight to flee before facing the horrific fate of the Huguenots at home, the author of the *Intelligencer* nevertheless did not deprive them of the opportunity to confront similar trials. In doing so, he was the first to offer in print a tale that became central to the grand narrative of the New Paltz descendant community. In the New World, it was not the Catholic Church that endangered the founders; rather, it was the savage, heathen Indians, who kidnapped the wife and three children of Louis DuBois in the midst of the Second Esopus War in 1663. Catherine Blanchan DuBois and her children were, in fact, taken captive during the conflict, as were Catherine's sister Maria Blanchan Crispell and her child, and the two children of Matthew Blanchan Jr., Catherine's brother. However, the essence of the story that had reportedly been transmitted orally down through the generations had little to do with the documentable facts. Through their mythologizing, descendants transformed the tale into one of Christian heroism that rivaled that of the Huguenot martyrs, reinforcing the belief that pious French-speaking Protestants served as bulwarks against the forces of evil in both the Old World and the New.

At the start of the Second Esopus War, the DuBois, Crispell, and Blanchan families were living in Nieuw Dorp (later Hurley), a few miles south of the main center of settlement in Wiltwijck (later Kingston). On June 7, 1663, Nieuw Dorp was burned to the ground, as was a considerable part of Wiltwijck. Those responsible for the destruction—the Esopus Indians—then took captive members of those families, along with thirty-seven others. Pieter Stuyvesant placed Captain Martin Kreiger in charge of the military efforts against the Esopus. Kreiger then dedicated himself to reclaiming the captives. After several months of intelligence gathering, searching, and negotiations, during which time some of the captives were returned, Kreiger learned of the location of a new fort that the Esopus were building. He assumed that some of the remaining captives were being kept there. On September 3, Kreiger led a rescue party, which included his military forces and "seven freemen," who arrived at the fort on September 5. An attack ensued, and many of the Esopus fled, making it possible for the rescue party to reclaim twenty-three of the captives. The party then plundered and destroyed the Indians' village and returned to Wiltwijck on September 7.[26]

Kreiger never mentioned who from the villages was included in the party, but the author of the *Intelligencer* series claimed that one of their number was Louis DuBois, who became the hero of his tale. The author writes that after months of separation, a "friendly Indian" informed DuBois of the location of his wife and children, whereupon "they immediately slung their knapsacks, shouldered their rifles, and calling their dogs, pursued their perilous journey—a small, but desperate and determined band." (A Wappingers Indian had indeed provided information about the new Esopus fort, but he gave that intelligence to Lieutenant Pieter van Couwenhoven, not DuBois.) According to the *Intelligencer*, the party had nearly reached the Indian encampment, when "coming near the spot, towards evening, Dubois being in advance alone, to guard against an ambuscade, discovered an Indian, partly concealed behind a tree, within a few feet of him. He was in the act of putting his arrow on his bow-string; but trembling through surprise or fear, he missed the notch of the arrow in applying it to the string, which Dubois observing, he sprang on him and despatched him with his sword without giving any alarm." The rescue party proceeded on to the Indian fort, arriving just as the Indians were preparing to burn Louis' wife, Catherine, to death at the stake. To prolong her life, the pious Catherine began to sing Psalm 137. Her choice was particularly appropriate, as the Israelites had chosen to sing that psalm to their Babylonian captors, who "required of us mirth, saying, 'Sing us one of the songs of Zion.'" Her devout singing momentarily stayed the hands of the Indians, a moment just long enough for the intrepid Louis DuBois to bravely charge into the fort and save his wife from a horrific death. Without her faith, and her courageous hero, she would have certainly perished.[27]

Other than the basic fact that a rescue party did reclaim the captives, little of this tale is included in the official journal of Captain Kreiger. Kreiger offers nothing to suggest that the Esopus were preparing to torture and kill Catherine DuBois, her children, and her kin. If something as dramatic and deadly as that almost transpired, it would seem strange that Kreiger failed to mention it. Kreiger's journal does indicate that the Esopus had told the white captives that if "the Dutch come thither, we will give you a knock and kill you all at once," but the most likely purpose for doing so would have been to relieve the Indians of their human burden, so that they could fight or escape more easily. Neither does he mention that DuBois was in the vanguard or that he was even there, although it is certainly possible that he did participate in the rescue.[28]

The only time Kreiger mentions DuBois is in an entry from the following month, in which he relates a far less "heroic" story of survival that perhaps inspired the story of how DuBois killed an Indian as the rescue party neared the fort. Kreiger reported that "Louis the Wallon went today to fetch his oxen . . . as he was about to drive home the oxen, three Indians, who lay in the bush and intended to seize him, leaped forth. When one of these shot at him with an arrow but only slightly wounded him, and Louis, having a piece of a palisade in his hand, struck the Indian on the breast with it so that he staggered back." The *Intelligencer* author did not know of this event, since he never consulted the documentary record, although he knew of its existence. The similarity between Kreiger's report on DuBois and the family legend therefore suggests that somewhat dubious stories of the war had indeed passed down through the families, which at least some of them accepted without any further evidentiary support.[29]

The author of the series provides little direct interpretation of the event, but he clearly links Catherine's potential murder to the Catholic oppressions of French Huguenots. Just as Catherine was threatened with death by fire, so too had the Huguenots in France been "thrown into fires, and when partly burnt, taken out." The tale also reflects contemporary romantic historicism, with the main actors representing piety and bravery. The author of the series also suggests the guiding hand of Providence in tune with the millenialist interpretation of the American past. The author remarks that "it was on this expedition" to recover Catherine that "they first discovered the Paltz lowlands," which led to the founding of the village of New Paltz, the establishment of which enabled them to worship according to their God-given Protestant faith in a free land. These linked and fanciful stories—persecution in France and near martyrdom in America, leading to the founding of a final permanent refuge—first offered in print in the 1840s, were not fundamentally questioned, but often enhanced, for well more than a century.[30]

The author of the *Christian Intelligencer* series offered additional "traditional" tales, many of which were ultimately found to be untrue or at least problematic. Their inaccuracy, however, never motivated descendants to question the core element of the grand narrative of persecution. For example, the *Intelligencer* series relates that "according to tradition, a gentleman by the name of Deyo, one of the twelve patentees . . . was reported to the French Papal authorities by his own wife. In the subsequent conduct of this woman, however, notwithstanding her treachery, a ray of affection is said to have shone forth; for when the gens-d'arms entered at the front door, she not only gave her husband notice, but as he fled through a back way, ran to a window in the second story, and putting her head out of the casement, exclaimed—'Adieu, Peter, adieu.'" This story is patently untrue. Pierre Deyo left his homeland as a child with his family some time before 1655, and he did not marry until 1675 when he and his recently widowed father, Christian, were living in Mutterstadt. The author was likely not aware of that bit of evidence, although he should have been aware that there was a host of American Deyos who descended from Pierre Deyo and his only wife, Agetta, who had come to America with him. Equally questionable is the story of patentee "Louis Bevier . . . [who] was on the eve of leaving France, [when] his own brother was so exasperated at him, (being doubtless a deluded Papist,) that he refused to reciprocate the most common civilities:

not condescending, on meeting him in the street, to notice him as much as to respond to the ordinary salutation of social courtesy, which was respectfully tendered by the emigrant." As Louis Bevier was born in the Palatinate within a Protestant family and community, such an event simply could not have occurred. These clearly questionable aspects of the traditional narrative should have brought it in its entirety into question, but for well more than a century, its core elements were never put to the test.[31]

As the *Intelligencer* series appeared in a newspaper, the ephemeral nature of the medium suggests that it likely reached relatively few eyes. It did, however, reach some members of the Pennsylvania branch of the DuBois family, inspiring them to explore their family history further. Several of these men, including William Ewing Du Bois, Rev. Robert Patterson Du Bois, Louis Du Bois, and Charles Du Bois, conducted additional research and later published a second history of New Paltz—the 1860 *Record of the Family of Louis Du Bois.* They began their research within their immediate families in Pennsylvania, but as they could derive little from tradition, they embarked on travels through New Jersey (where a son of patentee Abraham DuBois had settled early in the eighteenth century) and later New Paltz, which they visited in 1846. They also conducted documentary research in order to flesh out the stories they had heard from descendants through the course of their travels. The DuBois version was also probably not widely disseminated, as it was produced in very few numbers strictly for family use, but the *Record* was just the beginning of the DuBois family's historicizing.[32]

The first foray of the DuBois men into history making was relatively thin on interpretation and relied even less on rhetoric. In a limited way, they suggested that their ancestors had been inspired by God to remove to a land where He could be worshipped in freedom, linking their narrative to the providential interpretation of American history. They, like the author of the *Intelligencer* series, erroneously believed that Louis DuBois had been a persecuted French Huguenot rather than a Walloon from the Spanish Netherlands. They deduced that Louis, unwilling to "defile his conscience," fled persecution sometime around 1658, bringing his family to America in 1660 by way of Mannheim, an assertion that the author of the *Intelligencer* series would have patently denied. They assumed that Louis had been motivated to leave his homeland in about 1658 with the death of Oliver Cromwell, whom they believed had been keeping "a watchful eye" over Catholic France, such that persecutions would presumably have increased after his death.[33]

Thanking God for having guided Louis in his migrations, they beseeched "the same kind Providence which permitted our great and good *Paterfamilias* to be driven into exile, that he might in this land become the founder of a family of free citizens and true Christians." The DuBois men expressed their thankfulness for the fact that it was Louis' blood that flows through their veins." They further exalted him for his character, as one of "greater heart, in a good cause," although they did not suggest that Louis' character was an essential physical characteristic derived from his "blood." They argued that Louis led the founding of New Paltz so that "they might enjoy their proper language, customs and worship. Along with that, they had, of course, a purpose of improving their earthly condition." That latter point, while legitimate—and accurate—was virtually ignored by other descendants, at least in print, as it ran counter to the moral and political center of their narrative.[34]

The *Record* also included the story of the rescue of Catherine DuBois, although the authors mentioned it in a somewhat off-handed manner. Unlike the author of the *Intelligencer* history, the authors had not yet fully committed to that tradition. Quoting directly from the *Intelligencer* article, the authors of the *Record* remarked that Catherine's rescue from the stake "instead of being a part of this transaction, probably related to another Indian foray, of less account and of later date. At all events, we give it for what it is worth." These family historians appear to have questioned the accuracy of the folktale because they, unlike the author of the *Intelligencer* series, had read Kreiger's official journal, which said nothing of Louis or the impending murder of Catherine. They nevertheless wanted it to be true, which led them to contradict themselves. After first questioning the story, they immediately reversed their position, offering in print "the very words used by our mother, whose life, with that of her children, was saved by her song." The rescue myth, and its expression of the piety of their foremother, was apparently too compelling to dismiss entirely, although they were hesitant to accept it based solely on tradition. The overall tone of the *Record* is that the DuBois men considered their story strictly as a family story rather than a history of great import. Their approach would change dramatically in the coming years.[35]

Before that would occur, however, other descendants closer to New Paltz aimed to bring attention to their ancestors in ways that would later influence both the authors of the *Record* as well as their kinsmen. One mechanism that made this possible was the founding of the Ulster County Historical Society in 1859, through which patentee descendants offered a variety of romantic, providential, and historical interpretations of their ancestral past. In doing so, they began to argue that their forebears were not just of family or local significance but of national importance as well. The motivation for the creation of the Ulster County Historical Society was patriotism, and the founders beckoned the current generation to preserve historic papers, "relics," and "Legends or traditions" as tools to construct "a correct history of the State." The founders of the society "sincerely hope[d] that the pride of the people in, and their patriotic love for, their homes, will induce all cordially to assist in carrying out the objects of this Society." The dates for the meetings of the society were chosen to commemorate annually the anniversaries of two formative events in the history of the county: the burning of Kingston by British forces in the Revolution (October 16, 1777) and the "massacre" at Kingston (then Wiltwijck) on June 7, 1663, which was the beginning of the Second Esopus War and the date several of the New Paltz forebears had been taken captive.[36]

A. Bruyn Hasbrouck, a lawyer and former president of Rutgers College, served as the first president of the Ulster County Historical Society. In his founding address, he primarily and atypically considered the past through a historical lens, suggesting that the present was the result of past human actions and events. He declared that the colonial development of the region and the adoption of the 1777 New York Constitution in Kingston were stories that needed to be told, as "it will be one of the results of our enquiries to mark and define the influences of each upon our present condition and character." This historical method of interpretation ultimately had little impact on his nineteenth-century kinsmen. However, he had greater influence in his use of a romantic perspective, characterizing the story of Catherine DuBois's captivity and rescue as "a romantic tale well worthy of the pictured pages of Walter Scott." He remarked that the "lonely intrepid colonists who first ventured upon these savage-haunted wilds . . . kept alive and bright the reverence for religion, and the love of religious freedom, which, in the days of their ancestors, had been so signally displayed in Holland, under William of Orange, and in France, by the Huguenots under the murdered Coligny." In referencing the Dutch and the French, he feigned to claim a superior position for either, suggesting that no ethnocultural or ethnoracial group held a monopoly on the desire for liberty. He was even willing to honor Anglo-Americans as a people who embraced liberty and promoted its advancement. As a New Yorker, he proudly noted that the first New York state constitution was "the work of Jay" (a descendant of a French Huguenot) "and Hamilton and Morris." Nevertheless, Hasbrouck did declare that his ancestors had brought a "germ of civilization" to the American shores. He further remarked that "the seed thus sown in the forest by these humble and pious men, has ripened into the stern morality and strict religious observances which, in our day, are the marked characteristics of their descendants." Hasbrouck did not ascribe an ethnoracial quality to that "germ" or "seed," although others later would.[37]

The founding of the Ulster County Historical Society also provided a mechanism for other New Paltz patentee descendants to publically explore the history of their ancestors, including Edmund Eltinge, an 1835 graduate of Rutgers College and a lifelong resident of New Paltz. Eltinge first penned a story of early New Paltz in his 1862 version of the captivity narrative of Catherine DuBois, from whom Eltinge descended through her son Abraham, who had also been taken captive in the Esopus War. This story was very close to Eltinge's heart, so much so that he even commissioned a large oil painting for his home in the 1850s, depicting the near-burning of Catherine by the Indians. Apparently, however, Eltinge learned of the legend only after the 1846 publication of the story in the *Intelligencer*, suggesting that it was not a story that had descended within the families in New Paltz proper. In a letter he wrote in 1843 to a correspondent in Lancaster, Pennsylvania, who had written to Eltinge for information about the history of New Paltz, Eltinge included absolutely nothing of the legend. He merely noted that between the emigration of the earliest patentee immigrants and the acquisition of the New Paltz patent, "the Huguenots of Ulster spent a few years of unsettled life at Kingston and in the meantime explored the country." Neither did he suggest that the founding of New Paltz was linked to the rescue initiative. He merely remarked that "those [New York Huguenots] who were poor came to Kingston," suggesting that their decision to withdraw to the wilderness rather than to stay closer to the urban center was determined entirely by economics. Although Eltinge's 1843 comments suggest that the traditional narrative had apparently not been transmitted across the generations in New Paltz itself, many descendants would later claim that it had. Neither did Eltinge initially perceive the experience of his ancestors as having been particularly significant in American history, although that too changed over time.[38]

In Eltinge's hand, the story of the founders and the founding of New Paltz lost much of the anti-Catholicism of the *Intelligencer* version, as his was not primarily a religious narrative, although it certainly bore religious content. He did, however, follow the *Intelligencer's* providential interpretation, furthering the transformation of the story into an epic tale that represented the origins of American political identity. Following yet extending A. B. Hasbrouck's interpretation, Eltinge asserted that his ancestors had transported the supposed "germ" of liberty to the American shores. The patentees were "men who loved liberty," and driven by "the cruelties and barbarisms of tyranny of the old world," brought "in their breasts . . . the precious freedom as the basis of our confederated republic, which has grown into a form of beauty, strength and benignity, which has not its like on the globe." He further remarked that his ancestors had a particular "attachment to the principles of the Bible as the Grand Constitution of all government," and that "they carried in their bosoms a portion of the constituent elements of our great and glorious governmental fabric." He did believe that they possessed within themselves the "germ" of civic liberty, but he does not claim that that "germ" was physically inscribed in their bodies. For both Eltinge and Hasbrouck, the germ was more metaphoric than biologic.[39]

As Eltinge retold the story in the mode of a number of providential antebellum American historians, so too was his version linked to the romantic literary idiom of the time, with its inclusions of elements both picturesque and sublime. When the residents of Wiltwijck (Kingston) and Nieuw Dorp (Hurley) let down their guard against the possible depredations of the "children of the forest," they had lost their "fatal security! For now the savages had formed their hellish purposes, and were thirsting for the blood of these devoted pioneers." All those pioneers did not perish in the ensuing massacre, however, which later permitted the intrepid romantic hero and his pious, devoted wife to make their appearances as representative heroes for a contemporary audience. Leading the pursuit to reclaim his captive wife and children, "Lewis DuBois, whose ardor in the pursuit could not be excelled, moved on at the head of the party, more agile and strong than the others . . . [as a]n Indian secreted behind a tree, just at the moment he was discovered by DuBois, who let go his arrow upon him," killing the Indian on the spot. Arriving at the Indians' campsite, "on the very spot where faggots had been piled to execute these women," including Louis' wife, Catherine, the rescuers found "these devoted women [who] had resorted to singing psalms and hymns to buoy up their own spirits and breathe out their trust upon the All-wise Governor of the universe, and, singularly as it may appear, it was the means of prolonging the time of their intended final death by the savages." In the years that followed, when the founders of New Paltz made their fifteen-mile journey to their new home, it became clear that not only was God on their side but also nature itself: "On their way, doubtless, these pioneers breathed forth upon the gentle spring breezes their holy songs in which they dedicated themselves anew to the service of their Father in Heaven, whose providences seemed to lead them on to a happy home. Animate creation too seemed playful. The songs of birds and chirpings of squirrels and other game cheered them on their way."[40]

Eltinge and Hasbrouck expressed the belief that their ancestors were thoroughly committed to civil and religious liberty, and that their commitment significantly contributed to the development of the United States. Yet, like other romantic historians, their paradigm was sufficiently expansive to include the possibility that others could also have made important contributions, including those of Anglo-Saxon descent. They believed the American commitment to liberty and freedom was the product of the shared heritage and contribution of the French, Dutch, and English. Not thinking in an ethnoracially competitive manner, they found no need to claim that they and their non-English ancestors were uniquely important to the story of American liberty and freedom.

The descendants' construction of their history and its significance, however, became more racialized and exclusive when the descendants of Louis DuBois and his brother Jacques (who did not settle in Ulster County) organized a family reunion and public commemoration of the bicentenary of their ancestors' arrival in America, held in New Paltz in 1875. It is clear that by then, "blood" had taken upon a new deterministic role as DuBois descendants began to construct a genetic interpretation of Louis and his compatriots' legacy. Of course, they did not use the word "genetics," using such terms as "race" and "blood" instead; but by claiming that their forebear's experiences were dependent upon the biological characteristics of the ancestral "stock," they suggested that those essential characteristics were their physical birthright, defining their present as much as it defined the past. Such ideas reflected the growing contemporary American trend to conceive of American history as the progress of a race. The descendants of the New Paltz patentees, however, did not find the dominant Anglo-Saxonist racial narrative sufficient, so they constructed a new history for themselves in which their ancestors played the central role in establishing the ideals of the nation.[41]

As they reconstructed their history within a new racial paradigm, another influential voice joined their celebration—that of the Rev. Dr. Anson Du Bois, who was instrumental in "bringing the tribe together" for the reunion. Rev. Du Bois, an 1847 graduate of Rutgers and one-time president of the Dutch Reformed Church in America, rejoiced at the presence of so many descendants of the DuBois brothers, "though bearing other names, inherit as fully as ourselves the blood of our ancestors." This blood, he believed, was "more honorable than the blood of perjured, persecuting kings." He certainly was not alone in extolling the virtue of the racialized blood of their ancestors and thus their own as well. A similar perspective was offered in an anonymous poem of thanksgiving offered at the reunion, a poem which delves into the persecution of the Huguenots—a group of which the poet erroneously assumes the DuBois brothers had been a part—and their flight from their homeland. The poet remarked, "And here we meet to praise His name For all His mercies and His grace, And for the honor He vouchsafed to Louis, James [i.e., Jacques DuBois], and all our race." Dr. Henry A. DuBois, in commenting upon the "general characteristics of the race," similarly declared that his ancestors were guided by "piety, courage and honorable principles which they transmitted to their descendants." He further maintained that "amongst the earliest and very best settlers of this country, the Huguenots stand foremost as a race. Wherever they settled, north or south, they have been noted as virtuous and useful citizens, honorable men, and fearless upholders of civil and religious liberty." That Henry DuBois was thinking racially is also reflected in a reference to the "Teutonic Race" in his discussion of the origins of Anglo-American surnames, clearly demonstrating his awareness of the Anglo-Saxon myth. Cornelius DuBois, another attendee, likewise interpreted them through a racial paradigm, although he uncharacteristically referred to the DuBois family as "Walloons." He claimed that the Walloons "were by nature and descent a brave and hardy race." He nevertheless blurred the distinction between Walloons and Huguenots, suggesting that his ancestors were simultaneously both, remarking that "the Huguenots . . . were an intelligent as well as a religious and a chivalric race." For Cornelius DuBois, Walloons and Huguenots were apparently of the same race, being linked by their use of the French language, such that for him, language and racialized nationalism went hand in hand.[42]

Rev. R. Patterson Du Bois also asserted that races possessed particular attributes, which through descent remained "characteristics of the family." He pointed out that "this family have been so ramified with other names, so scattered abroad over the land, so diversified in their circumstances and surroundings, that we must expect to find with them, as with every other wide-spread race, a mingling of opposite kinds. Yet, with all this, something definite and positive may be properly said." In claiming such persistence in spite of the combining of races, Rev. R. Patterson Du Bois further suggested that the strength of the Huguenot blood was such that it could dominate those of other European racial groups. Using a Lamarckian theoretical paradigm to explain the transmission of acquired physical characteristics, R. Patterson Du Bois noted that the founders "were all well adapted to make them the hardy vigorous men they were, and [were able] to transmit the same iron constitution to their family." He further remarked that the patentees having been "self-governing and intelligent citizens . . . led to the transmission of the same character to those who have sprung from them." R. Patterson Du Bois was at variance with some of his kinsmen, however, as he was willing to claim that Huguenots were not alone in contributing to the civil and religious liberty of the American nation. He remarked that "the Huguenot and Dutch elements being diffused so early as the seventeenth century . . . have always been admitted by our country's historians to have brought to bear a most powerful influence for good in moulding the character of this whole American people. They greatly aided in making this a protestant nation. They helped to secure its liberty and independence."

His inclusion of the Dutch in the American story nevertheless did not serve to counter his racial claims.[43]

Many DuBois descendants construed the term "Huguenot" in racial terms, which on the surface seems rather peculiar, since the Huguenots were simply French adherents of Reformed Protestantism. However, in constructing race as they did, descendants could not have viewed Huguenots as simply French, as that would have required them to logically conclude that some French people promoted religious liberty while others religious intolerance. Since they believed that the desire for liberty inhered deep within the very bodies of the Huguenots, they were therefore forced to conclude that the Huguenots must be distinct from the French. This is not to say that the DuBois descendants never referred to themselves and their ancestors as French. For example, Anson Du Bois, in describing the wagons used to transport the patentee families, remarked that "they are unmistakably French-built . . . made by French mechanics, and loaded with French goods and furniture . . . and there were precious little French babies stowed snugly into them." In harping on the Frenchness of the people and their material culture, however, Du Bois was simply calling attention to the fact that his patentee ancestors were distinct from their Dutch neighbors, which became one of his primary concerns in later years. The DuBois descendants essentially blurred the distinction between French, Walloon, and Huguenot, as did other descendants, sometimes combining them into one, and sometimes dividing them into three separate races, depending upon the issue at hand, reflecting the protean character of race itself. Simply put, they *needed* to think of Huguenots, and thus themselves, as a distinct liberty-loving race. Otherwise, they would have been totally eclipsed by the descendants of Anglo-Saxon colonists who, according to the arguments of contemporary Anglo-American historians, had been ever attached to liberty, freedom, and self-government. If the patentee descendants were to prevent their own marginalization, then members of a distinct race of Huguenots they must be.[44]

All descendants, however, were not satisfied with the claim that the Huguenots were the only race to which the patentee descendants should give honor. The Harvard-educated Irving Elting, another descendant of patentees Louis and Abraham DuBois, chose to accentuate the historic importance of the Dutch "race" in both New York and the nation as a whole. Through twisted logic, he nevertheless found an important place in American history for his French-speaking New Paltz ancestors as well, and not just any place, but a supposedly central position.

Elting brought a new aspect of the racial myths of the United States' political origin to the fore, based on the Teutonic germ theory, a theory then being promoted by the American Herbert Baxter Adams and the Englishman Edward Freeman. For Adams and most of his followers, the exploration of the legacy of the Teutonic people had generally been focused upon early New England towns and their institutional life. Elting, however, aimed to broaden, and possibly even recenter, discussions of the supposed Teutonic past of America to include the Dutch and the political institutions they created in New Netherland/New York. He achieved some success, as his monograph,

"Dutch Village Communities on the Hudson River," was published in 1886 in Adams's own Johns Hopkins series in the history of political institutions.[45]

Elting's primary argument was that the Dutch "village communities" along the Hudson River shared Teutonic origins with the towns of New England. This was the case because both employed the concept of a "commons," which Teutonist historians argued was a vestige of the ancient Teutonic "Mark," which in turn was linked to the Teutons' legendary self-government. Perhaps, suggested Elting, the Dutch immigrants were even closer to the original source. Whereas Freeman had argued that the New Englanders had actually revived a dormant English sociopolitical system in the New World, Elting held forth that that system had never been submerged in "the forest regions of the Lower Palatinate east of the Rhine, and in those northern provinces of the Netherlands—Friesland, Groningen and Drenthe." (Not surprisingly, Drenthe was the birthplace of the American progenitor of the Eltinge family, Jan Eltinge.) Thus, "the liberty-loving Netherlanders had . . . preserved much of the freedom of the people, which the feudal system had tended to crush out." In the New World, they therefore established "village rights of common in regard to land [which] were accompanied . . . by rights of common participation in the deliberative assembly of the people." In a flourish harkening back to the romantic historians of a previous generation, Elting claimed that in the actions of New Amsterdam burghers who unanimously accepted taxes in November 1653, "one needs no great power of the imagination to fancy that he hears, in the unanimously spoken 'Yes!' of the Dutch assembly something very like the shaking of spears and clashing of shields with which the sturdy warlike Teutons signified assent to the plans of their chieftains in the open-air meetings of the tribe!" In his summation, he asserted that "from this more recent confederation of States in the Netherlands, one may derive by a continuous race-tradition, through the Dutch village communities on the Hudson river, that principle of the union of sovereign powers which gave form to our United States."[46]

Although Elting claimed that all of the Dutch immigrants to America helped to transfer the Teutonic ideals to the New World, he argued for a particular and perhaps unique contribution made by the Walloon/Huguenot patentees of New Paltz to the origins of American society and government. His commitment to the Teutonic germ theory was such that he was even able to interpret the history of his Walloon/Huguenot ancestors through such a lens, even though the patentees could in no way be considered scions of the Teutonic race. This argument was constructed out of three interrelated parts. The first was that Elting claimed that the Walloon patentees created a commons when they established their new community, as did their Dutch neighbors. That they did own commonly held lands is a fact, as subdivisions of the patent became private property only as they were parceled out to the patentees and their descendants, a process which took several generations.

The second arm of his three-pronged argument, however, was based on a highly questionable legend, which held that in New Paltz "the lands were first tilled in common and the proceeds were divided equally." Other family historians had referenced this "fact" in the past, but only as an interesting peculiarity. For Irving Elting, that aspect of the narrative was essential, as it fundamentally grounded his claims for the historical significance of the patentees. As common ownership of arable land was the cultural centerpiece of the Teutonic race, out of which self-government developed, he could claim that his ancestors had been primary transmitters of self-government to the American shores because they too owned and farmed land collectively. Irving Elting forcefully remarked that "perhaps no documents now exist which establish the evidence of this early cultivation in common of tracts of the arable land by the numerous co-owners, but tradition, both trustworthy and direct, places the matter almost beyond question." In reality, the question was anything but adequately answered, as the only evidence Elting had was limited and untrustworthy oral history. He claimed, "One of the worthy representatives of her Huguenot ancestors told the writer a few weeks ago that in her younger days she used frequently to hear an old resident of New Paltz relate how his mother . . . after becoming a widow . . . [took] her turn in caring for the common stock and crops, as her husband had done before." Elting did not indicate the age of that informant, but the story suggests that that widow who tended to the common fields and animals was doing so in the mid-eighteenth century at the earliest. It is absolutely certain that no one was raising stocks and crops communally at that point, if they ever had, but the point was too important for Elting's argument to interrogate it too closely.[47]

The third and most important element in Irving Elting's argument was his contention that the patentees governed their village through a perfectly democratic government: the Duzine. Its existence supposedly proved the Teutonic roots of the patentees' political organization, which further confirms their contribution to the political ideals of the United States. As previously explored, however, the Duzine did not represent the government of New Paltz. Rather, it was simply an efficient and legal means of managing a jointly held land patent, inspired by laws enacted by the Anglo-American colonial government.

Again, Elting was not the first to call attention to the Duzine, although he was the first to imbue it with racial significance. Rev. Charles Stitt, one-time pastor of the New Paltz Dutch Reformed Church, first published the story in 1862 in the collections of the Ulster County Historical Society. He presumably had collected it from patentee descendants. In documenting the story, Stitt attempted to bring the Duzine into the greater narrative of the United States, remarking that it was formed through "a *social compact* [emphasis in the original], no less remarkable than that which formed on board the May Flower [*sic*]." It was actually nothing of the sort, since it was not a civil government. Rev. Anson Du Bois offered a similar tale. In referring to the Duzine as the civil government, he pointedly noted that even though "we must assume the right of appeal to the colonial government, no such appeal is known to have been made, or disputed boundary, or internal feud to have disturbed the absolute harmony of the settlement." Du Bois's intention in relating the story was not to make historical connections between the Duzine and American self-governing political forms, but rather to suggest that the "absolute harmony" of life under the Duzine was an outgrowth of God's granting of a promised land to His chosen people. For the patentees, "in their deepest hearts they felt this to be a paradise, and the mercies of God in bringing them hither like his mercies to his ancient covenant people." Du Bois simply offered a corrective to the Anglo-American Protestants who claimed a particular, divinely ordained mission in America for their ancestors, as truly, Du Bois's ancestors were the favorites of God.[48]

Irving Elting also called upon the legend, but because the Duzine grounded the connections between the ancient Teutons, the patentees, and the origins of self-government in America, he had to take greater pains than others to prove that the Duzine represented the government. Such a proof was difficult for a trained historian such as Elting, since he was well aware that local governments had been created by provincial statutes. He also knew that the Duzine had not even been created until 1728, fifty years after the founding of New Paltz. To cover this problematic, Elting simply obfuscated by noting that the twelve patentee themselves were originally called "the Duzine" or "the Twelve Men," although no documents exist supporting such a contention. This assertion would become another standard myth. Elting nevertheless hedges, noting that "for more than a hundred years, the 'Twelve Men' or 'Duzine' of New Paltz, had *practically* [emphasis added] constituted the only legislative and judicial tribunal of the village. No doubt an appeal lay to the colonial government, but as far as is known, none seems to have been taken." Elting claimed that the Duzine's legislative function was evidenced by fencing requirements established in New Paltz in 1712 in response to county orders. He nevertheless failed to note that it was not the Duzine but "the inhabitants" of New Paltz who had created the regulations after having been instructed to do so by the county government. Elting further argued that the Duzine's supposed judicial powers lay in their power to divide land. Since no such decisions were ever appealed to the colonial provincial government, Elting deduced that the Duzine itself must have resolved any conflicts, even though there is no evidence to suggest that conflicts had ever arisen. In other words, the very lack of judicial records of the Duzine supposedly—and paradoxically—proved its judicial powers. Perhaps it could be argued that the Duzine did possess quasi-legal and quasi-judicial functions in regards to land divisions, but it did not possess legal and judicial authority, which clearly resided in the institutions that stemmed from the provincial government.[49]

While he asserted that the Dutch of New York preserved Teutonic "characteristics of early village community-life," he stressed his belief that the New Paltz patentees recreated the most Teuton-like practices in the New World by establishing a near-perfect form of democracy in the Duzine. If the New Paltz founders created a community based on the most ancient of Teutonic roots, and if the American democratic republic's sources could be found among the ancient Teutons, then New Paltz represented the most profoundly American community of any in North America. A challenge for Elting, however, was that he was fully aware that New Paltz had not been founded by those who could make any claim to being members of the Teutonic race. Yet he did find a solution to this problem, through which he linked both his Huguenot and Dutch ancestors through the lens of the Teutonic germ theory.

The culmination of his argument was that the Walloon founders of New Paltz "had probably gained familiarity with the free village community government, afterwards established here, during their residence on the banks of the Rhine of the German Palatinate," which, paradoxically, was actually ruled by the Elector Palatine. Irving Elting therefore could grandiosely argue that New Paltz represented the origins of the United States itself. He held forth that "from the banks of the Rhine, the germs of free local institutions, borne on the tide of western emigration, found here, along the Hudson, a more fruitful soil than New England afforded for the growth of those forms of municipal, state, and national government, which have made the United States the leading Republic among the nations."[50]

His argument would not be one that many other racially obsessed descendants could accept. Since Elting could in no way contend that his Huguenot/Walloon ancestors possessed the racial "germ" that advanced liberty, he essentially argued that they had been heavily influenced by their temporary yet close proximity to another race. Such an argument suggests that his French-speaking forebears must have been racially weak, if they were indeed vulnerable to the influence of another race. That was a suggestion that Anson Du Bois and others who promoted the racial value and contribution of the "Huguenot" patentees could never have accepted. For Elting, however, the Teutons were paramount, as they were the unique bearers of the germ of liberty and self-government. He therefore gripped his Teutonist interpretation as tenaciously as necessary, regardless of how it impacted the racial position of his Huguenot/Walloon ancestors. And indeed the power of that Teutonic germ was indescribable, as even merely brushing against it for a few years had utterly transformed his ancestors, enabling the patentees to create a government out of which a new republic was generated, perhaps the most important the world had yet seen.[51]

Chapter 7

SET in STONE

The various strains of providentialism, romantic nationalism, and racial determinism that led nineteenth-century descendants of the New Paltz founders to claim their ancestors' historical importance produced various interpretations of the New Paltz story. The events and experiences descendants highlighted, many of which were either fanciful or inaccurate, were offered not as evidence that needed to be interpreted but as proof of something they already knew existed: the power of God's guiding hand and/or the deterministic impact of race. Descendants did not construct their own historical paradigms but simply followed the theoretical frameworks created by other historians, both in the United States and Europe.

They did not, however, agree with the Anglo-American scholars who argued that Anglo-Saxons had been divinely ordained or racially determined to advance the cause of liberty in America. They argued for the powerful influence of their "Huguenot" and/or their Dutch forebears instead. But as descendants did not agree with the Anglo-Saxonists, they also did not agree with each other. They offered various perspectives as to which "race" they believed had been more significant in the history of America, primarily because they all did not privilege the same theories of history. Their basic narrative did not change, but their interpretations of it did. Edmund Eltinge interpreted the past through a providential and romantic nationalist lens, while Anson Du Bois held a providential and racial perspective. Irving Elting followed a racial paradigm exclusively, but as a Teutonist/Anglo-Saxonist, he remained committed to a very specific one at that. Each felt free to construct the past as he saw fit, and for many years, they did so without any overt conflict among themselves. That changed when descendants in the 1890s made the momentous decision to commemorate and honor their forebears publically. As each interpretation reflected a different perspective on the role specific ethnocultural groups played in the community's, and thus the nation's, past, only when the various interpretations of New Paltz's history were brought into conversation was the cohesiveness of the descendant community challenged. Once again, descendants of the founders would struggle to find a place for their non-Englishness in an Anglo nation. They did not all find the same solution, such that their experience continued to reflect the challenges the patentees and their descendants had been facing ever since New Paltz was founded.

Creating a National Audience

A primary figure in advancing the cause of history in the descendant community was Ralph LeFevre (1844–1925), the publisher and editor of the *New Paltz Independent* from 1869 through 1925. Beginning in the 1880s, LeFevre encouraged a lively public discussion in which the history and significance of the New Paltz founders were presented to and expounded upon by descendants throughout the United States. LeFevre had been heavily influenced by the earlier publications discussed above, and he furthered their reach by disseminating those stories and interpretations to a broader audience. He added a great deal more by collecting and publishing additional primary material, traditional stories, reminiscences, and genealogies related to the history of his ancestral community. The newspaper also served as a forum for other descendants to participate in the history-making process. LeFevre eventually compiled much of this history into book form. That work of antiquarianism reached an even broader audience, including some who had no ancestral connections to the village, as attested to by reviews that appeared in the *Nation*, the *New York Tribune*, and the *Brooklyn Daily Eagle*. His efforts and influence ultimately motivated the descendants to create sites of memory, which could serve as monuments to and for themselves and a source of inspiration for the public at large.[1]

LeFevre's interpretation of the New Paltz myths and legends is distinct from the earlier published New Paltz histories that influenced him, as he generally did not highlight one interpretation or theoretical perspective over another. Rather, he attempted to synthesize them, as demonstrated by the remarks he published on April 22, 1898. Those comments encapsulate the tone and substance of both the DuBois and the Elting/Eltinge histories. He offered these remarks following his attendance at a Huguenot Society of America dinner in New York City the previous week, held in honor of the 300th anniversary of the promulgation of the Edict of Nantes. LeFevre effused that "it is a generally recognized fact that no place on the continent is more dear to the Huguenot heart than New Paltz, because of the romantic circumstances of the settlement and because New Paltz remained for so long a period a distinctive Huguenot community, where the French language was spoken and used in church records." He further emphasized the significance of New Paltz by asserting that it "perhaps [was] the only place in America where the government was patriarchal and the authority of the original proprietors perpetuated in the Dusine." LeFevre stressed both the continuity of the history as well as his growing concern for historic preservation, noting that "even to the present day the old stone houses of the fathers remain to a great extent and some are still owned by their descendants." He further remarked upon other speeches given at the anniversary celebration, noting that "by the time they were ended no one could doubt that the old Huguenots were indeed a wonderful race. It is to be hoped that their descendants of the present day will try to imitate their virtues." While LeFevre referenced contemporary arguments on race, he also harkened back to the comments made by A. Bruyn Hasbrouck at the founding of the Ulster County Historical

Society. Both he and Hasbrouck suggested that their ancestors should provide inspiration, not that they had necessarily provided their descendants with a biological birthright. Although LeFevre did not fully imbibe the idea that culture was strictly based on genetics, it would have been impossible to employ the word "race" in the 1890s without implying to his audience its fixed and essentialist meanings.[2]

Through the *Independent*, LeFevre, like many other descendants, demonstrated that the significance of their "Huguenot" racial heritage was grounded in the supposed persecution of their ancestors, as well as their corresponding commitment to religious liberty. In December 1894, LeFevre wrote, "New Paltz [was] a little hamlet . . . where a handful of French Huguenots, fleeing from persecution had found a home and a refuge, where they might worship God in peace and rear their families in comfort." He erroneously took for granted that the patentee families were of those "half a million of subjects of the French king [who] left their native country and fled to foreign lands," after "1661, when Louis XIV himself assumed the reins of authority, until the formal revocation of the Edict of Nantes, in 1685, which was the last act in a series of persecutions." While LeFevre did note that Louis DuBois and Antoine Crispell had arrived in New Netherland a year before Louis XIV took control of his realm, he failed to consider the implications of that fact, since doing so would have undermined his interpretation. He likewise overlooked the fact that DuBois and Crispell had not even fled from a region under Louis' control. Like many other descendants, LeFevre consistently maintained a belief that his ancestors had fled persecution as Huguenots, even when available evidence conflicted with, or at the very least problematized, the legend.[3]

LeFevre did not adulate the Huguenots alone, as he also brought to the fore the supposed contribution of the scions of the Teutons in America, particularly through their efforts to advance civic liberty and self-government through the Duzine. In focusing upon the Duzine, he, like Irving Elting, simultaneously evoked not only the Dutch, who supposedly brought their own vision of self-government to the American shores, but the "Huguenot" patentees as well. LeFevre erroneously believed that the patentees "perpetuated the government of the Dusine bro't with them from the Rhine," such that "the government of New Paltz in the earliest period was evidently a pure Democracy." Again, like Elting, LeFevre claimed that the Duzine "exercised, to some extent, judicial as well as legislative Powers," even though he, too, was well aware that local officials were also elected according to provincial law. LeFevre likewise linked self-government and communal farming. He consistently referred to "evidence" that proved his assertions, although he demurred in highlighting what it comprised. This, of course, is not surprising, since such evidence did not exist.[4]

In a unique instance, attorney Frank Hasbrouck of Poughkeepsie questioned the myth that the Duzine possessed judicial authority, but he was the only contemporary of LeFevre who ever did. He also countered those who claimed that the patentees themselves had been called the Duzine. Hasbrouck correctly asserted that "the agreement of April 21st, 1728" functioned as the "charter of the Duzine," and that "the controversies were not of such character that they could be settled by the Dusine; but were settled by the courts of justice of those days." Hasbrouck nevertheless still maintained that the Duzine served as the town's government, although he failed to explore in what ways they actually governed or how the village was governed before the Duzine's creation. Although Ralph LeFevre published Frank Hasbrouck's legitimate protest, limited as it was, that protest fell on deaf ears.[5]

In bringing attention to their Huguenot and Dutch forebears, descendants provided a corrective to the Anglo-American historians' primary interest in the English Puritans as having been the basis for the American republic. The Hon. G. D. B. Hasbrouck, for example, noted that "the Puritan and the Hollander have always had a penchant for self-government, and could not long resist the tendency to try and set it up." Anson Du Bois was even less interested in the New Englanders than Hasbrouck, bemoaning that "I suppose that almost everybody has heard of Plymouth Rock. Is it not a good thing that they are gradually learning that there are other places where fidelity to religious principles and to all those civic and social virtues which elevate and adorn human life is as fully and as beautifully illustrated as in those now so worthily famous?" Ralph LeFevre similarly wanted to take the Puritans down a peg. He suggested that the Huguenots should claim the greatest attention, remarking that "no one will question that their memory is entitled to at least equal honor with that of the Puritans of New England." Charles Freer, of Warren, Ohio, went even further, claiming the superiority of his Huguenot ancestors over the Puritans, the latter who undertook their own persecutions. Although his mother, a "Vermont Yankee" was of the opinion that "what did not come over in the Mayflower and plant itself on Plymouth Rock, was not worth saving, indeed had no kind of business in America at all," he extolled the virtues of his Huguenot ancestors over the Pilgrims and Puritans. "Though they had been subject to endless persecutions," he remarked, "yet they were never persecutors, burnt no churches, abused no Catholics, hung no Quakers and burnt no witches."[6]

Those involved in constructing a history of New Paltz also viewed their collective past through a highly gendered lens, which would bear important implications for the commemoration of both the Walloon/Huguenot and Dutch legacies. With only one exception, articles in the newspaper stressed that descendants should honor the founding fathers exclusively; founding mothers were apparently just passive recipients of male agency and ideals. According to Ralph LeFevre, it was in "the old graveyard, where the Huguenot fathers sleep," although the mothers had found their eternal rest there as well. He later commented that "when the [commemorative] monument is built and the names of the Patentees placed on it, people will understand that . . . [it is] a memorial to the Huguenot fathers of the community." C. Elting Crispell noted that his interest in the history of New Paltz was due to the fact that "the faith and lives of our forefathers are read there, and we need not blush for the reading." Similarly, the Rev. R. Patterson Du Bois remarked that descendants possessed a "title to the truer nobility of the soul, which our Huguenot fathers have bequeathed us in the annals of an heroic devotion to their faith." If it was only the male founders of the village who carried the desire for liberty and piety, presumably those desires were only borne in the male line. As a result, descendants who lacked a patentee surname—which meant that they were connected to a patentee through a woman—would have a much looser claim to the patentees' legacy and a much greater desire to also honor their Dutch ancestors.[7]

The articles LeFevre published concerning the French/Walloon and Dutch legacy, as well as a more general discussion of New Paltz history, attracted interest from a diverse array of descendants from throughout the country, a fact of which LeFevre was exceedingly proud. LeFevre remarked in 1894 that "the letters which come to hand from different parts of the country certainly show that the work is appreciated." Again on July 19, 1895, LeFevre reported that "quite a number of letters have come to hand of late from persons who are interested in the early history of New Paltz." Such correspondents hailed from such diverse places as Chicago, Philadelphia, and New York City, as well as from rural Georgia and Pennsylvania. In May 1896, LeFevre published a more complete list, which included sixty-six individuals from thirteen states and the District of Columbia "who during [just] the past year have taken the Independent on account of its old time sketches, or have sent for back copies of the paper containing these sketches," or "who were warmly interested in the history of New Paltz, or of Ulster county."[8]

It was not only descendants who were interested in the village's history, a point which LeFevre did not refrain from publicizing. Those who corresponded with LeFevre included the Rev. Dr. David D. Demarest, who for much of the second half of the nineteenth century was a professor at the New Brunswick Theological Seminary and a trustee of Rutgers College. Another correspondent was Dr. Henry M. Baird, a professor at New York University and the author of three standard works concerning the history of the Huguenots in France. Included on that list is also the extremely wealthy philanthropist Mrs. Russell Sage, who apparently had a strong interest in Huguenot history, as she became an honorary member of the Huguenot Society of America in 1909. LeFevre also proudly noted that "we think we may claim that no newspaper articles published in this county have ever been so widely copied or commented upon, as those in the Independent concerning the early history of New Paltz. We learned not long since that one of these articles, published last fall, had been copied in the Albany Journal and the Biographical and Genealogical Record published in Philadelphia."[9]

Many descendants involved in creating a usable past soon became convinced that something as ephemeral as a newspaper was an insufficient tool of commemoration. Something more permanent and accessible was needed. Descendants came to believe that a physical memorial could serve as a pilgrimage site for ancestor-worshipping descendants, as well as for the general public. Many agreed and offered their resources to support the goal. But who was worthy of celebration? The Huguenots? The Dutch? Both? The answer to this question would not be unanimous, and this lack of consensus would lead to public conflict. Through their heated disputes, descendants demonstrated how their non-English western European heritage remained a challenge for those who lived in an Anglo-American world. That challenge would become only more powerful as racial rhetoric came to define history making in the late nineteenth century.

Mobilizing for Commemoration

The efforts to create a site of celebration and commemoration were initiated by Edmund Eltinge, who, in August 1893 proposed that a memorial monument be constructed. This idea was soon aired in the pages of the *Independent*, initiating a vigorous discussion within the descendant community. What Eltinge proposed was a stone monument that would be topped with "bronzed figures of a Hollander and a Huguenot with clasped hands," and to that end, he had secured a sketch for the monument from noted sculptor George Edward Bissell. According to Eltinge, a number of descendants warmly embraced both the idea of a monument as well as the proposed design, being "particularly pleased" with the overall concept.[10]

As soon as Eltinge proposed such a monument, however, descendants began to suggest and advocate for other forms of commemoration. One semi-anonymous descendant soon suggested that a "Pioneer Memorial Society" be formed to preserve the gravesites of early settlers of the New Paltz region, with a preference given first to the graves of the Huguenot founders. Such an effort would be "very worthy of those whose virtues and labors we wish to commemorate and would in its entirety be a fitting completion by their descendants of the important work they did." In contrast, Rev. James LeFevre of Middlebush, New Jersey, believed that "a fire-proof building, with historical and library compartments would be a profitable as well as suitable memorial."[11]

Ralph LeFevre took that idea one step further when he opined that "the best monument to the Huguenot settlers of New Paltz would be not a shaft of granite or marble, but one of the quaint old houses that our forefathers built, filled with relics of the olden times. A tablet could and should be placed on the wall, with the names of the twelve patentees and something concerning their history." As the editor and publisher of the newspaper, he ensured that others who favored the acquisition of a house were also heard. In the same issue of the newspaper that LeFevre proposed the acquisition of a house, he also printed a letter from Dr. John Deyo of Newburgh, New York, who suggested that "a better plan would be for all interested parties to subscribe to a fund to buy and preserve the old DuBois, Hasbrouck, Deyo and any other house originally occupied by the patentees, rather than put up a monument. The houses could be turned over to some Society or association in New Paltz and always prove an attraction and 'Mecca' to which all interested, and the outside world, could be invited to admire and inspect. They could be filled with relics."[12]

These discussions became more than theoretical when, in December 1893, a group of sixteen influential male descendants of the patentees came together to form the "Huguenot Patriotic Historical and Monumental Society of New Paltz." The Articles of Incorporation adopted by thirty-two men present at a subsequent meeting clearly stated the society's purposes, which included *all* of the many possible commemorative activities that had been discussed over the previous several months. Although the list of possible endeavors was not prioritized, the first stated in the Articles of Incorporation was also the first that had been suggested—a monument—a project that was near and dear to Edmund Eltinge's heart. The society therefore stated one of its primary goals as being "to record the virtues, and to perpetuate the memory of the Huguenot Patentees of New Paltz and of the early settlers on the New Paltz Patent by erecting and maintaining a suitable monument to the Patentees at New Paltz Village." Fifteen individuals were chosen to serve as trustees, including Ralph LeFevre (who would serve as president throughout the society's formative years), Edmund Eltinge, and Irving Elting, as well as members of the DuBois, Deyo, Bevier, and Hasbrouck families. While the majority of the thirty-two men who became charter members of the society possessed a patentee surname, all did not, as seven bore an Eltinge surname. Other early Ulster County families were also represented, including Van Wagenen and Clearwater, both of which were Dutch. Those without a patrilineal connection the to the founders were therefore also keenly interested in preserving the legacy of other "early settlers," as so stated in the society's goals, which were almost exclusively Dutch or other Batavianized European-Americans.[13]

After its formation, the trustees of the society immediately began to discuss future projects, beginning with the proposed George Bissell design for the monument. They also soon began to consider the "relative merits of different old stone houses in this village as store-houses of the relics of the early settlers of New Paltz." A committee of three was formed "to obtain refusal of properties for a House and a Monument site." As early as March, however, it became quite clear that the trustees of the society were at odds with each other as to which should come first. Edmund Eltinge moved that the first project be the erection of the monument, and although seconded, it was never voted upon because of too much dissension. Ralph LeFevre later reported that discussion had ranged even more broadly, as some believed that the society should concentrate on cemetery preservation, "where the bones of the early settlers repose," and another man suggested that a "tablet with the names of all the list of pastors should be placed in the Reformed church."[14]

The committee assigned to explore possible houses for acquisition reported in March that they believed that the so-called Jean Hasbrouck House was most appropriate. They also revealed that the owner, Jesse Elting, had offered it to the society for $3,500, although he was willing to contribute $500 of that price. Other houses on Huguenot Street that were considered and rejected included the Maria DuBois House and the Deyo House, both of which had been heavily altered, as well as the Samuel Bevier House, although the committee dismissed that structure as inappropriate due to its apparently poor condition. It appears that the committee never considered any house other than those on Huguenot Street, but that was probably due to their erroneous belief that the houses in the historic village core had been built by the patentees themselves. The committee opined that the most appropriate site for the monument was "the

Village triangle," a small plot of ground owned by the Village in front of the Jean Hasbrouck House.[15]

The first official meeting of the society after its legal establishment was held on April 25, 1894, at which time the members made the decision to begin caring for the burying ground immediately. They also agreed to acquire a safe to store the important historical records of the community, including the church records and the "papers of the Patentees." A fundraising committee was established for each of the patentee families, and the trustees authorized the publication and distribution of a solicitation letter written by Frank Hasbrouck of Poughkeepsie. In his missive, Hasbrouck noted the society's intention both to acquire a house and construct a monument, for which they intended to raise $10,000. The society expressed much confidence that their endeavor would move forward successfully, as "no difficulty is anticipated in easily and speedily raising that amount from the numerous descendants, of their generation, who feel proud of his descent from those sterling men of early days. It is hoped that every descendant whom this appeal reaches will contribute liberally according to their means." One thousand copies were to be printed and distributed by the family committees, the agents of which were called upon for their "persever[ance] and indefatigable determination. Success will be your Crown. The praise of succeeding generations your reward." They felt confident that success would be quickly achieved, as "it is not alone New Paltz, nor Ulster county; but descendants of all Huguenots are interested. And in the success of the undertaking every lover of the Huguenot name and of the Huguenot virtues should take a warm interest." The executive committee therefore set the date of October 1, 1894, for the payment of all pledges.[16]

Support for the initiative was in theory quite broad, but when funds were sought, support was neither quite as wide nor as deep as the society had hoped. As of August 1895, only $1,700 had been collected or pledged, less than one-fifth of the desired result. Many of the donors lived in the vicinity, but donations were also received from descendants in New York City, Chicago, Virginia, and Kansas. Those involved in the effort still expressed much hope for success, as "when such men as Messrs. Irving Elting and Frank Hasbrouck of Poughkeepsie . . . Edmund Eltinge and others, meet to organize a society, we know that it can hardly fail of success." There was apparently some discussion among the leadership concerning the possibility of seeking donations from those who had not descended from the patentees (LeFevre had noted the previous August that a local non-descendant had suggested such an approach), but the society hoped that they could remain exclusive. Given that the commemorative site would be dedicated to ancestor worship, which, by extension, implied the celebration of contemporary descendants as well, it is hardly surprising that descendants found no reason to include non-kin who happened to live in the community. Only after "a more complete canvass made of those who are descendants from the Huguenot patentees, others, residing in New Paltz, will be invited to contribute." Inclusivity would be sought only if economic necessity dictated.[17]

After two more years of fundraising, cash on hand and pledges had hardly increased. That fact did not deter LeFevre, who showed himself to be a savvy fundraiser. If nothing sells like success, he wanted his public to know that the society was clearly making progress toward its goal, with support from a geographically broad constituency of descendants. LeFevre carefully chose letters from donors to the fund from both near and far whose words might activate the philanthropic spirit of others. Most of these letters suggested that descendants should donate out of respect for their ancestors but secondarily as a means of supporting the economic development of New Paltz. One such letter came from William E. Du Bois of Maiden Lane, New York City, who remarked, "The main attraction at New Paltz we understand to be that this place was the home of his fathers. When the old stone house becomes a store house of antiquities and the monument to the early settlers is erected we doubt not that many descendants of the Huguenots who are now scattered over the country will take pleasure in visiting New Paltz and spending a vacation here. This should be inducement to our village people to subscribe to the Huguenot Memorial fund." LeFevre also printed a letter from New Paltz's former pastor, Rev. Ame Vennema, who had served the community from 1882 to 1886. Vennema understood perfectly that LeFevre was using these letters to demonstrate that there was sufficient support for the endeavor, which in turn would promote confidence that the project was indeed achievable. As Rev. Vennema wrote, "Now you may expect help from people living between the oceans east and west and between the lakes and gulf north and south. You can appeal with good grace to the many who, enriched with an inheritance of noble blood and sterling character for which they are indebted to their ancestry, have gone from among your midst and made their fortunes elsewhere, even in distant parts of our land. And if I do not misinterpret the letters . . . their authors are only waiting a convenient opportunity to convert and crystalize the sentiments of esteem and appreciation these letters contain, into something more substantial and enduring."[18]

In 1896, Ralph LeFevre also published an extended address of Rev. James LeFevre (of Middlebush, New Jersey), given to the Huguenot Society of America the previous year, as a means of offering his perspective through the words of another. In his address, James LeFevre retold with adulation the history of the village and its founders, and further related the efforts of the society to erect a monument and acquire the Jean Hasbrouck House. James LeFevre described the house, and the stone houses in general, as a symbol that accentuated the strength and commitment of the founders, who fled persecution and aimed to create a permanent home of religious and civil liberty—"a distinct commonwealth"—for their posterity. According to Rev. LeFevre, "the work [in the stone houses] is all substantial. There was evidently no slighting of work by mechanics in those days. The old settlers meant to stay, and they built their houses for themselves and their posterity." He implied that the founders' concern for their progeny should be balanced by the descendants' willingness to honor their ancestors by keeping their memory alive. Rev. LeFevre was even willing to tug on his auditors' conservative and nostalgic heartstrings (as Ralph LeFevre likewise aimed to do in republishing the address) to guilt them into donating, remarking that

> one of the sdadest [*sic*] things to be seen in this country is the giving up of landed estates; old homes. They are readily relinquished, sold out to anybody; even deserted and allowed to go to ruin. Ancestral acres held by old parchment deeds, substantial houses full of old heir-looms and fuller of old memories; the very floors still echoing the tread of some stalwart sire, and the rustle of a mother's bridal dress; the very walls throwing back one's own childhood laughter; sold, instead of held. No thought of making and keeping them a center of family affection, a rallying place and a resting place, for any and all of the latest generations; to which the childless Naomies might return for sympathy and the widowed Ruths for cheer.

Rev. LeFevre closed with a progress report concerning the raising of funds and an implicit request for more donations. In reprinting such words, Ralph LeFevre made a call for more support not only through his own pleas but through those of others as well.[19]

Although funds were not coming in as fast as desired, the society had reached a point in December 1896 that required its leaders to decide which of their ideas to execute first. The question as to whether a monument should be erected before a historic house was purchased nevertheless remained as controversial as it had been when first posed two-and-one-half years earlier. After going in circles yet again in a subsequent April 1897 meeting, the Board of Trustees decided that they would put the matter to a vote on May 11, 1897. Before that decision was to be made, Abraham Hasbrouck and Ralph LeFevre were appointed to discuss the current asking price for the Jean Hasbrouck House with its owner, Jesse Elting. However, the scheduled May vote was apparently never taken, and a final decision had not yet been made even three months later.[20]

It is not entirely clear why the issue remained such a contentious one. Ralph LeFevre's own preference was decidedly in favor of the purchase of the house, and he seems to have used his newspaper as a bully pulpit to advance his agenda. One argument he offered was that a house would generate more tourism than a monument, and thus a museum would be better for local economic development. In February 1898, for example, he noted that Washington's Headquarters in Newburgh received more than twenty thousand visitors a year, implying that the Jean Hasbrouck House would attract many visitors as well. LeFevre further remarked that "we really think that when the old house is fitted up as a museum of antiquities that it will be considered one of the most interesting places in the United States and that visitors from all parts of the country will come to New Paltz." William E. Du Bois agreed, suggesting that time was of the essence, urging that "a monument is a mere matter of dollars and cents and can be erected at any time and anywhere. . . . But the old houses, especially those with history behind them, are fast disappearing and few remain in their original state. They are, of course, no curiosity to people in New Paltz; but people from far and near will travel to see them, as they do at the present time to see the Senate house at Kingston,

Washington's Headquarters, Mount Vernon and the Huguenot house at San Augustine, Florida." Simply put, while the United States was replete with monuments, LeFevre believed that upon the creation of a house museum, "there will not be just such another place in the country."[21]

As much as he asserted that the transformation of a house into a commemorative site would generate tourism, LeFevre's commitment to the project was clearly based on more than dollars and cents. He cared deeply about honoring the supposed civil and religious legacy of his ancestors, but he found the houses particularly compelling. He believed that "in no other place in our country, the homesteads have been handed down in the family ever since the first settlement . . . the Huguenots kept their grip on their own old homesteads, and their conservatism we consider a more remarkable point." The houses served as a unique statement of continuity in a modernizing world. His interest in the past, as well as his research and publishing, was also topically more extensive, including his concern for his ancestors' role in the Revolution, which linked him to broader national trends. That was something that did not particularly concern his peers. He remarked how "it is surprising that nearly all recollections of the Revolutionary record of their ancestors has [*sic*] faded from the minds of men of the present generation." He further expressed his sadness that not only had information not been preserved, but that artifacts were also in short supply. His broader interests sometimes led him even to forget to include the word "Huguenot" in the society's name, a faux pas that other descendants could never have made. Instead, he sometimes referred to it as the "New Paltz Monumental and Historical Society" or the "New Paltz Memorial Society," revealing his concern for the community's history as a whole.[22]

LeFevre's desire for a museum house was predicated upon the belief that a house could express that broader history more fully than a didactic monument dedicated exclusively to honoring the founders' religious and civic lives. If the descendants created a "Huguenot Home"—not just a house—it could be "fitted up with antique furniture in parlor, sitting room and kitchen, to show just how the people lived 200 years ago." He remarked that "we know of no more interesting relics to be placed in the Memorial House in this village than the cradles, tables and furniure [*sic*] of all kinds, which the old people used in parlor, hall and kitchen." Inspired to create domestic scenes that had become popular beginning with the old-time kitchen at the Centennial Exposition, LeFevre cherished the artifacts both as connections to a homely past and as representations of the "vicissitudes of pioneer life" in an age of massive technological change. LeFevre likewise believed that historic documents and books, such as the many family Bibles collected for exhibition in a house, would likewise strengthen visitors' connection with the past. While a monument was one means of honoring the past, interaction with a unique and rare house furnished as a home would connect contemporary individuals emotionally to the past far more effectively, at least in LeFevre's eyes. Those who advocated for a monument apparently did not likewise perceive the power of historical objects, thinking instead that the purchase of a house would leave them with nothing more than a useless and meaningless responsibility and expense. LeFevre took pains to argue just the opposite, remarking that "nobody need think that the society will have an elephant on its hands."[23]

In total, LeFevre seems to have been much more aware of and more strongly motivated than his peers by those aspects of the Colonial Revival movement that involved the preservation and exhibition of material culture as one reaction to a changing present. His ideas were in tune with such historic preservationists as William Sumner Appleton and Wallace Nutting, as well as the work of newly formed patriotic and genealogical societies including the Daughters of the American Revolution (DAR; founded 1890, with a local chapter having been formed in Kingston in 1892) and the National Society of the Colonial Dames of America (founded 1891). He was clearly aware of the work of those female societies, which they partly accomplished through historic preservation. He even noted that the DAR chapter in Kingston was endeavoring to raise funds for "the purchase of an old stone house, to be used for the preservation of memorials." LeFevre thought the ladies might be best served by purchasing a house in New Paltz, as that town "has more historic old stone houses than we know what to do with."[24]

While LeFevre's clear preference was for purchasing the house before erecting a monument, he did not want to directly use his newspaper to advance his position. He even remarked disingenuously that "we wish it understood that we take no sides in this question," presumably using the first person plural in reference to the newspaper, the voice of which was essentially his own. That did not mean, however, that he was unwilling to indirectly push for his agenda, which he did by stressing the opinions of those who recommended the immediate purchase of the house, whom he claimed were in the majority. He also opined that "more money has been contributed by people living outside of New Paltz than by New Paltz people and the people who contributed the money ought to have the privilege of saying whether they preferred to have it used in the purchase of a house at once or to wait until enough is raised for both purposes." And the desires of those beyond the community were apparently clear: "The expression of opinion from people outside of New Paltz in regard to the proper action of the Huguenot Memorial Society, seems to be practically unanimous that the old stone house should be purchased now and the erection of the monument deferred." To advance this argument, LeFevre published letters that supported it, such as that of William E. Du Bois, who forcefully pointed out that "my contribution I intended for the purchase of the old house. . . . A monument can be erected later. But, first of all, I hope the old house will be purchased, restored and preserved in honor of our forefathers—a sort of object lesson to our children in these progressive times," such that he too referenced contemporary motivations for historic preservation. LeFevre further contended that "as Mr. DuBois is the largest contributor to the Memorial fund his views are entitled to special consideration," a point which permitted LeFevre to express support for the acquisition of a house without taking a forceful position himself.[25]

An apparent stumbling block to the purchase of the house was surmounted upon the death of Edmund Eltinge on December 1, 1897, as he had been the most prominent voice in favor of postponing the acquisition of a house until a monument had been erected. His passing was nevertheless mourned, and in February 1898, at the first meeting of the officers and executive committee after his death, the grateful partners in the commemorative endeavor noted that "the first thought and suggestion of such a memorial originated in his patriotic mind. While his pride in race, and his loyalty to his descent suggested a preference as to the character of that memorial, his liberality of spirit refused to dictate the acceptance of such preference as a donation of his allegiance to our society."[26]

In spite of their grief, the society's leaders moved right along, creating a committee "appointed to obtain old relics, old furniture, farm implements, books, papers, etc., to be placed in the building when the purchase is made," even though no vote had yet been taken concerning the purchase of the Jean Hasbrouck House. The society's leadership simply assumed its purchase was inevitable and would come sooner rather than later. Undated minutes recorded between April 13 and July 15 indicate further that the society's treasurer be "requested to collect all pledges and promises of money . . . by July 15th 1898," so that the house could be purchased by July 1. When a meeting of the officers and executive committee was convened on July 16, the seven attendees resolved "that the deed for the 'old house' be prepared and executed ready for delivery," even though a formal vote had still not been taken. Fundraising nevertheless continued in order to meet the $3,000 price tag: as of January 1899, eighty-six individuals had made donations, in amounts ranging from $2 to $210.68. An unexpected donation of $100 from Charles Lang Freer, a descendant unknown in the community but whose collection would ultimately form the Freer Gallery at the Smithsonian, brought them one step closer to their goal. Even though some individuals had specifically provided funds for the monument, the society's leadership chose to overlook their wishes, choosing instead to dedicate all monies as they saw fit. Finally, on January 7, 1899, almost five years after the society was formed, the purchase of the house was effected, and in the minutes of a February 1899 meeting, the purchase was treated simply as a fait accompli. Neither LeFevre, nor the society's records, reveal how the final decision to purchase the house had been made. President LeFevre, perhaps improperly, had achieved his goal: but in resolving one controversy, a much more intense one was beginning to brew, one that would bring the issue of race front and center.[27]

Who's on Top?

For much of the latter half of the nineteenth century, the discussion of the contribution of both the Huguenots and the Dutch to New Paltz history, and by extension to American history, was amicable. (Of course, their heritage was Walloon rather than French Huguenot, but for nineteenth-century descendants, that point was immaterial, since they uniformly constructed themselves as French Huguenots whose ancestors had faced persecution in France.) One reason for this was that all patentee descendants had ancestors in both groups. They were willing to acknowledge and honor both, but within limits, as they all did not agree as to the relative value of each group's contribution to the development of their ancestral village, their nation, and even humanity itself.

A consideration of this question of value was not merely academic, as it bore implications for descendants' vision of their own place in the contemporary world. This was the case because they believed that racial characteristics were patrilineal; if one bore a "Huguenot" or a Dutch surname, then by definition that person remained "Huguenot" or Dutch today. As Irving Elting remarked, the Jean Hasbrouck House "was purchased by the contributions not of Huguenots alone, nor even of Huguenot and Dutch together." Ralph LeFevre echoed this perspective when he remarked that Elting expressed "the Dutch standpoint," even though LeFevre knew that Elting's New Paltz heritage was rooted in the marriage of a "Huguenot" woman, Sara DuBois (the daughter of patentee Abraham DuBois), and a Dutch man, Roelof Eltinge. The European race of one's female ancestors apparently had no bearing on one's racial nature. Dr. John Coert DuBois offered a similar comment, remarking that "from my French descent, I joined the Huguenot Society; from my Dutch ancestry, I became a member of the Holland Society." Yet, he put a call out to "the Dutch descendants of Ulster" to donate to the commemorative efforts in concert with "the sons of the Huguenots," suggesting that they were distinct groups. To put this another way, descendants simultaneously considered themselves both French *and* Dutch, based on their genealogy, but also French *or* Dutch, a belief grounded in their gendered conceptions of race. If a descendant considered himself either French or Dutch, then his value today could be inferred from the presumed value of his patriline. And indeed this issue was primarily a question for and about men, since they believed that it was their forefathers and not their foremothers who were active agents in any historical processes.[28]

Conflict among the descendants over the relative value of the French and the Dutch began when, after a "hot discussion," at the April 10, 1899, annual meeting of the society, the officers and members in attendance voted to name the house "The Huguenot-Holland Memorial House," in recognition of the importance of both to the heritage of the community. The shock this decision engendered cannot be understated. The first to enter the public controversy was Rev. Anson Du Bois, who had been publicly acclaiming the racial heritage of the Huguenots since as early as 1875. As soon as he learned of the decision, he shot off a deeply heartfelt tirade to Ralph LeFevre, who immediately published the letter in his newspaper. Rev. Du Bois fulminated, "You can scarcely imagine with what surprise and pain I received your announcement. . . . Why at this late date divide honors equally between two parties when in all reason and fairness these honors belong wholly to one party, and not to the other?" Clearly the town was established by Huguenots rather than the Dutch, who, according to Du Bois, had no reason to strike out into the "wilderness . . . with savages and wild beasts for neighbors." As he again erroneously argued, it was his Huguenot ancestors "who had been driven from home, and country, and rights for their religious faith. They would go and camp down there in the woods upon the naked earth. They had their Bible their common heritage of sacrifices and sufferings, their hope in God and nothing else." He did acknowledge his own Dutch heritage, for he willingly "honor[ed] the Hollanders for what they have done, and for what they are, and [he did] not forget how large a proportion of [his] own blood flowed first in Holland veins." That fact, however, need not be commemorated, as "the intermarriage of our ancestors with the Dutch was neither a fault or a misfortune. It fell out so in the natural progress of the years. But it did not change the basal facts of the history. It did not endow the Dutch with what did not otherwise belong to them, and it did not take from the French what was clearly theirs." By stating that "our ancestors" intermarried with the Dutch, when he could have just as appropriately remarked that "our ancestors" had intermarried with the Huguenots, he connects himself most strongly with his French Protestant forebears, a connection made obvious by his surname.[29]

From Du Bois's perspective, the Dutch were insignificant in establishing a nation of liberty, either religious or civil, whereas the Huguenots had been essential. Echoing the early modern English critique of the Dutch, he remarked, "They migrated . . . wholly of their own choice to better their material interests," or as he had put it simply in 1875, the Dutch came for "*peltry* not *piety*." The Huguenots, on the other hand, had sought both religious and civil liberty, as evidenced by their establishment of the Duzine. He did not connect the desire for self-government with the Teutonic germ, implicitly suggesting that it was their piety and morality, drawn from their Huguenot faith, which motivated the creation of a government based on equality and fairness. Du Bois held forth that "here these people formed a government unlike any other government before or since, without law except their conscience and sense of right, without courts except as one neighbor admonished another, and without officer to enforce obedience except as the general sentiment came to dominate the personal will. . . . They formed a French church, called a French pastor, and used the French language for at least two generations." Theirs was a true religious community, not a political one, although their ideals carried sociopolitical implications. Du Bois emphatically claimed that both the desire for religious and civil liberty were essential characteristics of the Huguenot race, so upon their race alone could the principles of American liberty be grounded. He implicitly argued that the Huguenots were even superior to Anglo-Saxons, who did not universally believe in religious liberty. Therefore, he concluded, "Let us have the distinction and correct name, the name HUGUENOT, that alone, and let us maintain our unimpaired heritage in all that name implies." His commitment to this vision was such that he insisted that his overwrought voice be heard, but he strongly believed that he was not alone in thinking as he did, as "I would not have them take away from me my whole unbroken patrimony of family traditions if my protest can prevent it and I am deeply mistaken if I do not in this express the feelings of thousands of the descendants of the Patentees whose protest cannot be spoken."[30]

The vehemence of Du Bois's attack on the proposed name suggests an ethnoracial exclusiveness far removed from the more generous approach of the romantic historians of New Paltz, such as Edmund Eltinge. Eltinge's ideology did not preclude the possibility that multiple groups of people could bear a drive for liberty in their blood, hence he could recommend that both a Huguenot and a Hollander be placed on top of a proposed monument. Du Bois's ideology was far more restrictive than that of the romantics, as he adhered to a more racialized interpretation of ethnicity, as first articulated by contemporary "Anglo-Saxons," predicated on a perceived hierarchy even among various white western European groups. Du Bois therefore viewed the Huguenots as the apex of that hierarchy, with the New Paltz founders having been the very best of the lot. This ideology simply did not countenance equality between ethnoracial groups. If equality was possible, the racial hierarchy was not, in fact, real. Acknowledging the Dutch would therefore have brought into question, and even possibly destroyed, the concept of race as Du Bois understood it. It is no wonder that he was so angered by something as minor as the proposed name of a mere house museum.

In submitting this letter to the editor of the *Independent*, Du Bois found a sympathetic ear, that of Ralph LeFevre, even if LeFevre was not as race-obsessed as Du Bois. LeFevre remarked that his "own position is exactly that of Rev. Dr. Anson Du Bois. . . . The grandmother of the editor of the *Independent* was an Elting, but that fact does not change our views a particle." A number of letters from descendants promoting a similar perspective came across the editor's desk. One was from Rev. James LeFevre, who also believed that the proposed name was a "misnomer," although "in saying this [he did] not discard the Dutch blood in [his] viens [*sic*]." Rev. R. Patterson Du Bois also wrote to the newspaper, stressing that Du Bois's position was "unassailable." It is perhaps not surprising that ministers took a stand in favor of their French Protestant ancestors, but it was not only ministers who spoke out against memorializing the Dutch in the name of the memorial house. For example, the wealthy Chicago developer Mr. S. E. Gross pointedly remarked that "our Holland ancestors can afford to let them (the Huguenots) alone in their glory so far as the naming of the Memorial House is concerned. I have more Holland than I have Huguenot ancestry and I equally respect both, but the Huguenots were particularly a strange people in a strange land, fleeing from religious persecution and they deserve a particular memorial."[31]

Capt. R. G. DuBois of Washington, D. C., also stood in opposition to the inclusion of "Holland" in the proposed name, in a manner that referenced issues of both race and gender. Capt. DuBois opined that "having read carefully the communication of Rev. Anson Du Bois in regard to the name of the 'Huguenot Association' we believe his views are right. Let the descendants of the beneficieries [*sic*] of grand old Holland celebrate her glory under their own flag. Better American Huguenot, than Huguenot Holland Association. This would better accord with the history of the fathers and have a broader and more significant bearing for the future of the question than any other." That his ethnoracial identification was patrilineal is suggested not only by his reference to the "fathers," but also in his unwillingness to define himself, a man with a patentee surname but of both French and Dutch heritage, as one of the beneficiaries of "old Holland." He was a DuBois, and by definition, he was a Huguenot.[32]

Although many men articulated their disapproval of the proposed name to Ralph LeFevre, he was painfully aware that all descendants did not share their concern, as his had been the lone voice among the society's leadership against the inclusion of the word "Holland." Not surprisingly, the strongest response in favor of including Holland in the name of the house museum was that of Irving Elting. His gendered racial thinking practically compelled him to seek commemoration of his Dutch ancestors, as his Dutch surname did not entitle him to claim for himself the racial heritage of the Huguenots to the same degree as those who bore patentee surnames. But it was not his name alone that drove him to celebrate the Dutch, as he was the one who most forcefully argued for the importance of the Teutonic race in the development of American liberty and self-government. He claimed the Dutch brought in their bodies that essential germ. He did acknowledge the importance of the New Paltz founders in instituting self-government in New York, having been influenced by contact with Teutonic people in the Palatinate, but that did not mean that the patentees bore the same racial essence.[33]

In the midst of the controversy, Ralph LeFevre explained why the society had chosen such an inclusive name. He noted that "the ruling thought with those who voted to insert the word Holland in the name of the house was, we think that as the Eltings had been large contributors to the fund, something was due out of courtesy to the Dutch and that moreover something was due to the memory of Mr. Edmund Eltinge who started the movement for the erection of a memorial to the New Paltz settlers and whose first plan was the erection of a monument with a Huguenot and Hollander clasping hands." It is likely that those who opposed the inclusion of Holland in the name might have understood why the decision had been made to include both the Dutch and Huguenots in the name of the house, considering the recognized importance of the recently deceased Edmund Eltinge in the enterprise. That did not mean they would accept the decision without a fight.[34]

In spite of his belief that the Dutch should be honored alongside the Huguenots, Irving Elting offered a compromise. This move was supported by Judge Frank Hasbrouck, who, along with Irving Elting and Edmund Eltinge, had initiated the effort to raise funds for the construction of a monument. Irving Elting's suggested that both "Holland" and "Huguenot" be dropped, and the house simply be called the "New Paltz Memorial House," although he proposed this alternative grudgingly and somewhat snidely, at best. He sharply remarked, "If the Memorial is to be so strictly Huguenot in its character, would it not be fair, as well as courteous, for some of your previous correspondents to propose that the Association return the subscriptions made under the natural supposition that the memorial was to be a joint affair before they suggest that if the Dutch wish a Memorial, they may go apart and erect one." He also thought those who promoted the Huguenot connection were being stingy with their praise, by referencing the fact that the Dutch had welcomed the Huguenot immigrants into their midst: "Shall not those who are their descendants best honor their memory by emulating their liberality shown toward all with whom they were brought in contact?" Offended by contemporary Huguenots' exclusivity, he could not help but interject that the bricks used in the Jean Hasbrouck House's chimney were supposedly Dutch (which, in fact, they were not), and that the house was already being filled with many artifacts of Dutch-American origin.[35]

A week after LeFevre published the opinion of Irving Elting, LeFevre put an end to the discussion, at least in his newspaper, remarking that "no more communications are desired on this subject." LeFevre soon noted in the August 25, 1899, edition of his newspaper that "all parties seem to agree now that both Huguenot and Holland shall be dropped and the building called simply the 'New Paltz Memorial House.'" That official name stuck, but in common parlance, it became known simply as the "Memorial House."[36]

The Controversy Abates

After the controversy surrounding naming rights died down, and as strongly as such people felt about the issue, the issue of Huguenot over Dutch began to fade once the house was opened as a museum for the exhibition of donated or loaned objects. This is not surprising, as very few of the objects available for inclusion in the house demonstrated anything other than generic Euro-Americanism. Some of the first objects received for display included "a shovel for putting bread in an old fashioned brick oven, . . . and a candle mould and ancient bandbox." The "shovel" would have been an iron peal, and the "ancient" bandbox likely dated from the first half of the nineteenth century, neither of which possessed any French or Dutch cultural overtones. Rufus LeFevre donated an eighteenth-century winnowing basket purchased from a estate that was established in 1690 by Jacob Aast VanWagenen, which reportedly "was rich in Holland relics brought to this country" by the original owner, but none of those "Holland relics" were apparently donated to the museum. Other objects included a wolf trap; an eighteenth-century ladder-back armchair; and a wedding dress of "olden times." Other donated artifacts included a flintlock musket; some old newspapers; Peter DuBois's "captain's uniform and epaulets, worn in the old training days"; a collection of coins including American copper pennies, Canadian five-cent pieces, and "French coins, brought to this country by Margarita and Marie Reynolds . . . on their return from France"; and even "two or three fine geological specimens" from the town of Highland, which had once been part of New Paltz. The house was fast becoming the community's attic, even a cabinet of curiosities, rather than reflecting any particular ethnoracial heritage.[37]

This is not to say that nothing reflecting French or Dutch heritage was available and put on display at the Memorial House alongside more ethnoculturally generic material. The collecting patterns nevertheless represented a much greater degree of ethnoracial inclusiveness than was evident in the argument over naming rights for the house. One of the few categories of objects that did reflect non-English heritage was composed of documents written in French or Dutch, some of which were included in the so-called Patentees' Trunk, which were transferred from storage with the town clerk to the Memorial House. Early French and Dutch Bibles also reflected non-English culture, as did both copies of Huguenot historical medals donated by Judge A. T. Clearwater and a "head of lance, brought from Holland, by Jan Elting." Other items harkened back to the founding of New Paltz, which did invoke the founders' ethnicity, such as the legendary gun that Louis DuBois supposedly used during his attempt to reclaim his wife and children in the Second Esopus War. In total, though, the collection of objects primarily helped to fulfill Ralph LeFevre's goal of fitting up a house of yesteryear as a testament to pioneer days.[38]

A greater inclusivity was also shown by descendants when they contemplated an official opening for the house, which appears to have never taken place. Ralph LeFevre noted in his newspaper that in May 1900, a formal opening was being considered, to which would be invited "delegations from kindred organizations, such as the Huguenot Society in America, the Holland Society, and historical societies in neighboring counties." The formal opening was also intended to be suitably patriotic, although not in an ethnoracially exclusive manner. Even without an official opening, visitors began to arrive at the house, where they were given tours by Mrs. Donaldson, who, along with her husband, were taken on as live-in caretakers. Ralph LeFevre was eager to publicize the fact that visitation was on the rise, and not simply for descendants, but from many curious out-of-town visitors as well (see figure 7.1). Community booster that he was, LeFevre also marketed New Paltz by suggesting that visitors might want to come "from Dutchess county and elsewhere. The ride over the trolley is delightful, and two or

Figure 7.1. Visitors to the Jean Hasbrouck House, c. 1897–1899. Historic Huguenot Street, New Paltz, New York.

three hours can be spent in inspecting the normal school building, visiting the Memorial House, taking a look at the old houses and listening to the music in the casino." He also noted when others suggested a visit to New Paltz, such as the notice from the *Newark Evening News*, which he took the liberty of republishing in the *Independent*. A "J. J. B." suggested that those who were "sweltering in the city and breathing its confined air" might want to visit "the breezy hills" near New Paltz, with its "memorial house, which was built in 1712, and which has been set apart for the preservation of early relics and traditions."[39]

As the society began to collect objects for display in the Memorial House, the members continued to raise funds to fulfill the initial purpose of the society: erecting a monument. The original recommendation made by Edmund Eltinge, which had initially met with considerable support, had included bronze figures of a Huguenot and a Hollander clasping hands. By the time that planning for a monument began in earnest, the society's leadership had apparently scrapped the original proposal. It is not surprising that memorializing the Dutch forebears through the monument was apparently not given further consideration, given the intense discussions concerning the inclusion of both Huguenot and Hollander in the naming of the society's house museum. The proposed cost of such monument was another factor, as it was highly unlikely that the society could acquire additional donations needed to reach the $6,000 price tag of the monument as originally proposed. Instead, by the spring of 1903, the "general consensus of opinion [was] that an appropriate monument would be a large boulder for a base, surmounted by a large, rough piece of Shawangunk grit for a shaft [from the local Shawangunk Mountains], inlaid in which there should be a bronze tablet, bearing a suitable inscription." The plan "which met most favor was to construct a mound of stones some five or six feet high, laid up in cement. On this place the base of the monument about four feet thick and on top of that a shaft eleven or twelve feet high."[40]

Soon after the effort to raise funds for the erection of a monument began again in earnest, LeFevre published a heartfelt editorial from an anonymous correspondent named "A." Given the tone and content of the letter, it is certainly possible that the author was Anson Du Bois. The missive encapsulates both the persistent erroneous history and the supreme superiority complex that had surrounded both the literary and physical commemoration of the founders and their descendants. "A." clearly contended, as did many descendants, that the essence of the United States as a freedom-loving, self-governing, religious, moral, and classless egalitarian society practically burst forth fully formed in the little village of New Paltz, rendering it a paradise in miniature. "A." did not suggest that New Paltz served as the origin of American culture and society, although other descendants had done just that, but he or she did suggest how New Paltz represented all that was good in America. The founders' essential nature had produced a culturally and morally superior community, and through their efforts, they demonstrated the progress of humans as a species. "A." contended that New Paltz should serve as an example to surrounding communities, but if what "A." said about the village was true, it would be easy to see how the village might serve as a model not only for America but the world. The author reveals that this unique utopia had not been created by Anglo-Saxons, whose descendants falsely claimed their centrality in the creation of America and all it stood for. Rather, it was an Eden created by persecuted French-speaking Protestants from the Continent. Both descendants and visitors could therefore make of New Paltz a site of pilgrimage, where they could worship the true founders of America in the very spot where their feet had trod.[41] "A.'s" homily is worth quoting at length:

> Very few villages have greater reason for keeping up good appearances than New Paltz. In the first place it has a history, political, social and religious almost unique in our country. Buying its land from the aborigines and securing a Patent from the Colonial government the original Huguenot colony lived a century as a Democracy, without courts or lawyers. It was a union of church and state without bigotry or tyranny, having order without class distinction or social inequality and to-day, after two and a quarter centuries, it is a sort of Holy Land to scores, if not hundreds, in every part of America—the direct descendants in name or blood of the first settlers. . . . Her noble history, with many scores of ancestral homes, with a credit of two hundred years of comfort and piety, her scenery unsurpassed in vale, mountain and river, with trees that might have flourished in Eden and a climate suited to that realm, her intelligence, hospitality and fidelity to law and right a pattern to surrounding communities, may it not be rightly expected that she appear to the best advantage to all who come within her bounds, and that she takes pains to do so. . . . The New Paltz of to-day must be regarded as the practical outcome of some of the deepest principles of human growth and development. Its founders sought freedom, education and religion. They had fled from the operation of the opposites, or the perversion of these principles. The habits, traditions and isolated position of these people and the remarkable progress of country along these lines, have here left these principles to their natural fruitage. It must be to the credit of New Paltz if all these fruits appear here in their best form. Let every person and family do its best and the conditions will correspond with the purposes and hopes of the beginnings and a brighter chapter will be hard to find in human history.[42]

"A.'s" thoughts did not represent merely local boosterism, nor even a civil religion, but an almost limitless ancestor worship, which by extension extended to self-worship, since the legacy of the founders was the patrimony of the descendants. They who possessed the "name or blood" of the founders held as their rightful inheritance the unique characteristics of the progenitors. The extent to which "A." claimed his or her community's greatness seems almost absurd, but "A" made these comments in the context of ethnoracial competition that simply did not allow for a generous inclusivity, even among those of light-skinned European descent. The theory behind New Englanders' Anglo-Saxonism did not leave room for more than one at the top, so descendants of the New Paltz founders staked out their own claim for the highest tier.

Perhaps the editorial was what the descendant community needed in order to once again mobilize to commemorate their ancestors through a monument. Fundraising continued, and by April 1908, the shaft and rocks had been selected after an intense search for appropriate materials in the nearby Shawangunk Mountains. Soon the society purchased a memorial tablet made by the Gorham Company, which was set in the rough stone of the monument's shaft. The monument was finally unveiled on September 29, 1908, after more than fifteen years of dedicated effort (see figure 7.2). The descendants took noticeable pride in their accomplishment, even though the monument was "not pretty," according to Ralph LeFevre. He nevertheless believed "there is perhaps in the United States no finer boulder monument." LeFevre further opined that "the house and the monument together form a worthy memorial to the early settlers of New Paltz. The massive boulder monument conveys an idea of strength, permanence and substantiality. It looks as if it had stood there for ten thousand years and would stand ten thousand years longer." Descendant Judge A. T. Clearwater echoed LeFevre's perspective, remarking at the unveiling of the Patentees' Monument, "that I have seen many bowlders used as monuments in this and other countries, and I know

Figure 7.2. Unveiling of Huguenot Monument, September 29, 1908. Historic Huguenot Street, New Paltz, New York.

of none more impressive than ours. People who have no acquaintance with monumental bowlders have no comprehension how extremely insignificant some of them are." Even in their aesthetically unpleasing monument, the patentee descendants were unable to refrain from self-aggrandizement.[43]

The monument still stands today as a central point in the National Historic Landmark District of Huguenot Street, and it continues to misinform the public as to the origins of the village. It proclaims in bronze that the New Paltz patentees were "driven by religious persecution from their native France, exiles for conscience's sake." What is less evident is that it was never really aimed at commemorating the founders, but rather the descendants, who believed they bore within themselves the legacy of that desire for liberty. That was their biological birthright, such that by honoring their ancestors, they were simply honoring themselves.

"Provincial Pride"

In April 1904, from Japan, Miss Mary Deyo wrote to Ralph LeFevre a brief but revealing letter, which he found fit to reprint in his newspaper. In just a few words, she distills both why the patentee descendants had demonstrated such a deep commitment to honoring their forebears, as well as what their ancestors had provided their progeny across the centuries. Miss Deyo wrote, "We meet people from all the different parts of the United States out here, and I have been interested to notice that the Southerners, and especially the Virginians, seem more like 'our kind of folks' than those from other places and wonder if the Huguenot admixture in their ancestry and the intense provincial pride which we have in common has something to do with it." Certainly the similarities had nothing to do with the inclusion of Huguenots within the heritage of either those in the Old Dominion or in New Paltz. Yet, Miss Deyo did appreciate the "intense provincial pride" of those from both Virginia and New Paltz, each of whom sought to claim historical supremacy over New England Anglo-Saxonists. That pride was fundamentally based on the perception held by both the Virginians and the New Paltz descendants that they and their ancestors each formed and perpetuated the highest form of civilization in human history. For the descendants of the New Paltz founders, their "provincial pride" was grounded in their belief that their ethnoracial blood was superior to that of all other races. Being descendants of Huguenots—and thus Huguenots themselves—they claimed that they were a people more fully American than any other, moreso than either the Anglo-Saxons of the Northeast or of the South. In the race for racial superiority, there could be only one winner, and for the descendants of the New Paltz patentees, the winner was clear: themselves.[44]

The founders of New Paltz and their descendants never assumed the significance they deemed appropriate in the annals of the United States. As a National Historic Landmark district that eventually boasted seven house museums and a reconstructed church, Huguenot Street would indeed be visited by thousands of people annually. Still, few if any members of the general public ever honored the founders as the descendants hoped and even demanded. This is not surprising in the least, given that the village and its residents had very little influence on the historical development of the United States. This is not to say that Huguenot Street and its houses, artifacts, and archives are not special. Nor do I mean to suggest that the efforts of the descendants to preserve evidence of their forebears should not be treated with respect. What made and makes those descendants special is not who they were and are, but what they did and do. They created and continue to sustain a unique opportunity to tell a story of fluid creolization, which reflects an important aspect of American history in the heterogenous Middle Colonies. It is also a story that reveals that being a light-skinned American with other than Anglo-American roots created a host of shifting challenges that flowed across more than three centuries. Because of their success in preserving both legend and artifact, heritage and houses, the descendants of the New Paltz founders were and are important, although for reasons other than what they believed.

NOTES

Introduction

1. Jane Howard, "Can a Nice Novelist Finish First?" *Life*, November 4, 1966, 74.
2. 'Huguenot Street: "The oldest street in America with its original houses," (New Paltz, NY: n.d.).
3. Bertrand Van Ruymbeke, "The Walloon and Huguenot Elements in New Netherland and Seventeenth-Century New York: Identity, History and Memory," in *Revisiting New Netherland: Perspectives on Early Dutch America*, ed. Joyce D. Goodfriend (Leiden, The Netherlands: Brill, 2005), 41–56. Two of the founders, the brothers Jean and Abraham Hasbrouck, were from Calais, which was under French control by the end of the sixteenth century, such that according to Van Ruymbeke, they should be considered Huguenots rather than Walloons. However, it is unclear how they identified themselves. Eric Roth, '"where ye walloens dwell.' Rethinking the Ethnic Identity of the Huguenots of New Paltz and Ulster County, New York," *New York History* 89, no. 4 (Fall 2008): 347–373.
4. Ralph LeFevre, *History of New Paltz New York and its Old Families (From 1678 to 1820) Including the Huguenot Pioneers and Others who settled in New Paltz previous to the Revolution With an Appendix bringing down the history of certain families and some other matter to 1850*, 2nd ed. (Albany, NY: Fort Orange Press, Brandow Printing, 1909), 66.
5. Ibid.
6. Elizabeth LeFever, "Story of the Rescue of Catherine Dubois from the Indians and Settlement of New Paltz, New York," *Daughters of the American Revolution Magazine* 45, no. 4 (October 1914): 210–212; Cornelia DuBois, *The story of the Paltz: Being a brief history of New Paltz, N.Y., a compilation* (n.p.: privately printed, 1915), 20, 23, 30. Also see Ralph LeFevre, *History of New Paltz*, 2nd ed., 47–48, 59.
7. Ralph LeFevre, *History of New Paltz*, 2nd ed., 48; Cornelia DuBois, *The story of the Paltz*, 31.
8. Kenneth E. Hasbrouck and Erma R. DeWitt, *The Street of the Huguenots* (Goshen, NY: Bookmill on Windy Hill, 1952), 7–9.
9. Michael Kammen, *Colonial New York: A History* (New York: Charles Scribner's Sons, 1975), 145–146; Alice P. Kenney, *Stubborn for Liberty: the Dutch in New York*, (Syracuse, NY: Syracuse University Press, 1975), 112.

10. Paula Wheeler Carlo, *Huguenot Refugees in Colonial New York: Becoming American in the Hudson Valley* (Brighton, UK: Sussex Academic Press, 2005); Ralph LeFevre, *History of New Paltz*, 2nd ed., 6; Jon Butler, *The Huguenots in America: A Refugee People in New World Society* (Cambridge, MA: Harvard University Press, 1983); Carlo, *Huguenot Refugees.* Carlo seems to accept the descendants' assertion that the Duzine was the first government of the village, eliding her discussion of that institution with the local government, suggesting that they were somehow related. This is incorrect, as is discussed in chapter 1 (Carlo, *Huguenot Refugees*, 39–41). Carlo likewise suggests that the patentees and their descendants were independently minded in their religious affairs, motivating them to choose controversial ministers who were sometimes ordained outside of the Dutch Reformed establishment. This argument is also highly questionable, as is explored in chapter 5 (Carlo, *Huguenot Refugees*, 26, 48–54, 74–78, 174). When generalizing about cultural preservation in New Paltz, Carlo is rather vague, noting that "while not as pronounced, some ethnic homogeneity was preserved among the descendants of the founders of New Paltz as well" (*Huguenot Refugees*, 3). When she attempts to be more precise, her evidence is often weak. For example, concerning language, Carlo remarks, "Hence, by the 1720s and 1730s, an increasing number of New Paltz documents, including church records, were written in Dutch. It is very likely, however, that use of French, in conjunction with Dutch continued in private life among couples of mixed ethnicity even later into the century as was frequently the case in other immigrant communities." To support this statement, she cites only two primary documents (Carlo, *Huguenot Refugees*, 174). She further notes that "what is certain is that the English language made few significant inroads into this area until after the American Revolution," which, as is explored in chapter 4, is not accurate (*Huguenot Refugees*, 175).
11. Eric J. Roth, "Being Poor in New Paltz," *de Halve Maen* 79, no. 1 (Spring 2006); Eric J. Roth, 'where ye walloens dwell,' 362.
12. Larson supports his argument by referencing the historiography of the Dutch experience in colonial New York and New Jersey, including studies by David Steven Cohen, Firth Haring Fabend, Joyce D. Goodfriend, and Donna Merwick. Kenneth Hewes Barricklo and Neil Larson & Associates, "Historic Structure Report: The Abraham Hasbrouck House at the Huguenot Historical Society, New Paltz, NY," (unpublished report for the Huguenot Historical Society, 2003) 4:1–8, 21; Larson Fisher Associates and Crawford & Stearns, "Historic Structure Report for the Jean Hasbrouck House" (unpublished report for the HHS, 2007), 1.6–1.8.
13. John M. Murrin, "English Rights as Ethnic Aggression: The English Conquest, the Charter of Liberties of 1683, and Leisler's Rebellion in New York," in *Authority and Resistance in Early New York*, edited by William Pencak and Conrad Edick Wright (New York: The New-York Historical Society, 1988), 56–94.
14. Donna Merwick, *Possessing Albany, 1630–1710: The Dutch and English*

Experiences (Cambridge, UK: Cambridge University Press, 1990); Donna Merwick, *Death of a Notary: Conquest and Change in Colonial New York* (Ithaca, NY: Cornell University Press, 1999).

15. Randall Balmer, *A Perfect Babel of Confusion: Dutch Religion and English Culture in the Middle Colonies* (New York: Oxford University Press, 1989).
16. Dirk Mouw, "Moederkerk and Vaderland: Religion and ethnic identity in the Middle Colonies, 1690–1772" (PhD diss., University of Iowa, 2009), 615. Fabend notes that the newspaper of the Dutch Reformed Church, *The Christian Intelligencer*, first published in the 1820s, "introduc[ed] readers to forgotten or never-known chapters in Dutch political, cultural, and religious history . . . rekindle[ing] Dutchness in New York and New Jersey." She further notes that the "old Dutch ancestral customs" were preserved at least into the 1850s, but that "by the time of the Civil war, Dutchness in the Hudson Valley had become for many only a quaint memory." Firth Haring Fabend, "The Reformed Dutch Church and the Persistence of Dutchness in New York and New Jersey," in *Dutch New York: The Roots of Hudson Valley Culture*, ed. Roger Panetta (New York: Hudson River Museum, Fordham University Press, 2009), 137–158 (quotations at 148, 150, 155). For another of Fabend's explorations of Dutch cultural persistence, see Firth Haring Fabend, *A Dutch Family in the Middle Colonies, 1660–1800* (New Brunswick, NJ: Rutgers University Press, 1991).
17. Joyce D. Goodfriend, *Before the Melting Pot: Society and Culture in Colonial New York City, 1664–1730* (Princeton, NJ: Princeton University Press, 1992); David Steven Cohen, *The Dutch-American Farm* (New York: New York University Press, 1992); David Narrett, *Inheritance and Family Life in Colonial New York City* (Ithaca, NY: Cornell University Press, 1992).
18. John R. Stevens, *Dutch Vernacular Architecture in North America: 1640–1830* (West Hurley, NY: The Society for the Preservation of Hudson Valley Vernacular Architecture, 2005); Fabend, *A Dutch Family in the Middle Colonies*.
19. Susan Shaw Romney, *New Netherland Connections: Intimate Networks and Atlantic Ties in Seventeenth-Century America* (Chapel Hill: University of North Carolina Press, 2014); Evan Haefeli, *New Netherland and the Dutch Origins of Religious Liberty* (Philadelphia: University of Pennsylvania Press, 2012); Jaap Jacobs, *The Colony of New Netherland: A Dutch Settlement in Seventeenth-Century America* (Ithaca, NY: Cornell University Press, 2009); Janny Venema, *Beverwijck: A Dutch Village on the American Frontier, 1652–1664* (Helversum, The Netherlands: Veloren, 2003).
20. Robert Baron and Ana C. Cara, "Introduction: Creolization as Cultural Creativity," in *Creolization as Cultural Creativity*, eds. Robert Baron and Ana C. Cara (Jackson: University of Mississippi Press, 2011), 3–19; Charles Stewart, "Creolization: History, Ethnography, Theory," in *Creolization: History, Ethnography, Theory*, ed. Charles Stewart (Walnut Creek, CA: Left Coast Press, 2007), 1–25; Thomas Hylland

Eriksen, "Creolization in Anthropological Theory and in Mauritius," in *Creolization: History, Ethnography, Theory*, ed. Charles Stewart, (Walnut Creek, CA: Left Coast Press, 2007), 153–177. For a discussion of "creolization" in colonial America, see John Smolenski, *Friends and Strangers: The Making of a Creole Culture in Colonial Pennsylvania* (Philadelphia: University of Pennsylvania Press, 2010), 1–5. A few other historians of Dutch America, including Goodfriend, Narrett, and Cohen, have also suggested that creolization occurred in the region, even if they do not always use the term.

21. Eric J. Roth, '"The Society of Negroes Unsettled": A History of Slavery in New Paltz, NY," *Afro-Americans in New York Life and History* 27, no. 1 (January 2003): 27–54.

Chapter 1

1. Eric J. Roth, '"where ye walloens dwell"; Van Ruymbeke, "The Walloon and Huguenot Elements," 44; John Campbell, "The Walloon Community in Canterbury, 1625–1649" (PhD diss., University of Wisconsin, 1970), 6–10, 13–16.
2. Francis W. Cross, "History of the Walloon & Huguenot Church at Canterbury," in *Publications of the Huguenot Society of London*, vol. 15 (London: Huguenot Society of London, 1898): 24, 35–36, 82.
3. Cross, "History of the Walloon & Huguenot Church at Canterbury," 97, 121; Campbell, "The Walloon Community in Canterbury," 22, 24.
4. The Blanchan family was still in Armentières on August 14, 1642, when their son Maximilian was baptized. Gwenn F. Epperson, *New Netherland Roots* (Baltimore, MD: Genealogical Publishing Company, 1994), 136. The Blanchans baptized their daughter Magdelaine in the Walloon Church in Canterbury on May 16, 1647. Robert Hovenden, ed., "The Registers of the Walloon or Strangers' Church in Canterbury," in *The Publications of the Huguenot Society of London*, vol. 5, pt. 2 (Lymington, UK: C. T. King, 1894), 209.
5. Mattieu Blanchan was mentioned in the records of the Walloon Church in Canterbury in the 1649 marriage contract of his brother (Robert Hovenden, ed. "The Registers of the Walloon or Strangers' Church in Canterbury," 725). "Mannheim: Records of the French Congregation 1651–1710," unpublished translation by Ruth P. Heidgerd, New York (1978), available at the HHS library, New Paltz, NY. Heidgerd attributes Blanchan's move to Mannheim as having been motivated by the start of the civil war in England, although he moved not at the start of the war but towards its end. Ruth P. Heidgerd, "The Blanchans" (unpublished manuscript, c. 1970s), available at HHS library, New Paltz, NY.
6. Claus-Peter Clasen, *The Palatinate in European History: 1559–1660*, (Oxford: Basil Blackwell, 1963), 35–36; J. H. Clapham, "Charles Louis, Elector Palatine, 1617–1680: An Early Experiment in Liberalism," *Economica* n.s. 7, no. 28 (November 1940): 391; André Paul, "Les Réfugiés

Huguenots et Wallons dans le Palatinat du Rhin du XVIe Siècle a la Révolution," *Revue Historique* 157, fasc. 2 (1928): 267–268.

7. Clapham, "Charles Louis, Elector Palatine," 391–394; Roth, "where ye walloens dwell." Antoine Crispell was originally from St. Guin (now Sainghin-en-Weppes) and Louis DuBois from Wicres, both approximately ten miles southwest of Lille (Roth, "where ye walloens dwell," 351). The spelling of the patentee families' names in the seventeenth and eighteenth centuries is not uniform, but for the sake of consistency, they will be spelled as follows: DuBois, LeFevre, Deyo, Freer, Bevier, Crispell, Hasbrouck.
8. Roth, "where ye walloens dwell," 351. More detailed information on the Bevier family, compiled by family genealogist Dale André BeVier, was accessed December 4, 2013 at http://www.bevier.us.
9. Roth, "where ye walloens dwell," 351, 353; Van Ruymbeke, "The Walloon and Huguenot Elements," 44–48. Christian Deyo was taxed in Mutterstadt in 1655, as was the father of Abraham and Jean Hasbrouck. (Kenneth E. Hasbrouck and Ruth P. Heidgerd, *The Deyo (Deyoe) Family*, revised and edited by Carol Van Wagner, Esther Deyo Aldridge, and Nancy Gentile [New Paltz, NY: Deyo Family Association, 2003], x). While most of the founders of New Paltz were ethnic Walloons, it is believed that the Hasbrouck brothers were from Calais, a French port, so it is possible that the Hasbrouck brothers might have considered themselves French. If that was the case, it might be more appropriate to consider them Huguenots. However, they might have had ancestral connections with Lille, which suggests the possibility that they considered themselves Protestant Walloons (Roth, "where ye walloens dwell," 351, 353; Van Ruymbeke, "The Walloon and Huguenot Elements," 48–49). France occupied Lorraine, the home region of the LeFevre brothers, in the 1640s, but vacated it in 1648, only to occupy the region once again beginning in 1670. The LeFevre brothers united with the Dutch Reformed Church in Kingston in 1665 (Ralph LeFevre, *History of New Paltz*, 10, 20).
10. Edward O'Callaghan, *The Documentary history of the State of New York* (Albany, NY: Weed, Parson, & Co., 1850) 3:37. DuBois received twenty morgens and Crispell eight morgens; a morgen is a little larger than two acres. Crispell's was admittedly relatively small, but DuBois's grant was similar in size to that of several Dutch recipients, such as Roeloff Swartwout (twenty morgens) and Lambert Huyberts (twenty-one morgens). The largest grant was only thirty-four morgens. Augustus H. Van Buren, *A History of Ulster County Under the Dominion of the Dutch* (Kingston, NY: n.p., 1923), 130–131; Ralph LeFevre, *History of New Paltz*, 19.
11. Roth and Carlo have suggested that the 1667 outbreak of plague in the Palatine might have motivated some of the Walloon founders of New Paltz to emigrate, but the evidence for such a theory is only circumstantial. Roth, "where ye walloens dwell," 356; Carlo, *Huguenot Refugees*, 20. "French Letter," HHS. Translation in Dale BeVier, *The Bevier Family*, 54. (Roth's interpretation of the "French Letter" is in

error. He indicates the "Imperial" forces mentioned are the forces of the French crown, but the author is actually referencing those of the Holy Roman Empire. Roth also misinterprets the author's reference to "this city," which he indicates refers to Speyer. The reference is to Philipsburg. Roth, "where ye walloens dwell," 357.)

12. Van Buren, *A History of Ulster County*, 130–131; LeFevre, *History of New Paltz*, 12–19. The original "Indian Deed" and a recent translation by Kees-Jan Waterman are in the archives of the HHS. Both are also available at http://www.hrvh.org/cdm/compoundobject/collection/hhs/id/ 15/rec/8 (accessed April 20, 2014).
13. LeFevre, *History of New Paltz*, 107–108, 375–376; Abraham DuBois, "Will, October 1, 1731," New York County Probate Records, Liber 11, 175–179; Kenneth Hewes Barricklo and Neil Larson & Associates, "Historic Structure Report: The Abraham Hasbrouck House."
14. J. F. Bosher, "Huguenot Merchants and the Protestant International in the Seventeenth Century," *The William and Mary Quarterly*, 3rd series, 52, no.1 (January 1995): 77–102 (quotation at 78); Romney, *New Netherland Connections.*
15. Hugh Hastings, Edward Corwin, and James Holden, *Ecclesiastical Records, State of New York* (Albany: State of New York, 1901–1906), 5:3209 (henceforth, *ERNY*).
16. Dingman Versteeg, *Records of the Reformed Dutch Church of New Paltz, N.Y.*, vol. 3 in *Collections of the Holland Society of New York* (New York: Holland Society, 1894), 1–2, 6–65. The argument that a desire for land, rather than the establishment of an independent French-speaking community and congregation, was the driving force behind the creation of New Paltz is at variance with both traditional and scholarly interpretations (LeFevre, *History of New Paltz*, 11; and Carlo, *Huguenot Refugees*, 26).
17. LeFevre, *History of New Paltz*, 18. Overviews of the development of New York town and county government can be found in the WPA's *Transcriptions of early County Records of New York State: Minutes of the Board of Supervisors of Ulster County 1710/1 to 1730/1* (Albany, NY: The Historical Records Survey, 1939), x–xiv; and Nicholas Varga, "The Development and Structure of Local Government in Colonial New York," in *Town and Country: Essays on the Structure of Local Government in the American Colonies*, ed. Bruce Daniels (Middletown, CT: Wesleyan University Press, 1978), 186–215. The Duke's Laws originally allowed for eight overseers, but that number was reduced to four in 1665. The right for the town court to meet every few weeks was provided for in a 1665 addendum to the Duke's Laws, so was thus in effect when New Paltz was founded. *The Colonial Laws of New York from the Year 1664 to the Revolution* (Albany, NY: James B. Lyon, 1894), 1:74.
18. *Colonial Laws*, 1:121–122, 125–128, 237–238, 539–542. This 1683 legislation (*Colonial Laws*, 1:131–133) did not affect the office of constable, which continued uninterrupted throughout the eighteenth century. For a brief time after October 18, 1701, the role of the elected supervisor was transferred to the justices of the peace (*Colonial Laws*,

1:459), although that law was repealed by the assembly on November 27, 1702 (*Colonial Laws*, 1:523–525), through an act that repealed all laws passed since August 1, 1701, thus apparently reverting to the 1691 legislation. The November 27, 1702, law was itself repealed by the Queen on June 26, 1708, but by then, the 1703 law concerning the election of officials was in force. The provisions concerning the election of officials and their responsibilities and duties were reinforced by an additional 1743 act, which exclusively addressed Ulster County (*Colonial Laws*, 3:320–325).

19. *Colonial Laws*, 1:225–226, 3:320–325. The 1684 law that confirmed the continued election of constables also authorized towns to elect more than one constable if they deemed necessary (*Colonial Laws*, 1:146–147). However, a 1743 act stipulated that New Paltz was allowed to elect only one constable. (Legislation was passed allowing other towns to each elect two constables [including Goshen in Orange County (1743), and Rochester and Marbletown in Ulster County, (1753)], but no similar legislation was passed for New Paltz [*Colonial Laws*, 3:326; *Colonial Laws*, 3:947–948].) Nevertheless, the New Paltz townspeople began electing two constables in 1761. Other legislation that affected New Paltz included a 1701 act that allowed for the additional appointment of town surveyors of highways by the county justices of the peace (*Colonial Laws*, 1:471–472) or by the assembly (beginning in 1729 with *Colonial Laws*, 2:504–506); the latter were of limited duration and thus often revived (sometimes with alterations). In 1721, the assembly again gave the "Free-holders and Tenants in Possession of every Town, Mannor and Precinct" the right to establish by majority vote rules for fences and to elect annually two persons to be fence "Viewers or Overseerers [*sic*]." The law was to be in force only for seven years and "from thence to the end of the next Sitting of the Generall Assembly," but was continued by further legislation, including chapter 528 in 1728, which allowed for the election of a many fenceviewers as deemed necessary (*Colonial Laws*, 2:64–67; *Colonial Laws*, 2:481–485). Legislation creating the position of overseer of the poor was passed in 1743 (*Colonial Laws*, 3:320–325).

20. County documents indicate that New Paltz was electing assessors as early as 1701 and supervisors as early as 1702, if they had not been doing so earlier (*Transcriptions of early County Records of New York State: Minutes of the Board of Supervisors of Ulster County 1710/1 to 1730/1*). A 1702 tax receipt indicates that collectors were in place in New Paltz at that time. A constable had also been elected by 1703, as indicated by a warrant from a justice of the peace to the unnamed constable commanding patentee Pierre Deyo to appear before a justice of the peace ("Charles Broadhead to Constable of New Paltz," March 3, 1703 [Deyo Family Papers (*1675–1870*], HHS). The earliest record indicating that New Paltz was following appropriate fence legislation is 1712, when the "inhabitants of ye Niew Pals" met to create fence rules, in response to an order of the constable. This agreement also indicated that fences would be inspected by "the Viewers of fences." (LeFevre, *History of New*

Paltz, 66–68). LeFevre erroneously indicates that it was the Duzine who "made rules in regard to fence building," (*History of New Paltz*, 69), as the rules were actually created by all of the inhabitants. Eric Roth suggests that the New Paltz community governed itself according to its own ethno-religious ideals when it came to providing for the poor, thus outside of English sociocultural constructs. He supports such an argument by noting that the deacons of the New Paltz congregation were providing for the poor as early as 1698, if not earlier, in accordance with the ecclesiastical structure of the Walloon Reformed Church (Roth, "Being Poor in New Paltz"). While this may have been the case, it is highly unlikely that deacons alone provided for the poor in the early years of the community, as by the opening years of the eighteenth century, the townspeople were electing officers whose role, in part, was aimed at the establishment of a government-sanctioned and government-organized means of "maintaining the poore" throughout the county. Taxes were collected in each town for such a purpose even before the 1743 law provided for the election of overseers who managed such support. (Evidence suggests that the nearby Ulster County towns of Hurley and Marbletown elected overseers of the poor even before the 1743 enabling legislation, such that New Paltz might have done so as well.) Before the election of overseers, perhaps one of the other elected officials oversaw the dispersal of poor relief, since they had been responsible for its collection. In other words, even if the New Paltz congregation chose to provide support for the poor, they likely did so in addition to that provided by the local government, which had been constructed according to English political ideals.

21. The first directive produced by the provincial legislature in regard to the division of jointly held patents was a 1708 act entitled "An Act for the easier Partition of Lands in Joint Tennancy or in Comon." Prior to the passage of that act, the heirs of those who had received patents were required, if following proper legal procedures, to present a Writ of Partition to the court. However, according to the 1708 legislation, this "should Still leave them uncapable of reaping [for] themselves or procuring to her Majty or Other's that Certain Advantage Accrueing by Settlements, and Improvements," presumably because this action still did not permanently and legally divide the land. This 1708 law provided that those with rights to commonly held undivided land henceforth had the right to divide the land by majority vote into portions to which they were legally entitled and to draw lots for such subdivisions in the sight of three "Indifferent" persons. This law essentially stood in effect from its passage until September 1, 1718, with a brief lapse in 1715. After the 1708 law finally lapsed, a related law was enacted in October 1718, with the primary difference being that the new law stipulated that only "assignees of full shares of Patentees," rather than all of those whom had a right to any part of the tract of land, had the right to decide by majority vote how to divide commonly-held land equally. How these "assignees" were to be chosen and how those full shares were to be divided among those with partial rights, were not made clear in the law. This law was in

effect only until November 1, 1721, but in 1726 another similar "Act for the Easier partition of Lands held in Common and promoting the Settleing and Improvement thereof & for Confirming the former Divisions of the Settled Townships of this Colony" was passed. This new law also addressed the fact that without it, patentees and their heirs were still not legally able to divide their lands. The new law, however, had the potential for taking the division of lands outside the hands of the heirs, as it allowed for those with rights to such tracts of land to elect by majority vote nine "substantiall Freeholders & Inhabitants" of the county who would effect the division, with the possibility existing that those "substantial" men were not heirs as well. *Colonial Laws*, 1:882, 2:329–337.

22. The agreement that created the Twelve Men allowed for elections (as in the 1726 act), although not of indifferent persons, rather of representatives of those with a real interest in the land (thus more in tune with the both the 1708 and 1718 acts). It was somewhat akin to the 1718 law in that the elected individuals would each represent one of twelve patentees, similar to the "assignees of full shares" as in that law. LeFevre, *History of New Paltz*, 70–75.
23. LeFevre, *History of New Paltz*, 73. Paula Carlo implies that the 1728 agreement, which served as the founding document for the Twelve Men, provided for an immediate division of the then-undivided land, but the division to which she refers was not accomplished until 1760 (Carlo, *Huguenot Refugees*, 39).
24. See Roth ("where ye walloens dwell," 354, 356, 364) for information as to other French-speaking families who lived in the region. Of the four children of patentee Pierre Deyo, three married "Dutch" individuals (two from the Clearwater family and one VanBommel). The remaining son was the only one who married someone of French ancestry, Marie LeConte; however, she was also known by the Dutch version of her surname, deGraff, possibly suggesting a Dutch cultural identification. Five of these six children of patentee Louis DuBois married those of "Dutch" descent [Vernooy (2), Van Meteren, Foochen, Matthysen], and the one child who married a patentee family member married a Hasbrouck. Two of Louis Bevier's children married Hasbroucks, one married a Vernooy, and the two who married those of mixed French/Walloon and Dutch heritage married children from unions of Montany/de Hooges and Blanchan/Van Schoonhover. Of Abraham Hasbrouck and his wife Maria Deyos's children, one married a person of Walloon background (DuBois), two married within the "Dutch" families (Schoonmaker and Van Wagenen,) and two married individuals of mixed French/Walloon and Dutch ancestry (Deyo/Clearwater and DeLange/VanSchaick). Data concerning marriages is derived from Versteeg, *Records of the Reformed Dutch Church of New Paltz*, and family genealogies.
25. The statistics concerning marriage patterns over time are derived both from marriage dates and the date of the earliest baptism for a child that resulted from such unions, although such baptismal dates may not reflect the baptism of a couple's first child (and thus not relate directly to

their marriage date). A starting date of 1750 was chosen for an analysis of marriage patterns, as that date marks a time when the New Paltz congregation began having regular, uninterrupted services of a minister, such that the marriage and baptismal records after that date are far more comprehensive than they had been previously. The year 1750 was also chosen because it reflects the ethnic state of the community before the development of a substantially British neighborhood in the eastern portion of the patent as a result of the c. 1760 settlement of the river lands and the 1763 "new division," which is explored below. Eighteen marriages in which the wife's maiden name is not indicated in the New Paltz church records have been excluded. Seven of the 216 unions in which the surnames of both spouses were recorded have also been excluded. Six of these seven involved marriages that included individuals in which the non-patentee partner possessed a common English surname that could be found in New York before 1675 [Cooper, Ketcham, Wolsey, Wood (3)], but it is not clear whether such individuals descended from such immigrants or if they themselves or their forebears arrived more recently. The name Emmanuel Consalis was also not included in the statistics, as being of Spanish derivation, it is difficult to classify in the other groupings. Twelve men and thirteen men in the "Dutch" group married partners with a British surname. The names in the "Dutch" or non-British category are, with the number of occurrences: Alsdorf (1), Blanchan (4), Bos (1), Bruyn (3), Burger (2), Cantine (1), Decker (3), Devaal (1), Dewitt (3), Eccert (1), Ein (5), Elmondorph (1), Eltinge (10), Evert (1), Goetschuis (2), Griffin (1), Hardenbergh (7), Helm (2), Hofman (1), Hog (1), Hoogland (1), Huey (1), Jansen (2), Jumens (1) Kool (1), Kritsinger (2), Krom (1), Lenjee (1), Low (3), Manny (1), Masten (1), Ostrander (2), Palmetier (1), Pawling (1), Perhemis (1), Relyea (2), Roosa (1), Rutsen (1), Sax (1), Schoonmaker (5), Schut (2), Sluyter (4), Smedes (1), Swart (2), Terbush (1), Terwilliger (14), Van Aaken (1), Vandermerken (1), Van Keuren (1), Van Vliet (2), Van Wagenen (8), Vernoy (3), Viele (1), Wirtz (1). Broadhead (3), an English name, is also included in the "Dutch" group as the progenitor was in Kingston (Wiltwijck) before the English conquest. The British names (all occur only once except those noted) are: Ancton, Auchmoody, Bennet, Bodine (2), Clark, Donaldson, Elmore, Green, Harris, McDonald (2), McKinley, Mitchell, Parker, Perkins, Saxton, Tilson, Waring, Webb, Weller, Winfield, York (3).

26. A list of fathers with British surnames who had children baptized in the New Paltz church include, but are not limited to, Allen, Barrett, Brannen, Bussy, Callahan, Canneway, Carney, Carson, Coleman, Demsy, Ellis, Elmore, Ferris, Flagler, Forgeson, Forman, Forster, Gallasbie, Gedney, Graham, Irwin, Jones, Kern, Kidney, Mackey, Mahony, Masters, McCaby, McClaghley, McNeel, Myer, Myers, Owens, Philips, Poor, Quick, Robertson, Rogers, Russel, Scott, Stevens, Tamkins, and Wells. Unions between spouses both of whom had British surnames include Allen/Donaldson (1753), Callahan/Johnson (1757); Whiller/Killy, [Wheeler/

Kelly] (1769) Danelson [probably Donaldson]/Robertson (1786); Countryman/Conneway (1789) (the date in parenthesis indicates the earliest record of such unions).

27. The seven women with British birth names who became church members are Elizabeth Wood (1752), Magdalena (Auchmoody) Low (1753), Cathrina (Broadhead) DuBois (1761), Rachel (Auchmoody) Bevier (1784), Maria (York) Bevier (1784) Maria (Wells) Lemonjon (1786), and Syntje (Strickland) Wesmuller (1792). Three of the six with strong patentee/"Dutch" connections were married to men with patentee surnames; two of these three were themselves daughters of patentee women (Maria York Bevier and Rachel Auchmoody Bevier), and the third (Cathrina Broadhead DuBois) was from a family with Ulster county roots dating back to the Nieuw Nederland period. The fourth, Magdalena (Auchmoody) Low, also had a mother born with a patentee surname, and she was married to a man with a Germanic surname (Low) with strong connections to the patentees. The remaining two were also married to non-British men. It is possible that Elizabeth Wood was Dutch-identified as well. As noted earlier, the surname "Wood" was found in New York before 1675, but as it was a not-uncommon name, it is not known if the Wood family in New Paltz is related to the early Wood immigrant(s) or possibly a family who arrived later. The eight men with British surnames include James Auchmoody, husband of Maria Deyo, and Jacobus their son; Moses York, husband of Maria Freer, and their son Johannes; and Wessel Broadhead. Also included were Pieter York (perhaps a brother of Moses), William Jenkins (who became a member in 1800, and had originally been a church member in Ramapo, New Jersey), and Daniel Graham, who became a member in 1778.

28. One hundred eighty-nine out of the 239 (78 percent) times a person was elected to serve as elder or deacon, the person chosen had a patentee surname.

29. LeFevre, *History of New Paltz*, 89, 92. The 1712 tax was based on an assessment for all real and personal property. Although the 1728 tax does not specifically state that the tax was to be based on both real and personal property, it nevertheless likely was, as that was the general practice (see, for example, *Colonial Laws*, 2:173–188 and *Colonial Laws*, 2:254–272). The men included in the 1712 tax list that developed close connections to the patentee families included father and son Tunis Jacobse and Jacob Clearwater (the father, Tunis, used only his patronymic), who were closely connected to the Deyo family: Jacob was married to Marie Deyo, daughter of patentee Pierre Deyo, and Jacob's sister Elsie had married Pierre's eldest son, Abraham. Jan Terpenning, also included in the 1712 list, was married to Esther Freer, granddaughter of Hugo Freer, the patentee. That husbands marrying into patentee families attained high social status was at least the case for the husbands of Elias Ean and Jan Terpenning, as is clear from their fathers-in-law's wills. The two additional men of Dutch background who lacked any obvious connections to the founding families in 1712 were Hendrick Van Weye and Gerrit Lambertse. The patentee community

held 99 percent of the assessed wealth in 1712 (£1,875 out of £1,895). In 1728, twenty-one of thirty-three taxables (64 percent) had patentee surnames. Of the remaining twelve, six were of Dutch background who were or had been married to a person from a patentee family (including Peter Low, who was married to Catherine DuBois [granddaughter of patentee Louis]; Roelof Elting, Esq., who was wed to Sara DuBois, daughter of patentee Abraham DuBois; and Mattys Slecht, who married Maria Madaleen Crispell). These six increased those of or in the orbit of the patentee families at that time to 82 percent. Three of the remaining six included August Vandemark (who may not have been connected to the founding families but was of Dutch descent) and Anthony Westbrook and Nicholas Roosa (whose families would later be united with patentee families through marriage), all of whom had Dutch heritage or had been integrated into the local "Dutch." ("Roosa" was a Dutch surname, and Westbrooks were found in New York before 1675, and thus possibly had a Dutch identity as well.) Several Westbrooks later married patentee women, and Nicholas Roosa's daughter later married Abraham Hardenbergh, who lived on land that was ultimately annexed to New Paltz. Although no Hardenberghs were taxed as being from New Paltz in 1728, they ultimately became very much part of the New Paltz community after the death of Abraham Hardenbergh's first wife; his second wife, whom he married in 1752, was Mary Hasbrouck, daughter of Hardenbergh's neighbor Joseph Hasbrouck. The other two taxables were a non-resident (Col. Jacob Rutson) and a freeholder on the Garland Patent that abutted New Paltz (Garret Keeteltas). The assessed wealth of the patentee community in 1728 was £1,133 of £1,145, or 99 percent.

30. LeFevre, *History of New Paltz*, 94–96. The 1765 taxes were assessed for all real and personal property. Fifty-two of 112, or 46 percent, had patentee surnames. Those of Dutch surnames who had integrated with the patentee families through marriage include Ean, Eltinge, Low, Hardenbergh, Terwilliger, and Van Wagenen. Hardenbergh and Low are more precisely German, but by 1765, the Hardenberghs had become part of the local "Dutch." Those of "Dutch" background that were within the patentee orbit without marrying into the patentee families include another Van Wagenen (Abraham), the widow of a Dutch man (Marynus Van Aken) and a man likely of Huguenot or Walloon background (Michael De Vou). Seventy-six of 112 taxables, or 68 percent, were therefore in the patentee orbit.

31. Examples of those with British surnames include Dean, Donaldson, Elsworth, Gray, Gilbert, Sergeant, Mackay, Wheeler, and Woolsey. The surnames Dean, Elsworth, and Woolsey were found in New York before 1675, so it is conceivable that they had been impacted by Dutch culture or possessed a Dutch identity. Germanic names include Presslar, Hass, and Wasemiller; French or Walloon names include such as Palmiter/Polmitier and Pontinear. Of the thirty-four names of the newcomers, at least eighteen were not found in New Paltz just over thirty years later (based on the 1798 Direct Tax schedules). Six of those eighteen names

(Hubble, Hurs, Hurta, Nap, Stover, and Wyard) cannot even be found in the county just over a decade later, as evidenced by the Revolutionary War militia lists. Of the thirty-six households of newcomers, twenty-six were assessed £2 or less; eighteen of those twenty-six only £1 or less. As a point of comparison, twenty-seven of the seventy-six taxables in the majority group were assessed between £10 and £30, four between £30 and £50, and eight between £50 and £71 3s. Abraham Donaldson was assessed at £17 14s. It is possible that Abraham Donaldson could be considered part of the patentee group, since at one point he served as a member of the Twelve Men for the share of Louis DuBois, but his ancestry is unclear. It is possible that he was a descendant of Catherine DuBois, the daughter of patentee Abraham DuBois, who married a William Donaldson in 1728 and later moved to Lancaster, Pennsylvania, although the DuBois family genealogy provides no information as to whether they had any offspring and if so, if any returned to New Paltz.

32. LeFevre, appendix to *History of New Paltz*, 26–27.
33. The patentee group included 149 out of 407 taxables, or 37 percent. That number includes a few individuals who had been living in the village as early as 1772 and possibly had integrated into the "Dutch" community without having married into a patentee family, evidenced by their contribution to the construction of a new church structure in that year. Ulster County "Dutch" names include such as Dewitt, Decker, Dumont, Delemetre, Vanhoesen, Vanvliet, and Vanstienbergh. Dumont and Delemetre were of French heritage rather than Dutch, but by the end of the eighteenth century, any sense of Frenchness had been eclipsed years before. One hundred and twenty-seven out of 166 new surnames were represented only once. Ninety-seven of the patentee group owned or leased houses that were worth at least one hundred dollars, and likewise did seventy-eight of the 259 newcomers. Sixty-five, or 44 percent of the patentee group owned houses valued at over three hundred dollars.
34. Nominees and elected officials without patentee surnames whose families had intermarried with patentee families were from such families as Hardenbergh, Eltinge, Newkirk, Ean, Low, and later in the 1760s, Van Wagenen and Terwilliger. The four officials elected between 1751 and 1759 who neither had a patentee surname nor had married into the patentee families were Abraham Vandemerke (whose family had connections in New Paltz as early as 1728), who served as tax collector three times; Matthew Allen, who was nominated as assessor twice and served once; Johan Jury Rang, a "Belgian" who settled in nearby Shawangunk and was a member of the New Paltz church (LeFevre, *History of New Paltz*, 500–501), although never elected; and Jonathan Tomkins, nominated once as surveyor of highways in 1758, but not elected. Those of the "river side" who were nominated or elected between 1760 and 1762 were living on lands along the river that had been divided in 1745, suggesting that it was not until about 1760 that those lands were settled. In 1761, William Elsworth and Israel Coolson were nominated as "Surveyor Highway River" (Elsworth was elected).

and Leonard Lewis was elected constable "At River Side." Peleg Ransom and Valentine Perkins (Parkin, Parkus) were elected as fenceviewers at the "river" in 1762, and Leonard Lewis was again elected as constable. Beginning in 1762, however, no geographic designations were indicated for the office of constable, although presumably constables were still chosen for particular areas, as several individuals were elected who lived near the river (Lewis, Andrew Mackey, and Peleg Ransom). Fenceviewers, however, continued to be divided both in and after 1763 and between those at the river side (such as Peleg Ransom, James Tuttle, and Eliazer Cole) and the "paltz" side, and a pound master was elected in 1763 and 1766 only for the river side of the community.

35. Thirty individuals were elected to fill fifty-eight terms of high office between 1790 and 1795; twenty-three were from the patentee group (77 percent), while seven (23 percent) were newcomers. One of the clerks—George Wirtz—was a newcomer, but he had married a woman of the patentee group (Esther Hasbrouck). Wirtz was also related to several ministers of the Goetschius family who served in the town. The overseers elected during the 1790–1795 period not from within the patentee community were Elisha Lister, Solomon Waring, Zopher Perkins, Isaac Bodine, and Benjamin Rasel; only Rasel served more than once. Of the other fifteen assessors who served alongside Ransom, one served three times, five served twice, and the remaining nine each served once.
36. See note 1.

Chapter 2

1. The literature on property and gender in the Walloon region of Europe is rather limited, but includes Emmanuel Le Roy Ladurie, "A System of Customary Law: Family Structures and Inheritance Customs in 16th-Century France," in *Family and Society: Selections from the Annales Economies, Sociétés, Civilisations*, eds. Robert Forster and Orest Ranum, trans. Elborg Forster and Patricia M. Ranum (Baltimore, MD: Johns Hopkins, 1976), 75–103, and Martha Howell, "Rewriting Marriage in Late Medieval Douai," *Romanic Review* 86, no. 2 (March 1995), 307–337 (quotations at 308 n.3 and 310).
2. The principle by which children did inherit in place of their deceased parent is referred to as *représentation*.
3. The principle by which Dutch parents transferred control of the family estate to the surviving spouse while there were minor children in the house was called *boedelhouderschap*.
4. Studies of ethnicity, gender, law, and property in New Netherland and colonial New York include Linda Briggs Biemer, *Women and Property in Colonial New York: The Transition from Dutch to English Law, 1643–1727* (Ann Arbor, MI: UMI Research Press, 1983); David Narrett, "Dutch Customs of Inheritance, Women, and the Law in Colonial New York City," in *Authority and Resistance in Early New York*, eds. William Pencak and Conrad Edick Wright (New York: New-York Historical Society, 1988),

27–55; David Narrett, "Men's Wills and Women's Property Rights in Colonial New York," in *Women in the Age of the American Revolution*, eds. Ronald Hoffman and Peter J. Albert (Charlottesville: University of Virginia, 1989), 91–133; David Narrett, *Inheritance and Family Life in Colonial New York City* (Ithaca, NY: Cornell University Press, 1992); Martha Dickinson Shattuck, "A Civil Society: Court and Community in Beverwijck, New Netherland, 1652–1664" (PhD diss., Boston University, 1993) in particular, see 140–191; Susan Elizabeth Shaw, "Building New Netherland: Gender and Family Ties in a Frontier Society" (PhD diss., Cornell University, 2000); Michael E. Gherke, "Dutch Women in New Netherland and New York in the Seventeenth Century" (PhD diss., West Virginia University, 2001); Adriana E. van Zwieten, "A little land . . . to sow some seeds: Real Property, Custom, and Law in the Community of New Amsterdam" (PhD diss., Temple University, 2001).

5. For an overview of women and property rights in the British colonies in America, see Marylynn Salmon, *Women and the Law of Property in Early America* (Chapel Hill: University of North Carolina Press, 1986). For a discussion of *feme covert* status, see in particular Narrett, "Men's Wills," 106, and Salmon, *Women and the Law of Property in Early America*, 14–18. For a discussion of separate estates, see Salmon, *Women and the Law of Property in Early America*, 81–104.
6. Salmon, *Women and the Law of Property in Early America*, 18, 141–147.
7. Narrett, "Men's Wills," 127–128.
8. Carole Shammas, Marylynn Salmon, and Michel Dahlin, *Inheritance in America from Colonial Times to the Present* (New Brunwick, NJ: Rugers University Press, 1987), 41–62.
9. Louis DuBois and Catherine Blanchan, "Will, October 13, 1676," Deed Book 2 ("Kingston Papers"), 246–247, accessed September 24, 2013, http://www.co.ulster.ny.us/archives/dutchsearchscreen.html. If either survivor remarried and produced additional offspring, half of the remaining half (i.e., one-quarter of the whole estate) would ultimately be inherited by them, with the result being that the heirs from the first marriage would inherit a total of only three-quarters of the estate. As Catherine was forty-seven at the time she and her husband composed their will, it was unlikely that she would produce any more heirs; but Louis was fifty at the time, and they apparently wanted to provide for the possibility that he might father more children if, by chance, Catherine preceded him in death.
10. Louis DuBois, "Will, March 31, 1686," Ulster County Land Records, Deed Book AA, 39. In Ulster County, the last mutual will that was probated was written in 1683, in New York City in 1693, and in Albany, 1709 (Narrett, "Dutch Customs of Inheritance," 34).
11. Louis DuBois, "Will, March 27, 1694," Ulster County Land Records, Deed Book AA, 167–168.
12. Louis DuBois and Catherine Blanchan, "Will, October 13, 1676"; Louis DuBois, "Will, March 31, 1686"; Louis DuBois, "Will, March 27, 1694";

Louis DuBois, "Codicil, February 22, 1696," Ulster County Land Records, Deed Book AA, 169–170. Between 1694 and 1696, Louis apparently had started to distribute his real estate, so he executed a codicil in 1696 that directed some of his children to make various payments to the estate for certain lands they had already received, such that the total value of the estate could then be divided equally. Although it is impossible to know whether the payments represented the exact market value of the land he gave to each of his children, the estate was nevertheless still distributed in eight equal parts.

13. Hugo Freer, "Will, September 4, 1698," transcribed in the appendix to LeFevre, *History of New Paltz*, 68–70; Christian Deyo, "Will, August 10, 1676," Deed Book 2 ("Kingston Papers"), 243; Christian Deyo, "Will, October 15, 1687," Ulster County Land Records, Deed Book AA, 65; Antoine Crispell, "Will, November 6, 1707," Ulster County Land Records, Deed Book AA, 425–428.
14. Louis Bevier, "Will, September 12, 1715," Louis Bevier Papers, HHS; Louis Bevier, "Will, May 2, 1720," Ulster County Land Records, Deed Book CC, 111–113.
15. Jean Hasbrouck, "Will, August 26, 1712," Ulster County Land Records, Deed Book BB, 375– 378; "Indenture, January 2, 1705," between Mary DuBois and Jean Hasbrouck, HHS.
16. It is possible, although unlikely, that some of the property Mary received included land. Jean Hasbrouck refers to land between that of his daughter Mary and Abraham DuBois ("heet stuck Landt Leggende tusschen het Landt van: Abraham Dubois en myn doghter Mary"), but it is unclear whether he was referring to land that he had given to her or to land that had been owned by Mary's deceased husband, Isaac DuBois, which Mary administered.
17. Hendricus Deyo, "Will, December 4, 1724," Levi Hasbrouck Family Papers: The Locust Lawn Collection, translated. David Wilkin, February 2003. The original French is "ma famme margriste demeurera en la plaine Posesiont de toute me bien pour en jouir paisiblement Durant sont veuage seant quel soit oublige de rendre Conte a me enfant." Andries Lefevre, "Will, April 19, 1738," in Gustave Anjou, *Ulster County, N.Y. probate records in the office of the surrogate, and in the county clerk's office at Kingston, N.Y. : a careful abstract and translation of the Dutch and English wills, letters of administration after intestates, and inventories from 1665, with genealogical and historical notes, and list of Dutch and Frisian baptismal names with their English equivalents* (New York: Anjou, 1906), 1:153–154.
18. Daniel DuBois, "Will, September 12, 1747," Daniel and Simon DuBois Family Papers (1695–1864), HHS. (The original French is "ma femme Marie demeurera en la pleine possession et Jouissance de tous mes biens mouvable et ymmouvables . . . pour en jouir paisiblement Durant son veufage sans quelle soit oblige den render Conte a mes Enfans ny a personne quy que e soit.") Daniel DuBois had similarly provided for his wife in his previous 1729 will (Daniel DuBois, "Will, August 16, 1729,"

transcribed in Anjou, *Probate*, 1:114–116). Hendricus DuBois, "Will, June 21, 1774," transcribed in Anjou, *Probate*, 1:158–159; Abraham LeFevre, "Will, July 3, 1790," Ulster County Will Book A, 309–310.

19. Andries Lefevre, "Will, April 19, 1738," in Anjou, *Probate*, 1:153–154; Simon LeFevre, "Will, September 6, 1743," New York County Probate Records, Liber 16, 385–387.
20. Noah Eltinge, "Will, August 16, 1782," New York County Probate Records, Liber 37, 362–368.
21. Hugo Freer, "Will, February 12, 1707," transcribed in Anjou, *Probate*, 1:78–79; Daniel DuBois, "Will, August 16, 1729" (in the original French, "elle aura un tiers dans les revenus de toutes mes terres aussy elle aura une negresse trois or quatre vaches trous Cheveaus et tous les meubles de ma maison"); Henry DuBois, "Will, May 26, 1784," Ulster County Will Book A, 85–86; Simon LeFevre, "Will, September 6, 1743."
22. Jacob Hasbrouck, "Will, June 7, 1720," Levi Hasbrouck Family Papers: The Locust Lawn Collection, HHS; Jacob Hasbrouck, "Will, March 2, 1732," Levi Hasbrouck Family Papers: The Locust Lawn Collection, HHS; Andries Lefevre, "Will, April 19, 1738"; Jonathan DuBois, "Will, July 14, 1746," New York County Probate Records, Liber 17, 9; Jacobus Bevier, "Will, February 18, 1774," New York County Probate Records, Liber 29, 109–111; Daniel LeFevre, "Will, September 4, 1784," transcribed in Anjou, *Probate*, 2:47.
23. Joseph Hasbrouck, "Will, January 23, 1723/24," in Kenneth Hasbrouck, *The Hasbrouck Family in America*, 35–36 (original document in private collection); Abraham Deyo, "Will, September 20, 1724," Ulster County Land Records, Deed Book CC, 293–294 (the original French was "mais sy elle ces venoit a se Remarier alor elle sera oblige de rendre tous a mon fist Abraham); Simon DuBois, "Will, July 24, 1756," Daniel and Simon DuBois Family Papers (1695–1864), HHS; Daniel Hasbrouck, "Will, January 24, 1759," Ulster County Wills in the Office of the Surrogate, A: 201–205.
24. John (Jan) Hasbrouck, "Will, May 7, 1768" (1770 translation by executor Abraham LeFevre), HHS; Jacob Hasbrouck Jr., "Will, August 3, 1776," Levi Hasbrouck Family Papers, The Locust Lawn Collection, HHS.
25. Josiah Eltinge, "Will, April 4, 1767," (1784 fair copy), Roelof J. and Ezekiel Elting Family Papers, HHS; Peter Deyo, "Will, June 16, 1791," Ulster County Wills in the Office of the Surrogate, A: 265267; Johannis Freer, "Will, September 1, 1796," transcribed in Anjou, *Probate*, 1:158.
26. Abraham DuBois, "Will, October 1, 1731," New York County Probate Records, Liber 11, 175–179.
27. Roelof Eltinge, "Will, October 29, 1745," New York County Probate Records, Liber 16, 251–255; Benjamin Hasbrouck, "Will, July 7, 1796," HHS.
28. Elsie Hasbrouck, "Deed, June 1, 1754," in Kenneth Hasbrouck, *The Hasbrouck Family in America*, 37 (manuscript in private collection); Margrietje Eltinge Bevier, "Will, 1793," "Will, 1796," "Will, 1799," "Will, 1805," and "Indenture, 1776," as well as a June 6, 1787, document

in which she indicated that her eldest son, Solomon, had not fulfilled his part of the contract with her (Hendricus DuBois Family Papers, HHS). Versteeg, *Records of the Reformed Dutch Church of New Paltz*, 34.

29. Jacob Hasbrouck, "Will, June 7, 1720." (The original Dutch is "sal in volle possessie en besitt van myn gehee[le] staat blyve gedurende de tut van haar weduwelyke staat sonder Eenige Rekenschap te sulle geven aan myn Erfgenamen.")
30. Jacob Hasbrouck, "Will, March 2, 1732"; Jacob Hasbrouck, "Will, September 25, 1747," New York County Probate Records, Liber 23, 206–208.
31. Catherine Cottin, "Will, July 23, 1712," Ulster County Land Records, Deed Book BB, 323–324; "Indenture, January 20, 1713," Ulster County Land Records, Deed Book BB, 325–326.
32. Maria Hasbrouck, "Will, July 30, 1729," HHS. In the original French, Maria Hasbrouck's bequest to her son reads, "il ma entreteneu en mon vielle agee et a este mon consolasion." Catharina Freer, "Will, September, 22, 1781," Ulster County Probate Records, Box 14; Wyntje Hasbrouck, "Will, June 23, 1781," Ulster County Wills in Office of Surrogate, A: 162–163.
33. Elsie Hasbrouck, "Deed, June 1, 1754," in Kenneth Hasbrouck, *The Hasbrouck Family in America*, 37 (manuscript in private collection); "Indenture, March 9, 1781," Hendricus DuBois Family Papers, HHS. When Mathusalem DuBois, Jacob DuBois, and John Van Wagenen were granted letters of administration during the minority of Garret and Methusalem DuBois Jr. (sons of Henry and Rebecca DuBois) on April 28, 1788, the surrogate noted that Rebecca DuBois had previously renounced her power of executrix on June 5, 1787 (Anjou, *Probate*, 2:33).
34. In 1713, Maria still paid taxes as head of household, when her children ranged in age from twenty-four to twenty-nine; there is no evidence to suggest that her sons disputed her matriarchal status. Maria DuBois posthumously received four seats in the church, presumably because she was a substantial donor; only one other person received more. "List of New Paltz Taxpayers, 1712," LeFevre, *History of New Paltz*, 89; Mary DuBois, "Release, February 14, 1718/19," in LeFevre, *History of New Paltz*, 293–294; Versteeg, *Records of the Reformed Dutch Church of New Paltz*, 2–3. Maria Hasbrouck's eldest son, Joseph, also donated to the church, but he resided outside of the New Paltz patent on his own farm. "New Paltz Tax Payers in 1728," LeFevre, *History of New Paltz*, 92.
35. Simon LeFevre, "Will, September 6, 1743"; Versteeg, *Records of the Reformed Church of New Paltz*, 34. Petronella had not received any real property in New Paltz from her father, Joseph Hasbrouck.
36. Maria Eltinge, "Release of Dower," Roelof J. and Ezekiel Elting Family Papers, HHS; "1798 Federal Direct Tax, New Paltz schedules," HHS.
37. Christian Deyo, "Will, February 1, 1687"; Hendricus Deyo, "Will, December 4, 1724"; Daniel DuBois, "Will, August 16, 1729"; Daniel DuBois, "Will, September 12, 1747" (which stipulated that all of his real estate and the bulk of his personal property were to be divided among his three sons and one daughter, with the only exception being that he

gave his three sons his horses, with his eldest receiving one more than each of his brothers); Simon LeFevre, "Will, September 6, 1743," in Anjou, *Probate*, 2:140. (The values of livestock are based on the 1774 inventory of the estate of Abraham Bevier [Hendricus DuBois Family Papers, HHS].) Simon DuBois, "Will, July 24, 1756"; John (Jan) Hasbrouck, "Will, May 7, 1768"; Henry DuBois, "Will, May 26, 1784"; Hugo Freer, "Will, January 15, 1728."

38. Jacob Hasbrouck, "Will, September 25, 1747," New York County Probate Records, Liber 23, 206–208; Samuel Bevier, "Will, April 3, 1750," New York County Probate Records, Liber 21, 307–309; Noah Eltinge, "Will."
39. Louis Bevier, "Will, September 12, 1715"; Louis Bevier, "Will, May 2, 1720"; Andries Lefevre, "Will, April 19, 1738." Andries LeFevre inherited land from his father, his unmarried and childless uncle (also a patentee), and his mother. Daniel Hasbrouck, "Will, January 24, 1759." In 1756, Solomon DuBois bequeathed large farms to his three surviving sons, with Benjamin receiving about three thousand acres in the town of Catskill in Greene County, New York, and Cornelius and Hendricus receiving farms in New Paltz; the latter two also each received an equal share in their father's rights to undivided New Paltz lands. Together, his three sons would have to pay their two sisters £100 each, with an additional £100 to the heirs of another sister who was deceased. Solomon carefully noted that he did not provide a similar bequest of £100 to his other daughter, Jacomyntje, as she had already received such a sum from the widow of her deceased brother, Isaac, to whom Solomon had given land in Pennsylvania. Solomon DuBois noted that "I have thought fit to make mention of the same that they may not seem to be wronged in their proportion of my Estate." Again his choice would have had little to do with a fear of fragmentation, thusly reflecting ethnocultural concerns. Solomon DuBois, "Will, 1765." In 1774, one of Solomon's sons Hendricus, likewise gave land to his three sons (and helped the fourth purchase a farm), for which they would have to financially compensate their three sisters and the children of a fourth sister who had already died. (His fifth daughter, Rachel, received only one-fifth of her father's right to certain church pews; what motivated this disparity is impossible to say.) Hendricus DuBois, "Will, June 21, 1774." Other men who devised their property in a comparable manner were Abraham Bevier, who in 1763 devised his real estate to his two sons, directing them to pay a total of £300 to their five sisters, with all seven sharing equally in the moveable estate. Abraham Bevier, "Will, May 13, 1763," Hendricus DuBois Papers, HHS. Benjamin Hasbrouck (1796) gave his land to his three sons, who in turn were to pay two of their four sisters £50, and their other two sisters the annual interest of £50, with each child receiving one-seventh of their father's personal estate. Benjamin Hasbrouck, "Will, July 7, 1796."
40. Samuel Bevier, "Will"; Hendricus DuBois, "Will, June 21, 1774"; Benjamin Hasbrouck, "Will, July 7, 1796."
41. Joseph Hasbrouck, "Will, January 23, 1723/24." The Guilford Patent

was not directly in New Paltz, but abutted an additional patent that Louis DuBois, the patentee, had received bordering the New Paltz patent. For functional purposes, it was part of the town of New Paltz. Abraham Hasbrouck's being so privileged substantially impacted his eventual rise to the status of, according to Edward Countryman, a local "chieftain" (Edward Countryman, *A People in Revolution: The American Revolution and Political Society in New York, 1760–1790* [Baltimore, MD: Johns Hopkins University Press, 1981], 245). Cornelius DuBois, "Will, November 6, 1780," transcribed in Anjou, *Probate*, 1:160–161; Peter Deyo, "Will."

42. Narrett, "Men's Wills," 120, 122; Christian Deyo, "Will, October 15, 1687" (An estimate for the value of a rijksdaalder can be found at http://www.coins.nd.edu/ColCoin/ColCoinIntros/Rix-Dollar.intro.html [accessed March 28, 2014]); Hugo Freer, "Will," (includes in the original French, "hugue Frere son fils aisnes aura dix pieces de huit pour son droit d'aisnes"); Jacob Hasbrouck, "Will, June 7, 1720" (a translated portion of which reads, "I give to my oldest son Jean a pound current money of New York for the right of primogeniture without him having or pretending anything more"). John (Jan) Hasbrouck, "Will, May 7, 1768"; Jacobus Bevier, "Will, February 18, 1774"; Jonathan DuBois, "Will, July 14, 1746"; Daniel DuBois, "Will, September 12, 1747"; Abraham LeFevre, "Will, July 3, 1790"; Abraham DuBois, "Will, October 1, 1731" (which includes the following bequest to his eldest son in the original Dutch: "mijn oudste soon Abraham sal hebben en genieten voor syn eerste geboorte en syn gehoorsamhyt uyt mijn staat voor of te som vantive hondert poundt courrant gelt van dese proventie").
43. Antoine Crispell, "Will"; Louis Bevier, "Will, May 2, 1720"; Hugo Freer, "Will, January 15, 1728."

Chapter 3

1. A list of craftsmen necessary for the construction of a stone house in Ulster County can be derived from the records of Louis Bevier of nearby Marbletown related to the 1751 construction of a one-room addition to his stone house. Neil Larson, "Building a Stone House in Ulster County, New York," *Newsletter of the Society for the Preservation of Hudson Valley Vernacular Architecture* 15, no. 4–6 (April–June 2011): 5–11. For a brief discussion of "primary" and "secondary" characteristics of domestic structures, see Cohen, *The Dutch-American Farm*, 37.
2. "1798 Federal Direct Tax, New Paltz schedules," HHS.
3. Jeroen van den Hurk, "Imagining New Netherland: Origins and Survival of Netherlandic Architecture in Old New York," (PhD diss., University of Delaware, 2006) 4, n. 5. Architectural historians Neil Larson (whose work is extensively cited below) and John Stevens (John R. Stevens, *Dutch Vernacular Architecture in North America: 1640–1830* [West Hurley, New York: The Society for the Preservation of Hudson Valley

Vernacular Architecture, 2005]) do not seem to question the "Dutchness" of New Paltz architecture, while Jeroen van den Hurk does (van den Hurk, "Netherlandic Architecture," 321–323).

4. The following analysis of independent domestic architecture in the Netherlands is drawn primarily from the work of Henk D. Zantkuyl, "The New Netherlands Town House," *New World Dutch Studies: Dutch Arts and Culture in Colonial America, 1609–1776*, eds. Roderic H. Blackburn and Nancy A. Kelley (Albany, NY: Albany Institute of History and Art, 1987), 143–160; van den Hurk, "Netherlandic Architecture"; Kenneth Hewes Barricklo and Neil Larson & Associates, "Historic Structure Report: The Abraham Hasbrouck House"; and Larson Fisher Associates and Crawford & Stearns, "Historic Structure Report for the Ezekiel Elting House" (unpublished report for the Huguenot Historical Society, 2007).
5. Stevens, *Dutch Vernacular Architecture*, 16–17, 117, 178–179; Cohen, *The Dutch-American Farm*, 31.
6. Room nomenclature is varied in both the primary and secondary literature. The room nomenclature employed here is based on a 1648 New Netherland building contract cited in Zantkuyl, "The New Netherlands Town House," 153–154. The house reconstruction in figure 3.4 is based on a 1646 contract between Cornelis van Tienhovern and his housewright, Reynier Dominicus (Zantkuyl, "The New Netherlands Town House," 151–152), van den Hurk, "Netherlandic Architecture," 179–181.
7. Jeroen van den Hurk's analysis of Nieuw Nederland building contracts reveals no evidence that the term "binnenhaard" was used in the colony, although the term "opkamer" was, van den Hurk, "Netherlandic Architecture," 177–182.
8. Fred B. Kniffen, "Folk Housing: Key to Diffusion," in *Readings in American Vernacular Architecture*, eds. Dell Upton and John Michael Vlach (Athens: University of Georgia, 1986), 11–13; Leland M. Roth, *A Concise History of American Architecture* (Boulder, CO: Westview Press, 1979), 15; Abbott Lowell Cummings, "Inside the Massachusetts House," in *Readings in American Vernacular Architecture*, eds. Dell Upton and John Michael Vlach (Athens: University of Georgia, 1986), 219–239; William H. Pierson Jr., *American Buildings and Their Architects: The Colonial and Neoclassical Styles* (New York: Oxford University Press 1970), 1:48.
9. van den Hurk notes that there were actually four different types of bent systems employed in Dutch houses, based on a very clear nomenclature, although American architectural historians generally refer to all such bents as "anchor beam bents." van den Hurk further notes that only one type of bent is a true anchor beam bent, or *ankerbalgebint*. A true anchor beam bent is in the shape of an H, in which the transverse beam is inserted through the post, with a "tongue" protruding out the other side. In houses, such anchor beam bents were generally employed only when an *uitlait* was present, as otherwise the tongue would be exposed to the elements and thus be prone to rot (van den Hurk, "Netherlandic Architecture," 154–159).

10. Archaelogist Joseph Diamond (a professor at the State University of New York at New Paltz) presented on "the onsite discovery of both an earth-fast or 'post-in-ground' style house from the 17th century and a pit house uncovered north of the DuBois Fort" on 4/18/2013 at Historic Huguenot Street, accessed February 15, 2016, https://www.facebook.com/events/604988689515730/. Barricklo and Larson, "Historic Structure Report: The Abraham Hasbrouck House," 4.3; Sean E. Sawyer, "Constructing the Tradition of Dutch American Architecture, 1609–2009," in *Dutch New York: The Roots of Hudson Valley Culture*, ed. Roger Panetta (New York: Fordham University Press, 2009), 94; John R. Stevens, "DuBois House," *Newsletter of the Society for the Preservation of Hudson Valley Vernacular Architecture* 12, no. 8–10 (August–October 2009): 10–12.
11. The Jacob (Jean) Hasbrouck House is owned by HHS. The date that Jean Hasbrouck had his house built is based on a 1677 cutting date for the tree from which the lintel for the fireplace in the basement kitchen was hewn. Larson Fisher Associates and Crawford & Stearns, "Historic Structure Report for the Jean Hasbrouck House," 1.3.
12. "1798 Federal Direct Tax, New Paltz schedules," HHS.
13. The Maria DuBois house is owned by HHS. It is generally known today as the "DuBois Fort" and sometimes the "Daniel DuBois House," but it was actually built when the widow Maria, the mother of Daniel, had attained control of the family estate after the death of her husband, Isaac. John G. Waite Associates, "Dubois Fort: Historic Structure Report," (unpublished report for the Huguenot Historical Society, 2003). (See pages 76–77 for sketches by Douglas Bucher). Stevens, *Dutch Vernacular Architecture*, 86.
14. Neil Larson, "National Register of Historic Places Registration Form: Abraham & Maria LeFevre House," prepared May 12, 2006; Helen Wilkinson Reynolds, *Dutch Houses in the Hudson Valley before 1776* (New York: Holland Society, 1929), 210, 262. It is not clear in the photograph in Reynolds whether the mow door was still in place in the gable of this house, or whether it had already been replaced with a window, a common nineteenth-century alteration. For reference to the term "wenteltrap," see van den Hurk, "Netherlandic Architecture," 184.
15. The Daniel Hasbrouck and Samuel Bevier Houses are both owned by HHS. The Daniel Hasbrouck House has generally been known as the "Abraham Hasbrouck House"; Daniel was the son of Abraham and inherited his father's home lot. However, Abraham had died four years before the first room of the house was constructed. The house would be most appropriately named for Maria Hasbrouck, Abraham's wife, as it was built when she managed her deceased husband's estate. Barricklo and Larson, "Historic Structure Report: The Abraham Hasbrouck House"; Stevens, *Dutch Vernacular Architecture*, 190, 191. John Stevens compiled a list of front-gable houses in June 2006, totaling only twenty-two, only eight of which were built after 1739: "Newsletter," *Society for the Preservation of Hudson Valley Vernacular Architecture* 9, no. 6–7 (June/July 2007): 7. Zink notes that the primary entrance of a rural Dutch house was sometimes moved from the front gable to a side

elevation when the house lacked an *uitlat*, although he does not provide evidence to support such an assertion: Cifford Zink, "Dutch Framed Houses in New York and New Jersey," *Winterthur Portfolio* 22 no. 4 (Winter 1987): 265–294.

16. van den Hurk, "Netherlandic Architecture," 180. The interior entrance to the Daniel Hasbrouck *kelderkeuken* was likely created in the early years of the house.

17. van den Hurk, "Netherlandic Architecture," 185–187; Thomas R. Ryan, "Cultural Accommodations in the Late-Eighteenth-Century Architecture of Marbletown, New York," in *Shaping Communities*, vol. 6, *Perspectives in Vernacular Architecture*, (1997): 137–149 (see in particular, n. 24, p. 148); Barricklo and Larson, "Historic Structure Report: The Abraham Hasbrouck House," part 4.5–6; LeFevre, *History of New Paltz*, 272–273; Reynolds, *Dutch Houses*, 198, 255; *Newsletter of the Society for the Preservation of Hudson Valley Vernacular Architecture* 8, no. 7 (July 2006): 3–5.

18. The dendrochonological dating for structural members of the second addition to the Daniel Hasbrouck house is not as definitive as those for the earlier two rooms. However, there is evidence to suggest that one of the smaller beams used in the house was formed from a tree felled in 1734, the same year Daniel Hasbrouck married Wynje Deyo. Barricklo and Larson, "Historic Structure Report: The Abraham Hasbrouck House," 4.20. For a discussion of typicality in design, see Reynolds, *Dutch Houses* and Ryan, "Marbletown," 137–141, who refutes Reynolds.

19. Stevens, *Dutch Vernacular Architecture*, 225–227. Figure 3.23 reflects the original conditions of the Ten Eyck House; figure 3.22 reveals a later rear addition. The 1775 Hendricus DuBois House, which is no longer extant, was likely similar in form to the Jacob Hasbrouck House, according to architectural historian Neil Larson, who has studied the nineteenth-century house that incorporated some repurposed building materials from the Hendricus DuBois House (Neil Larson, personal communication, 2007).

20. Zantkuyl, "The New Netherlands Town House," 149–150. The architectural term "Georgian" is actually a misnomer, but will be employed here as a shorthand for the center-hall double-pile plan. For a more precise description of English architectural styles, see Pierson, *American Buildings*, 61–156, and James D. Kornwolf, *Architecture and Town Planning in Colonial America* (Baltimore, MD: Johns Hopkins University Press, 2002), 2:513–525, 2:957–1008.

21. Neil Larson, "National Register of Historic Places Registration Form: Abraham & Maria LeFevre House."

22. Ibid.

23. The land on which Daniel Deyo built his house was acquired for him in 1763 (LeFevre, *History of New Paltz*, 266–267). The Freer-Louw House is owned by HHS. Edward R. Cook and William J. Callahan, "Dendrochronological Analysis of the Freer-Low House, New Paltz, New York," (unpublished report for the HHS, 2008); Larson Fisher Associates and Ted Bartlett, for Crawford & Stearns, "Historic Structure Report

for the Freer-Louw House," (unpublished report for the Huguenot Historical Society, 2011).

24. Abraham D. Deyo was recorded as D. Abraham Deyo in the 1798 tax list.
25. Barricklo and Larson, "Historic Structure Report: The Abraham Hasbrouck House," 4.11–4.12; "Newsletter," *Society for the Preservation of Hudson Valley Vernacular Architecture* 8, no. 8 (August 2006): 5; Stevens, *Dutch Vernacular Architecture*, 69–73.
26. H. J. Louw, "The origin of the sash-window," *Architectural History* 26 (1983): 47–72, 144–150; Stevens, *Dutch Vernacular Architecture*, 73.
27. "Newsletter," *Society for the Preservation of Hudson Valley Vernacular Architecture* 8, no. 9 (September 2006): 4; Stevens, *Dutch Vernacular Architecture*, 70, 71, 314–317; Barricklo and Larson, "Historic Structure Report: The Abraham Hasbrouck House," 4.11–4.22. The windows pictured are early nineteenth-century replacements of those from 1734; one of the 1734 window frames is still in place beneath early nineteenth-century wood facing.
28. van den Hurk points out that "American scholars usually consider the jambless fireplace a prototypical element of Dutch colonial architecture. However, this type of fireplace was used not only by the Dutch but also by other Europeans." ("Netherlandic Architecture," 195). While this may be the case, the jambless fireplace was the fireplace of choice in the Dutch cultural region of New York before the region was influenced by English architecture, such that the association between the jambless fireplace and Dutch-American architecture remains apt.
29. Larson, "National Register of Historic Places Registration Form: Abraham & Maria LeFevre House." For a discussion of other examples in which both jambless and jambed fireplaces were built at approximately the same time, see Stevens, *Dutch Vernacular Architecture*, 95, 176–177.
30. Neil Larson, "Building a Stone House in Ulster County, New York in 1751"; Stevens, *Dutch Vernacular Architecture*, 314–317 (Stevens suggests a mid-eighteenth century date for the alteration made to the Samuel Bevier House based on the surviving original lower sash that remains in situ); Heirs of Samuel Bevier and Josiah Eltinge, "Indenture, May 12, 1760," Roelof J. and Ezekiel Elting Family Papers, HHS.
31. Larson Fisher Associates and Crawford & Stearns, "Historic Structure Report for the Jean Hasbrouck House," 1.26–1.30.
32. Larson Fisher Associates and Ted Bartlett, for Crawford & Stearns, "Historic Structure Report for the Freer-Louw House"; Barricklo and Larson, "Historic Structure Report: The Abraham Hasbrouck House," 4.25.
33. The Terwilliger House is part of the collection of Locust Lawn, Gift of Annette Innis Young, owned by Locust Grove, Poughkeepsie, New York. Crawford & Stearns and Neil Larson, "Historic Structure Report for the Evert Terwilliger House" (unpublished report for the Huguenot Historical Society, 2005), 1.4. How Terwilliger acquired the land from Freer is unknown, but a 1759 deed references Evert Terwilliger's earlier acquisition of the land in fee simple (Ulster County Deeds, Book FF, 412, noted by Neil Larson in Crawford & Stearns and Neil Larson, "Historic

Structure Report for the Evert Terwilliger House," 1.3). John Stevens does not include the Terwilliger House in his June 2006 list of front-gable houses, as he included only those "examples [which were] known to the preparer at the time of compilation (June 22, 2006): there are probably more," ("Newsletter," *Society for the Preservation of Hudson Valley Vernacular Architecture* 9, no. 6–7 [June/July 2007]: 7).

34. When the Terwilliger House was reconfigured, a new beam from a tree felled in 1755 was inserted, so the structural work must have been performed after that date (Crawford & Stearns and Neil Larson, "Historic Structure Report for the Evert Terwilliger House," 1.13).

35. The architectural historian for the Terwilliger House, Neil Larson, has argued that the purpose of this reconstruction was merely to provide private spaces for the newly married Jonathan and his wife, Mary, as his parents were still alive when the son married, rather than an attempt to follow contemporary Anglo-American domestic architectural practices (Crawford & Stearns and Neil Larson, "Historic Structure Report for the Evert Terwilliger House," 1.13). Private spaces, however, could have been provided without the labor-intensive reconstruction of the house. The two rooms of the house could have provided this, or the new (kitchen) addition could have served as a separate area for the newlyweds (and their forthcoming children), without having to reconfigure the original spaces. This is what occurred in the Daniel Hasbrouck House when the final room was constructed.

36. For a discussion of the Wynkoop House, see Roderic H. Blackburn, Geoffrey Gross, and Susan Piatt, *Dutch Colonial Homes in America* (New York: Rizzoli, 2002), 154–161, and Reynolds, *Dutch Houses*, 287.

37. "Newsletter," *Society for the Preservation of Hudson Valley Vernacular Architecture* 4, no. 2 (March 2002) and 4, no. 5 (June 2002). The precise date of the construction of the stone portions of Thornwood is not known, but the presence of rose-headed nails in the frame addition suggest it was built "in the late eighteenth century."

38. Larson, "National Register of Historic Places Registration Form: Abraham & Maria LeFevre House"; John R. Stevens, "Christian and Marytje [*sic*] Deyo house: 374 Springtown Road, New Paltz, Ulster Co., New York, *Society for the Preservation of Hudson Valley Vernacular Architecture* 14, no. 1–3 (January–March 2011), 3–4.

39. Neil Larson, "Town of New Paltz Landmark Nomination Form, Benjamin & Maria Hasbrouck House, 88 Manheim Blvd., New Paltz, NY." Once again, Larson argues this change in the form of the Dutch-American house in New Paltz suggests modernization rather than creolization of Dutch and English forms. In an attempt to avoid interpreting the evolution of domestic architecture in New Paltz as representing the adoption or adaptation of English culture, he even suggests a possible connection between the form of the Benjamin and Maria Hasbrouck house and Hudson Valley German-American architecture on the east side of the Hudson River, although he is careful not to argue for any causal connection. The Lucas Van Wagenen House stands on the west side of Huguenot Street between

the Maria DuBois House (DuBois Fort) and the Reformed Church.

40. Dell Upton explores how a modern center hall was incorporated into the two-room Anglo-Virginian house in a manner that paralleled the Dutch-American development (Dell Upton, "Vernacular Domestic Architecture in Eighteenth-Century Virginia," in *Readings in American Vernacular Architecture*, eds. Dell Upton and John Michael Vlach [Athens: University of Georgia, 1986], 315–336), but the two forms developed independently. Neil Larson estimates that the Hardenbergh House under discussion was built c. 1790 (Larson Fisher Associates and Crawford & Stearns, "Historic Structure Report for the Ezekiel Elting House," 1.16). It certainly was in existence by the 1798 direct tax. LeFevre claims that the house was built by Abraham Hardenbergh (*History of New Paltz*, 457–459), who would have been only thirteen in 1790 and twenty-one in 1798. Given his age in the 1790s, the house was likely not built by Abraham but by his father, John A. Hardenbergh (Stevens, *Dutch Vernacular Architecture*, 56–57).

41. The Ezekiel Eltinge House (sometimes known as the "LeFevre House") is owned by HHS. Its gambrel roof was destroyed in a storm in the late nineteenth century and was replaced with a pitched roof. The manuscript schedules for the 1798 Federal Direct Tax for New Paltz indicate that the typical one-story profile remained dominant through the eighteenth century, even among the elite. Of the houses of 380 separate homeowners or tenants, only eight houses were listed as consisting of two floors, while three additional houses were one-and-one-half stories in height, together representing just 3 percent of the houses in the village. This is clearly much less than that found in nearby New England in 1798, such as in Worcester County, where about one-third of the houses were two stories in height (Jack Larkin, *The Reshaping of Everyday Life, 1790–1840* [New York: Harper & Row, 1988], 112). As such, there is no evidence that any New Paltz house would have been perceived as essentially English Georgian as of 1798, in either its elite or vernacular variations, as would have been seen across wide stretches of New England.

42. Both Henry Glassie and Dell Upton explore a similar process of how modern design principles can be incorporated into a vernacular architectural paradigm, resulting in idiosyncratic combinations of tradition and modernity: Henry Glassie, "Eighteenth-Century Cultural Process in Delaware Valley Folk Building," in *Readings in American Vernacular Architecture*, ed. Dell Upton and John Michael Vlach (Athens: University of Georgia, 1986), 394–425 and Dell Upton, "Vernacular Domestic Architecture in Eighteenth-Century Virginia," in *Readings in American Vernacular Architecture*, eds. Dell Upton and John Michael Vlach (Athens: University of Georgia, 1986), 315–336.

43. Roelof J. and Ezekiel Elting Family Papers, HHS; Larson Fisher Associates and Crawford & Stearns, "Historic Structure Report for the Ezekiel Elting House," 1.38–1.39.

44. Locust Lawn is part of the Collection of Locust Lawn, Gift of Annette Innis Young, owned by Locust Grove, Poughkeepsie, New York. John A.

Bonfide, "National Register of Historic Places Registration Form: The Locusts," prepared June 1996.

45. Robert M. Toole, Neil Larson, and Arthur Jay Hibbs, "Historic Landscape Report and Landscape Master Planning for Locust Lawn (unpublished report for the HHS, 2002), 8.
46. Fitchen, *The New World Dutch Barn*, ed. Gregory D. Huber (Syracuse, NY: Syracuse University Press, 2001), 159, 180; Cohen, *The Dutch-American Farm*, 28, 32, 90; Stevens, *Dutch Vernacular Architecture*, 117; Theodore H. J. Prudon, "The Dutch Barn in America: Survival of a Medieval Structural Frame," in *Readings in American Vernacular Architecture*, eds. Dell Upton and John Michael Vlach (Athens: University of Georgia, 1986), 204–218.
47. Neil Larson references one surviving Dutch barn in New Paltz that might have been included in the 1798 tax list. Neil Larson, "An Inventory of Dutch Barns in the Town of New Paltz in 1798," *Newsletter of the Dutch Barn Preservation Society* 10, no. 1 (Spring 1997): 1; "1798 Federal Direct Tax, New Paltz schedules," HHS.
48. A few non-Dutch *barns* were owned by men with Dutch and non-English names who did not have long-term connections with New Paltz, including Vanwagenen, Vanvliet, Dumont, Leroy, Polmitier, and Weismeller.
49. A very small number of *Dutch barns*, seven to be precise, had a side-to-side ratio that exceeded the average of the *barns* (four 40x30 at 1:1.33, one 48x36 at 1:1.33, one 48x35 at 1:1.37, and one 36x26 at 1:1.38).
50. In "true hybrid Dutch-Anglo" barns, the bents were oriented parallel to the side, rather than parallel to the gable as in the "classic" Dutch barn. Larson, "An Inventory of Dutch Barns in the Town of New Paltz in 1798"; Fitchen, *The New World Dutch Barn*, ed. Gregory D. Huber, xxvi.
51. Fitchen, *The New World Dutch Barn*, ed. Gregory D. Huber, xxx.
52. Many essays in Dell Upton and John Michael Vlach, eds., *Readings in American Vernacular Architecture*, (Athens: University of Georgia, 1986) attest to the theory that vernacular architecture changes slowly because stylistic changes must be accompanied by changes in the function and social geography of domestic spaces.

Chapter 4

1. "The Diary of Abraham Hasbrouck," in *The Earliest Records of the Hasbrouck Family*, ed. Kenneth Hasbrouck (New Paltz, NY: privately printed, 1992).
2. Ralph LeFevre, *History of New Paltz*, 59.
3. A translation of the "Indian Deed" appears in LeFevre, *History of New Paltz*, 12–13. The original manuscript is in the New Paltz Town Records (1677–1932), HHS.
4. "Contract, 1707," Jean Cottin Papers, HHS; "Kripplebush Fence Agreement (1708)," New Paltz Town Records (1677–1932); "Town Meeting Minutes (1712)," New Paltz Town Records (1677–1932);

"Road Construction Agreement (1739)," New Paltz Town Records (1677–1932); "Land Division agreement (ca. 1720–1730)," New Paltz Town Records *(1677–1932)*; "Contract for Button and Ladle Molds (ca. 1720–1730)," New Paltz Reformed Church Records (1683–1892).

5. The only Dutch will composed after 1743 dates from 1768.
6. While the 1751 letter does not stipulate when the church was led by lay readers who delivered printed sermons in French, one purpose of the letter was to explain to Classis how the church was organized before the arrival of Rev. Johannes van Driessen in 1731. Thus the period referenced is the early decades of the eighteenth century. Hugh Hastings, Edward Corwin, and James Holden, *ERNY*, 5:3209. Versteeg, *Records of the Reformed Dutch Church of New Paltz*, 2. The title of the Jean Hasbrouck's book of Psalms is *Les Pseumes de David Mis en Rime Françoise* (Paris: Antoine Cellier, 1667) in Bible and Religious Book Collection, HHS. Jean Hasbrouck's New Testament was noted in a "Catalogue of Loan Exhibition Under Auspices of Wiltwick Chapter D. A. R., Given in Honor of the Annual Meeting of the New York State Historical Association, September 12, 13, and 14, 1911, Kingston, N.Y.," *Proceedings of the New York State Historical Association*, v. 11 (n.p.: New York State Historical Association, 1911), 274. Although Elizabeth Hasbrouck Bevier (the subsequent owner of her father's book of sermons) and her husband, Louis Bevier, moved to nearby Marbletown in 1715, the family kept close connections with New Paltz as late as 1720, if not later. Katherine Bevier, *The Bevier Family, A History of the Descendants of Louis Bevier Who came from France to America in 1675 after a sojourn of ten years in the Palatinate and settled in New Paltz, New York* (New York: Tobias A. Wright, 1916), 64–68. In the original French, Abraham Deyo noted that his testament was in French, but did not stipulate the language of the other two books ("un testament fancoij et on livre de sermon en un Livr a Saume"). Abraham Deyo, "Will, September 20, 1724," Ulster County Land Records, Deed Book CC, 293–294. Andries LeFevre, "Will, April 19, 1738," Anjou, 1:153–154.
7. *ERNY*, 5:3209. Jean Tebenin, "Will," 1719, and Tebenin, "Will," 1730, Jean Tebanin Papers (1700–1730), HHS.
8. Versteeg, *Records of the Reformed Dutch Church of New Paltz*, 3. Both LeFevre (*History of New Paltz*, 141–142) and Carlo (*Huguenot Refugees*, 50) claim that van Driessen was Belgian. The belief that he was Belgian seems to have been created by a New Paltz minister, who in 1860, misinterpreted van Driessen's 1727 ordination certificate (Charles H. Stitt, "History of the Huguenot Church and Settlement at New Paltz," in *Collections of The Ulster County Historical Society* 1, no. 3 ([Kingston, NY: Hommel & Lounsbery, 1862], 196). Gabriel P. Disosway, writing for the American Dutch Reformed Church (in *The Earliest Churches of New York and its Vicinity* [New York: James G. Gregory, 1865], 401), also indicates that van Driessen was from Belgium, but he notes that he based this on the statement made by Charles Stitt. Edward Tanjore Corwin (*A Manual of the Reformed Church in America, [formerly Ref.*

Prot. Dutch Church] 1628–1902 [New York: Board of Publication of the Reformed Church in America, 1902], 819–820) also indicated that van Driessen was educated in Belgium but does not provide the source of this information. The ordination certificate provided by the Congregational ministers meeting at Yale refers to "Johannem Van Driessen Belgicum Lug. Batavorum educatum." The term "Belgicum" refers to his ethnicity/place of origin. The term is a form of the place name "Belgica," a general Latin term for the Netherlands, both northern and southern; thus, the certificate does not suggest that van Driessen was from what became the country of Belgium any more than it refers to another place in the United Provinces. "Lug. Batavorum educatum" refers to his place of education: the full place name, Lugdunum Batavorum, references Leyden. Another American church history reports that van Driessen was "born in Holland in 1697" (*A History of the Classis of Paramus of the Reformed Church in America* [New York: Board of Publication of the Reformed Church in America, 1902], 174), but that is the only publication so far uncovered that indicates his place of birth, and as such, cannot be corroborated. Van Driessen had sought ordination from the Classis of Amsterdam in 1719 with forged certificates from his professors at Groningen. "Johannes van Driessen to Jacob Hasbrouck, April 9 1748," Levi Hasbrouck Family Papers: The Locust Lawn Collection, HHS; Versteeg, *Records of the Reformed Dutch Church of New Paltz*, 80.

9. The "Guimar Family Bible" ("Bible 169," Bible Collection, HHS), printed in Utrecht in 1712, includes genealogical records of Esther Guimar, wife of Philip DuBois (b. 1689), who was the son of Isaac DuBois and Maria Hasbrouck. Philip DuBois and Esther Guimar lived most of their married life in Rochester, but Philip's brother Daniel (b. 1684), a life-long New Paltz resident, also recorded his marriage in the "Guimar Family Bible." The births of Philip, Daniel, and their brother Benjamin (b. 1687) are also recorded in the Bible, obviously after the fact, but such records suggest the possibility that the Bible was originally owned by their mother, Maria Hasbrouck DuBois. The current location of the Petrus LeFevre Bible is unknown. Abraham Deyo, "Will, September 20, 1724." In his Bible ("Bible 184," HHS), Jan Ean wrote, "1730 meij de 9 heb yk det boockge kregen," or "1730 may the 9th I received the book." The Caty Van Wagenen religious book is known as the "Elias Ean Prayer Book" ("BIB 108," HHS). The Terwillger/Freer Bible is known as the "Hugo Freer Bible" ("BIB 008," HHS). "Hendricus DuBois Bible" ("BIB 301," HHS). The Eltinge book includes the following entry: "Josia Eltinge Syn Boeck Magdalena Eltinge haer Boeck 1734" ("Bible 017," HHS). Andries LeFevre, "Will, April 19, 1738," in Anjou, 1:153–154. The sale of Tebenin's effects occurred in November 1733; the vendue list appears in Abraham Hasbrouck, "Ciphering Book," stored in the Ciphering Book Collection, HHS.

10. The last consistory installed during van Dreissen's pastorate was that of May 1736 (Versteeg, *Records of the Reformed Dutch Church of New Paltz*, 65). Stitt, "History," 197. For sources related to the Goetschius

family, see chapter 5 below. LeFevre, *History of New Paltz*, 144–145; Corwin, *Manual*, 887.

11. LeFevre, *History of New Paltz*, 147–148, 156–158; Stitt, "History," 205–206. Although Stitt may not always be trusted, as it was he who first recorded that van Driessen was "Belgian," his statement that Stephen Goetschius alternated between Dutch and English seems credible, as it is likely that Stitt had been able to speak with some individuals who had firsthand knowledge of Stephen Goetschius's service in New Paltz.
12. It has traditionally been said that the schoolmasters were hired by the New Paltz congregation and that the church building also served as the schoolhouse (LeFevre, *History of New Paltz*, 22–26; Carlo, *Huguenot Refugees*, 103). Charles W. Baird, *History of The Huguenot Emigration to America* (New York: Dodd, Mead & Co., 1885), 2:92–93. In 1689, the proprietors of the patent gifted Cottin a small "shack" and the right to harvest wood, as well as rights of pasturage (Original deed, in French, in Hugo Freer Family Papers, 1677–1721, HHS). Cottin lived in New Paltz for several more years after he ceased serving as a teacher, selling his land in New Paltz in 1701, around the time he relocated to Kingston, where he became a merchant. The Cottin account books are in the archives of the First Reformed Church of Kingston, New York. Tebenin's 1719 and 1730 wills are in Jean Tebanin Papers (1700–1730), HHS.
13. A reference to Pierre Simon appears in the New Paltz Church Records ("Promissory Note," April 19, 1736, New Paltz Reformed Church Records [1683–1892], HHS). Jean Meschines is mentioned in 1739 in the ciphering book kept first by Abraham Hasbrouck. When the book was subsequently used by Jacob Hasbrouck for recording deacons' accounts, he noted that he paid tuition to Jean Meschines's school for his son Isaac. The Abraham Hasbrouck ciphering book has been erroneously attributed to an Abraham who was a descendant of Jean Hasbrouck and who also had a son named Isaac. The ciphering book actually appears to be that of Abraham Hasbrouck, son of Solomon Hasbrouck and grandson of patentee Abraham Hasbrouck, as the book was also used by Solomon Hasbrouck in his capacity as deacon (Versteeg, *Records of the Reformed Dutch Church of New Paltz*, 65). It is not clear whether Abraham and his father, Solomon, used the book simultaneously or consecutively.
14. An additional ciphering book, kept by Peter LeFevre Jr. from 1779 to 1781, survives. All ciphering books referenced are included in a synthetic Ciphering Book Collection in the archives of HHS.
15. Joseph Coddington, a descendant of Puritan founders of Massachusetts Bay, was born in 1730 in Woodbridge, Middlesex County, New Jersey. John Coddington, his great-grandfather, had settled in Woodbridge, an Anglo community not far from Staten Island, soon after King Philip's War (in which he took part). An August Vandemark was taxed in New Paltz in 1728 (LeFevre, *History of New Paltz*, 92). The earliest reference to Coddington that clearly indicates he was the schoolmaster is the will of Rev. Johannes Mauritius Goetschius, written July 4, 1770, for which Coddington signed as a witness (Johannes Mauritius Goetschius, "Will,"

July 4, 1770, *Collections of the New-York Historical Society for the Year 1898* [(New York: New-York Historical Society, 1899], 405). LeFevre, *History of New Paltz*, 96, 102, 217; Versteeg, *Records of the Reformed Dutch Church of New Paltz*, 104.

16. For a discussion of the Coetus-Conferentie dispute, see chapter 5.
17. "Louis Bevier Bible," ("BIB 352," HHS); "Jean Hasbrouck Bible" ("BIB 349," HHS); Jacob Hasbrouck's *Histoire des Martrys* ("BIB 059," HHS); "Guimar Family Bible," ("BIB 169," HHS).
18. "Jan Ean Bible," ("BIB 184," HHS); "Hendricus DuBois Bible" ("BIB 301," HHS); Eltinge "Prayer Book" ("BIB 017," HHS).
19. "Elias Ean Prayer Book," "BIB 108," HHS. It is unclear whether Evert Terwilliger or his wife, Sara Freer, inscribed the family records in their Bible ("Hugo Freer Bible," "BIB 008," HHS). The birth dates of the group that used Dutch extended for over a century, between 1686 through 1791. The bulk (nineteen) of those had birth dates relatively evenly distributed between 1710 and 1755, with three each before and after that period. For those that used English, their birth dates stretched between 1720 and 1782. Seven of the eighteen were born between 1720 and 1755, eight in the 1760s, two in the 1770s, and one in 1782. "Jacob Hasbrouck Bible," ("BIB 006," HHS).
20. "Cornelius Decker Bible" ("BIB 359," HHS); Petrus LeFevre Bible (current location unknown). The only Bible in the collection of HHS that was in use in the second half of the eighteenth century in which the text and the family records were both in English is the 1784 Bible of Jacob J. Hasbrouck, great-grandson of patentee Jean Hasbrouck ("BIB 012," HHS).
21. "Elias Ean Prayer Book," ("BIB 108," HHS); "Cornelius Decker Bible" ("BIB 359," HHS); Petrus LeFevre Bible (current location unknown).
22. More precisely, the Pierre Deyo documents are composed of twelve receipts, three short statements of obligations, and one short request for payment. Seven documents are in French, and six in English. The Pierre Deyo receipts in French include records of transactions with Abraham DuBois, August Jay, James Barré, Pierre Vanbomollo, Rulland, Gacherie (no first names indicated for the last two). The merchants involved with the transactions recorded in English were Thomas Delanall, John Delanall, and John White, and their agent William Haines. The transactions in Dutch were with Jacob Decker and one with Robert Story, a "koopman" in New York City. Deyo Family Papers (1675–1870), HHS. Three additional receipts in French are included in the Louis Bevier receipts, but as they are for official payments of taxes, they have not been included in the count. Louis Bevier Papers (1675–1719), HHS.
23. The sixteen receipts in French (dating 1691–1721) in the Hugo Freer collection recorded business with ten individuals, the New Paltz congregation, and two unidentified persons. The Dutch documents in the Hugo Freer receipts number twenty-two, noting business transactions with twenty-one individuals. They date from 1696 to 1732. Two receipts in English in the Hugo Freer papers record transactions with Jean Cottin (1707) and Stephen DeLancey (1717). Hugo Freer Family Papers

(1677–1721); Freer Family Papers, Haviland-Heidgerd Historical Collection, Elting Memorial Library, New Paltz, NY.

24. Two of the French receipts in the DuBois papers refer to transactions with Jacob Hasbrouck and Juryan Tappan; the third receipt is not signed. The six Dutch receipts in the DuBois papers involve business affairs with three men with Dutch surnames. Daniel and Simon DuBois Family Papers (1695–1864), HHS.
25. The four Dutch receipts of Simon DuBois include three Dutch surnames (Petrus Low, Cornelius Elmendorph, and Johannes Mauritius Goetschius [the Batavianized minister in New Paltz from 1760–1771]). The English receipts involved twenty-seven to twenty-nine individuals (one receipt is anonymous and one is illegible). Daniel and Simon DuBois Family Papers (1695–1864), HHS. The Dutch receipts in the Abraham Deyo papers date from 1752, 1760, and 1762. In the Abraham Deyo receipts, the surnames of those with names from English-speaking ethnicities are McClaghry and Carman. Deyo Family Papers (1675–1870). The English receipts of Johannes Freer from 1750–1775 number six (with three individuals), while seven were in Dutch (with five persons). The English receipts of Jonas Freer from 1783–1790 records transactions with sixteen people. Wilhelmus and Moses Hasbrouck Family Papers (1753–1897), HHS.
26. Deyo Family Papers (1675–1870). The thirty-three English receipts record contained in the construction records for the church involve transactions with twenty-seven individuals.
27. Louis Bevier Family Papers: The Elizabeth Wright Collection (1721–1929), HHS. The book of accounts concerning Andries Bevier and two letters to Philip DuBois are contained in the Louis Bevier Family Papers: The Rutgers Collection (1687–1921), a photocopied collection, HHS. "Louis Bevier to Abraham Hasbrouck, July 31, 1744," in Louis Bevier Family Papers: The Rutgers Collection (1687–1921), HHS; "Louis Bevier to Moses Depue, November 16, 1761," in Louis Bevier Family Papers: The Rutgers Collection (1687–1921), HHS.
28. "Tryntje Bevier to Cornelius DuBois, January 31, 1760," Josiah DuBois Family Papers, HHS; Hendricus DuBois Jr., "Account Book," Hendricus DuBois Family Papers, HHS; Jannetje DuBois, "Account Book," Hendricus DuBois Family Papers, HHS; William E. Du Bois, "Bringing the Tribe Together," in *Bi-Centenary Reunion of the Descendants of Louis and Jacques Dubois (Emigrants to America, 1660 and 1675) at New Paltz, New York, 1875* (Philadelphia, PA: Rue & Jones, 1876), 82.
29. The Solomon Eltinge letters (dated December 24, 1776, February 22, 1777, August 29, 1778, December 8, 1778, January 25, 1779, and June 22, 1783) are in the Cornelius Eltinge Family Papers, 1727–1820, in the Haviland-Heidgard Historical Collection, New Paltz Public Library, New Paltz, NY (Collection: 13.ELT.2). The R. J. Eltinge letters are in the Roelof J. and Ezekiel Elting Family Papers, HHS. The letter from R. J. Eltinge to his son was dated September 29, 1783, and to his wife, January 11, 1784. The merchant account records and diary are also in

the Roelof J. and Ezekiel Elting Family Papers. HHS.

30. Abraham Hasbrouck offers an interesting comment on the knowledge of French in the later eighteenth century, noting that his niece Catharine Bruyn (1759–1776) "spoke Dutch, English and French tolerably well." It is very unlikely that this suggests the survival of French in the region, as Catherine was not from New Paltz; and even if she were, she was born long after French had ceased to be a language of communication or worship. As an elite young woman, perhaps she received some training in French. "The Diary of Abraham Hasbrouck," in *The Earliest Records of the Hasbrouck Family*, ed. Kenneth Hasbrouk (New Paltz, NY: privately printed, 1992); "Abraham Hasbrouck to Brother Bruyn, March 11, 1748," Joseph and Jacob J. Hasbrouck Family Papers, HHS; "Noah Eltinge to Abraham Hasbrouck, Lewis Bevier Junior and Jacob Hasbrouck Junior, February 13, 1753 (or possibly 1763)." Levi Hasbrouck Family Papers: The Locust Lawn Collection (1672–1968), HHS.
31. The date of the sale and Isabella's age are both approximate, based on her own recollections. Olive Gilbert, *Narrative of Sojourner Truth*, ed. Margaret Washington (New York: Vintage, 1993), 3, 6–7; Carleton Mabee with Susan Mabee Newhouse, *Sojourner Truth: Slave, Prophet, Legend* (New York: New York University Press, 1993), 5.
32. William Strickland, *Journal of a Tour in the United States of America, 1794–1795*, ed. J. E. Strickland (New York: The New-York Historical Society, 1971), 102.

Chapter 5

1. The folktale of Hendricus DuBois is recorded in Benjamin Myer Brink's, "The Coetus and Conferentie Controversy," *Olde Ulster: An Historical & Genealogical Magazine* (February 1905): 38. "IDHOS," or "In Den Heeren Ontslapen," appears on two graves in the old New Paltz Cemetery on Huguenot Street.
2. Randall Balmer, *A Perfect Babel of Confusion: Dutch Religion and English Culture in the Middle Colonies* (New York: Oxford University Press, 1989).
3. Dirk Mouw, "Moederkerk and Vaderland: Religion and Ethnic Identity in the Middle Colonies, 1690–1772" (PhD diss., University of Iowa, 2009).
4. Joyce D. Goodfriend, *Before the Melting Pot: Society and Culture in Colonial New York City, 1664–1730* (Princeton, NJ: Princeton University Press, 1992); Firth Haring Fabend, "The Reformed Dutch Church and the Persistence of Dutchness in New York and New Jersey," in *Dutch New York: The Roots of Hudson Valley Culture*, ed. Roger Panetta (New York: Hudson River Museum, Fordham University Press, 2009), 137–158.
5. Carlo, *Huguenot Refugees*, 50–51, 174–176. Carlo notes that the congregation "exhibited a remarkable degree of independence since the ministers they selected were from the more controversial quarters of the Dutch Reformed Church" (174).
6. For a published translation of the records relating to the construction, see Versteeg, *Records of the Reformed Dutch Church of New Paltz*, 2–3.

The reading of printed sermons is referenced in a 1751 letter from New Paltz to the Classis of Amsterdam (*ERNY*, 5:3209).

7. Versteeg, *Records of the Reformed Dutch Church of New Paltz*, 3, 80; *ERNY*, 4:2572, 5:3208–3211.
8. *ERNY*, 4:2564, 2572–2573, 2580–2581, 2606–2608, 2610–2612.
9. Edward Tanjore Corwin, *A Manual of the Reformed Church in America, (formerly Ref. Prot. Dutch Church) 1628–1902* (New York: Board of Publication of the Reformed Church in America, 1902), 20–21; Gerald F. De Jong, *The Dutch Reformed Church in the American Colonies* (Grand Rapids, MI: Wm. B. Eerdmans, 1978), 180–181. For further insight into the limits of the Classis of Amsterdam's authority over American congregations, see, for example, the documents relative to the early ministry of Rev. Bernardus Freerman (*ERNY*, 2:1348–1349, 1384–1385, 3:1469–1471, 1532–1539, 1647). For a further analysis of conflict between American congregations and ministers and the Classis of Amsterdam, see the discussion below of the ministry of Rev. Johannes Henricus Goetschius on Long Island.
10. *ERNY*, 4:2571–2573, 2580–2581.
11. Ibid., 4:2572; 5:3208–3211.
12. Ibid., 5:3208–3211.
13. Ibid., 4:3116–3118.
14. James I. Good, *History of the Reformed Church in the United States, 1725–1792* (Reading, PA: Daniel Miller, 1899), 171–182, 279–287; Joseph Henry Dubbs, *The Reformed Church in Pennsylvania*, part 9 (Lancaster: Pennsylvania-German Society, 1902), 105–108; Ruth and William Heidgerd, "The Goetshy Family: European Notes, By Ruth & William Heidgerd on their trip to Salez Switzerland, 1968," accessed May 19, 2014, http://www.goetchius.com/ limpingmessenger.htm.
15. Good, *Reformed Church*, 182–184, 188; Charles R. Roberts and J. D. Schindel, *History of the Egypt Church* (Allentown, PA: Lehigh County Historical Society, 1908), 4–8; William J. Hinke, "A History of the Goshenhoppen Reformed Charge," part 29 of *Pennsylvania: The German Influence in its Settlement and Development* (Lancaster: Pennsylvania-German Society, 1920), 117–119; Joseph Henry Dubbs, *The Reformed Church in Pennsylvania*, 108–109; William J. Hinke, editor, *Life and Letters of the Rev. John Philip Boehm: Founder of the Reformed Church in Pennsylvania, 1683–1749* (Philadelphia, PA: Reformed Church in America, 1918), 53–54, 277–280, 284; Heidgerd, "Goetschy Family"; *ERNY*, 4:2684–2685, 2718.
16. Good, *Reformed Church*, 188–189; William J. Hinke, "Life and Works of the Rev. Peter Henry Dorsius," in a *Collection of Papers Read before the Bucks County Historical Society* 5 (1926): 44–53; Robert Arnoud Naborn, "Eilardus Westerlo (1738–1790): From Colonial *Dominee* to American *Pastor*" (Academisch Proefschrift, Vrije Universiteit, 2011); Hinke, *Boehm*, 53–54; *ERNY*, 4:2741, 2743–2745, 2798–2800.
17. When Goetschius was later asked why he believed that Dorsius had the right to ordain, Goetschius responded that "it seemed to him that he had,

because Do. Dorsius said that he corresponded with the Synod of South Holland. 2nd, That Do. Dorsius thought that he might make use of the position held by Voetius, namely, That in a country where there was no Synod or Classis, one minister might make another minister" (*ERNY*, 4:2782). In concluding that he could ordain ministers because there was no local classis, Dorsius seems to have been influenced by remarks made by Rev. Johannes Wilhelmius of Leiden to a theology student of Dorsius's acquaintance with whom he traveled to America in 1737. This student, Johannes Vermanus Van Basten, had chosen to seek opportunities for serving in the British colonies before having been ordained. Before he left Rotterdam for Pennsylvania, however, he queried Wilhelmius as to how he might be ordained in America. According to Good, Wilhelmius replied that "as a member of classis he could not license him, but he thought that Dorsius, together with one or two ministers in America, could do that, as there was as yet no classis there." It is very likely that Van Basten subsequently reported Wilhelmius's opinion to Dorsius, as Dorsius's comments to Goetschius reflect such a perspective; it is therefore possible that Dorsius took Wilhelmius's opinion as authorization (Good, *Reformed Church*, 192). Rev. Freerman believed Dorsius's claim that he had been authorized to ordain (*ERNY*, 4:2752–2753), while Rev. Gualtherus DuBois of New York City was more skeptical (*ERNY*, 4:2754–2757). *ERNY*, 4:2765–2767, 2776–2777.

18. It is not known precisely when Goetschius's congregations became aware of the opinion of Classis as to Dorsius's authority, which was contained in a September 9, 1741, letter to the congregation at Midwout (Flatbush), a copy of which was sent with Rev. Johannes Arondeus when he left Amsterdam for Long Island in May 1742. It probably began circulating in the colony in the fall of that year, as the congregations in Port Jervis, Minisink, and Walpack, in the lower Hudson Valley, noted in 1743 that they had become aware of the Classical letter at that time. It concerned them as well, because Dorsius had also ordained their minister, Johannes Fryenmoet, in 1741. Goetschius's congregations on Long Island likely would have had access to it even earlier than did those congregations in the Hudson Valley, as Arondeus served congregations very close to those of Goetschius (*ERNY*, 4:2801–2803). *ERNY*, 4:2781–2783.
19. Balmer, *A Perfect Babel*, 123–127; *ERNY*, 4:2782–2787.
20. *ERNY*, 4:2788–2793, 2827–2828, 2839–2844, 2857–2861, 2883–2899, 2939–2940, 2944–2949, 3033. For an outside assessment of the bitter factionalism, see the letter of Rev. Johannes Ritzema to the Classis of Amsterdam, of June 16, 1746, in which Ritzema extols the sincerity and commitment of Goetschius and encourages Classis not "to decide against this gentleman, who is, indeed, like a bird in a snare, attacked by many." Ritzema likewise confirms that Goetschius came to understand that he was misled by Dorsius, but also that Goetschius's pietism offended many, remarking that "he was one of the best of domines. But when he learned the sin of such easy going, when he chastised others for this, and in the fear of the Lord endeavored to convert them: then they came to

the kernel (of divine truth), and for this reason, chiefly, I am inclined to think, most of the agitations of his opponents, if not all, sprung up" (*ERNY*, 4:2913–2916). For a more extended treatment of the Goestchius affair, see Kenneth Shefsiek, "'Make an end of my misery': Rev. Johannes Henricus Goetschius and the negotiation of authority in Eighteenth-Century Dutch New York," *de Halve Maen* 88, no. 2 (Summer 2015): 27–34.

21. How Goetschius learned of New Paltz's need is not entirely clear, but it possible that he was encouraged to visit by Jonathan DuBois (the great-grandson of patentee Louis DuBois), who was born in Pittsgrove, New Jersey, in 1727 and raised in the Presbyterian Church. He may have been a student of Dorsius. (He was ordained and installed as Dorsius's successor at Neshaminy in 1752). At some time in the mid- to late-1740s, Jonathan DuBois traveled to New Paltz to seek financial support from his relatives in order to pursue his studies for the ministry. It was possibly during that trip that DuBois learned of the absence of ministerial leadership in New Paltz and later facilitated communication between that congregation and Goetschius (Howard G. Hageman, *Two Centuries Plus*, vol. 13 of *The Historical Series of the Reformed Church* [Grand Rapids, MI: Wm. B. Eerdmans, 1984], 6). Corwin, *Manual*, 319; Richard Wynkoop, *Wynkoop Genealogy in the United States of America* (New York: Knickerbocker Press, 1904), 60; Mouw, "Moederkerk," 629; *ERNY*, 5:3164–3165. *ERNY*, 4:3116–3118.
22. *ERNY*, 4:3135, 3141–3146.
23. Ibid., 5:3160–3161, 3184–3186, 3108–3212, 3251–3254, 3267–3274.
24. Ibid., 5:3208–3212, 3251–3254, 3263, 3267–3274. Versteeg, *Records of the Reformed Dutch Church of New Paltz*, 4; De Jong, *The Dutch Reformed Church*, 114–115.
25. Goetschius likely preached for the first time on June 4, 1749, the day he baptized Zacharias, the son of Daniel Hasbrouck and Wyntje Deyo. When precisely he began to offer the Lord's Supper is unknown, but Mancius reported in April 1750 that Goetschius had begun to officiate at the sacrament at some point since the two first met for discussion in 1749. Goetschius's 1751 visit lasted at least from April 12 through April 21, as he performed marriages on April 12, 14, 16, and 21, and accepted new members on April 19. While J. H. Goetschuis was not the only minister who served from time to time in New Paltz in the early 1750s, it is quite likely that he was the minister who accepted all of those who joined during the period when he periodically served. (Theodorus Frelinghuysen Jr. visited in January 1751 and February 1753; Benjamin Meinema, pastor in Poughkeepsie, served in New Paltz in September 1752 and May 1753; and Johannes Fryenmoet visited in October 1750, January 1752, and November 1753.) Goetschius even returned to assist New Paltz sometime after Vrooman left in 1754 to serve the Schenectady congregation (Charlotte Taylor Luekhurst, transcriber, "Marriage Records of the Reformed Protestant Dutch Church of Schenectady, N.Y.," [unpublished, 1917]). Goetschius was in New Paltz on August 22, 1756,"

when the consistory met and discussed the time for the election of a new consistory; he was presumably there six days later, when Jacob Rutsen Hardenbergh was once again accepted into the congregation, along with his wife Dina (the widow of Rev. Johannes Frelinghuysen, Hardenbergh's teacher). Both became members of the congregation upon presentation of certificates. Versteeg, *Records of the Reformed Dutch Church of New Paltz*, 66, 74, 96; *ERNY*, 4:3116–3118, 5:3211.

26. Mouw, "Moederkerk," 153–242; De Jong, *The Dutch Reformed Church*, 185–187.
27. Mouw, 253–254; De Jong, 188.
28. Mouw, 255–260; De Jong, 190–191.
29. Mouw, 255–263; De Jong, 189–191.
30. Mouw, 254–273.
31. Mouw, 275–303; De Jong, 191–198.
32. Mouw, 304–315; De Jong, 198–202.
33. Mouw, 315–327; De Jong, 202–204.
34. Corwin mentions that J. M. Goetschius began practicing as a doctor as soon as he arrived in the New World, but this is impossible, given that he was still a child when he immigrated (*Manual*, 492).
35. *ERNY*, 5:3534, 3550, 3553, 3659, 3687–3689, 3708–3710; LeFevre, *History of New Paltz*, 147; Versteeg, *Records of the Reformed Dutch Church of New Paltz*, 10–12.
36. Mouw, "Moederkerk," 328–426. In reference to the Hardenbergh Commission, see in particular *ERNY*, 6:3883–3886.
37. Versteeg, *Records of the Reformed Dutch Church of New Paltz*, 5; *ERNY*, 6:3925–3930.
38. "New Paltz Consistory to Hendricus DuBois, July 25, 1765, August 3, 1765, and August 19, 1765," Hendricus DuBois Family Papers, HHS; "Membership of the New Paltz Church to Hendricus DuBois, August 31, 1765," *Records of Reformed Church of New Paltz*, trans. Berthold Fernow, New York Historical and Genealogical Society, New York; Versteeg, *Records of the Reformed Dutch Church of New Paltz*, 2.
39. Versteeg, *Records of the Reformed Dutch Church of New Paltz*, 7, 20–22; Mouw, "Moederkerk," 430.
40. Versteeg, 6–9, 23–34; Mouw, 454.
41. The core membership of the Conferentie church centered upon closely related branches of the DuBois, Eltinge, and Low families (table 5.1). The leading members of the church were Hendricus DuBois and his wife, Jannetje Houghtaling; Hendricus's sister Magadalena and her husband, Josiah Eltinge (grandson of Abraham DuBois); and Josiah's brother Noah and Noah's wife, Jacomyntje Eltinge. Hendricus's former brother-in-law Petrus Low (whose first wife was Hendricus's deceased sister, Catherine) and his wife, Deborah Van Vliet, also joined. As for the younger generation, five of Hendricus and Jannetje DuBois's eight children became members (and an additional son Mathuselem attended but did not join), and five of Magdalena and Josiah Eltinge's six surviving children joined (with the sixth probably having been too young to do

so). Noah and Jacomyntje Eltinge's only child, Sara, joined, as did her husband, Dirk Wynkoop. The Low family was not so thoroughly represented in the younger generation. Clearly, family was a defining factor in the Second Church, and since the adult children were possibly following the lead of their parents, it is the elder generation's motivations that possibly reveal most about the meaning behind the ecclesiastical dispute. Versteeg, *Records of the Reformed Dutch Church of New Paltz*, 13–15, 76; Mouw, "Moederkerk," 448–462.

42. Hendricus DuBois, "Will, June 21, 1774," transcribed in Anjou, *Probate*, 1:158–159; "Indenture, March 9, 1781," Hendricus DuBois Family Papers, HHS.
43. Noah Eltinge, "Will, August 16, 1782," New York County Probate Records, Liber 37, 362–368.
44. Josiah Eltinge, "Will, April 4, 1767," (1784 fair copy), Roelof J. and Ezekiel Elting Family Papers, HHS.
45. Josiah Eltinge, "Will, April 4, 1767," (1784 fair copy), Roelof J. and Ezekiel Elting Family Papers, HHS.
46. Hendricus DuBois Jr., "Account Book," Hendricus DuBois Family Papers, HHS; Jannetje DuBois, "Account Book," Hendricus DuBois Family Papers, HHS; Cornelius Eltinge Family Papers, Haviland-Heidgard Historical Collection, New Paltz Public Library, New Paltz, NY.
47. See chapter 3 for further information concerning the Abraham DuBois/ Josiah Eltinge and 1775 Hendricus DuBois Houses, both no longer extant. The Noah Eltinge House was on the property upon which Peter Eltinge's house (later named "The Locusts") was built. John A. Bonfide, "National Register of Historic Places Registration Form: The Locusts," prepared June 1996.
48. New Paltz Town Records (1677–1932), HHS; Versteeg, *Records of the Reformed Dutch Church of New Paltz*, 40–42.
49. The justices of the peace had been given the legal right to demand that those whose allegiance they deemed questionable take such an oath, although the oath as prescribed had primarily been aimed at Catholics. It is possible that Meyer was influenced by his wife's family to take a position against the Conferentie, as he was married to Rachel Hardenbergh, sister of Rev. Jacob Rutsen Hardenbergh of the Coetus. Meyer had traveled to New York together on the same ship as Rev. Hardenbergh when the latter returned from his ill-fated meeting with religious authorities in the Netherlands. Pawling and Bevier were trustees of the nearby town of Marbletown, as was Jacob Hasbrouck, Jr. (Colonel Abraham Hasbrouck's second cousin). Marius Schoonmaker, *The History of Kingston New York. From its Early Settlement to the Year 1820*, (New York: Burr Printing House, 1888), 216–217; Mouw, "Moederkerk," 436–438. For an account of the dispute, see in particular "The So-Called Trial of Rev. Hermanus Meyer, Oct. 9, 10, 1764," in *ERNY*, 6:3955–3959.
50. The Diary of Abraham Hasbrouck," in *The Earliest Records of the Hasbrouck Family*, ed. Kenneth Hasbrouk (New Paltz, NY: privately printed, 1992).

51. "The Diary of Abraham Hasbrouck," 18–19; Abraham Hasbrouck, "Will, September 5, 1785," in Kenneth Hasbrouk, *The Earliest Records of the Hasbrouck Family*, 47–52.
52. Jacob Hasbrouck Jr., "Will, August 3, 1776," Levi Hasbrouck Family Papers, The Locust Lawn Collection, HHS. See chapter 3 for further discussion of the Jacob (Jean) Hasbrouck Sr. and Jacob Hasbrouck Jr. Houses.
53. Abraham Hasbrouck, "Will, September 5, 1785," in Kenneth Hasbrouk, *The Earliest Records of the Hasbrouck Family*, 53–58; Jacob Hasbrouck Jr., "Will, August 3, 1776," Levi Hasbrouck Family Papers, The Locust Lawn Collection, HHS.
54. The wealth of the leaders of the Conferentie faction placed them at the top of local society, with Josiah Eltinge ranked second, Hendricus DuBois sixth, and Noah Eltinge ninth out of a total of 108 taxables, according to a 1765 tax list. Major Jacob Hasbrouck Jr. and Colonel Abraham Hasbrouck were ranked fifth and first respectively in 1765. Abraham Hasbrouck's assessment was based only on his farm, which represented only a fraction of his total wealth. LeFevre, *History of New Paltz*, 94–96.
55. LeFevre, *History of New Paltz*, 94–96; New Paltz Town Records (1677–1932), HHS. It is worth noting that motivations behind party affiliation were likely not monolithic and thus to generalize about the motivating factors across class and gender lines, for example, might be inappropriate. Furthermore, the archival record is, as is not unusual, weighted towards the wealthiest members of the community, so an analysis is possible only for those of the highest status in New Paltz. Nevertheless, such a comparison is particularly important because it reveals that the schism was a conflict that pitted elites against each other, rather than a struggle between those of different social ranks.
56. "Account Book," Hendricus DuBois Jr., Hendricus DuBois Family Papers, HHS.
57. Josiah Eltinge's son Roelof Josiah became a merchant, and in a fragment of an account book for 1768–1769, Josiah Eltinge had a credit for three firkins of butter valued at 7.0.3 ½, which partially offset purchases amounting to 15.13.11 (Roelof J. and Ezekiel Family Papers, HHS), suggesting that Josiah's trade was primarily local. Tradition holds that Josiah Eltinge was a merchant as well, but in a 1772 bond between Josiah and Roelof Josiah, the father is referred to as "yeoman" and the son "merchant" (Roelof J. and Ezekiel Family Papers, HHS).
58. Thomas S. Wermuth, *Rip Van Winkle's Neighbors: The Transformation of Rural Society in the Hudson River Valley, 1720–1850* (Albany, NY: SUNY Press, 2001); Thomas S. Wermuth, "Rural Elites in the Commercial Development of New York: 1780–1840," *Business and Economic History* 23, no. 1 (Fall 1994): 71–80.
59. For a more extensive exploration of English anti-Dutch bias, see chapter 6 of Kenneth Shefsiek, "Stone House Days: Constructing Cultural Hybridity in the Hudson Valley" (PhD diss., University of Georgia, 2010), 211–230.

60. Schoonmaker, *History of Kingston*, 175; *New York in the Revolution as Colony and State* (Albany, NY: J. B. Lyon, 1904), 1:199; Berthold Fernow, *New York in the Revolution* (Albany, NY: Weed, Parsons, 1887), 1:287–288.

Chapter 6

1. Edmund Eltinge, "An Account of the Settlement of New Paltz by the Huguenots," *Collections of the Ulster Historical Society* 1, part 1 (1860), 40.
2. As this ultimate assimilation of the patentee community into an Anglo-American culture occurred after the American Revolution, it is possible that the war influenced ethnocultural change in New Paltz, at least to some extent. The patentee community did predominately support the war, and their commitment to an independent Anglo-American nation might have motivated them to absorb its broader culture. However, since descendants were increasingly making use of Anglo-American culture long before the Revolutionary War, at most it might have increased only the speed of its acceptance. As for changes in language use, LeFevre remarked, "During this time the French language was giving way and the Dutch taking its place"; descendant Cornelia Dubois used identical language to explain this transition (Ralph Lefevre, *History of New Paltz*, 59; Cornelia DuBois, *The story of the Paltz*, 21). Abraham Bruyn Hasbrouck noted simply in 1860 that the patentee families "worship[ped] in the French language for about one-half a century—and then the French language, being much lost, the descendents of the Walloons had divine service in the Dutch language" (Abraham Bruyn Hasbrouck, "Address," *Collections of the Ulster Historical Society* 1, part 1 [1860], 35). DuBois descendants also casually remarked in 1860 that "the first church, we were told, was a log hut; its successor, besides passing from French to Dutch, was built on a different spot" (Robert Patterson Du Bois, and William Ewing Du Bois, *Record of the family of Louis Du Bois, who emigrated from France to America in 1660* [Philadelphia, PA: J. C. Clark & Son, 1860], 24). That the Dutch matriarch had been forgotten is evidenced by the names later given to the Maria DuBois and the Abraham/Daniel Hasbrouck Houses. Both were constructed when women managed the family estate, but in the case of the Maria DuBois House, her house came to be known simply as the DuBois Fort, and the house built when Maria Hasbrouck managed her deceased husband's estate came to be known as the Abraham Hasbrouck House. When precisely these names came to be used is unclear, but there is no suggestion that nineteenth-century descendants were aware that the houses were built when women controlled the family assets (LeFevre, *History of New Paltz*, 294, 369). As for the decay and demolition of early houses, see for example, LeFevre, *History of New Paltz*, 305–306, 411, 475.
3. All objects in Locust Lawn are part of the Collection of Locust Lawn, Gift of Annette Innis Young, owned by Locust Grove, Poughkeepsie, New York. Neil Larson, with R. M. Toole, "Locust Lawn Historic Landscape

Report," (unpublished report for the Huguenot Historical Society, 2002); *New Paltz Independent* (henceforth, *NPI*), August 5, 1887; Douglas Bucher for John G. Waite Associates, "Historic Furnishings Plan for Locust Lawn" (unpublished report for the Huguenot Historical Society, 2003), 42, 75, 102–103.

4. Abraham Bruyn Hasbrouck, "Address," 34; John G. Waite Associates, "Dubois Fort: Historic Structure Report," report prepared for the Huguenot Historical Society, 2003, 14–25.
5. The Deyo House is owned by the Huguenot Historical Society, New Paltz, New York. *NPI*, January 3, 1902; *NPI*, March 7, 1902; *NPI*, September 15, 1905; LeFevre, *History of New Paltz*, 2.
6. Abraham Bruyn Hasbrouck, "Address," 28, 34, 36; Anson Du Bois, "The Life and Times of Louis Dubois," in *Bi-Centenary*, 13; Irving Elting, "Dutch Village Communities on the Hudson River," *Johns Hopkins University Studies in Historical and Political Science: Municipal Government and Land Tenure* 4, no. 1 (1886): 53; *NPI*, September 29, 1893; *NPI*, November 9, 1894; *NPI*, August 18, 1899; *NPI*, June16, 1899.
7. Reginald Horsman, *Race and Manifest Destiny: The Origins of American Racial Anglo-Saxonism* (Cambridge, MA: Harvard University Press, 1981), 9–24; Rogers Smith, *Conflicting Visions of Citizenship in U.S. History* (New Haven, CT: Yale University Press, 1997), 48–49.
8. George M. Fredrickson, *Racism: A Short History* (Princeton, NJ: Princeton University Press, 2002), 70–74; Horsman, *Race*, 25–42; John Higham, *Strangers in the Land: Patterns of American Nativism, 1860–1925* (New Brunswick, NJ: Rutgers University Press, 1955), 9–10, 133–134; Dorothy Ross, *The Origins of American Social Science* (New York: Cambridge University Press, 1991), 24–25.
9. Horsman, *Race*, 158–186; David Levin, *History as Romantic Art: Bancroft, Prescott, Motley, and Parkman* (Stanford, CA: Stanford University Press, 1959), in particular 3–45, 74–92 (quotation at 11).
10. Thomas F. Gossett, *Race: The History of an Idea in America* (Oxford: Oxford University Press, 1997), 84–95; Ross, *The Origins of American Social Science*, xiv–50 (quotation at 28).
11. T. J. Jackson Lears, *No Place of Grace: Antimodernism and the Transformation of American Culture, 1880–1920* (Chicago, IL: University of Chicago Press, 1981), 20–24 (quotation at 20); Gossett, *Race*, 95–175; Ross, *The Origins of American Social Science*, 53–97; Edward Norman Saveth, "Race and Nationalism in American Historiography: The Late Nineteenth Century," *Political Science Quarterly* 54, no. 3 (September 1939): 421–441; Richard Hofstadter, *Social Darwinism in America*, rev. ed. (New York: George Braziller, 1959), 170–200; Bluford Adams, "World Conquerors or a Dying People? Racial Theory, Regional Anxiety, and the Brahmin Anglo-Saxonists," *Journal of the Gilded Age and Progressive Era* 8, no. 2 (April 2009): 189–215.
12. Henry Sumner Maine, *Village-Communities in the East and West* (London: John Murray, 1876), 81; Herbert Baxter Adams, "The Germanic Origin of New England Towns," *Johns Hopkins University Studies in*

Historical and Political Science 1, no. 1 (1883): 16.

13. Herbert Baxter Adams, "Germanic Origin," 13, 23.
14. Herbert Baxter Adams, "Germanic Origin," 8, 27–28; Edward A. Freeman, "An Introduction to American Institutional History," *Johns Hopkins University Studies in Historical and Political Science* 1, no. 1 (1883): 15.
15. Barbara Miller Solomon, *Ancestors and Immigrants: A Changing New England Tradition* (Chicago, IL: University of Chicago Press, 1956), 1–81; James M. Lindgren, *Preserving Historic New England: Preservation, Progressivism, and the Remaking of Memory* (New York: Oxford University Press, 1995), 3–13.
16. Michael D. Clark, "More English than the English: Cavalier and Democrat in Virginia Historical Writing," *Journal of American Studies* 27, no. 2 (August 1993): 187–206; Catherine W. Bishir, "Landmarks of Power: Building a Southern Past in Raleigh and Wilmington, North Carolina 1885–1915," in *Where These Memories Grow: History, Memory, and Southern Identity*, ed. W. Fitzhugh Brundage (Chapel Hill: University of North Carolina, 2000), 141–168; James M. Lindgren, *Preserving the Old Dominion: Historical Preservation and Virginia Traditionalism* (Charlottesville: University Press of Virginia, 1993) (in particular, see 91–152); James M. Lindgren, "'For the Sake of our Future': The Association for the Preservation of Virginia Antiquities and the Regeneration of Traditionalism," *The Virginia Magazine of History and Biography* 97, no. 1 (January 1989): 47–74.
17. Grace Elizabeth Hale, *Making Whiteness: The Culture of Segregation in the South, 1890–1940* (New York: Pantheon, 1998), 75–79; Thomas Denenberg, *Wallace Nutting and the Invention of Old America* (New Haven, CT: Yale University Press, 2003), 171–175.
18. Fredrickson, *Racism*, 11–12, 56–82; Gossett, *Race*, 68–83.
19. David R. Roediger, *Working Toward Whiteness: How America's Immigrants Became White* (Cambridge, MA: Basic Books, 2005), 3–34; Horsman, *Race and Manifest Destiny*, 116–138.
20. Only once did any of the early leaders in the efforts to commemorate New Paltz suggest that commemoration was necessary so as "to inculcate and foster the sentiments of patriotism in these coming generations and by this means assimilate and digest the hordes of foreigners, now coming to our shores, most of whom are entirely ignorant of our early history and of the fundamental principles, underlying our Government and laws" (Ralph LeFevre, *NPI*, September 13, 1915). The only other time a leading figure in the New Paltz commemorative activities addressed the issue of immigrants was when, in a 1908 speech to the members of the Holland Society, their president, Frank Hasbrouck, suggested that contemporary immigrants were anything but the dregs of humanity. He argued that current Americans should be sensitive to the challenges that present-day immigrants faced as they wrenched themselves away from their homes in search of better lives, just as the ancestors of the Holland Society members had done centuries earlier (*Year Book of the*

Holland Society of New York 1908 [New York: Knickerbocker Press, 1916], 105–117). In creating the myth of the Dutch origins of American identity, the patentee descendants were not entirely alone. As Annette Stott has demonstrated, Americans reveled in "Holland Mania" for a short period beginning in the late nineteenth century, leading to a revisionist history centered around the Dutch contribution to America. However, as she bases her conclusions primarily on an exploration of art and design, Stott perhaps overstates her case. Annette Stott, *Holland Mania: The Unknown Dutch Period in American Art and Culture* (Woodstock, NY: Overlook Press, 1998).

21. "The Huguenots of Ulster County, No. 1," *The Christian Intelligencer* 16, no. 40 (April 16, 1846), (henceforth *TCI*); "The Huguenots of Ulster County, No. 2," *TCI* 16, no. 41 (April 23, 1846); "The Huguenots of Ulster County, No. 3," *TCI* 16, no. 42 (April 30, 1846); "The Huguenots of Ulster County, No. 4," *TCI* 16, no. 43 (May 7, 1846). Johannes Hornbeck Bevier was born in Wawarsing, New York (approximately twenty miles from New Paltz), educated at the Theological Seminary of New Brunswick, and served as pastor of the Shawangunk Reformed Church from 1831 to 1843 (located about twenty-five miles from New Paltz). He left Shawangunk in 1843 to assume the editorship of the *Intelligencer*, a post he held until 1852. E. W. Bentley, *Historical Discourse Read before the Classis at its Meeting in the Reformed Dutch Church, Port Jervis, April 20, 1875* (Ellenville, NY: James O. Fisher, 1875), 10. Bevier did not simply relate traditions that might have descended in his immediate family, as he also referred to a "correspondent" designated as "O. P.," whom he does not identify but liberally quotes.
22. "Huguenots," *TCI*, April 16, 1846; *TCI*, April 23, 1846; Nancy Lusignan Shultz, *Fire & Roses: The Burning of the Charlestown Convent, 1834* (New York: The Free Press, 2000); Abraham Garret Bevier (attributed), *The Indians: or Narratives of Massacres and Depredations on the Frontier, in Warwasink and its vicinity during the American Revolution Interspersed with Reflections on the Providence of God* (Kingston, NY: Bradley & Wells, 1846), 70. That Johannes Bevier would have been familiar with the perspective of his cousin Abraham Garret Bevier is beyond doubt, as his cousin's anti-Catholic attack appeared in another publication available for purchase at the office of the Reformed Church's magazine, of which Johannes Bevier was editor.
23. Through his use of quotation marks, the author of the *Christian Intelligencer* series indicates that some of his material is derived from other secondary sources that addressed the Huguenot experience, but he does not provide bibliographic information. However, this quotation, which appeared in "Huguenots," *TCI*, April 23, 1846, can be found in American Sunday-School Union, Committee of Publication, *History of the Huguenots*, (Philadelphia, PA, 1844), 198–201. Abraham Garret Bevier, *Indians*, 69.
24. "Huguenots," *TCI*, April 23, 1846.
25. "Huguenots," *TCI*, April 23,1846; *TCI*, April 30, 1846. Intriguingly, the

only "fact" he supplies to support his contention that the founders began to flee to the Palatinate only in the 1670s is that "the first birth, *on the records of the Bevier family, in this country*, is dated 1674 (emphasis original)." Not only does that fact not prove exactly when the Beviers left their homeland, it also does not suggest anything as to how long they lived in the German state. More importantly, it was not even a fact. The document upon which this assertion was based is a March 1675 letter from Louis and Marie Bevier's pastor in the Palatinate, which they acquired in preparation for their emigration to the New World. That document confirms both their marriage and the 1674 birth of their first daughter as having taken place in Die Pfalz, not America, as the author claimed.

26. Martin Kreiger, "Journal of the Second Esopus War," accessed February 15, 2014, http://www.hudsonrivervalley.org /library/pdfs/articles_books_essays/EsopusJournal1663.pdf.
27. "Huguenots," *TCI*, April 30, 1846. Another story that involves the death of an Indian at the hands of DuBois also exists, but it was printed only once and did not become part of the common stock of traditional lore. That story was recorded by another descendant, Yale University professor William Henry Brewer, who indicated that according to his family tradition, DuBois murdered the Indian not as he was reaching the Indian encampment but when the Esopus warriors attacked DuBois in his house in Nieuw Dorp, when members of the women and children of DuBois's extended family were taken captive. Professor Brewer writes, "The story was that he, (DuBois) was within the house, the Indians trying to enter; DuBois ran the leader through and pinned him to the door post." Brewer further claims that the very sword was in the position of his uncle, Peter DuBois. *NPI*, February 26, 1904; "William Henry Brewer Papers," at the New York Botanical Garden," accessed November 1, 2013, http://library.nybg.org/ finding_ guide/archv/brewer_ppb.html.
28. Martin Kreiger, "Journal of the Second Esopus War."
29. Martin Kreiger, "Journal of the Second Esopus War." The author of the *TCI* series was aware that some archival records of the war survived, as he noted that "it is said an account of this irruption may be found on the Historical Records, vol. 1, p. 168, in the office of the Secretary of State, at Albany" (*TCI*, April 30, 1846).
30. "Huguenots," *TCI*, April 23, 1846.
31. "Huguenots," *TCI*, April 23, 1846. A variant of the Bevier tale exists, in which it is claimed that Louis Bevier returned to France to claim an inheritance, during which time he happened on the road to meet his Catholic uncle, who refused to acknowledge him. Who this supposed "uncle" was is unclear. He could not have been Bevier's father's sibling, as his father was not from France. He may have had a Catholic uncle in his mother's family, as she was from the Picardy region of France and could still have had brothers living there. However, as Louis never lived in France, he would have been a stranger to any uncle he passed on the road, Catholic or otherwise, who therefore would have not known that this passerby on the street was his kin. Kenneth Hasbrouck, *The Bevier*

Family: The Descendants of Louis Bevier, Patentee of New Paltz, New York (New Paltz, NY: The Huguenot Historical Society, 1970), 4.

32. Robert Patterson Du Bois and William Ewing Du Bois, *Record of the family of Louis Du Bois*.
33. Ibid., 8, 22.
34. Ibid., 8, 17, 20, 76.
35. Ibid., 14–16.
36. Abraham Bruyn Hasbrouck, "Address," 21–24.
37. Ibid., 21–24, 26, 31.
38. Edmund Eltinge, "An Account of the Settlement of New Paltz by the Huguenots," in *Collections of the Ulster Historical Society* 1, no. 1 (1860): 40–48; Irving Elting, "Dutch Village Communities on the Hudson River," *Johns Hopkins University Studies in Historical and Political Science: Municipal Government and Land Tenure* 4, no. 1 (1886): 62; Edmund Eltinge to I. Daniel Rupp, February 25, 1843, as quoted in I. Daniel Rupp, *History of Lancaster County* (Lancaster, PA: Gilbert Hills, 1844). Later, in the 1890s, the most comprehensive chronicler of New Paltz, Ralph LeFevre, was perhaps rather sensitive to the possible critique that the "traditional" narrative may not have been as traditional as descendants claimed, and twice he took pains to note that it was indeed a widely shared story. He noted that "by recent inquiry we learn that Grand-father Peter LeFevre [d. 1830] used to tell that same story with all its particulars to his children so we no longer have doubts concerning its truthfulness" (*NPI*, November 9, 1894). He also related that "it will be noted that these important points in the story [of Catherine's rescue] as preserved among the Decker family [of Bruynswick, 16 miles from New Paltz], who have always lived in the locality agree with the tradition among the New Paltz people" (*NPI*, October 7, 1898). Since these statements were made fifty years after the story was first put in print, it is certainly possible that that half-century could have unconsciously produced an invented tradition of more recent vintage.
39. Edmund Eltinge, "Account," 40, 41, 46.
40. Edmund Eltinge, "Account," 41–47; Levin, *History as Romantic Art*, 3–22, 49–73.
41. *Bi-Centenary Reunion of the Descendants of Louis and Jacques Dubois*.
42. William E. Du Bois, "Bringing the Tribe Together," in *Bi-Centenary*, 79; Anson Du Bois, "Address of the President," in *Bi-Centenary*, 12; "Rev. Anson Du Bois, D.D.," *New York Times*, May 5, 1905; Anson Du Bois "The Life and Times of Louis Dubois," in *Bi-Centenary*, 70; "Hymn of Thanksgiving," in *Bi-Centenary*, 15; Henry A. DuBois, "The Family Surname," in *Bi-Centenary*, 38, 39, 43, 44; Cornelius Du Bois, "Our History in Europe," in *Bi-Centenary*, 19, 27, 36.
43. Robert Patterson Du Bois, "The Characteristics of the Family," in *Bi-Centenary*, 73, 77, 78.
44. Anson Du Bois, "The Life and Times of Louis Dubois," in *Bi-Centenary*, 62.
45. Irving Elting graduated from Harvard A.B. Class of 1878 and LL. B. Class of 1881. *Quinquennial Catalogue of the Officers and Graduates of*

Harvard University, 1636–1895 (Cambridge, MA: Harvard University Press, 1895), 329. Irving Elting, "Dutch Village Communities on the Hudson River," *Johns Hopkins University Studies in Historical and Political Science: Municipal Government and Land Tenure* 4, no. 1 (1886): 5–68. The monograph was also published in a separate edition. Previous to the publication of Elting's *Dutch Communities*, Elting presented his paper during the second annual meeting of the American Historical Association in 1885. Herbert Baxter Adams, "Report of the American Historical Association, at Saratoga, September 8–10, 1885," in *Papers of the American Historical Association* (New York, G. P. Putnam's Sons, 1886), 463–474.

46. Irving Elting, "Dutch Village Communities," 9, 11, 25.
47. Edmund Eltinge, "Account," 47; Anson Du Bois, "Life and Times of Louis Dubois," in *Bi-Centenary*, 64; Irving Elting, "Dutch Village Communities," 53, 54.
48. Stitt also attempted to link religion and civil self-government. He again associated the New Paltz founders with principles that guided many early residents of New England, who many argued brought to America the principles upon which the United States was later founded. He could do so, however, only by turning the word "religious" into an adverb, and using it in a manner that had nothing to do with religion. Stitt noted that the patentees seem "to have combined the religious as well as the civil element. They religiously selected the above mentioned twelve of the brethren as 'the Duzine,' or Twelve Patentees, of which one was Chief or President, who were invested with the functions of legislators and judges in the little Christian community" (Stitt, "History of the Huguenot Church," 189). Anson Du Bois, "Life and Times of Louis Dubois," in *Bi-Centenary*, 64, 65.
49. Irving Elting, "Dutch Village Communities," 55, 60.
50. Ibid., 66, 68.
51. Ibid., 67.

Chapter 7

1. LeFevre received his education at the New Paltz Academy and later at the State Normal School in Albany (Carol A. Johnson and Marion W. Ryan, *Images of America: New Paltz* [Charleston, SC: Arcadia, 2001]), 110; Carol A. Johnson, *Images of America: New Paltz Revisited* (Charleston, SC: Arcadia, 2010), 65. *NPI*, May 27, 1904; June 24, 1904; June 3, 1904.
2. *NPI*, April 22, 1898.
3. *NPI*, December 28, 1894; LeFevre, *History of New Paltz*, 5–6. In the 1890s, LeFevre published a number of articles and letters from other descendants based on similar conclusions. In a January 1896 address before the Huguenot Society of America, later published in the *Independent*, the Rev. James LeFevre also spoke of "these Patentees [who] had fled in former years from the French persecutions to find a home in the Lower Palatinate along the Rhine" (*NPI*, November 13, 1896). Louis Bevier, a

descendant of the patentee of the same name, wrote about his ancestor in 1899, erroneously remarking that "in early manhood he embraced the doctrines of the Reformation, and, with his ardent temperament, he soon drew down upon himself so much opposition, and eventually persecution, that he could no longer remain in safety at home, so, with some Huguenot friends, he took refuge in the Palatinate" (*NPI*, April 7, 1899). Anson Du Bois also claimed that his ancestors had faced and reacted against persecution, commenting that "not one of the New Paltz families found a refuge from persecution in Holland," presumably because they had done so through their relocation to the Palatinate (*NPI*, June 16, 1899).

4. In referencing the two record books of the Duzine, one of which documented land divisions and the other lawsuits concerning the boundaries of the patent, LeFevre remained convinced that although "there are no records of other action which they may have taken concerning other matters . . . there is reason to believe that some action was taken and no permanent record kept." He also claimed that "there is good evidence that in the early settlement the land was worked in common . . . Grote Bontecoe"—an area in New Paltz settled by an early generation of LeFevres where Ralph LeFevre was born—"was certainly worked by the settlers in common, and there is good reason to believe that other lands were also so worked," although he failed to provide any further evidence. *NPI*, July 20, 1894; April 22, 1898; LeFevre, *History of New Paltz*, 66, 69, 70; LeFevre, appendix to *History of New Paltz*, 16.
5. In the pages of the *Independent*, James LeFevre and Anson Du Bois expressed their beliefs that the twelve patentees themselves were called the "Duzine" (*NPI*, February 7, 1896; November 13, 1896; November 20, 1896). *NPI*, December 1, 1893.
6. *NPI*, July 20, 1894; February 7, 1896; July 9, 1898; November 26, 1897.
7. Ibid., July 26, 1895; April 15, 1898; December 29, 1899; June 8, 1900.
8. Ibid., March 23, 1894; July 19, 1895; July 26, 1895; May 22, 1896. A few examples suggest the broad interest LeFevre had helped to generate among descendants. Mr. S. E. Gross, a wealthy real estate investor and, according to LeFevre, a "big hearted Chicago millionaire," wrote that "I am a descendant of Matthew Blanshan, Louis DuBois and Christian Deyo. I feel honored in my descent from these worthy people and wish to participate in the commendable efforts of yourself and others of the descendants to perpetuate their memory" (*NPI*, December 28, 1894). LeFevre also published that "Mr. R. C. DuBois, writes from his home at Meridian Hill, Washington, D.C., under date of March 16th—'I thank you for the copy of the Independent of February 9th, '94, containing letters by Louis Bevier and reference to certain publications of your journal containing history of early settlers, etc., etc. Please send me a copy of each number. You may have still some on hand, and if you can obtain any number not on your files that is of interest in a historical point of view I shall be glad to have you do so" (*NPI*, March 23, 1894). In a letter to LeFevre and his newspaper, Rev. C. Elting Crispell, of Spring Valley, New York, commented, "I am pleased to be recognized as one interested in the early history of New Paltz. I am interested

in all that pertains to it. . . . There is a lawful and becoming ground of pride for us in that history. Our ancestors looked beyond 'food and raiment for themselves and their children.' And so do we. Let us continue to promote the civil interests, to foster the educational advantages, and, above, all to labor for religious advantages and privileges of the New Paltz," although what kind of privileges New Paltz needed are unstated (*NPI*, July 26, 1895). And although not a correspondent with LeFevre until somewhat later, the wealthy Detroit industrialist and philanthropist Charles Lang Freer—art collector and benefactor to the Smithsonian and descendant of patentee Hugo Freer—kept in his personal papers clippings from the *Independent* on historical matters. Colleen Hennessey and Rachael Cristine Woody, "A Finding Aid to The Charles Lang Freer papers at the Freer Gallery of Art and Arthur M. Sackler Gallery Archives" (2002), accessed May 8, 2013, http://www.asia.si.edu/ archives/finding_aids/freer.html.

8. *NPI*, March 24, 1894; August 3, 1895; May 22, 1896; John Riddle, "Guide to the David D. Demarest Letters, 1837–1850," Special Collections and University Archives, Rutgers University Libraries, October 1997, accessed May 5, 2013, http://www2.scc.rutgers.edu/ead/uarchives/demarest_df.html; *Proceedings of the Huguenot Society of America*, vol. 6 (New York: Huguenot Society of America, 1909), 28.
9. *NPI*, November 17, 1893.
10. Ibid., August 25, 1893; October 20, 1893.
11. Ibid., November 24, 1893.
12. The other purposes referenced in the founding documents of the society included "by marking and preserving the marks of the burial places of early settlers: by marking and preserving historical sites and buildings: by acquiring ownership of such sites and buildings together with relics, documents and papers, and by founding & maintaining thereon and therewith a Museum: or Museums, by discovering collecting, and preserving documents and information respecting the New Paltz Patent and its early settlers and by publishing the same." "Minutes, Huguenot Patriotic Historical and Monumental Society of New Paltz," HHS.
13. "Minutes," HHS, 3–4; *NPI*, April 13, 1894.
14. "Minutes," HHS.
15. *NPI*, April 27, 1894; May 4, 1894; July 29, 1894; "Minutes," HHS.
16. " Minutes," HHS; "Treasurer's Account Book," Huguenot Patriotic Historical and Monumental Society of New Paltz, HHS, New Paltz, NY; *NPI*, August 17, 1894; April 12, 1895.
17. "Minutes," HHS; *NPI*, November 1, 1895; May 29, 1896.
18. *NPI*, November 13, 1896; November 20, 1896.
19. "Minutes," HHS; *NPI*, December 11, 1896; April 16, 1897; August 20, 1897.
20. *NPI*, September 10, 1897; February 25, 1898; June 24, 1898.
21. LeFevre, *History of New Paltz*, v–vi, 2; *NPI*, April 13, 1894; September 14, 1894; November 9, 1894; August 20, 1897; October 8, 1897; March 11, 1898; June 24, 1898.
22. *NPI*, September 13, 1895; October 8, 1897; January 13, 1899; May 29, 1899.
23. While LeFevre referred to the activities of ladies' patriotic organizations

only after his society purchased the Jean Hasbrouck House, the historic preservation goals of the local DAR were likely a topic of public discussion for some time before the purchase. *NPI*, July 15, 1898; May 18, 1900. Alan Axelrod, ed., *The Colonial Revival in America* (New York: Winterthur-Norton, 1985); James Lindgren, *Preserving Historic New England*; Joseph Conforti, *Imagining New England: Explorations of Regional Identity from the Pilgrims to the Mid-Twentieth Century* (Chapel Hill: University of North Carolina Press, 2001); Thomas Andrew Denenberg, *Wallace Nutting and the Invention of Old America*.

24. *NPI*, September 10, 1897; November 26, 1897; July 2, 1898.
25. "Minutes," HHS.
26. "Minutes," HHS; "Treasurer's Account Book," HHS; *NPI*, April 15, 1898; June 24, 1898; July 1, 1898; July 29, 1898; September 30, 1898; January 13, 1899.
27. *NPI*, July 14, 1899; July 21, 1899; August 4, 1899; August 11, 1899; September 8, 1899.
28. "Minutes," HHS; *NPI*, June 16, 1899.
29. *NPI*, June 16, 1899; Anson Du Bois, "Life and Times of Louis Dubois," in *Bi-Centenary*, 59.
30. *NPI*, June 30, 1899; July 7, 1899; July 21, 1899; August 4, 1899; August 11, 1899.
31. Ibid., August 18, 1899.
32. Ibid., August 4, 1899; August 11, 1899; September 8, 1899.
33. Ibid., June 30, 1899.
34. Ibid., August 11, 1899.
35. Ibid., August 18, 1899; August 25, 1899.
36. Ibid., June 16, 1899; January 19, 1900; June 1, 1900; June 29, 1900; August 24, 1900; October 19, 1900; October 27, 1900; March 22, 1901. One critic even remarked upon the generic collection of objects, noting that "as the matter stands now we have a very fine old stone house and a growing assortment of relics and old documents, but a stranger visiting the house may not understand it as a memorial to the Patentees at all, as there is nothing about the house or grounds to indicate such a thing" (*NPI*, June 8, 1900).
37. Ibid., July 6, 1894; June 16, 1899; July 2, 1899; February 2, 1900.
38. Ibid., May 25, 1900; July 13, 1900; July 27, 1900; August 24, 1900; August 7, 1900.
39. *NPI*, April 17, 1903; "Minutes," HHS.
40. *NPI*, July 31,1903.
41. Ibid.
42. "Minutes," HHS; *NPI*, April 17, 1908; August 22, 1908; October 2, 1908; October 16, 1908.
43. *NPI*, May 27, 1904.

BIBLIOGRAPHY

Published Primary Sources

Adams, John. *The Flowers of Modern Travels, Being Elegant, Entertaining and Instructive Extracts, Selected from the Works of the Most Celebrated Travellers.* Boston, MA: John West, 1797.

Aglionby, William. *The Present State of the United Provinces of the Low-Countries: as to the Government, Laws, Forces, Riches, Manners, Customes, Revenue, and Territory, of the DUTCH.* London: John Starkey, 1669.

Anjou, Gustave. *Ulster County, N.Y. probate records in the office of the surrogate, and in the county clerk's office at Kingston, N.Y.: a careful abstract and translation of the Dutch and English wills, letters of administration after intestates, and inventories from 1665, with genealogical and historical notes, and list of Dutch and Frisian baptismal names with their English equivalents.* 2 vols. New York: Anjou, 1906.

Benson, Adolph B., ed. and trans. *Peter Kalm's Travels in North America: the English Version of 1770 Revised from the original Swedish and edited by Adolph B. Benson With A Translation of New Material from Kalm's Diary Notes.* New York: Wilson-Erickson, 1937.

Carr, William. *The Travellours Guide and Historians Faithful Companion.* London: Eben Tracy, 1695.

Chamberlayne, Edward. *The present state of England.* London: William Whirwood, 1683.

Clark, George. *Observations Upon the United Provinces of the Netherlands by William Temple.* Oxford: Clarendon Press, 1972.

Colden, Cadwallader. *The letters and papers of Cadwallader Colden.* 10 vols. New-York Historical Society Collection. New York: 1918–1936.

The Colonial Laws of New York from the Year 1664 to the Revolution. 5 vols. Albany, NY: James B. Lyon, 1894.

"The Diary of Abraham Hasbrouck." In *The Earliest Records of the Hasbrouck Family.* Edited by Kenneth Hasbrouk. New Paltz, NY: privately printed, 1992.

de Beer, E. S., ed. *The Diary of John Evelyn.* Oxford: Clarendon Press, 1955.

de Chastellux, Marquis. *Chastellux Travels in North America in the Years 1780, 1781.* Translated by Howard C. Rice Jr. Chapel Hill: University of North Carolina Press, 1963.

de Warville, Jacques-Pierre Brissot. *A Critical Examination of the Marquis de Chastellux's Travels in North America.* Philadelphia, PA: Joseph James, 1788.

de Warville, Jacques-Pierre Brissot. *New travels in the United States of America, 1788.* Edited by Durand Echeverria. Cambridge, MA: Belknap Press of Harvard University Press, 1964.

Defoe, Daniel. *The Complete English Tradesmen in Familiar Letters.* 2nd ed. 1727. Reprint, New York: August M. Kelley, 1969.

The Dutch Drawn to Life. London: Thomas Johnson, 1664.

"Edmund Eltinge to I. Daniel Rupp, February 25, 1843," as quoted in I. Daniel Rupp, *History of Lancaster County.* Lancaster, PA; Gilbert Hills, 1844.

Felltham, Owen. *A brief Character of the Low-Countries under the States Being three weeks observation of the Vices and Vertues of the Inhabitants.* London: Henry Seile, 1652.

Fernow, Berthold, ed. *New York in the Revolution.* Albany, NY: Weed, Parsons, 1887.

Goetschius, Johannes Mauritius. "Will, July 4, 1700." In *Collections of the New-York Historical Society for the Year 1898,* 405. New York: New-York Historical Society, 1899.

Goldsmith, Oliver. "The Traveller; or a Prospect of Society." N.p. (America): n.p., 1768.

Halsey, Francis W., ed. *A Tour of the Hudson, the Mohawk, the Susquehanna, and the Delaware in 1769, being the Journal of Richard Smith of Burlington, New Jersey.* 1906. Reprint, Fleischmanns, New York: Purple Mountain Press, 1989.

Hamilton, Alexander. *Itinerarium,* published as *Gentleman's Progress: The Itinerarium of Dr. Alexander Hamilton 1744.* Edited by Carl Bridenbaugh. Chapel Hill: University of North Carolina for the Institute of Early American History and Culture, 1948.

Hasbrouck, Kenneth, ed., *The Earliest Records of the Hasbrouck Family.* New Paltz. NY: Huguenot Historical Society, 1992.

Hastings, Hugh, Edward Corwin, and James Holden. *Ecclesiastical Records, State of New York,*7 vols. Albany: State of New York, 1901–1916.

Hinke, William J., ed. *Life and Letters of the Rev. John Philip Boehm: Founder of the Reformed Church in Pennsylvania, 1683–1749.* Philadelphia, PA: Reformed Church in America, 1918.

Hovenden, Robert, ed. "The Registers of the Walloon or Strangers' Church in Canterbury." In *The Publications of the Huguenot Society of London.* Vol. 5, pt. 2. Lymington, UK: C. T. King, 1894.

Hume, David. "Of National Characters." In *Essays, Moral and Political.* 3rd ed. London: A. Millar, 1748.

Ireland, Samuel. *A Picturesque Tour Through Holland, Brabant, Part of France, Made in the Autumn of 1789.* London: T. Egerton, 1796.

Irving, Washington. *A History of New York, from the Beginning of the World to the End of the Dutch Dynasty, by Diedrich Knickerbocker,* rev. ed. A. L. Burt Company, n.d.

Johnson, Warren. "Journal 1760–1761." *Papers of Sir William Johnson.* Vol. 13. Edited by Milton Hamilton. Albany: State University of New York, 1962.

Journal of the votes and proceedings of the General Assembly of the colony of New York. Began the 9th day of April, 1691 and ended the 23d of December, 1765. New York: H. Gaine, 1764–1766.

Kreiger, Martin. "Journal of the Second Esopus War." Accessed February 15, 2014. http://www.hudsonrivervalley.org/library/pdfs/articles_books_essays/EsopusJournal1663.pdf.

A Late Voyage to Holland. London: John Humphreys, 1691.

Marshall, Joseph. *Travels through Holland, Flanders, Germany, Denmark, Sweden, Lapland, Russia, The Ukraine, and Poland in the Years 1768, 1769, and 1770.* 2 vols. London: J. Almon, 1772.

Moll, Herman. *Twenty four new and accurate maps of the several parts of Europe.* London: J. Nicholson, c. 1707.

Mountague, William. *The Delights of Holland: or, A Three Months Travel about that and the other Provinces.* London: John Sturton, 1696.

New Paltz Independent.

New York in the Revolution as Colony and State. Vol. 1. Albany, NY: J. B. Lyon, 1904.

O'Callaghan, Edward B. *The Documentary history of the state of New York.* 4 vols. Albany, NY: Weed, Parsons & Co., 1850–1851.

Payne, John. *New and Complete System of Universal Geography, Describing Asia, Africa, Europe and America.* Vol. 3. New York: John Low, 1800.

Peers, Richard. *The English Atlas. Volume 4. Containing the Description of the Seventeen Provinces of the Low-Countries, or Netherlands.* London: Moses Pitt, 1682.

"Philip Mazzei to Thomas Jefferson, April 8, 1781." In *The Papers of Jefferson.* Vol. 5. Edited by Julian P. Boyd, et al. Princeton, NJ: Princeton University Press, 1952ff.

Radcliffe, Ann. *A Journey made in the Summer of 1794 through Holland and the Western Frontier of Germany, with a return down the Rhine.* London: G. G. and J. Robinson, 1794.

Reresby, John. *Memoirs & Travels of Sir John Reresby Bart.* London: Kegan, Paul, Trench, Trubner & Co, 1904.

Richard, John. *A Tour from London to Petersburgh, from thence to Moscow, and return to London by way of Courland, Poland, Germany and Holland.* London: T. Evans, 1778.

Roberts, Kenneth, and Anna M. Roberts, trans. and ed. *Moreau de St. Mery's American Journey 1793–1798.* Garden City, NY: Doubleday, 1947.

Seabury, Samuel. *Letters of a Westchester Farmer.* New York: Rivington, 1774.

Smith, Jr., William. *The history of the Province of New-York.* Edited by Michael Kammen. Cambridge, MA: Harvard University Press, 1972.

Strickland, William. *Journal of a Tour in the United States of America, 1794–1795.* Edited by J. E. Strickland. New York: The New-York Historical Society, 1971.

Transcriptions of early County Records of New York State: Minutes of the

Board of Supervisors of Ulster County 1710/1 to 1730/1. Albany, NY: The Historical Records Survey, 1939.

Varick, Richard. "Richard Varick to Colonel Hardenbergh, June 20, 1783." In *Encyclopedia of Biography of New York*, 134. Edited by Charles Elliott Fitch. New York: The American Historical Society, 1916.

Versteeg, Dingman. "Kingston Papers." Edited by Peter R. Christoph, Kenneth Scott, and Kenn Stryker-Rodda. Baltimore, MD: Genealogical Publishing Company, 1976.

Versteeg, Dingman, ed. and trans. *Records of the Reformed Dutch Church of New Paltz, N.Y.* Vol. 3 of the *Collections of the Holland Society of New York*. New York: Holland Society, 1894.

Watson, Winslow C., ed. *Men and Times of the Revolution; or, Memoirs of Elkanah Watson, including Journals of Travels in Europe and America, from 1777 to 1842, with his Correspondence with Public Men and Reminiscences and Incidents of the Revolution.* New York: Dana and Company, 1856.

Weld, Jr., Isaac. *Travels Through the States of North American and the Provinces of Upper and Lower Canada, during the Years 1795, 1795, and 1797.* London: John Stockdale, 1799.

Wraxall, Peter. *An Abridgment of the Indian Affairs Continued in Four Folio Volumes, Transacted in the Colony of New York, from Abridgment in the year 1678 to the year.* Edited by Charles Howard McIlwain. Cambridge, MA: Harvard University Press, 1915.

Wright, Frances. *Views of Society and Manners in America.* Edited by Paul R. Baker. Cambridge, MA: Belknap Press of Harvard University Press, 1963.

Year Book of the Holland Society of New York 1908. New York: Knickerbocker Press, 1916.

Unpublished Primary Sources

Bevier, Louis, Papers (1675–1719). Huguenot Historical Society, New Paltz, NY.

Bevier, Louis, Family Papers: The Elizabeth Wright Collection (1721–1929). Huguenot Historical Society, New Paltz, NY.

Bevier, Louis, Family Papers: The Rutgers Collection (1687–1921). Photocopied collection, Huguenot Historical Society, New Paltz, NY.

Bible and Religious Book Collection. Huguenot Historical Society, New Paltz, NY.

Ciphering Book Collection (c. 1730–1849). Huguenot Historical Society, New Paltz, NY.

Cottin, Jean, Papers. Huguenot Historical Society, New Paltz, NY.

Deyo Family Papers (1675–1870). Huguenot Historical Society, New Paltz, NY.

DuBois, Daniel and Simon, Family Papers (1695–1864). Huguenot Historical Society, New Paltz, NY.

Dubois, Hendricus, Family Papers (1702–1927). Huguenot Historical Society, New Paltz, NY.

Dubois, Josiah, Family Papers. Huguenot Historical Society, New Paltz, NY.

Elting, Roelof J. and Ezekiel, Family Papers (1723–1908). Huguenot Historical Society, New Paltz, NY.

Eltinge, Cornelius, Family Papers. Haviland-Heidgerd Historical Collection. Elting Memorial Library, New Paltz, NY.

Freer Family Papers. Haviland Heidgerd Historical Collection. Elting Memorial Library, New Paltz, NY.

Freer, Garret, Family Papers. Huguenot Historical Society, New Paltz, NY.

Freer, Hugo, Family Papers (1677–1721). Huguenot Historical Society, New Paltz, NY.

Hasbrouck, Joseph and Jacob J., Family Papers (1723–1860). Huguenot Historical Society, New Paltz, NY.

Hasbrouck, Levi, Family Papers: The Locust Lawn Collection (1672–1968). Huguenot Historical Society, New Paltz, NY.

Hasbrouck, Wilhelmus and Moses, Family Papers (1753–1897). Huguenot Historical Society, New Paltz, NY.

"Mannheim: Records of the French Congregation 1651–1710." Unpublished translation by Ruth P. Heidgerd, New York (1978), available at the Huguenot Historical Society library, New Paltz, NY.

"Membership of the New Paltz Church to Hendricus DuBois, August 31, 1765." Records of the Reformed Church of New Paltz. Translated by Berthold Fernow. New York Historical and Genealogical Society, New York.

"Minutes," Huguenot Patriotic Historical and Monumental Society of New Paltz." Huguenot Historical Society, New Paltz, NY.

"New Paltz Consistory to Hendricus DuBois, August 19, 1765." Records of the Reformed Church of New Paltz. Translated by Berthold Fernow. New York Historical and Genealogical Society, New York.

New Paltz Reformed Church Records (1683–1892). Huguenot Historical Society, New Paltz, NY.

New Paltz Town Records. Huguenot Historical Society, New Paltz, NY.

New York County Probate Records.

"1798 Federal Direct Tax, New Paltz schedules." Huguenot Historical Society, New Paltz, NY.

Tebanin, Jean, Papers (1700–1730). Huguenot Historical Society, New Paltz, NY.

"Treasurer's Account Book." Huguenot Patriotic Historical and Monumental Society of New Paltz, Huguenot Historical Society, New Paltz, NY.

Ulster County Land Records.

Ulster County Wills in the Office of the Surrogate.

Published Secondary Sources: Books

American Sunday-School Union, Committee of Publication. *History of the Huguenots.* Philadelphia, PA, 1844.

Appleby, Joyce Oldham. *Economic Thought and Ideology in Seventeenth-Century England.* Princeton, NJ: Princeton University Press, 1978.

Archdeacon, Thomas J. *New York City, 1664–1710: Conquest and Change.* Ithaca, NY: Cornell University Press, 1976.

Axelrod, Alan, ed. *The Colonial Revival in America.* New York: Winterthur-Norton, 1985.

Baird, Charles W. *History of The Huguenot Emigration to America.* New York: Dodd, Mead & Co., 1885.

Balmer, Randall. *A Perfect Babel of Confusion: Dutch Religion and English Culture in the Middle Colonies.* New York: Oxford University Press, 1989.

Bentley, E. W. *Historical Discourse Read before the Classis at its Meeting in the Reformed Dutch Church, Port Jervis, April 20, 1875.* Ellenville, NY: James O. Fisher, 1875.

Bevier, Abraham Garret Bevier. *The Indians: or Narratives of Massacres and Depredations on the Frontier, in Warwasink and its vicinity during the American Revolution Interspersed with Reflections on the Providence of God.* Kingston, NY: Bradley & Wells, 1846.

BeVier, Dale André. *The Bevier Family: Its History and Genealogy.* N.p.: privately printed, c. 2000. (Available in the library of the Huguenot Historical Society.)

Bevier, Katherine. *The Bevier Family. A History of the Descendants of Louis Bevier Who came from France to America in 1675 after a sojourn of ten years in the Palatinate and settled in New Paltz, New York.* New York: Tobias A. Wright, 1916.

Biemer, Linda Briggs. *Women and property in Colonial New York: the transition from Dutch to English law 1643–1727.* Ann Arbor, MI: UMI Research Press, 1983.

Blackburn, Roderic H., and Nancy A. Kelley, eds. *New Word Dutch Studies: Dutch Arts and Culture in Colonial America 1609–1776, Proceedings of the Symposium Organized by the Albany Institute of History and Art, Albany, August 2–3, 1986.* Albany, NY: Albany Institute of History and Art, 1987.

Bonney, Richard. *Political Change in France under Richelieu and Mazarin: 1624–1661.* Oxford: Oxford University Press, 1978.

Butler, Jon. *The Huguenots in America: a refugee people in new world society.* Cambridge, MA: Harvard University Press, 1983.

Carlo, Paula Wheeler. *Huguenot refugees in colonial New York: Becoming American in the Hudson Valley.* Brighton, UK: Sussex Academic Press, 2005.

Chartier, Roger. *The Cultural Origins of the French Revolution.* Translated by Lydia G. Cochrane. Durham, NC: Duke University Press, 1991.

Clasen, Claus-Peter. *The Palatinate in European History: 1559–1660.* Oxford: Basil Blackwell, 1963.

Clearwater, Alphonso T. *The History of Ulster County, New York.* Kingston, NY: W. J. Van Deusen, 1907.

Cohen, David Steven. *The Dutch-American Farm.* New York: New York University Press, 1992.

Corwin, Edward Tanjore. *A Manual of the Reformed Church in America, (formerly Ref. Prot. Dutch Church) 1628–1902.* New York: Board of Publication of the Reformed Church in America, 1902.

Coalter, Jr., Milton J. *Gilbert Tennent, Son of Thunder: A Case Study of Continental Pietism's Impact on the First Great Awakening in the Middle Colonies.* Westport, CT: Greenwood Press, 1986.

Conforti, Joseph. *Imagining New England: Explorations of Regional*

Identity from the Pilgrims to the Mid-Twentieth Century. Chapel Hill: University of North Carolina Press, 2001.

Cross, Francis W. "History of the Walloon & Huguenot Church at Canterbury." Vol. 15, *Publications of the Huguenot Society of London*. London: Huguenot Society of London, 1898.

Countryman, Edward. *A People in Revolution: The American Revolution and Political Society in New York, 1760–1790*. Baltimore, MD: Johns Hopkins University Press, 1981.

De Jong, Gerald F. *The Dutch Reformed Church in the American* Colonies. Grand Rapids, MI:Wm. B. Eerdmans, 1978.

Dennenberg, Thomas Andrew. *Wallace Nutting and the Invention of Old America*. New Haven, CT: Yale University Press, 2003.

De Vries, Jan. *The Dutch Rural Economy in the Golden Age, 1500–1700*. New Haven, CT: Yale University Press, 1974.

Disosway, Gabriel P. *The Earliest Churches of New York and its Vicinity*. New York: James G. Gregory, 1865.

Dubbs, Joseph Henry. *The Reformed Church in Pennsylvania*, pt. 9. Lancaster: Pennsylvania German Society, 1902.

DuBois, Cornelia. *The story of the Paltz: Being a brief history of New Paltz, N.Y., a compilation*. N.p.: privately printed, 1915.

Du Bois, Robert Patterson, and William Ewing Du Bois. *Record of the family of Louis Du Bois, who emigrated from France to America in 1660*. Philadelphia, PA: J. C. Clark & Son, 1860.

Epperson, Gwenn F. *New Netherland Roots*. Baltimore, MD: Genealogical Publishing Company, 1994.

Eze, Emmaneul Chukwadi. *Race and the enlightenment: a reader*. Cambridge, MA: Blackwell, 1997.

Fabend, Firth Haring. *A Dutch Family in the Middle Colonies, 1660–1800*. New Brunswick, NJ: Rutgers University Press, 1991.

Fitchen, John. *The New World Dutch Barn: The Evolution, Forms, and Structure of a Disappearing Icon*. 2nd ed., with new material by Gregory D. Huber. Syracuse, NY: Syracuse University Press, 2001.

Fredrickson, George M. *Racism: A Short History*. Princeton, NJ: Princeton University Press, 2002.

Fried, Marc B. *The Early History of Kingston & Ulster County, N.Y.* Marbletown, NY: Ulster County Historical Society, 1975.

Gilbert, Olive. *Narrative of Sojourner Truth*. Edited by Margaret Washington. New York: Vintage, 1993.

Good, James I. *History of the Reformed Church in the United States 1725–1792*. Reading, PA: Daniel Miller, 1899.

Goodfriend, Joyce D. *Before the Melting Pot: Society and Culture in Colonial New York City, 1664–1730*. Princeton, NJ: Princeton University Press, 1992.

Gossett, Thomas F. *Race: The History of an Idea in America*. Oxford: Oxford University Press, 1997.

Greven, Philip J. *Four Generations: Population, Land and Family in Colonial Andover Massachusetts*. Ithaca, NY: Cornell University Press, 1970.

Gross, Geoffrey, Susan Piatt, and Roderic H. Blackburn. *Dutch Colonial Homes in America.* New York: Rizzoli, 2002.

Haefeli, Evan. *New Netherland and the Dutch Origins of Religious Liberty.* Philadelphia: University of Pennsylvania Press, 2012.

Hageman, Howard G. *Two Centuries Plus.* Vol. 13 of *The Historical Series of the Reformed Church.* Grand Rapids, MI: Wm. B. Eerdmans, 1984.

Hasbrouck, Frank. *The History of Dutchess County New York.* Poughkeepsie, NY: S. A. Matthieu, 1909.

Hasbrouck, Kenneth E. *The Bevier Family: The Descendants of Louis Bevier, Patentee of New Paltz, New York.* New Paltz, NY: The Huguenot Historical Society, 1970.

———. *A Guide to Huguenot Street and Preservation Efforts of The Huguenot Historical Society New Paltz, N.Y.* rev. ed. New Paltz, NY: Huguenot Historical Society, 1987.

———. *The Hasbrouck Family in America, with European Background,* 3rd ed. New Paltz, NY: Privately printed, 1986.

Hasbrouck, Kenneth E., and Erma R. DeWitt. *The Street of the Huguenots.* Goshen, NY: Bookmill on Windy Hill, 1952.

Hasbrouck, Kenneth E., and Ruth P. Heidgerd. *The Deyo (Deyoe) Family.* Revised and edited by Carol Van Wagner, Esther Deyo Aldridge, and Nancy Gentile. N.p.: privately printed, 2003. (Available in the library of the Huguenot Historical Society.)

Heidgerd, William. *The American Descendants of Chrétien Du Bois of Wicres, France.* Revised and edited by Du Bois Family Association, Inc. New Paltz, NY: privately printed, 1998. (Available in the library of the Huguenot Historical Society.)

Higham, John. *Strangers in the Land: Patterns of American Nativism, 1860–1925.* New Brunswick, NJ: Rutgers University Press, 1955.

Hine, C. G. *History and Legend Fact, Fancy and Romance of the Old Mine Road: Kingston, N.Y. to the Mine Holes of Pahaquarry.* N.p.: C. G. Hine, 1909.

Hinke, William John. "A History of the Goshenhoppen Reformed Charge." Part 29 of *Pennsylvania: The German Influence in its Settlement and Development.* Lancaster: Pennsylvania-German Society, 1920.

A History of the Classis of Paramus of the Reformed Church in America. New York: Board of Publication of the Reformed Church in America, 1902.

Hofstadter, Richard. *Social Darwinism in America,* rev. ed. New York: George Braziller, 1959.

Horsman, Reginald. *Race and Manifest Destiny: The Origins of American Racial Anglo-Saxonism.* Cambridge, MA: Harvard University Press, 1981.

Israel, Jonathan I. *Dutch primacy in world trade, 1585–1740.* Oxford: Clarendon Press,1990.

Jacobs, Jaap. *The Colony of New Netherland: A Dutch Settlement in Seventeenth-Century America.* Ithaca, NY: Cornell University Press, 2009.

Johnson, Carol A. *Images of America: New Paltz Revisited.* Charleston, SC: Arcadia, 2010.

Johnson, Carol A., and Marion W. Ryan. *Images of America: New Paltz.* Charleston, SC: Arcadia, 2001.

Kammen, Michael. *Colonial New York: A History.* New York: Charles Scribner's Sons, 1975.

———. *Mystic Chords of Memory: The Transformation of Tradition in American Culture.* New York: Knopf, 1991.

Kenney, Alice P. *Stubborn for Liberty: the Dutch in New York.* Syracuse, NY: Syracuse University Press, 1975.

Klein, Milton M. *The politics of diversity: essays in the history of colonial New York.* Port Washington, NY: Kennikat Press, 1974.

Kornwolf, James D. *Architecture and Town Planning in Colonial America.* Baltimore, MD: Johns Hopkins University Press, 2002.

Kulikoff, Allan. *Tobacco and Slaves.* Chapel Hill: University of North Carolina Press, 1986.

Larkin, Jack. *The Reshaping of Everyday Life, 1790–1840.* New York: Harper & Row, 1988.

Lears, T. J. Jackson. *No Place of Grace: Antimodernism and the Transformation of American Culture, 1880–1920.* New York: Pantheon, 1981.

LeFevre, Ralph. *History of New Paltz, New York and its Old Families (From 1678 to 1820) Including the Huguenot Pioneers and Others who settled in New Paltz previous to the Revolution With an Appendix bringing down the history of certain families and some other matter to 1850.* 2nd ed. Albany, NY: Fort Orange Press, Brandow Printing, 1909.

Lemon, James T. *The Best Poor Man's Country: A Geographical study of Early Southeastern Pennsylvania.* New York: Norton, 1972.

Levin, David. *History as Romantic Art: Bancroft, Prescott, Motley, and Parkman.* Stanford, CA: Stanford University Press, 1959.

Lindgren, James M. *Preserving Historic New England: Preservation, Progressivism, and the Remaking of Memory.* New York: Oxford University Press, 1995.

———. *Preserving the Old Dominion: Historical Preservation and Virginia Traditionalism.* Charlottesville: University Press of Virginia, 1993.

Mabee, Carleton with Susan Mabee Newhouse. *Sojourner Truth: Slave, Prophet, Legend.* New York: New York University Press, 1993.

Maine, Henry Sumner. *Village-Communities in the East and West.* London: John Murray, 1876.

Matson, Cathy. *Merchants and Empire: Trading in Colonial New York.* Baltimore, MD: Johns Hopkins University Press, 1998.

McManus, Edgar J. *A History of Negro slavery in New York.* Syracuse, NY: Syracuse University Press, 1966.

Meeske, Harrison F. *From Vernacular to Spectacular.* Fleischmanns, NY: Purple Mountain Press, 2007.

Merwick, Donna. *Death of a notary: conquest and change in colonial New York.* Ithaca, NY: Cornell University Press, 1999.

———. *Possessing Albany, 1630–1710: The Dutch and English Experiences.* Cambridge, UK: Cambridge University Press, 1990.

Miller, Myrtle Hardenbergh. *The Hardenbergh Family: A Genealogical*

Compilation. New York: The American Historical Company, Inc., 1958.

Narrett, David. *Inheritance and Family Life in Colonial New York City*. Ithaca, NY: Cornell University Press, 1992.

Nobles, Gregory. *American Frontiers: Cultural Encounters and Continental Conquest*. New York: Hill and Wang, 1997.

Norton, Thomas Elliot. *The Fur Trade in Colonial New York, 1686–1776*. Madison: University of Wisconsin Press, 1974.

Otterness, Philip. *Becoming German: The 1709 Palatine Migration to New York*. Ithaca, NY: Cornell University Press, 2004.

Otto, Paul. *The Dutch-Munsee Encounter in America: The Struggle for Sovereignty in the Hudson Valley*. New York: Berghahn, 2006.

Pierson, Jr., William H. *American Buildings and their Architects*. Vol. 1, *The Colonial and Neoclassical Styles*. New York: Oxford University Press, 1970.

Pincus, Steven C. A. *Protestantism and Patriotism: Ideologies and the making of English foreign policy, 1650–1668*. Cambridge, UK: Cambridge University Press, 1996.

Pointer, Richard. *Protestant Pluralism and the New York experience: a study of eighteenth-century religious diversity*. Bloomington: Indiana University Press, 1988.

Prak, Maarten. *The Dutch Republic in the Seventeenth Century: The Golden Age*. Translated by Diane Webb. New York: Cambridge University Press, 2005.

Price, J. L. *Dutch Society 1588–1713*. Harlow, UK: Longman, 2000.

Proceedings of the Huguenot Society of America, Vol. 6. New York: Huguenot Society of America, 1909.

Quinquennial Catalogue of the Officers and Graduates of Harvard University, 1636–1895. Cambridge, MA; Harvard University Press, 1895.

Reynolds, Helen Wilkinson. *Dutch Houses in the Hudson Valley before 1776*. New York: Holland Society, 1929.

Rink, Oliver. *Holland on the Hudson: An Economic and Social History of Dutch New York*. Ithaca, NY: Cornell University Press, 1986.

Ritchie, Robert C. *The Duke's Province: A Study of New York Politics and Society, 1664–1691*. Chapel Hill: University of North Carolina Press, 1977.

Roberts, Charles R., and J. D. Schindel. *History of the Egypt Church*. Allentown, PA: Lehigh County Historical Society, 1908.

Roediger, David R. *Working Toward Whiteness: How America's Immigrants Became White*. Cambridge, MA: Basic Books, 2005.

Romney, Susan Shaw. *New Netherland Connections: Intimate Networks and Atlantic Ties in Seventeenth-Century America*. Chapel Hill: University of North Carolina Press, 2014.

Rosen, Deborah A. *Courts and Commerce: Gender, Law, and the Market Economy in Colonial New York*. Columbus: Ohio State University Press, 1997.

Ross, Dorothy Ross. *The Origins of American Social Science*. New York: Cambridge University Press, 1991.

Roth, Leland M. *A Concise History of American Architecture*. Boulder, CO: Westview Press, 1979.

Salmon, Marylynn. *Women and the Law of Property in Early America.* Chapel Hill: University of North Carolina Press, 1986.

Schama, Simon. *The Embarrassment of Riches: An Interpretation of Dutch Culture in the Golden Age.* New York: Knopf, 1987.

Schoonmaker, Marius. *The History of Kingston New York. From its Early Settlement to the Year 1820.* New York: Burr Printing House, 1888.

Shammas, Carole, Marylynn Salmon, and Michel Dahlin. *Inheritance in America from Colonial Times to the Present.* New Brunswick, NJ: Rutgers University Press, 1987.

Shepherd, William R. *Historical Atlas.* New York: Henry Holt and Company, 1911.

Shultz, Nancy Lusignan. *Fire & Roses: The Burning of the Charlestown Convent, 1834.* New York: The Free Press, 2000.

Smith, Rogers. *Conflicting Visions of Citizenship in U.S. History.* New Haven, CT: Yale University Press, 1997.

Smolenski, John. *Friends and Strangers: The Making of a Creole Culture in Colonial Pennsylvania.* Philadelphia: University of Pennsylvania Press, 2010.

Solomon, Barbara Miller. *Ancestors and Immigrants: A Changing New England Tradition.* Chicago, IL: University of Chicago Press, 1956.

Stevens, John R. *Dutch Vernacular Architecture in North America: 1640–1830.* West Hurley, NY: The Society for the Preservation of Hudson Valley Vernacular Architecture, 2005.

Stott, Annette. *Holland Mania: The Unknown Dutch Period in American Art and Culture.* Woodstock, NY: Overlook Press, 1998.

Stoye, John. *English Travellers Abroad, 1604–1667: Their Influence in English Society and Politics*, rev. ed. New Haven, CT: Yale University Press, 1989.

Sylvester, Nathaniel B. *History of Ulster County.* Albany, NY: Everts & Peck, 1880.

Tanis, James. *Dutch Calvinistic Pietism in the Middle Colonies: A Study in the Life and Theology of Theodorus Jacobus Frelinghuysen.* The Hague, The Netherlands: Martinus Nijhoff, 1967.

Van Buren, Augustus H. *A History of Ulster County Under the Dominion of the Dutch.* Kingston, NY: n.p., 1923.

Van Deursen, A. T. *Plain Lives in a Golden Age: Popular Culture, Religion and Society in Seventeenth-Century Holland.* Translated by Maarten Ultee. Cambridge, UK: Cambridge University Press, 1991.

Van Strien, C. D. *British Travellers in Holland During the Stuart Period.* Leiden, The Netherlands: E. J. Brill, 1993.

van Zanden, Jan Luiten. *The Rise and Decline of Holland's Economy: Merchant Capitalism and the Labour Market.* Manchester: Manchester University Press, 1993.

van Zandt, Roland, ed. *Chronicles of the Hudson: Three Centuries of Travelers' Accounts.* New Brunswick, NJ: Rutgers University Press, 1971.

Venema, Janny. *Beverwijck: A Dutch Village on the American Frontier, 1652–1664.* Helversum, The Netherlands: Veloren, 2003.

Wermuth, Thomas S. *Rip Van Winkle's Neighbors: The Transformation of*

Rural Society in the Hudson River Valley, 1720–1850. Albany: State University of New York Press, 2001.

White, Richard. *The Middle Ground: Indians, Empires, and Republics in the Great Lake Region, 1650–1815.* Cambridge, UK: Cambridge University Press, 1991.

Wynkoop, Richard. *Wynkoop Genealogy in the United States of America.* New York: Knickerbocker Press, 1904.

Published Secondary Sources: Articles and Book Chapters

Adelman, Jeremy and Stephen Aron. "From Borderlands to Borders: Empires, Nation-States, and the People in Between in North American History." *The American Historical Review* 104, no. 3 (June 1999): 814–841.

Adams, Bluford. "World Conquerors or a Dying People? Racial Theory, Regional Anxiety, and the Brahmin Anglo-Saxonists." *Journal of the Gilded Age and Progressive Era* 8, no. 2 (April 2009): 189–215.

Adams, Herbert Baxter. "The Germanic Origin of New England Towns." *Johns Hopkins University Studies in Historical and Political Science: Local Institutions* 1, no. 1 (1883): 5–38.

Ames, Kenneth. Introduction to *The Colonial Revival in America*, edited by Alan Axelrod, 1–14. New York: Norton, 1985.

Baron, Robert and Ana C. Cara. "Introduction: Creolization as Cultural Creativity." In *Creolization as Cultural Creativity*, edited by Robert Baron and Ana C. Cara, 3–19. Jackson: University of Mississippi Press, 2011.

Bieleman, Jan. "Dutch agriculture in the Golden Age, 1570–1660." In *The Dutch Economy in the Golden Age: Nine Studies*, edited by Karel Davids and Leo Noordegraaf, 159–185. Amsterdam, The Netherlands: Het Nederlandsch Economisch-Historisch Arcief, 1993.

Bishir, Catherine W. "Landmarks of Power: Building a Southern Past in Raleigh and Wilmington, North Carolina 1885–1915." In *Where These Memories Grow: History,Memory, and Southern Identity*, edited by W. Fitzhugh Brundage, 141–168. Chapel Hill: University of North Carolina Press, 2000.

Brink, Benjamin Myer. "The Coetus and Conferentie Controversy." *Olde Ulster: An Historical & Genealogical Magazine* (February 1905): 37–51.

Bosher, J. F. "Huguenot Merchants and the Protestant International in the Seventeenth Century." *The William and Mary Quarterly*, 3rd ser., 52, no. 1 (January 1995): 77–102.

Carr, Lois Green, and Lorena S. Walsh. "The Planter's Wife: The Experience of White Women in Seventeenth-Century Maryland." *William and Mary Quarterly*, 3rd ser., 34 (1977): 542–572.

"Catalogue of Loan Exhibition Under Auspices of Wiltwick Chapter D.A.R., Given in Honor of the Annual Meeting of the New York State Historical Association, September 12, 13 and 14, 1911, Kingston, N.Y." In *Proceedings of the New York State Historical Association* 5. N.p.: New York State Historical Association, 1911.

Clapham, J. H. "Charles Louis, Elector Palatine, 1617–1680: An

Early Experiment in Liberalism." *Economica*, n.s. 7, no. 28 (November, 1940).

Clark, Michael D. "More English than the English: Cavalier and Democrat in Virginia Historical Writing." *Journal of American Studies* 27, no. 2 (August 1993): 187–206.

Cohen, David Steven. "How Dutch Were the Dutch of New Netherland?" *New York History* 62, no. 1 (January 1981): 43–60.

Cummings, Abbott Lowell. "Inside the Massachusetts House." In *Readings in American Vernacular Architecture*, edited by Dell Upton and John Michael Vlach, 219–239. Athens: University of Georgia Press, 1986.

de Vries, Jan. "The Labor Market." In *The Dutch Economy in the Golden Age: Nine Studies*, edited by Karel Davids and Leo Noordegraaf, 56–78. Amsterdam, The Netherlands: Het Nederlandisch Economisch-Historisch Arcief, 1993.

Du Bois, Anson. "Address of the President." In *Bi-Centenary Reunion of the Descendants of Louis and Jacques Dubois (Emigrants to America, 1660 and 1675) at New Paltz, New York, 1875*, 11–15. Philadelphia, PA: Rue & Jones, 1876.

———. "The Life and Times of Louis Dubois." In *Bi-Centenary Reunion of the Descendants of Louis and Jacques Dubois (Emigrants to America, 1660 and 1675) at New Paltz, New York, 1875*, 44–71. Philadelphia, PA: Rue & Jones, 1876.

Du Bois, Cornelius. "Our History in Europe." In *Bi-Centenary Reunion of the Descendants of Louis and Jacques Dubois (Emigrants to America, 1660 and 1675) at New Paltz, New York, 1875*, 16–36. Philadelphia, PA: Rue & Jones, 1876.

Du Bois, Henry A. "The Family Surname." In *Bi-Centenary Reunion of the Descendants of Louis and Jacques Dubois (Emigrants to America, 1660 and 1675) at New Paltz, New York, 1875*, 38–44. Philadelphia, PA: Rue & Jones, 1876.

Du Bois, Robert Patterson. "Characteristics of the Family." In *Bi-Centenary Reunion of the Descendants of Louis and Jacques Dubois (Emigrants to America, 1660 and 1675) at New Paltz, New York, 1875*, 73–79. Philadelphia, PA: Rue & Jones, 1876.

Du Bois, William E., "Bringing the Tribe Together." In *Bi-Centenary Reunion of the Descendants of Louis and Jacques Dubois (Emigrants to America, 1660 and 1675) at New Paltz, NewYork, 1875*, 79–88. Philadelphia, PA: Rue & Jones, 1876.

Elting, Irving. "Dutch Village Communities on the Hudson River." *Johns Hopkins University Studies in Historical and Political Science: Municipal Government and Land Tenure* 4, no. 1 (1886): 5–68.

Eltinge, Edmund. "An Account of the Settlement of New Paltz by the Huguenots." *Collections of the Ulster Historical Society* 1, no. 1 (1860): 40–48.

Eriksen, Thomas Hylland. "Creolization in Anthropological Theory and in Mauritius." In *Creolization: History, Ethnography, Theory*, edited by Charles Stewart, 153–177. Walnut Creek, California: Left Coast Press, 2007.

Fabend, Firth Haring. "The Reformed Dutch Church and the Persistence of Dutchness in New York and New Jersey." In *Dutch New York: The Roots of Hudson Valley Culture*, edited by Roger Panetta, 137–158. New York: Hudson River Museum, Fordham University Press, 2009.

Faber, J.A. "The Decline of the Baltic Grain Trade in the Second Half of the Seventeenth Century." *Acta Historiae Neerlandica* 1 (1966): 108–131.

Freeman, Edward A. "An Introduction to American Institutional History." *Johns Hopkins University Studies in Historical and Political Science: Local Institutions* 1, no. 1 (1883): 5–39.

Gherke, Michael. "Toward a More Inclusive History of Early American Women: The Example of Married Women in New Netherland and New York in the Seventeenth Century." *The Hudson River Valley Review* 23, no. 2 (Spring 2007): 1–15.

Glassie, Henry. "Eighteenth-Century Cultural Process in Delaware Valley Folk Building." In *Readings in American Vernacular Architecture*, edited by Dell Upton and John Michael Vlach, 394–425. Athens: University of Georgia Press, 1986.

Goodfriend, Joyce D. "Archibald Laidlie and the Transformation of the Dutch Reformed Church in Eighteenth-Century New York City. *Journal of Presbyterian History* 81, no. 3 (Fall 2003): 149–162.

Hasbrouck, Abraham Bruyn, "Address." *Collections of the Ulster Historical Society* 1, no. 1 (1860): 25–39.

Hinke, William John. "A History of the Goshenhoppen Reformed Charge, Montgomery County, Pennsylvania (1727–1819)." In *A Narrative and Critical History Prepared at the Request of The Pennsylvania-German Society* 29, 96–111. Lancaster, PA: Pennsylvania-German Society, 1920.

———. "Life and Works of the Rev. Peter Henry Dorsius." In *Collection of Papers Read before the Bucks County Historical Society* 5 (1926): 44–53.

Hollister, Joan, and Sally M. Schultz. "The Elting and Hasbrouck store accounts: a window into eighteenth-century commerce." *Accounting History* 12, no. 4 (2007): 417–440.

Howard, Jane. "Can a Nice Novelist Finish First?" *Life*, November 4, 1966.

Howe, Adrian. "The Bayard Treason Trial: Dramatizing Anglo-Dutch Politics in Early Eighteenth-Century New York City." *The William and Mary Quarterly*: 3rd ser., 47, no. 1 (January 1990): 57–89.

Howell, Martha. "Rewriting Marriage in Late Medieval Douai," *Romanic Review* 86, no. 2 (March 1995): 307–337.

"The Huguenots of Ulster County, No. I," *The Christian Intelligencer* 16, no. 40 (April 16, 1846).

"The Huguenots of Ulster County, No. II," *The Christian Intelligencer* 16, no. 41 (April 23,1846).

"The Huguenots of Ulster County, No. III," *The Christian Intelligencer* 16, no. 42 (April 30, 1846).

"The Huguenots of Ulster County, No. IV," *The Christian Intelligencer* 16, no. 43 (May 7, 1846).

"The Huguenots of Ulster." *The Continental Monthly* 4, no. 1 (April 1862).

Israel, Jonathan. "Review." Review of *The Rise and Decline of Holland's Economy: Merchant Capitalism and the Labour Market*, by Jan Luiten van Zanden. *The English Historical Review* 3, no. 441 (April 1996): 458–459.

Kaplan, Wendy. "Traditions Transformed: Romantic Nationalism in Design, 1890–1920." In *Designing Modernity: The Arts of Reform and Persuasion 1885-1945*, edited by Wendy Kaplan, 19–47. New York: Thames & Hudson, 1995.

Kenny, Peter M. "Flat Gates, Draw Bars, Twists and Turns: New York's Distinctive Early Baroque Oval Tables with Falling Leaves." In *American Furniture*, edited by Luke Beckerdite, 107–136. Hanover, NH: Chipstone, 1994.

Kniffen, Fred B. "Folk Housing: Key to Diffusion." In *Readings in American Vernacular Architecture*, edited by Dell Upton and John Michael Vlach, 3–26. Athens: University of Georgia Press, 1986.

Larson, Neil. "Agrarian Changes: Learning from Barn Additions." *Dutch Barn Preservation Society Newsletter* 1, no. 2 (Fall 1998).

———. "Building a Stone House in Ulster County, New York in 1751." *Newsletter of the Society for the Preservation of Hudson Valley Vernacular Architecture* 15, no. 4–6 (April–June 2011): 5–11.

———. "An Inventory of Dutch Barns in the Town of New Paltz in 1798." *Newsletter of the Dutch Barn Preservation Society* 10, no. 1 (Spring 1997).

Ladurie, Emmanuel Le Roy. "A System of Customary Law: Family Structures and Inheritance Customs in 16th-Century France." In *Family and Society: Selections from the Annales Economies, Sociétiés, Civilisations*, edited by Robert Forster and Orest Ranum, translated by Elborg Forster and Patricia M. Ranum, 75–103. Baltimore, MD: Johns Hopkins University Press, 1976.

Lefever, Elizabeth. "Story of the rescue of Catherine Dubois from the Indians and the Settlement of New Paltz, New York." *Daughters of the American Revolution Magazine* (October 1914): 210–212.

Lefevre, Ralph. "The Huguenots—The First Settlers in the Province of New York." *The Quarterly Journal of the New York Historical Association* 2, no. 1 (January 1921): 177–185.

Lindblad, J. Thomas. "Foreign Trade of the Dutch Republic in the Seventeenth Century." In *The Dutch Economy in the Golden Age: Nine Studies*, edited by Karel Davids and Leo Noordegraaf, 219–249. Amsterdam, the Netherlands: Het Nederlandsch Economisch-Historisch Archief, 1993.

Lindgren, James M. "'For the Sake of our Future': The Association for the Preservation of Virginia Antiquities and the Regeneration of Traditionalism." *The Virginia Magazine of History and Biography* 97, no. 1 (January 1989): 47–74.

Louw, H. J. "The origin of the sash-window." *Architectural History* 26 (1983): 47–72, 144–150.

Matson, Cathy. "'Damned Scoundrels' and 'Libertisme of Trade': Freedom and Regulation in Colonial New York's Fur and Grain Trade." *The William and Mary Quarterly*, 3rd ser.,51, no. 3 (July 1994): 389–418.

Murrin, John M. "English Rights as Ethnic Aggression: The English Conquest, the Charter of Liberties of 1683, and Leisler's Rebellin New York." In *Authority and Resistance in Early New York*, edited by William Pencak and Conrad Edick Wright, 56–94. New York: New-York Historical Society, 1988.

Narrett, David. "Dutch Customs of Inheritance, Women, and the Law in Colonial New York City." In *Authority and Resistance in Early New York*, edited by William Pencak and Conrad Edick Wright, 27–55. New York: New-York Historical Society, 1988.

———. "Men's Wills and Women's Property Rights in Colonial New York." In *Women in the Age of the American Revolution*, edited by Ronald Hoffmann and Peter J. Albert, 91–133. Charlottesville: University of Virginia, 1989.

Noordegraaf, Leo. "Dutch Industry in the Golden Age." In *The Dutch Economy in the Golden Age: Nine Studies*, edited by Karel Davids and Leo Noordegraaf, 131–157. Amsterdam, The Netherlands: Het Nederlandsch Economisch-Historisch Archief, 1993.

Noordegraaf, Leo, and Jan Luiten van Zanden. "Early modern economic growth and the standard of living: did labour benefit from Holland's Golden Age?" In *A Miracle Mirrored, The Dutch Republic in European Perspective*, edited by Karel Davids and Jan Lucassen, 410–437. Cambridge, UK: Cambridge University Press, 1995.

Parmenter, Jon. "Onenwahatirighi Sa Gentho Skaghnughtudigh": Reassessing Haudenosaunee Relations with the Albany Commissions of Indian Affairs, 1723–1755." In *English Atlantics Revisited: Essays Honouring Professor Ian K. Steele*, edited by Nancy Rhoden, 235–283. Montreal, QC: McGill-Queens University Press, 2007.

Paul, André. "Les Réfugiés Huguenots et Wallons dans le Palatinat du Rhin du XVIe Siècle a la Révolution." *Revue Historique* 157, fasc. 2 (1928).

Pestana, Carla Gardina. "Cruelty and Religious Justifications for Conquest in the Mid-Seventeenth-Century English Atlantic." In *Empires of God: Religious Encounters in the Early Modern Atlantic*, edited by Linda Gregerson and Susan Juster, 37–57. Philadelphia: University of Pennsylvania Press, 2011.

Pincus, Steven C. A. "From Butterboxes to Wooden Shoes: The Shift in English Popular Sentiment from Anti-Dutch to Anti-French in the 1670s." *The Historical Journal*, 38, no. 2 (June 1995): 333–361.

Prudon, Theodore H. J. "The Dutch Barn in America: Survival of a Medieval Structural Frame." In *Readings in American Vernacular Architectures*, edited by Dell Upton and John Michael Vlach, 204–218. Athens: University of Georgia, 1986.

Roberts, Benjamin Roberts. "Unraveling Frijenmoet: An Adolescent Dutch Reformed Minister in Colonial New Jersey." *de Halve Maen* 75, no. 2 (Winter 2002): 69–76.

Roth, Eric J. "Being Poor in New Paltz." *de Halve Maen* 79, no. 1 (Spring 2006).

———. "'The Society of Negroes Unsettled': A History of Slavery in New Paltz, NY." *Afro-Americans in New York Life and History* 27 no. 1 (January 2003): 27–54.

———. "'where ye walloens dwell': Rethinking the Ethnic Identity of the Huguenots of New Paltz and Ulster County, New York." In *New York History* 89, no. 4 (Fall 2008) 347–373.

Ryan, Thomas R. "Cultural Accommodations in the Late-Eighteenth-Century Architecture of Marbletown, New York." *Perspectives in Vernacular Architecture: Shaping Communities* 6 (1997): 137–149.

———. "Revisioning the Ulster County Cultural Landscape From the 1798 Federal Direct Tax." In "Newsletter," *Society for the Preservation of Hudson Valley Vernacular Architecture* 15, no. 4–6 (April/May/June 2012): 3–14.

Saveth, Edward Norman. "Race and Nationalism in American Historiography: The Late Nineteenth Century." *Political Science Quarterly* 54, no. 3 (September 1939): 421–441.

Sawyer, Sean E. "Constructing the Tradition of Dutch American Architecture, 1609–2009." In *Dutch New York: The Roots of Hudson Valley Culture*, edited by Roger Panetta, 93–136. New York: Fordham University Press, 2009.

Schultz, Sally M., and Joan Hollister. "Single-Entry Accounting in Early America: The Accounts of the Hasbrouck Family." *Accounting Historians Journal* 31, no. 1 (June 2004): 141–174.

Shefsiek, Kenneth. "Governing New Paltz: Scholarship and the commemoration of colonial New York ethnic heterogeneity." *New York History* 91, no. 3 (Fall 2010): 295–314.

———. "'Make an end of my misery': Rev. Johannes Henricus Goetschius and the negotiation of authority in Eighteenth-Century Dutch New York." *de Halve Maen* 88, no. 2 (Summer 2015): 27–34.

———. "A Suspected Loyalist in the Rural Hudson Valley: The Revolutionary War Experience of Roeloff Josiah Eltinge," *The Hudson River Valley Review* 20, no. 1, (Summer 2003): 27–51.

Sinclair, Peter, ed. "Newsletter." *Society for the Preservation of Hudson Valley Vernacular Architecture* (November 1999).

———, ed. "Newsletter." *Society for the Preservation of Hudson Valley Vernacular Architecture* (September 2000).

———, ed. "Newsletter." *Society for the Preservation of Hudson Valley Vernacular Architecture* (March 2002).

———, ed. "Newsletter." *Society for the Preservation of Hudson Valley Vernacular Architecture* (June 2002).

———, ed. "Newsletter." *Society for the Preservation of Hudson Valley Vernacular Architecture* (May 2004).

———, ed. "Newsletter." *Society for the Preservation of Hudson Valley Vernacular Architecture* (June 2004).

———, ed. "Newsletter." *Society for the Preservation of Hudson Valley Vernacular Architecture* (July 2004).

———, ed. "Newsletter." *Society for the Preservation of Hudson Valley Vernacular Architecture* (September 2004).

———, ed. "Newsletter." *Society for the Preservation of Hudson Valley Vernacular Architecture* (June 2005).

———, ed. "Newsletter." *Society for the Preservation of Hudson Valley Vernacular Architecture* (November 2005).

———, ed. "Newsletter." *Society for the Preservation of Hudson Valley Vernacular Architecture* 8, no. 5 (May 2006).

———, ed. "Newsletter." *Society for the Preservation of Hudson Valley Vernacular Architecture* 8, no 7 (July 2006).

———, ed. "Newsletter." *Society for the Preservation of Hudson Valley Vernacular Architecture* 8, no. 8 (August 2006).

———, ed. "Newsletter." *Society for the Preservation of Hudson Valley Vernacular Architecture* 8, no. 9 (September 2006).

———, ed. "Newsletter," *Society for the Preservation of Hudson Valley Vernacular Architecture* 9, no. 6–7 (June/July 2007).

Stevens, John R. "Christian and Marytje Deyo house: 374 Springtown Road, New Paltz, Ulster Co., New York." *Society for the Preservation of Hudson Valley Vernacular Architecture* 14, no. 1–3 (January–March 2011): 3–4.

———. "DuBois House," in "Newsletter," *Society for the Preservation of Hudson Valley Vernacular Architecture* 12, no. 8–10 (August–October 2009): 10–12.

———. "Gable-fronted Dutch-American houses" in "Newsletter," *Society for the Preservation of Hudson Valley Vernacular Architecture* 9, no. 6–7 (June/July 2007): 7.

———. "Report on a trip to the Netherlands and Germany," in "Newsletter," *Society for the Preservation of Hudson Valley Vernacular Architecture* (October 2000).

Stewart, Charles. "Creolization: History, Ethnography, Theory." In *Creolization: History, Ethnography, Theory*, edited by Charles Stewart, 1–25. Walnut Creek, California: Left Coast Press, 2007.

Stitt, Charles H. "History of the Huguenot Church and Settlement at New Paltz." *Collections of The Ulster County Historical Society* 1, no. 3 (1862): 184–209.

Upton, Dell Upton. "Vernacular Domestic Architecture in Eighteenth-Century Virginia."In *Readings in American Vernacular Architecture*, edited by Dell Upton and John Michael Vlach, 315–336. Athens: University of Georgia, 1986.

Van Ruymbeke, Bertrand. "The Walloon and Huguenot Elements in New Netherland and Seventeenth-Century New York: Identity, History and Memory." In *Revisiting New Netherland: Perspectives on Early Dutch America*, edited by Joyce D. Goodfriend, 41–56. Leiden, The Netherlands: Brill, 2005.

Van Slyke, J. G. "The Huguenots of Ulster County." *Proceedings of the Huguenot Society of America* 2 (1891): 224–236.

van Zandern, Jan Luiten. "Did Holland's Golden Age Breed Inequality?" In *Income and wealth inequality in the Netherlands, 16th–20th century*, edited by Lee Soltow and Jan Luiten van Zanden, 23–54. Amsterdam, The Netherlands: Het Spinhuis, 1998.

Varga, Nicholas. "The Development and Structure of Local Government in

Colonial New York." In *Town and Country: Essays on the Structure of Local Government in the American Colonies*, edited by Bruce Daniels, 186–215. Middletown, CT: Wesleyan University Press, 1978.

Voorhees, David William. "In the Republic's Tradition: The Persistence of Dutch Culture in the Mid-Atlantic Colonies after the 1664 English Conquest." *de Halve Maen* 74, no. 3 (Fall 2001): 49–54.

Wermuth, Thomas S. "New York Farmers and the Market Revolution: Economic Behavior in the Mid-Hudson Valley, 1780–1830." *Journal of Social History* 32, no. 1 (Autumn 1998): 179–196.

———. "Rural Elites in the Commercial Development of New York: 1780–1840." *Business and Economic History* 23, no. 1 (Fall 1994): 71–80.

Wheeler, Robert G. "The Albany of Magdalena Douw." *Winterthur Portfolio* 4 (1968): 63–74.

Wheeler, Walter Richard. "Dating Buildings Using Dendrochronology." *Dutch Barn Preservation Newsletter* 17, no. 2 (Fall 2004).

Zacharasiewicz, Waldemar. "National Stereotypes in Literature in the English Language: A Review of Research." *REAL: The Yearbook of Research in English and American Literature* 1 (1982): 75–120.

Zantkuyl, Henk D. "The New Netherlands Town House." In *New World Dutch Studies: Dutch Arts and Culture in Colonial America, 1609–1776*, edited by Roderic H. Blackburn and Nancy A. Kelley, 143–160. Albany, NY: Albany Institute of History and Art, 1987.

Zink, Clifford W. "Dutch Framed Houses in New York and New Jersey." *Winterthur Portfolio* 22, no. 4 (Winter 1987): 265–294.

Unpublished Secondary Sources: Articles, Dissertations, and Reports

Barricklo, Kenneth Hewes, and Neil Larson & Associates. "Historic Structure Report: The Abraham Hasbrouck House at the Huguenot Historical Society, New Paltz, NY." Unpublished report for the Huguenot Historical Society, 2003.

Bonfide, John A. "National Register of Historic Places Registration Form: The Locusts." Prepared June 1996.

"William Henry Brewer Papers," at the New York Botanical Garden. Accessed November 1, 2013. http://library.nybg.org/finding_guide/archv/brewer_ppb.html.

Bucher, Douglas for John G. Waite Associates. "Historic Furnishings Plan for Locust Lawn." Unpublished report for the Huguenot Historical Society, 2003.

Campbell, John. "The Walloon Community in Canterbury, 1625–1649. PhD diss., University of Wisconsin, 1970.

Carlo, Paula Wheeler. "The Huguenots of Colonial New Paltz and New Rochelle: A Social and Religious History." PhD diss., City University of New York, 2001.

Coddington Genealogy. http://freepages.genealogy.rootsweb.ancestrycom/~coddingtons.

Cook, Edward R., and William J. Callahan. "Dendrochronological Analysis of the Abraham & Maria LeFevre House, Gardiner, Ulster County, New York." Unpublished report for the owners, February 2006.

———. "Dendrochronological Analysis of the Bevier-Elting House, New Paltz, New York." Unpublished report for the Huguenot Historical Society, 2004.

———. "Dendrochronological Analysis of the Freer-Low House, New Paltz, New York." Unpublished report for the Huguenot Historical Society, 2008.

Cook, Edward R., Paul J. Krusic, and William J. Callahan. "Tree-Ring Dating of the Abraham Hasbrouck House in New Paltz, New York." Unpublished report for the Huguenot Historical Society, 2003.

Crawford & Stearns and Neil Larson. "Historic Structure Report for the Evert Terwilliger House." Unpublished report for the Huguenot Historical Society, 2005.

Gehring, Charles. "The Dutch Language in Colonial New York: An Investigation of a Language in Decline and its Relationship to Social Change." PhD diss., Indiana University, 1973.

Gherke, Michael E. "Dutch Women in New Netherland and New York in the Seventeenth Century." PhD diss., West Virginia University, 2001.

Heidgerd, Ruth P. "The Blanchans." Unpublished manuscript, c. 1970s (available at Huguenot Historical Society library, New Paltz, NY.)

Heidgerd, Ruth P., and William Heidgerd. "The Goetshy Family: European Notes, By Ruth & William Heidgerd on their trip to Salez Switzerland, 1968." Accessed May 19, 2014. http://www.goetchius.com/limpingmessenger.htm.

Hennessey, Colleen, and Rachael Cristine Woody. "A Finding Aid to The Charles Lang Freer papers at the Freer Gallery of Art and Arthur M. Sackler Gallery Archives." Freer Gallery of Art and Arthur M. Sackler Gallery, 2002.

Larson, Neil. "National Register of Historic Places Registration Form: Abraham & Maria LeFevre House." Prepared May 12, 2006.

Neil Larson and Associates. "Furnishing Plan for the Jean [Jacob] Hasbrouck House, New Paltz, Ulster County, New York." Unpublished report for the Huguenot Historical Society, 2004.

Larson Fisher Associates and Ted Bartlett, for Crawford & Stearns. "Historic Structure Report for the Freer-Louw House." Unpublished report for the Huguenot Historical Society, 2011.

Larson Fisher Associates and Crawford & Stearns. "Historic Structure Report for the Ezekiel Elting House." Unpublished report for the Huguenot Historical Society, 2007.

———. "Historic Structure Report for the Jean Hasbrouck House." Unpublished report for the Huguenot Historical Society, 2007.

Luekhurst, Charlotte Taylor, transcriber. "Marriage Records of the Reformed Protestant Dutch Church of Schenectady, N.Y." 1917.

Mouw, Dirk. "Moederkerk and Vaderland: Religion and Ethnic Identity in the Middle Colonies, 1690–1772." PhD diss., University of Iowa, 2009.

Naborn, Robert Arnoud. "Eilardus Westerlo (1738–1790): From Colonial *Dominee* to American *Pastor*." Academisch Proefschrift, Vrije Universiteit, 2011.

Riddle, John. "Guide to the David D. Demarest Letters, 1837–1850." Special Collections and University Archives, Rutgers University Libraries. October 1997.

Roth, Eric J. "From Protestant International to Hudson Valley Provincial: A case study of language use and ethnicity in New Paltz, New York, 1678–1834." Unpublished paper for the Huguenot Historical Society, 2004.

———. "The Walloons of Ulster County, NY: Forging an Ethnic Identity in Colonial America." Unpublished paper for the Huguenot Historical Society, 2007.

Shattuck, Martha Dickinson. "A Civil Society: Court and Community in Beverwijck, New Netherland, 1652–1664." PhD diss., Boston University, 1993.

Shaw, Susan Elizabeth. "Building New Netherland: Gender and Family Ties in a Frontier Society." PhD diss., Cornell University, 2000.

Shefsiek, Kenneth. "Another House on Huguenot Street: The Discovery of the Dubois-Elting House." Unpublished paper for the Huguenot Historical Society, 2002.

Toole, Robert M., Neil Larson, and Arthur Jay Hibbs. "Historic Landscape Report and Landscape Master Planning for Locust Lawn." Unpublished report for the Huguenot Historical Society, 2002.

van den Hurk, Jeroen. "Imagining New Netherland: Origins and Survival of Netherlandic Architecture in Old New York." PhD diss., University of Delaware, 2006.

Van Zweiten, Adriana E. "'A little land . . . to sow some seeds': Real Property, Custom, and Law in the Community of New Amsterdam." PhD diss., Temple University, 2001.

John G. Waite Associates. "Dubois Fort: Historic Structure Report." Unpublished report for the Huguenot Historical Society, 2002.

Wenger, Mark. "The Jean Hasbrouck House: A Social and Architectural Study." Unpublished report for the Huguenot Historical Society, 2004.

INDEX

Note: Page numbers in italics indicate illustrations; those with a *t* indicate tables.

Adams, Henry, 178
Adams, Herbert Baxter, 178–179, 194
Aix-la-Chapelle, Treaty of (1668), 19
Allen, Matthew, 235n34
Alva, Duke of, 18
American Revolution, 262n2
Andros, Edmund, 1, 17, 23, 26, 118
Anglo-American architecture, 1, 7, 163, 164, 173, *174*, 248n40; Georgian style of, *85*, 85–87, *86*, 93, 96–99, 101, 106–111, *107*, 245n20
Anglo-American culture, 11, 15–16; exceptionalist myth of, 176–177, 181–182
Antonides, Vincentius, 145, 148
Appleton, William Sumner, 210
Arondeus, Johannes, 148, 257n18
Articles of Capitulation (1664), 37, 42
Auchmoody, Christian, 32
Auchmoody, Daniel, 32
Auchmoody, Jacobus, 158t
Auchmoody, James, 32
Auchmoody, Maria Deyo (James's wife), 32

Balmer, Randall, 8, 142, 143, 148
Bancroft, George, 177
barns, *68*, 68–70, *69*, 111–115, *112*, 249nn48–50
Baumfree family, 135
Bayard, William, 166
Beekman, Cornelius, 132
Benjamin, Asher, 108
Berry, Mary DuBois, 172
Beveridge, Albert, 178
Bevier family, 20, 22, 266n25
Bevier, Abraham, 59
Bevier, Abraham Garrett, 183–184
Bevier, Andries, 45
Bevier, Elizabeth Hasbrouck (Louis II's wife), 44–46, 120, 236n35
Bevier, Jacobus, 60–61
Bevier, Johannes Hornbeck, 182, 265n21
Bevier, Louis (the elder, father of Louis the patentee), 20
Bevier, Louis (patentee, ca. 1647–1720), 20–22, 29, 130–131, 130t, 188; wills of, 44–45, 58–59, 61
Bevier, Louis II (son of Louis the patentee, 1684–1753), 120
Bevier, Louis III (son of Louis II, 1717–1772), 93, 133, 162
Bevier, Margrietje Eltinge (Abraham's wife), 52
Bevier, Marie LeBlanc (wife of Louis the patentee), 20, 22
Bevier, Samuel, 150; house of, 76–81, *77–79*, 205; will of, 58, 59

Bevier, Tryntje Low (Philip's wife), 133
Bill of Rights, 178
binnenhaard ("inner hearth"), *67*, 67–68, 70, 243n7
Bissell, George Edward, 204
Blanchan, Magdelaine Joire (Matthieu's wife), 19–21
Blanchan, Matthew, Jr., 185
Blanchan, Matthieu, 19–21, 23–24, 23t, 226n5
Bodine, Isaac, 236n35
Boel, Henricus, 145
Bogardus, William R., 123
Bosher, J. F., 24
Brewer, William Henry, 266n27
Broadhead, Abraham Deyo, 173
Bruyn, Catharine, 255n30
business records, 129–133, 130t, 132t
Butler, Jon, 6

Carlo, Paula Wheeler, 6–7, 143, 146, 149, 224n10
churches. *See* First Church of New Paltz *and* Second Church of New Paltz
civil liberties, 176–184, 191, 197–198, 201–202, 213
Civil War (U.S.), 180
Classis of Amsterdam, 8, 126, 141–142, 153; J. H. Goetschius and, 147–149, 151; J. M. Goetschius and, 155; Johannes van Driessen and, 144–145, 151
Clearwater, Alphonso T., 217, 220–221
Clinton, George, 167
Coddington, Catherine van der Marken (Joseph's wife), 125
Coddington, Joseph, 32, 125, 252n15
Coetus-Conferentie dispute, 8, 15, 126, 141–143, 150–154; Dutch culture and, 159–161, 167; English culture and, 162–165; schism caused by, 141–142, 155–159, 158t, 259n41
Cohen, David Steven, 9, 10
Cole, Eliazer, 236n34
Colonial Revival movement, 210
Columbia University, 154
commemoration projects, 204–211
Congregationalists, 144, 145
Consalis, Emmanuel, 232n25
Coolson, Israel, 235n34
Cottin, Jean, 54, 124, 252n12
Crispell family, 20, 22
Crispell, Antoine, 20, 23, 23t; birthplace of, 227n7; marriage of, 20; will of, 44, 61
Crispell, C. Elting, 202, 270n7
Crispell, Elizabeth (Antoine's daughter), 44
Crispell, Jan (Antoine's son), 44
Crispell, Jannetje (Antoine's daughter), 44
Crispell, Maria Blanchan (Antoine's wife), 20, 185
Cruger, Henry, 166

Daillé, Pierre, 25, 120, 143–144
Dankers, Jasper, 71
Darwin, Charles, 178
Daughters of the American Revolution, 210, 271n23
de Bonrepos, David, 25, 120, 144
Decker, Catherine, 170
Decker, Cornelius, 129
DeLancey, Oliver, 166
Demarest, David D., 203
Depuy, Moses, 133
Devolution, War of, 19
Deyo, Abraham I (1676–1725), 49, 120–122; house of, 173, *174*
Deyo, Abraham II (1710–1777), 131–132, 132t
Deyo, Abraham III (1734-1766), 131–132, 132t
Deyo, Abraham D., 89
Deyo, Agatha Nickol (Pierre's wife), 23t

Deyo, Christian (patentee), 22, 23t; wife of, 21; will of, 44, 57, 60
Deyo, Christian (Pierre's son), 44
Deyo, Cristoffel, house of, 102, *103*
Deyo, Daniel, house of, *88*, 245n23
Deyo, Elizabeth Helm (Peter's wife), 51
Deyo, Elsie Clearwater (Abraham I's wife), 49
Deyo, Frederick, house of, *100*, 100–101
Deyo, Hendricus, 46, 47, 57
Deyo, Jannetje Wibau (wife of Christian the patentee), 21, 23t
Deyo, John, 204
Deyo, Levi, 60
Deyo, Margriste vanBommel (Hendricus's wife), 46
Deyo, Marie, 121
Deyo, Mary, 221
Deyo, Nathaniel, 89
Deyo, Peter, 51, 60
Deyo, Philip, 125
Deyo, Pierre, 22, 23t, 29, 60, 130t, 187
Deyo, William, 132
Deyo House (Benjamin's?), 80, *81*
Diamond, Joseph, 244n10
Donaldson, Abraham, 32, 235n31
Dorsius, Petrus Hendricus, 147–149, 155, 257nn17–20
dower rights, 40–41, 46–52. *See also* property rights
DuBois family, 20–22; Second Church of New Paltz and, 158t, 159, 168
DuBois, Abraham (patentee), 21, 23t; Duzine and, 27; house of, 73, 169; New Jersey lands of, 24
DuBois, Abraham, Jr., 61
DuBois, Anne Hue (wife of Philip), 158t
Du Bois, Anson, 175, 192, 194, 196–201, 212–214, 218–220, 269n3
DuBois, Catharyntie LeFevre (Simon's wife), 49
DuBois, Catherine Blanchan (wife of Louis), 20, 21, 23t, 29, 185–187, 189, 190; will of, 41–42, 54
Du Bois, Charles, 188
DuBois, Cornelia, 3–4, 262n2
DuBois, Cornelius, 193
DuBois, Cornelius (1707–1781), 60, 133
DuBois, Cornelius, Jr. (1750–1834), 60
DuBois, Daniel (1684–1752), 131; marriage of, 57–58, 61, 127
DuBois, Daniel, Jr. (Daniel's grandson, b. 1750), 132
DuBois, Diana, 158t
DuBois, Gualtherus, 145, 148, 257n17
DuBois, Hendricus, Jr. (1743–1784), 58, 158t, 159, 161, 165–166
DuBois, Hendricus, Sr. (1710–1780), 159–161, 165; Bible of, 128; house of, 83, 161, 245n19; offices held by, 164; Second Church of New Paltz and, 141, 156–159, 158t, 168; will of, 47, 52, 55, 59, 159
DuBois, Henry, 48
DuBois, Henry A., 193
DuBois, Isaac, 21, 23, 45, 55
DuBois, Jacob, 158t
DuBois, Jacques, 192–193
DuBois, Jannetje Houghtaling (Hendricus Sr.'s wife), 55, 128, 158t, 159, 161
DuBois, John Coert, 212
DuBois, Jonathan, 49, 61
DuBois, Josiah, 94
DuBois, Lanetta Elting, 173
DuBois, Leah, 158t
DuBois, Louis, 23t, 118, 185–189,

192–193; birthplace of, 227n7; wife of, 20, 21, 29; will of, 41–44, 53, 54
DuBois, Margaret Deyo (wife of Abraham the patentee), 22, 23t, 56, 62; inheritance of, 51, 52
DuBois, Maria (Mary) Hasbrouck (Isaac's wife), 45–46, 55; house of (DuBois Fort), *73*, 73–76, *74*, 102, *104*, 205, 244n13, 262n2
DuBois, Maria LeFevre (wife of Isaac's son Daniel), 47
DuBois, Methusalem, 55, 159
DuBois, Peter, 216
DuBois, Philip (Hendricus Sr.'s son, b. 1734), 158t
DuBois, Philip (Isaac's son, 1689–1764), 133, 251n9
DuBois, Rachel, 158t
DuBois, Rebecca Van Wagenen (Hendricus Jr.'s wife), 55, 62, 240n33
DuBois, R. G., 214
Du Bois, Robert Patterson, 175, 188, 193–194, 202–203, 214
DuBois, Simon, 131, 132t; will of, 49, 58
DuBois, Solomon, 133, 134, 158t; will of, 59, 241n39
DuBois, Tryntje Gerritson (Solomon's wife), 158t
Du Bois, William Ewing, 188, 207, 208, 210
DuBois Fort. *See under* DuBois, Maria Hasbrouck
Duke's Laws, 26, 228n17
Dutch-American architecture, 1, 7, 161, 163–164
Dutch-American culture, 16, 175–176; Anglo-Saxon exceptionalism and, 181–198; preservation of, 159–161
Dutch Reformed Church, 4, 182; after Great Awakening, 8, 120; ordination in, 145, 147–149, 257n17; Walloon Reformed Church of New Paltz and, 141–152. *See also* Coetus-Conferentie dispute
Duzine (Twelve Men), 3, 5, 118, 196–197; creation of, 27–28, 197, 231n22; Anson Du Bois on, 213; Frank Hasbrouck on, 201–202; Ralph LeFevre on, 200, 201

Ean, Abraham, 128
Ean, Caty Van Wagenen (Jan's wife), 122, 129
Ean, Elias, 31, 233n29
Ean, Jan, 122, 128
Ean, Lysbeth Crispell (Elias's wife), 31, 56
Edict of Nantes, 200; Revocation of, 2, 5, 25, 183, 201
Elizabeth I, English queen, 17–18
Elsworth, William, 236n34
Elting, Irving, 175, 194–199, 201; commemoration projects of, 205, 206, 212, 215
Elting, Jan, 217
Elting, Jesse, 172–173, 205
Eltinge family, 158t, 159, 205
Eltinge, Abraham, 158t
Eltinge, Annetjen, 158t
Eltinge, Catharyntje, 158t, 160
Eltinge, Cornelius, 158t
Eltinge, Edmund, 190–192, 199; commemoration projects of, 204–206, 210–211, 214, 215
Eltinge, Ezekiel, 161; house of, 73, 106–108, *107*, 248n41
Eltinge, Jacomyntje (Noah's wife), 48, 158t
Eltinge, Jannetje LeSueur (William's wife), 158t
Eltinge, Josiah, 128, 134, 158t, 160, 261n54; house of, 173; languages of, 161; as moneylender, 166, 261n57; offices held by, 164; will of, 51, 160

Eltinge, Josiah R. (Roelof Josiah's son), 73, 112
Eltinge, Magdalena DuBois (Josiah's wife), 51, 128, 158t, 160
Eltinge, Maria Low (Roelof Josiah's wife), 56–57, 158t
Eltinge, Noah, 51, 158t, 160, 161, 164, 261n54; will of, 47–48, 58
Eltinge, Peter, *108*
Eltinge, Roelof, 51, 158t, 212
Eltinge, Roelof Josiah, 56, 134, 158t, 261n57; house of, 93–94, 108. *See also* Bevier, Samuel, house of
Eltinge, Sara DuBois (Roelof's wife), 43–44, 158t, 212
Eltinge, Solomon, 134, 158t, 161
Eltinge, William, 158t
English law, 25–27; inheritance rights in, 27, 39–46, 49–50
Esopus Indians, 17, 23, 118; war with, 185–187, 189, 190, 217, 266n27

Fabend, Firth Haring, 8–9, 143
feme covert status, 39, 160, 237n5
fireplaces, *94*, 97, *98*, *99*; jambless, *92*, 93, 96, 163, 246n28
First Church of New Paltz, 24–25, 141, 143–152, 155–159, 258n21, 258n25; baptisms in 30–31, 232n26; membership of 31, 151–152, 233n27; church offices in, 31, 233n28. *See also* Coetus-Conferentie dispute
Frederick III, elector of Die Pfalz, 20
Frederick IV, elector of Die Pfalz, 20
Frederickson, George, 180–181
Freeman, Edward, 178, 179, 194, 195
Freer, Agetta (Johannis's wife), 51
Freer, Charles, 202
Freer, Charles Lang, 211, 270n7
Freer, Hugo (patentee), 21, 22, 23t, 24, 44
Freer, Hugo, Sr. (son of Hugo the patentee), 61, 130t, 131; will of, 48, 58
Freer, Jannetje Wibau (wife of Hugo the patentee), 21, 22, 23t
Freer, Johannes (Johannis), 51, 132t
Freer, Jonas, 156
Freer-Louw House, 71, 88–89, *89*, 94, 169
Freerman, Bernardus, 147
Frelinghuysen, Theodorus, Jr., 155
Frelinghuysen, Theodorus, Sr., 147, 153, 154
Fryenmoet, Johannes Casparus, 122–123, 150, 257n18

gender issues, 202–203; property rights and, 15, 37–53, 159–164; racial theories and, 212, 215
Georgian architecture, *85*, 85–87, *86*, 93, 96–99, 101, 106–111, *107*, 245n20. *See also* Anglo-American architecture
German Reformed Church, 147, 155
Glassie, Henry, 248n42
Glorious Revolution (1688), 176
Goetschi, Moritz (1686–1735), 146–147
Goetschius, Elizabeth DuBois (Stephen's wife), 104
Goetschius, Johannes Henricus (1718–1774), 123, 143, 146–153, 157, 158, 257nn17–20, 258n25
Goetschius, Johannes Mauritius (1724–1771), 32, 123, 155–158
Goetschius, Stephen, 123, 126, 136; house of, 104, *105*
Goodfriend, Joyce D., 9, 10, 143

government, town, 25–27, 228n18–20; county, 26, 228n18–20; colony, 25–27, 228n18–19
Graham, Daniel, 31
Granger, Gideon, 108–109, *110*
Great Awakening, 8, 31, 142, 151–152
Gross, Samuel E., 214
Guilford Patent, 60, 134, 162, 242n41
Guimar, Esther, 251n9

Haefeli, Evan, 10
hallenhuis, 68, 111
Hamilton, Alexander, 190
Hardenbergh family, 135, 260n49
Hardenbergh, Annetje LeFevre (Charles's wife), 135, 136
Hardenbergh, Charles, 135, 136
Hardenbergh, Jacob Rutsen, 152, 155–156
Hardenbergh, Johannes, Jr. (Colonel), 135
Hardenbergh, Johannes, Sr. (Major), 135
Hardenbergh, Johannes III (d. 1799), 135
Hardenbergh, John A., 104–107, *106*
Hardenbergh, Maria DuBois (Johannes Jr.'s wife), 135
Hardenbergh, Maria LeFevre (Johannes III's wife), 135
Haring family, 9
Hasbrouck family, 21–22
Hasbrouck, Abraham (b. 1722), 124, 133
Hasbrouck, Abraham (Colonel, 1707–1791), 60, 117, 134, 162–164, 166–167
Hasbrouck, Abraham (patentee, ca. 1650–1717), 21–24, 23t, 29; birthplace of, 223n3, 227n9; wife of, 22, 56. *See also* Hasbrouck, Daniel, house of
Hasbrouck, Abraham Bruyn (1791–1879), 172, 174–176, 189–192, 200–201, 262n2
Hasbrouck, Anna Deyo (Jean's wife), 22, 23t
Hasbrouck, Benjamin, 51–52, 59, 125
Hasbrouck, Daniel, 150; house of, 71, 76–81, *77*, *78*, *80*, *92*, 93, 169; will of, 49, 59
Hasbrouck, Elsie Schoonmaker (Joseph's wife), 52, 117; inheritance of, 49, 54–55
Hasbrouck, Esther Bevier (Jacob Sr.'s wife), 45, 49, 52–53, 133
Hasbrouck, Frank, 201–202, 206, 215, 264n20
Hasbrouck, G. D. B., 202
Hasbrouck, Hylah Bevier (Levi's wife), 170–172, *173*
Hasbrouck, Jacob, Jr. (Major, 1728–1806), 128–129, 162; house of, *101*, 110–111, 163–164; will of, 50, 164
Hasbrouck, Jacob, Sr. (1688–1761), 124, 133; house of, 73, *82*, 82–87, *83*, *91–94*; wills of, 49, 52–53, 58, 60
Hasbrouck, Jacob J., 129
Hasbrouck, Jan, 50, 58, 60
Hasbrouck, Jannetje DuBois (Jacob Jr.'s wife), 50
Hasbrouck, Jean, 21, 22, 23t; birthplace of, 223n3, 227n9; books of, 120; house of, 2, 16, 71–73, 82, 170, 205–206, 209–218, *217*; will of, 45–46, 57. *See also* Hasbrouck, Jacob, Sr., house of
Hasbrouck, Joseph, 49, 116–117
Hasbrouck, Josiah, 128, 129; house of, 101, 108, *109*, 111, 164, 169, *171*
Hasbrouck, Kenneth E., Sr., 4–5
Hasbrouck, Levi, 170–172
Hasbrouck, Lydia (Benjamin's wife), 51–52

Hasbrouck, Maria Bevier (Isaac's wife), 94
Hasbrouck, Maria Deyo (wife of Abraham the patentee), 22, 23t, 54–56, 117
Hasbrouck, Rachel van Wagenen (Jan's wife), 50
Hasbrouck, Solomon, 56
Hasbrouck, Wyntje Deyo (Daniel's wife), 49, 54, 81, 121
Hasbrouck, Zacharias, 258n25
Hay, John, 178
Herder, Johann Gottfried von, 176–177
Holland Society, 212, 217, 264n20
Hosmer, James K., 178, 179
Howell, Martha, 37–38
Hue, Margaret, 158t
Huguenots, 24–25, 182–185, 194, 201; Puritans and, 202. *See also* Walloons
Huguenot Historical Society, 1–5, 16
Huguenot Patriotic Historical and Monumental Society of New Paltz, 204–205, 209
Huguenot Society of America, 200, 217
Huyberts, Lambert, 227n10

"Indian Deed," 228n12
inheritance laws, 27, 230n21; primogeniture and, 41, 60–61. *See also* property rights
insteek ("upper room"), *67*, 67–68, 70
Irish immigrants, 179, 181

Jacobs, Jaap, 10
Jay, John, 190
Jorisse, Madeline Brisson, 23t
Kammen, Michael, 5
Kenney, Alice P., 5
kelderkeuken, 68, 70, 80, 245n16
Kings College, 154
Kingston, N.Y., 9, 21, 22; during American Revolution, 189; church of, 24, 25, 144–146, 149–154; Dutch name of, 4; Abraham Hasbrouck's house in, 162–163, 166; Second Esopus War and, 185–186
Kreiger, Martin, 185–187, 189

Lamarckism, 193
Lambertse, Gerrit, 233n29
language, 15, 117–139, 162–163, 169, 216; Carlo on, 224n10; Fabend on, 225n16; LeFevre on, 262n2; surnames and, 30t, 213; used in business records, 129–133, 130t, 132t; used in religious life, 24, 120–124, 127–129, 161–162, 200, 262n2; used in schools, 124–126, 137; used in wills, 119–120, 119t, 160, 164
Larson, Neil, 6–7, 111; on Jacob Hasbrouck House, 245n19; on "modernization," 247n39; on Terwilliger House, 247n35
Lears, T. J. Jackson, 178
LeConte, Marie, 29, 231n24
LeFevre, Abraham, 47, 52, 61; house of, *76*, *87*, 87–88, 93, *102*
LeFevre, Andries (patentee), 21, 22, 23t
LeFevre, Andries (son of Simon the patentee, 1679–1738), 46, 47, 49, 59, 121
LeFevre, Catharine Cantine (Daniel's wife), 62
LeFevre, Cornelia Blanchan (wife of Simon's son Andries), 46
LeFevre, Elizabeth, 3–4
LeFevre, Elizabeth Deyo (wife of Simon the patentee), 22, 23t
LeFevre, Jacob (1760–1817), 129
LeFevre, James, 204, 207–208, 214
LeFevre, Maria Bevier (Abraham's wife), 47, 53

LeFevre, Mattys, 122
LeFevre, Peter, Jr. (b. 1759), 125
LeFevre, Petronella Hasbrouck (wife of Simon the patentee's grandson Simon), 47, 52, 56
LeFevre, Petrus (1720–1806), 122, 129
LeFevre, Philip, 102
LeFevre, Ralph, 3–5, 117, 136, 173, 175, 200–203; commemoration projects of, 204–221, 264n20; on family folklore, 267n38
LeFevre, Rufus, 216
LeFevre, Simon (patentee), 21, 22, 23t
LeFevre, Simon (Simon the patentee's grandson, 1710–1743), 47, 48, 53, 56, 58
Levin, David, 177
Lewis, Leonard, 236n34
Lister, Elisha, 236n35
Livingston, Robert, 144
Livingston, Robert G., 163
Lodge, Henry Cabot, 178
los hoes, 68, *68*
Louis XIII, French king, 3, 185
Louis XIV, French king, 2, 3, 5, 25, 183–185, 201
Louis, Charles, elector of Die Pfalz, 20
Low family, 157–159, 158t. *See also* Freer-Louw House
Low, Catherine DuBois (Petrus's first wife), 158t
Low, Christina McMullen (Simeon's wife), 158t
Low, David, 158t
Low, Deborah Van Vliet (Petrus's second wife), 157, 158t
Low, Elizabeth, 158t
Low, Isaak, 157, 158t
Low, Jannetje Van Heyning (Matthew's wife), 158t
Low, Johannes, 88–89, 158t
Low, Judith Van Vliet (Solomon's first wife), 158t
Low, Matthew, 158t
Low, Petrus, 157, 158t
Low, Rebecca Freer (Johannes's wife), 88–89, 158t
Low, Sarah Bosch (Solomon's second wife), 158t
Low, Simeon, 94, 158t
Low, Solomon, 158t

Mackey, Andrew, 236n34
MacPhaedris-Warner House, *85*
Magna Carta, 179
Maine, Henry, 177–178
Mancius, G. W., 149–150, 154
Mannheim, 14, 20, 21
Mary I, English queen, 17
Mazarin, Jules, 185
"Memorial House." *See* Hasbrouck, Jean, house of
Merwick, Donna, 7–9
Meschines, Jean, 124, 252n13
Meyer, Hermanus, 162
Meyer, John H., 123
Moll, Herman, *18*
Motley, John, 177
Mouw, Dirk, 8, 10, 142–143, 154, 157
Murrin, John, 7

Narrett, David, 9, 10, 60
Neely family, 135
Nutting, Wallace, 210

opkamer, 68–70, *80*, 80–82, 104

Palatinate (Die Pfalz), 14, 17, 20
Parkman, Francis, 177
Parson Capen House, *71*, *72*
Patentees Monument, 3, 16, 204–205, 210–211, 218–221, *220*
Pawling, Levi, 162
Perkins, Valentine, 236n34
Perkins, Zopher, 236n35
Philip II, Spanish king, 17–18
pit house, 71, 244n10
poor relief, 6, 27, 124; Roth on, 230n20

Presbyterian Church, 144, 147, 258n21
Preslar, Jonathan, 35
property rights, 27, 178–179, 195–196, 230n21; dower rights and, 40–41, 46–52; gender issues with, 15, 37–53, 159–164; primogeniture and, 41, 60–61
Puritans, 16, 179, 180, 202

Queens College. *See* Rutgers College

racial theories, 13, 175–178, 180–181, 198–201, 212–214; gender and, 212, 215
Rang, Johan Jury, 235n34
Ransom, Peleg, 35, 236n34
Rasel, Benjamin, 236n35
ravestissement principle, 38
Revolutionary War (U.S.), 262n2
Ritzema, Johannes, 257n20
Roediger, David, 181
Romney, Susanah Shaw, 10, 24
rookhuis, *67*
Roosevelt, Theodore, 178
Ross, Dorothy, 177
Roth, Eric, 6–7, 227n11, 230n20
Rutgers College, 152, 172, 203
Rysdyk, Isaak, 157

schools, 252n12; languages used in, 124–126, 137
Schryver, Martinus, 135
Second Church of New Paltz, 141, 156–159; membership of 157–158, 158t, 259n41. *See also* Coetus-Conferentie dispute
Simon, Pierre, 124, 252n13
slaves, 13–14; housing of, 73, 76, 80, 82, 110; in wills, 45, 48, 49, 52
Slecht, Mattys, 234n29
Smitt, Hendric, 31
social Darwinism, 178
Society of the Colonial Dames of America, 210
Spencer, Herbert, 178
stairs in houses, 75–76, *77*, 97, *98*
Stevens, John R., 9
Stitt, Charles, 196, 268n48
Stott, Annette, 265n20
stove, five-plate, *75*, 80, 82, 96, 109–110
Strickland, William, 136
Stuyvesant, Pieter, 185

Tacitus, 176, 178
Tebenin, Jean, 121, 122, 124
Ten Eyck, Matthew, 83, *84*, 245n19
Tennant, William, 147
Terpenning, Jan, 233n29
Terwilliger, Evert, 81, *95–99*, 100, 170, 247nn33–35
Terwilliger, Jonathan, 96–100
Thirty Years' War, 19–21
"Thornwood" House, *100*, 100–101
Tienhoven, Cornelius, 71
Tomkins, Jonathan, 235n34
Truth, Sojourner, 135–136
Tuttle, James, 236n34
Twelve Men. *See* Duzine

Ulster County Historical Society, 189–190, 196, 200–201
Union of Utrecht (1579), 17, 18
Upton, Dell, 248n40, 248n42

Van Basten, Johannes Vernanus, 257n17
Van Buren, Augustus H., 227n10
Van Cleck, Tryntie, 58
van Couwenhoven, Pieter, 186
Vandemerke, Abraham, 235n34
van den Hurk, Jeroen, 243n3; on anchor beam bents, 243n9; on jambless fireplace, 246n28
Vanderlyn, Nicolas, 132
van Driessen, Johannes, 121–122, 124, 133, 143–146, 149–151; birthplace of, 250n8
van Driessen, Petrus, 122, 144–146

Van Ruymbeke, Bertrand, 223n3
Van Wagenen, Jacob Aast, 216
Van Wagenen, Lucas, 104, *105*
Van Wagenen, Peter, 158t
Van Wagenen, Sara Low (Peter's wife), 158t
Van Weye, Hendrick, 234n29
Vas, Petrus, 145–146, 149–150
Vennema, Ame, 207
Vennema, Janny, 10
voorhuis, 67, 68, 70, 80, 94, 96, 97, 101
Vrooman, Barent, 123, 151

Walloons, 2–3, 6–7, 181–198; in Canterbury, England, 17–19, 226nn4–5; churches of, 2, 3, 24–25, 29, 120, 141–152; culture of, 14–15, 25, 35–36, 175–176; diaspora of, 14, 17–22. *See also* Huguenots
Waring, Solomon, 236n35
wenteltrap, 76, 77
"Westover" (house of William Byrd II), 85, *86*
Wibau, Touissant, 23t
Wilhelmius, Johannes, 257n17
wills, 53, 62; languages used in, 119–120, 119t, 160, 164; women's rights and, 15, 37–53, 159–164
Wiltwijck. *See* Kingston, N.Y.
Winckelman, Johannes, 68
windows in houses, 81, 89–94, *90–93*, 106, 163
Wirtz, Esther Hasbrouck (George's wife), 236n35
Wirtz, George, 236n35
Wood, Elizabeth, 31, 233n27
Wynkoop, Cornelia, 48, 58
Wynkoop, Cornelius, *86*, 87, 100
Wynkoop, Dirck D., 47–48, 158t
Wynkoop, Geertje, 48
Wynkoop, Sara Eltinge (Dirck's wife), 47–48, 158t
Wynkoop House, 247n36

Yale University, 144, 145
York, Johannes, 31

zijkammer ("sideroom"), *67*
Zink, Clifford, 245n15